About the editors

Catherine Alexander is a professor of anthropology at Durham University. Most of her work is concerned with shifting configurations of state, market, society and the third sector. This has also informed her work on waste. She has published on the community waste and recycling sector in Britain and waste as material and metaphor in Kazakhstan. Her current research is on attempts to revitalize Kazakhstan's nuclear energy industry, reusing expertise and equipment left over from the Cold War.

Joshua Reno is an assistant professor of anthropology at Binghamton University and is primarily interested in the intersections between environmental issues and science and technology. He conducted his doctoral fieldwork on transnational waste circulation and mega-landfills, their transformation of landscapes, lives and communities in rural Michigan, and their relationship to environmental politics and neoliberalism. From 2008 to 2010 he studied emerging European technologies in the fields of health and the environment, their innovation, contestation and governance. He has written articles on waste, energy, communication and material culture.

ECONOMIES OF RECYCLING

The global transformation of materials, values and social relations

edited by Catherine Alexander and Joshua Reno

Zed Books

LONDON | NEW YORK

Economies of Recycling: The global transformation of materials, values and social relations was first published in 2012 by Zed Books Ltd, 7 Cynthia Street, London N1 9JF, UK and Room 400, 175 Fifth Avenue, New York, NY 10010, USA

www.zedbooks.co.uk

1007245109

FSC
www.fsc.org
MIX
Paper from
responsible sources
FSC® C013604

Set in OurType Arnhem and Monotype Futura by
Ewan Smith, London
Index: ed.emery@thefreeuniversity.net
Cover designed by Rogue Four Design
Printed and bound by CPI Group (UK) Ltd, Croydon,
CR0 4YY

Distributed in the USA exclusively by Palgrave Macmillan, a division of St Martin's Press, LLC, 175 Fifth Avenue, New York, NY 10010, USA

A catalogue record for this book is available from the British Library
Library of Congress Cataloging in Publication Data available

ISBN 978 1 78032 195 0 hb
ISBN 978 1 78032 194 3 pb

Contents

Figures

Acknowledgements

The editors are grateful for the editorial support from Zed Books, particularly the enthusiastic help of Jakob Horstmann, our first editor, and Tamsine O'Riordan, our diligent second editor. We also thank Francisco Calafate, Elena Gonzalez-Polledo, Alan Howard, Alaina Lemon, Stephen Nugent and Elena Resnick.

We acknowledge the support of an ESRC grant (RES 000-23-0007), not only for the writing of much of this book but also for much of the underlying research in Alexander's, Crang et al.'s, Reno's, Norris's and Garcier's chapters.

Sections of Chapter 2 have appeared previously in N. Gregson, M. Crang, F. Ahamed, N. Akhter and R. Ferdous (2010) 'Following Things of Rubbish Value: "End-of-life ships", "chock-chocky furniture" and the Bangladeshi middle class consumer', *Geoforum* 41(6): 846–54 and are reused by kind permission from Elsevier.

Sections of Chapter 4 have appeared previously as X. Tong and J. Wang (2004) 'Transnational Flows of E-Waste and Spatial Patterns of Recycling in China'. Reprinted with permission from *Eurasian Geography and Economics*, 45(8): 608–21. ©Bellwether Publishing Ltd, 8640 Guilford Road, Columbia, MD 21046. All rights reserved.

Introduction

CATHERINE ALEXANDER
AND JOSHUA RENO

Recycling is the process by which previously used objects and materials are converted into something else, rather than discarded;[1] since the 1970s, it has been a keystone of environmental reform. However, keeping stuff in place while it is revalued can be problematic and expensive. Because of improvements in global transport and the rising costs of environmental compliance, it is often more cost effective to dump or recycle waste products in places with less severe environmental and labour regulations. The discards of wealthier countries do more than pollute other places, however; they enter subsidiary markets, create employment and provide materials for construction booms. As we explore in this volume, it is essential to keep these multiple perspectives on recycling in view simultaneously.

In a sense, all artefacts are remade from their original form in nature into what Marxists have termed a 'second nature' (Lukacs 1971; Adorno 1973): moving from a state of nature to a social world. Recycling assumes such powerful moral and political salience today because it appears to intercede in this transformation and corruption of nature, substituting existing artefacts and materials for the production of originals. Karl Marx (1998), however, also argued that the appropriation of nature is not a one-way process, but, in turn, fundamentally transforms human beings. Accounting for recycling cannot be reduced to limited environmental or material consequences; we also need to consider how remaking remakes us all.

The goal of the book The central theme of this book is the transformation and revaluation, in the broadest sense, of materials, objects, spaces and the people who carry out this work. Such change may come as a result of new contexts or social relations, or it may be through modification or disassembly and reassembly. As we explore different accounts of materials being transported and worked upon around the globe, however, we need to maintain the tension between seeing the world as simply so much matter and energy in a constant state of becoming, and acknowledging those moments where recognizable forms emerge, those places where things, for good or ill, come to rest. Throughout, we pay close attention to the astonishing variety of experiences, and organizational forms of labour, that recycling work draws out. Thus, the positive experience of crafting a basket for domestic use out of a rubber tyre may be juxtaposed with the marginalized labour of female, migrant workers in textile reprocessing factories in India or the dangerous disassembly of towering end-of-life ships. The once valued skills of care and repair often fit awkwardly with the urge to have the latest technology or garment; but such conspicuous consumption may also provide opportunities for other people and places to benefit practically and politically from reuse. In the case of the world's rag-picking cooperatives, for example, remaking other people's discards has led to forms of labour organization which are developing into a major force in their own right.[2] Thus to Gay Hawkins's (2006) account of the production of the self-as-recycler, we add the diversities of recycling practices and people.

Our eleven ethnographic chapters unpack global flows of materials (and ideologies) and localized practices of recycling in different parts of the world. By tracking these various flows and revealing what happens on the ground, the stories we often hear about the global economy, that it can be divided up into winners and losers, gains and losses, producers and consumers, become untenable. In their place, we offer accounts of global economies of recycling – patchy, tenuous and wondrously creative – that defy simple moral narratives.

In the first half of this introductory chapter we address several perspectives on material retransformation, before turning, in the second half, 'Economies of recycling', to the chapters themselves and the broader themes to which they speak. We start by outlining what is new about contemporary recycling before considering the emergence of organized, large-scale, urban recycling. As historians have noted, recycling is repeatedly 'discovered' with little reference to earlier mass-organized collection and repurposing systems. We suggest that many of these moments of 'discovery' appear alongside social and economic crises. In the section entitled 'Thinking with recycling' we show how the rupture between traditional societies and the modern, signalled by the First World War, was accompanied by an intense interest by avant-garde artists and writers in the idea of reconfiguration rather than evolutionary development. In the twentieth and twenty-first centuries, the arts have thus frequently used recycling, if not in so many words, as a metaphor or a way of representing the world. Representing recycling itself has proved challenging and of prime importance in accounting for and reducing waste: we therefore go on to consider interventions to model the complex, open-ended process of material transformation as matter and energy. While providing powerful heuristics for gauging the volume of materials moving around the world, these models and representations turn out to be as partial as the fine-grained, ethnographic accounts in our chapters. Both approaches are needed to gain a meaningful understanding of the processes and effects of recycling.

Contemporary stories of recycling In recent decades, recycling has shot up the global political agenda. By arresting, or at least reducing, the plunder of the world's resources through the substitution of existing materials, recycling offers two benefits: economic thrift and environmental care. Has it really taken so long to get this far? Under various guises, recycling has long been with us, but its continual disappearance and reappearance is a complex story and the nuances bear attention. The easy, too easy perhaps, moral and economic win-win of exhortations to householders and industry to recycle their waste becomes more complicated once we consider how recycling is carried out, where materials go to be revalued and reinserted into mainstream material flows, and the traces that are left behind as all this stuff swirls around the world: localized concentrations of toxic wastes, lingering, uncanny memories or imaginaries of previous material incarnations, and the harm done to the bodies of labourers who carry out this work, which is often dangerous and unprotected. People as well as things are remade through waste work. But there are also limits to just how often people and materials can be stretched, broken down and put together again, retooled for new economic regimes.[3]

At the very least, this raises the question of what exactly 'good environmental practice' means for different people, in different places. As many of the chapters in this volume show, claims of resource efficiency or sustainability through material recycling often omit accounts of what happens to the places and people where recycling occurs. Risk, danger and pollution are all too often simply displaced to other places and glossed over in feel-good accounts of recycling ships, re-enriching uranium for energy production, or reusing surplus clothes and equipment tossed aside in the quest for the latest fashion in consumer technology.

What is new in the contemporary story of recycling is the sheer scale of global trades in used materials. In the first decade of the twenty-first century, the largest export from the world's biggest economy (the

United States) to the next-biggest economy (China), was scrap (Allen 2010; Minter forthcoming). New technologies, broadly understood, have also changed economies of recycling dramatically on many fronts. Technical developments have improved the range of materials and quality of energy that can be recovered. Other innovative technologies, such as consumer electronics, present new kinds of objects with potentially valuable components to be ripped out and reused once the mobile phone, laptop or other once desirable electronic good is no longer wanted (Gabrys 2011). Novel technologies of governance reach into the heart of the domestic arena to orchestrate practices of sorting and segregating discards. Another new form of social technology, national and international regulations aimed at controlling toxic waste dumping, boosting material and energy recovery and tracking the movement of stuff, often has the unintended effect of rendering many material flows opaque or invisible. The cost of legal compliance drives many material discards into informal or black market exchanges: the links between waste disposal and criminality are well known (Block 1985; Massari and Monzini 2004; Hill 2006). The naming and categorization of stuff affects what can be done with it and where it can go. Accordingly, as materials move between categories (now waste, now scrap, now shoddy, now nuclear, now commodity), as well as through exchanges, it can become hard to track, quantify and accurately represent mass material movements.

The chapters in this volume engage ethnographically with some of these flows and their local encounters. This discloses both a sharply different view of global economic relationships from conventional narratives and unexpected connections between households and international trades, commodity prices and demands, core industrial regions and peripheries, and geographically dispersed technologies of recovery. Familiar economic geographies and understandings of how the global economy works are upturned as the developed North becomes a source for scrap/raw materials; marginal regions add value before (re)finished goods are sold, sometimes back to where the scrap came from. This is sharply different from the old imperial geography where colonial margins were often first plundered for raw materials and then forced to buy back finished, value-added goods,[4] or, in the 1990s, were dispossessed again of resources and lands by capitalist powers bent on further accumulation (Harvey 2003). Newly emerging economies such as the BRIC countries (Brazil, Russia, India and China), hungry for infrastructural materials, are key destinations for metal scrap. In this new geography, the Middle East suddenly appears as a central brokering node in the collection of scrap before it is sent on for sorting elsewhere. There are many levels of connection. Rag-picking collectives in Latin America are keenly aware of commodity prices being set in the London Metal Exchange (Calafate n.d.): futures trading affects their livelihood. Familiar divisions of global North and South, developed and un(der)developed regions, cease to hold. Viewed from the perspective of recycling, margins and peripheries appear in kitchens, city margins, workplaces and regions within and across nation-states, with startling links to each other.

For example, in the mid-2000s new household recycling schemes were introduced in Britain. In part, this was to satisfy public demand for green legislation, as well as to meet an obligation to the EU to reach reduction targets for landfilled waste. A less reported reason was that the price of recycled plastic was rising in China, where imported and domestic bottles were being broken down into pellets, remade into things such as plastic carrier bags and resold, at a profit, back to Europe (Vidal 2004). But these market arrangements tilt both ways. When consumer demand dropped precipitously in the West with the 2008 global financial crisis, many of China's plastic, paper and metal recycling industries suffered heavy losses (Branigan 2009), as did their many suppliers: the informal scrap collectors and dealers of Romania, Brazil, the Philippines and elsewhere (Chaturvedi 2009; Thorpe 2009).

While recycling is assuming new forms and affecting people's lives and economies in new ways, there is also a long history of engagements with material reconfiguration that is often ignored, and from which can be derived distinct, but complementary, insights into the contemporary global recycling economy. In the next part of the introduction we therefore give an overview of the history of how large-scale, organized, urban recycling, which now characterizes most forms of remaking and reuse on a global scale, emerged. We go on to consider how recycling has been used to represent the social world – and how recycling has been represented in turn. The key point that connects these histories, methods and representations to contemporary recycling discourse is the extent to which the *idea* of a perfect cycle is taken for reality. Material recycling necessarily involves physical degradation and uses energy to make things into other things. It is also an inevitably open-ended social process (see Graeber, this volume).

Histories and representations of recycling

Contemporary economies of recycling cannot be understood without accounting for the progressive rationalization and externalization of urban waste practices and the sweeping social changes that accompany them. The large-scale production of waste that cannot be reabsorbed by domestic or agricultural practices, and thus must be systematically collected and disposed of, is a phenomenon of urbanization, and one that intensified with the rapid growth of industrialized northern European cities in the late eighteenth century (Melosi 1981). While the first sewerage systems for human waste are old, according to Mumford (1961: 75) the cities of ancient Mesopotamia were characterized by 'the slack rural ways of disposing of rubbish and excrement', which 'became a menace in crowded urban quarters' so that 'for thousands of years city dwellers put up with defective, often quite vile, sanitary arrangements, wallowing in rubbish and filth' (ibid.).[5]

In early modern Europe, political intervention in the collection of human wastes began to couple centralized regulation of material excess with the elaboration of a private/public dichotomy: the individuation and concealment of acts of waste production and the social distribution of control over their product. There is a whole history of human waste, from shit to hair and latterly tissue (Parry 2007), and how it has been appropriated, recycled and commodified. One such alternative history interprets human waste as possessing latent value, highlighting links between the control of property rights in shit and the discipline of individual bodies (see Reno, this volume). Thus, for Laporte (2000), François I's 1530 Edict sought to both cleanse the French language and make each person responsible for readying their own 'private' shit for regular public collection and use as fertilizer. Here, the increasing centralization of political control over words and bodies relies on the externalization of that control to grammarians and waste collectors, apparent in struggles between these agents of semiotic and corporeal normalization and the general populace (see Reid 1991). Across the Channel, the English Crown similarly asserted its rights to the waste products of the urban population. In 1626, Charles I mandated the collection of urine-soaked earth from privies so that saltpetre (potassium nitrate) could be extracted for gunpowder (O'Brien 2007; Jewitt 2011).[6]

The 150 years after the 1750s were characterized first by the rise of liberalism, with its emphasis on private enterprise, individual sovereignty, responsibility and possession; secondly, by the expansion of industrial cities; and thirdly, by the concomitant increase in industrial and domestic wastes, principally fire ash. The collection of ash became a booming business as fine dust was used to make marshy soil cultivable and coarse ash was converted into bricks (see Velis et al. 2007) to build more houses as cities began to consume themselves.

Furthermore, gleaning, picking over, sorting and recovering value from urban waste as a survival strategy took the form of what would now be called 'waste streams' (Herbert 2007; Gordon 1890). Thus Mayhew (2010 [1851]) lists and classifies (in a carefully precise descending order of status): mudlarks, dredgermen and sewer hunters (toshers), bone grubbers, bottle finders, dustmen, rag-and-bone men (also known as totters), nightsoil men and others.

With the intensification of capitalism, urban gleanings, as a right of the poor, were steadily reorganized and reduced in London (Linebaugh 2003). Dickens's *Our Mutual Friend* shows simultaneously how a fortune could be made from dust and the maligned existence of those scrounging for what wastes remained in the margins of the metropolis. This is also the time when material waste, scavenging and low status became structurally aligned (Stallybrass and White 1986; Morris 2002). As 'health became public', Barnes (2006) argues, proper governance in Paris was tied to ideas of cleansing the body politic of disease and impure lifestyles. Stedman Jones (1976) shows, furthermore, that the idea of a social residuum was born in the 1880s: irrecoverable, parasitic, the undisciplined lumpenproletariat – incapable of useful production. In other words, such people were thought beyond redemption; they could not be valorized, recycled or transformed to serve in the new social order. Where there's muck there may be brass, as the old adage goes, but, in England at least, there's rarely class.

These socio-material transformations reveal the steady separation of laudable but publicly invisible practices of household thrift, reusing and recycling material (Strasser 2000) – later to become the object of policy and moral discourse – and practices beyond the household, whether performed by poor gleaners or middle-class reformers. This separation was reinforced by the rise of sanitation engineers, a product both of growing urban municipal intervention and the valorization of technological expert knowledge. This meant even more externalization of technical control over the material excess that had once belonged to domestic and agricultural domains and, later, to the gleaning economies of the urban poor. This professionalization of urban waste disposal was the start of a struggle between local communities and disposal enterprises, which prefigured late twentieth-century environmental justice movements (Clark 2007). Just as the fireplace and its ash gave way to the public incinerator, the closed tip or sanitary landfill replaced the profitable dust piles of *Our Mutual Friend*, further marginalizing those directly involved in the 'dirty trades' of recovery (Zimring 2004).

The municipal accent here, then, was on whisking urban rubbish out of sight and disposing of it efficiently (Maxwell 1898; Clark 2008). In parallel, however, in the twentieth century, public and policy concern with recycling regularly coincided with periods of political, economic and moral crisis, which gave rise to material shortages, before the return to periods of relative plenty. Thus, during the Second World War, intensive recycling was practised at a household, community and civic level in Europe (Herbert 2007: 32–3; Cooper 2008, 2009). The communist bloc continued to coordinate household and municipal recycling practices (Gille 2007). The ascendancy of disposal technologies and their expert attendants perhaps explains why the episodic nature of publicly organized recycling is repeatedly forgotten and there is constant surprise as, time and again, historians uncover more subtle material engagements and, indeed, more profound ways of thinking through the implications of reconfiguring the world, as the next section discusses.

Thinking with recycling What happened between the periods of liberal and neoliberal political economies is remarkable for its radical reconceptualization of the material and social world and the place of humans in it. Simply put, this was the moment when modernity emerged, uniting humankind with a common experience but also presenting 'a unity of disunity: it pours us all into a maelstrom of perpetual disintegration and renewal, of struggle and contradiction, of ambiguity and anguish' (Anderson 1984: 97). The interwar years, particularly the 1920s and early 1930s, were a period of intellectual and political experimentation that both drew on, and affected, the arts and sciences in thinking about human and material relations, the nature of time and the meaning (or lack of it) of human progress. For Lefebvre (1991), around 1910 a certain space was shattered, the space of common sense and common knowledge (see also Berman 1983).

The interwar years saw a coalescence across quite different domains in rethinking how the world was structured and experienced. Is it too much to suggest that the way the world was briefly thought about was tantamount to recycling (see Gregson 2009)? Archaeology, psychoanalysis, collage, literary modernism and anthropology all became ways of engaging with and understanding a world characterized by uncertainty, multiplicity and polyvalence.

In place of single narratives, trajectories and viewpoints came tumbling assemblages of fragments, multiple perspectives and voices. Around the movement of literary modernism clustered writers such as James Joyce and Virginia Woolf, experimenting with the effect of an individual's consciousness as it made sense of a stream of disparate thoughts, overheard voices, observations, recollections. The city, remnants of old and new blended together, was the modernist locus par excellence; the place of the epiphany or Woolf's 'moment of being', when the present was irradiated with senses of other times and places. Cubism again fractured the whole, showing different spatial angles, different temporalities contained within the momentary assemblage of a recognizable object or person. Archaeologists uncovered many-layered cities: Schliemann's Troy being the most noteworthy. Dawdy (2010: 761) explores the potency of the 'archaeological metaphor' for early twentieth-century thinkers such as Walter Benjamin and Freud – and for critical theory. Freud, a keen amateur Egyptologist, was partly inspired by excavations of places that revealed traces of former material and social lives through the coexistence of multiple sites to formulate notions of a multilayered conscious and the uncanny. He described psychoanalysis as a method of divining 'secret and concealed things' from 'the rubbish heap of our observations' (Ginzburg 1980: 10). The modern discipline of anthropology also emerged in the 1920s and was part of this conversation of finding alternatives to dominant narratives, meaning in margins and unconsidered trifles, and giving equal weight to multiple viewpoints. The fluidity of people and things appeared as never before.

The 1920s was also a period of radical experimentation with the materials, processes and products of art: Dada, surrealism, the futurists and Soviet constructivism delighted in taking apart the known world and reassembling the familiar into strange concurrences. André Breton, one of the founders of the surrealist movement, was an early practitioner of collage, literally meaning 'to stick together' from the French *coller*. Collages, or assemblages, were typically created from found objects, reassembled to create a work of art: a new configuration and a new context for component parts. The second great burst of artistic assemblage from found, rejected or broken scraps again appeared after the Second World War, culminating in the 1961 exhibition *The Art of Assemblage* in New York's Museum of Modern Art; San Francisco was another centre for assemblage art from the 1940s onwards (Whiteley 2010). Increasingly, industrial detritus was incorporated into these installations; in 1960s Chicago, John Chamberlain used parts from wrecked cars. The aftermath of each twentieth-century world war challenged the power hegemonies that gave rise to it and the idea of progress, replacing them, however briefly, with ideas of ephemerality, equality and contingency.

Cinematic montage techniques inspired the German cultural critic Walter Benjamin, who took them farther as a means of uncovering an image of history through its detritus (*Abfall*)[7] in the present, each trivial scrap an index to a greater whole, material traces that held the past. *The Arcades Project* (Benjamin 2002) is the most famous example of his textual simulation of collage, juxtaposing quotations and found segments of text. But earlier works also show an interest in defying genre. Benjamin's historical philosophy, apparently grounded in materialism, showed in its practice that 'progress' was merely material rearrangement, endless recycling.

In his 1930 review of Siegfried Kracauer's novel *Die Angestellten* (The Salaried Masses), Benjamin describes his 'technique of garbage collection': 'A rag-picker who picks up garbage early in the gray morning. Muttering darkly to himself, getting a bit drunk, he spears the remains of speeches and fragments of words with his stick, and throws them into his cart. ... He is the morning garbage collector, but this morning is the morning of the day of the revolution.'[8]

Just as all great civilizations end in dust, Benjamin imagined modernity rising only to fall again, or, following Marx, 'all that is solid melts into air' (Berman 1983).

The sense that things do not develop, but are only rearranged, underscored artistic and philosophical activity in the 1920s and served to challenge ideas of evolutionary social progress. Many of the emerging social sciences reflected and reinforced this way of seeing the world.

One exception was the emergence of economics, where the modern notion of the national economy in its contemporary sense, as an object of state monitoring and intervention, was being developed by Keynes and others (Mitchell 2002). Here a vision of material relationships as endless cyclic repetition, as the chaotic rising and falling of wages and profits resulting in ever-worsening depressions, was linked to a philosophy of control and planning. Of all this period's imaginative representations, this had the most enduring influence. Even after Keynes's views lost their popularity, the idea of The Economy, represented in terms of unemployment statistics, monetary policies and commodity prices, allowed a belief in the possibility of progress to live on.

Matter and energy Economics began as the study of household (*oikos nomos* literally meaning 'the rules of the household'), and a sense of how to keep household matters in balance (see Graeber, this volume). With Alfred Marshall, this notion of material balance shifted to a more abstract, mathematicized notion of equilibrium. Swedberg comments of classical political economy that 'while the actors in Smith and Marx still live in a material world, the material dimension is little theorized and taken for granted' (2008: 76), going on to note that 'What also makes objects disappear from the analysis is ... [the] steady focus on the market at the expense of everything else in economic life' (ibid.: 78). It is this displacement of things in their social context by mathematical abstraction or a focus on energy and matter which is the subject of this section.

Increasingly, twentieth-century economists had backgrounds in mathematics, especially statistics and probability theory, which explains why some have likened the modern discipline more to physics than to a human science or the moral philosophy it had been (Mackenzie 2006). Physics is shaped by a hypothesis of constant reconfiguration. The principle of the conservation of energy is summarized by the first law of thermodynamics: energy is not lost but converted into other forms. Similarly, the law of conservation of mass, or matter, states that mass remains constant over time, it just changes in form. The key to both principles is the context of a closed system, hence their centrality to chemistry, chemical engineering and industrial systems. Thus, chemistry is, in large part, the study of the transformation of matter, or recycling, in its broadest sense. One focus of industrial chemistry is on material and energy inputs and outputs to a given process. Based on the principle that, for each process or system, inputs and outputs are equal in mass and energy, the inevitable lack of equivalence can be accounted for by losses, inefficiencies or entropy (dispersed energy); this therefore indicates where to concentrate effort on minimizing loss or wastage. This is the notion of material or mass balance, which identifies the total mass entering and leaving a given process.

Effectively, this is material accounting and is typically used alongside several other techniques such as Life Cycle and Triple Bottom Line Assessment to represent material and energy movement and transformation (see Alexander 2012; Alexander and Smaje 2008). Mass balance has proved a powerful and popular heuristic for tracking material flows through geographic regions and industrial sectors or for following one element or type of object; in all these cases it is worth noting that the emphasis has shifted from closed to open systems. Nevertheless, mass balance is often seen as a prerequisite for intervention into material processes: identifying then reducing wastage through recycling.

From the idea that ecologies are natural closed systems, the term 'industrial ecology' was created (Frosch and Gallopoulos 1989; Socolow et al. 1994). The aim was to shift from open industrial processes producing waste material and dissipated energy to closed loops where wastes and energy outputs would form inputs to another process. Unused energy and materials, in other words, would be endlessly transformed, recycled, within the physical limits of entropy prescribed by the second law of thermodynamics. As with many instances, borrowing ideas from one domain to act as instrumental metaphors in another usually puts them under considerable strain. Ecosystems are rarely closed, and manufacturing industry is based on production; outputs leaving the system are its *raison d'être*. In another extrapolation from biological or ecological systems to mechanical ones, Ayres (1989a, 1989b) came up with the term 'industrial metabolism'. These metaphorical exchanges are based on the idea that systems analysis can explain social, biological, chemical and physical worlds alike.

In order to track the movement of matter and energy through industrial or other systems a form of Material Flow Analysis (MFA) was developed in the early 1990s, which was later adopted by the EU's Sustainability Unit (see Schmidt-Bleek et al. 1998). MFA aims to quantify materials and energy used in production and consumption, including 'hidden flows'. That is, where the mass or energy of the product is less than the input, then these hidden flows of wastes and by-products account for the difference. In the drive to represent and evoke material movement through metaphors or images, such hidden material flows are called the 'ecological rucksack': the displaced environmental impact that shadows each final product (Clift and Wright 2000). Along similar lines, Rees (1992) and Rees and Wackernagel (1996) added the notion of an ecological footprint, later refined to carbon, energy, water, etc., footprints, to indicate the broader environmental effects of a given region or process. The implications for recycling policy are potentially profound. The use of primary resources and energy together with the co-production of waste materials can be compared with similar products using recycled materials to identify the most resource-efficient process. In theory, then, MFA can demonstrate where recycling can reduce energy inputs, pollutants and waste. Further, whereas the social sciences have tended to concentrate on objects as discrete entities rather than materials constantly in a state of becoming (Ingold and Hallam 2007), industrial ecology restores the equally necessary focus on matter in motion.

The ability of these computational models to measure environmental impacts with apparent precision has made them a popular source of data for policy-makers and firms tasked with addressing corporate social and environmental responsibility (Gille 2007; Alexander 2005). Ironically, perhaps, these approaches of MFA and industrial ecology also pose a challenge to conventional models of the world economy, especially as many of the tools of economic measurement and analysis were originally intended to interpret and manage the affairs of a nation-state. With these approaches,[9] political divisions and connections are set aside in favour of a rigorously materialist analysis of matter circulating and transforming. This is a depoliticized view of the world that ignores local politics, economies and indeed people (Posch 2004). By shifting the scale of analysis to carbon, mass and energy, political boundaries and regulations can disappear or, at the very least, be backgrounded. But these are among the very things that determine where and how materials move: the transport infrastructure which carries them, the regulations that surround them or cause them to move into less detectable, underground flows.

Theoretically, MFA can be carried out at different scales. One key problem is that the variables used to measure the full impact of a process are necessarily selective: once one moves beyond a relatively closed system it is simply not possible to embrace all effects. The ways in which quantitative analyses are initially framed, furthermore, may anticipate the outcome.

Aside from their possible misinterpretation, one problem with some of these models is their selective use of thermodynamics. If the throughput of matter and energy is the primary focus of a given account, for example, then any *irreversible* changes that occur, such as entropy that resists a return to equilibrium, may not be accounted for (see Gößling-Reisemann 2008). For example, a significant problem with recycling is the tendency for recyclates to become less and less usable with every iteration of the cycle, as Norris's chapter in this volume illustrates so vividly. While some kind of end-product may be produced from most transformations, it becomes less economically viable to do so in terms of cost, energetics and the waste produced. Effective recycling is not infinite. Irreversible processes of degradation resist any attempt to model the simple substitution of one form of matter or energy for another. One way of accounting for this difficulty is by adjusting models to allow for irreversible dynamics. For example, the Waste Input Output model developed by Nakamura and Kondo (2002) combines a Life Cycle Assessment focus on environmental impacts with the input-output model, commonly used in economics to measure interdependency between economic sectors within a national or regional economy. One clear benefit of such combined approaches is that they have the potential to reveal unexpected connections between The Economy and waste management practices, including the various points where revalued materials re-enter and later exit economic circulation. A second advantage of such a methodology is that it highlights the gradual processes of environmental degradation and resource depletion of materials leaving and re-entering economic processes (see Takase et al. 2005).

Partial representations One of the limitations of computational models is that their social entanglements are often disregarded. This is particularly clear when MFA and input-output modelling are used to produce graphic representations. In terms of global waste flows, mapping datasets in this way can obscure what lies behind their production. For example, some of the best efforts at representing waste flows have come from international organizations, such as the European Environment Agency (EEA), the United Nations Environment Programme (UNEP) and the Basel Convention. In each case, datasets are provided, in part, by the very institutions that fund and support analysis. In other words, a particular collectivity must first exist and mandate a certain degree of data collection among its members in order to make the conditions for material flow accounting possible.

In the second of two Vital Waste Graphics reports supported by the Basel Convention and UNEP, for example, this limitation is clearly stated (Bournay and UNEP/GRID-Arendal 2006). In an analysis of global waste trade routes, evidence showing that Germany is the greatest recipient of waste among OECD countries is not only limited owing to the absence of black market data, it is complicated further by differential capacity among member states to report on waste data and by the lack of an obligation on them to participate at all. In a recent report (EEA 2009) the European Environment Agency claims that waste transfers are rising globally. This may be true, again, but it is difficult to be certain because the apparent 'rise' is partly explained by the gradual improvement in reporting techniques and EU guidance to member states, of which the Vital Waste Graphics document is a part.

Similar problems arise over what is included in representations of material flows or economic relationships, not just how well these elements can be measured. If analyses consider only energy or carbon, for example, they erase the lives of people implicated in the movement of waste and polluted landscapes, and people who are free from such processes and environments. Just as methods are partial in all senses, so too are the data representations they produce. The problem with such waste data is not merely that there are not enough but that there will always be blind spots. MFA is one form of analysis among others, including ethnography and other more qualitative methods, which are, in turn, limited in scope. For this reason, the contributions in this volume should be seen as another set of partial representations. Only by taking them all together is it possible to glimpse a larger human economy, within which material flows, objects and their analysis are made meaningful for human life in a globally connected world (see Hart et al. 2010).

Economies of recycling

In the first half of this introduction we explored different approaches to what could be called 'recycling' that have re-emerged throughout history. Rag-pickers, environmentalists, artists and engineers, employing distinct yet complementary perspectives, all seem to agree that 'recycling' offers new ways of imagining and engaging with the world. With this book, it is our contention that thinking about recycling, together with the world economy, allows us to productively rethink both. To imagine 'economies' as more than linear processes of commodity extraction, exchange and destruction, as profoundly shaped by acts of remaking, helps us to understand 'recycling' as an economically productive enterprise no less lucrative and no less morally complex than other modes of material transaction.

In order to apply this strategy further, in the second half of this introduction we consider the challenges that contemporary forms of remaking, discussed in the chapters that follow, offer to familiar economic categories such as neoliberalism, labour, property and value. Just as approaches to recycling have differed historically, contributors to this volume explore moments of remaking that differ materially and geographically.

The variations between the chapters can partly be explained by the diverse methods and perspectives employed by the authors, but they also suggest additional ways of thinking about economy and remaking together, which are derived from the local perspectives of the social actors discussed. Converting objects into new forms and uses can be so morally contentious that some of the people introduced in this book would eschew the label 'recycling' altogether (e.g. Halvorson's informants), to challenge the implication that the work they do involves the reuse of waste. Others might similarly contend that what they do is not 'economic' precisely because their labour is unpaid and generally devalued (e.g. those in Fredericks's and Faulk's chapters).

And yet, despite their heterogeneity, there are common threads that emerge throughout these chapters, which are discussed in terms of how they realign and refocus familiar economic concepts.

Environmentalism and economic policy As is clear from the first half of this introduction, the historiography of recycling focuses largely on the West, suggesting a need for wider global investigation of the sort offered here. But there is also good reason for a book with such aspirations to begin with European history. The period between the 1970s and the present, with which most of our chapters are concerned, is often characterized in terms of the reappearance of the eighteenth-century liberal emphasis on low central regulation, private commerce and individual rights, together with individual responsibility. The difference is that contemporary neoliberal governments have actively intervened to promote and deregulate private enterprise, while maintaining political control. In the aftermath of the Soviet Union's collapse, this neoliberalism gained global supremacy. What filled the global vacuum of Cold War policy was a vision of capitalism as the natural movement of market forces, whose growth required the spread of private ownership and the selective repeal and reform of state regulations.

The rise of neoliberalism has been an important narrative for the analysis of global economic relationships. But what the chapters here reveal is how neoliberal or post-liberal policies have developed in productive tension with new environmental regulations during the post-Cold War period, creating new market opportunities in their wake. As the energy crisis in the early 1970s renewed concern with husbanding materials and resources, environmental lobbyists challenged the continual growth required by capitalist relations.[10] The environmental movement began with social protest (usually against dumping toxic wastes) in capitalist (Bryant 1995; Gandy 1994), socialist (French 1990; Baumgartl 1993) and other rapidly urbanizing regimes (Broadbent 1998) alike. It should not be forgotten that many economists also responded to the challenge to rethink material economies at this crucial moment and resist the rise of neoclassical economics (Meadows et al. 1972; Daly 1973; Georgescu-Roegen 1971, 1979a; Dasgupta and Heal 1974, 1979; Socolow 1974, Stiglitz 1974).

By the 1980s, the resulting intensification of environmental regulation in wealthier countries made the cost of transport for offshore disposal cheaper than domestic options. This market outcome was crystallized in the infamous leaked memo signed by Lawrence Summers, then World Bank chief economist, in 1991, which stated: 'I think the economic logic behind dumping a load of toxic waste in the lowest wage country is impeccable and we should face up to that.' Despite the 'impeccability' of this market solution, in the late 1980s environmental justice movements grew to oppose the transboundary dumping of toxic waste in poorer countries, after several well-publicized incidents. This led to regional agreements such as the Bamako Convention (1991), which formally banned the practice in Africa, and was institutionalized on a global scale through the Basel Convention on transboundary wastes (1992), which forbade exporting toxic wastes to non-OECD countries.

But new global environmental policies did not simply block trades from happening, they enabled new markets to emerge. The limits of the Basel Convention[11] are those exports deemed to have a 'reuse' and which are therefore not regarded as mere transboundary wastes by importing nations, but as a potential source of resources (Clapp 2001). In their chapter, Crang et al. illustrate how taking things apart can also open up new markets and economic possibilities. They follow end-of-life ships as they are sent for disassembly to Bangladesh, where environmental and labour regulation is more flexible. Partly because massive container ships are icons of globalization, their disposal offers a striking metaphor for the less visible works of disassembly and immobility upon which global economies also depend. As the ships are broken up, furthermore, they produce new-for-old objects for middle-class Bangladeshi households and the construction industry. At the same time, these practices of disassembly are shaped by the uncertain terrain of environmental regulation: whether or not countries might ban sending end-of-life ships to places like Bangladesh, creating work and secondary markets but despoiling the beaches and seas with pollution through appalling labour conditions.

What has shaped contemporary economies of recycling is not only the unequal relationship between rich and poor areas of the world, but the emergence of transactions that complicate such overly simplistic geopolitical separations. From the 1980s, neoliberal philosophy spread (often as part of the conditions attached to international loans) to postcolonial and post-socialist contexts. For those whom this benefited, this led to an increasing demand for materials for infrastructural expansion, energy and consumer goods. This is why, in addition to relatively lax environmental regulation, India and China are primary destinations for various recyclable waste streams.

Despite the view that the traffic in wastes continues unimpeded by state intervention, Tong and Wang (this volume) demonstrate the complex policy arrangements that allow the flow of e-waste to China's coastal cities, but which simultaneously call into question the moral standing of the various electronics recyclers who profit from it. Like container ships, digital electronics goods are popular icons of global connection and their disposal reshapes China's coastal industries just as ship-breaking does the outskirts of Chittagong. New forms of e-waste are also challenging for the toxicity involved in their disassembly and transformation into revalued things. Chinese recycling is shown to have an important role in rural industrialization and to have fraught relations with international environmental NGOs because of the contaminants involved in e-waste recycling. Further, with the rise of China's ideology of the Circular Economy, the environmental credentials of various recyclers are under pressure and the e-recycling industry is forced to adapt its image and practice to overlapping regimes of legal, economic and media circulation.

There is money to be made in recycling economies but there are also new regulatory forms being developed at different levels from Basel, either self-imposed by companies wishing to promote images of producer responsibility or enforced by new national and sub-national protocols. Wastes continue to flow from wealthy to poor countries, not only in the absence of regulation, but also through regulatory channels. In his contribution, Garcier discusses how the moral promise of recycling in the nuclear energy industry, as its regulations are currently structured, succeeds by redistributing contamination risks from France to Russia. Concerns about environmental security and nuclear weapon development also shape the moral economy of spent nuclear fuel. While the French company is applauded for its moral and environmental care in re-enriching spent fuel, the place where this is performed ends up as a toxic sink. Thus, he demonstrates that following the rules for proper recycling does not preclude the destruction of places and may indeed act to block such pollution from view.

The destinations of recyclables are foregrounded in these three chapters. These places may not be the ultimate destination for the extracted materials, which may be resold in turn in a new product form. Rather, these are destinations because there is always something that lingers behind after processes of complex material disassembly. The moral conundrum of these global recycling economies is that they create work and follow existing regulations, yet may localize toxic pollution and hazardous working conditions in poorer countries on behalf of richer ones. There is a danger (as in Summers's memo) that the geopolitical divisions upon which this trade is predicated will be naturalized as if they were merely the work of the market's invisible hand distributing risks and wealth as it should. But it is also the work of regulations that have produced new economic enterprises and transactions, and continually realign global divisions of labour, in tension with these visions of natural, unfettered markets.

The lure of remaking The image of the downtrodden, Third World waste-picker regularly circulated through news media is a familiar one; it shows people living on the edge, attempting to survive in the midst of unspeakable tragedy (see Reno 2009: 32). Undignified and unproductive, merely scrounging off the scraps of others, the figure of the trash-picker (often a woman or a child) appears as the ideal counterpoint to the masculinized vision of industrial labour. Exploring recycling economies reveals the surprising significance of apparently small and undignified acts of collection and revaluation. Scavenging is, in fact, one of the most important sources of informal employment in the world (see Medina 2000).

The image of the waste-picker also exoticizes practices of remaking. But the labour of reusing materials to extend the life of an object or make another is familiar enough to most; literally so, that is, familial. Such labour was a central plank in household economies: worn sheets were restitched with French seams sides to the middle, clothes cut down for children, woollen garments unpicked for yarn; houses bore signs of neat patching from hoarded scraps (Pember-Reeves 2008 [1913]; Whiteley 2010; Strasser 2000). While such domestic crafts may often be tedious to perform, there is sometimes also pleasure to be found through the skilled labour involved. Re-creating can also be recreation; the positive affect of some acts of remaking should not be underestimated, as Alexander's and Bear's chapters show. Such skills of material attentiveness, prized in contexts of shortage, can lose their value where capitalism privileges productive and consumptive destruction over care and repair. Humans and their labour, as well as objects and landscapes, are discarded, cast off. As these chapters show, alongside narratives of material plenty and excess for some, there is also loss and decay in the midst of overwhelming transition, particularly of built environments and infrastructures.

But the relationship between labour and waste also opens up new possibilities for social protest and imagination in the wake of socio-economic upheaval. Bear's chapter examines the physical signs of deterioration in objects, landscapes and humans and the active processes of destruction wrought by capitalism along the Hooghly river, in West Bengal. For Bear, waste not only signifies loss but is a call to action as workers attempt to assert the creativity of human labour against the forces of decline associated with post-liberal structural reforms.

The retraction of state services accompanying the availability of new markets and goods has led to crises of waste disposal throughout the developing world, where municipal services cannot keep pace with rising rates of urbanization. In the absence of public collection services, some NGOs attempt to make individual citizens and communities responsible for their own waste collection. Fredericks and Faulk discuss the destruction of place and community through neoliberal reforms, and subsequent attempts to restore place and humanity through labour. Fredericks investigates attempts by international NGOs to convert Dakar's municipal garbage services into the responsibility of communities, especially women, who are to be converted into Senegalese entrepreneurs in place of a provisioned social infrastructure of waste removal. These projects rehearse the familiar alignment of low-status waste work with social divides in terms of class, gender, race and place. Despite the best intentions of these NGOs, ridding communities of waste is not easily recycled into an entrepreneurial and empowering form of community work. Rather, in the context of Dakar, it becomes devalued and unpaid labour, not the source of new values and collective expression.

Elsewhere, private industry replaces public services, which creates new problems for those who wish to reuse materials. With the rise of a global scrap market, for example, waste becomes prime fodder for privatization, an unregulated commons to which informal recyclers and larger firms struggle for access. Faulk recounts how the wasted landscape of Buenos Aires is recovered by its denizens, having been abandoned by the rollback of public welfare. The workers' movements she discusses seek to regain legitimacy through the recuperative power of their labour as they attempt to restore a hotel to live in together, as both a sign of their human worth and a way of resisting marginalization. In her account, hotels remade into habitable homes through community-led projects, and things reconstituted for sale, confront and resist the wasting of people, places and things, of which the state is accused (see also Bauman 2003).

Norris's evocative description of the environment in which migrant women dismantle garments for recycling in Panipat conveys the strident contradictions of these run-down, polluting factories. Surrounded by gloriously vivid mounds of colour, children suffer from dust-related respiratory conditions; their mothers labour long hours for little money, dependent on a 'jobber', or middleman, for work security. Most striking perhaps is how the skilled work of deconstructing complex clothing is carried out with kitchen tools and devalued to the point that the women are infantilized with presents of sweets in return for handing over valuables to their jobber.

Even devalued, however, labour with wastes in the most marginal of places can be interpreted as a meeting place between global markets and local concerns. In Millar's discussion of Jardin Gramacho, Rio de Janeiro's primary garbage dump (the largest in Latin America), marginal lives are still significant. Focusing on the tales of three *catadores*, or waste-pickers, Millar shows how lives on the urban and global margins are closely connected to centres of power and calculation that shape global prices of recovered materials. Millar avoids the easy narrative that overstates the power or nobility of those who sort and collect waste at dumps, but, by tracking their activities and transactions, she shows how the *catadores* reach beyond immediate survival to shape the lives of others, including Rio de Janeiro's citizens, who both provide the *catadores* with growing amounts of their refuse and marginalize them from mainstream society.

The places where recycling and waste work occur are typically marginal. Andrea Palladio, the celebrated sixteenth-century architect, compared the layout of a house to that of the human body, noting that the 'ignoble but essential parts are hidden' (Ackerman 1966: 57). The analogy can be extended to cities, countries and regions. Margins, in this sense, operate at a number of different levels, each servicing the more beautiful and exposed parts of society: markets, waste dumps, cemeteries and carnival were all traditionally linked to urban edges – socially subversive, troubling and essential. The rubbish dumps of Dakar and Rio de Janeiro are located on the edges of the cities that provide them with wastes. Broader global geographies link Chittagong to other ports; textile reprocessing factories first to the outskirts of Panipat and then to a wealthy Europe and Scandinavia; the Siberian city of Seversk accepts the depleted fuel of French electricity generation; and China's coastal areas and rural hinterlands take up the electronic detritus of Europe and America.

Considering the relationship between power centres and margins reveals dependencies that reach both ways. Commodity futures prices for raw and recovered materials affect scrap and recycling activities, which, in turn, feed economies with revalued materials and objects.

In such tightly knit relationships, it is hard to distinguish completely who is dependent upon whom. What is clear, however, is that there is little recompense for those who directly labour to extract potentially valuable elements from used-up industrial or consumer goods; it is the brokers and dealers, quite different kinds of marginal figures, who get the most monetary return. And yet, the possibility of remaking something never fails to attract willing hands and imaginations.

Property rights and obligations Recent forays into questions of property have begun to explore the mutability and ephemerality of property objects. The idea of assemblages, particular configurations of the socio-technical, material, regulative and so on, is a useful way of querying the extent to which we can limit and so define the object to which rights are sought – or denied; this is key. While most of the debates on property rights have concerned themselves with *rights* over things, shifting the focus to waste and recycling reveals an underbelly of problematic and unanswered questions, often concerning *obligations*. From biblical injunctions (Psalms 128:2) through Locke (1960) and onwards, the emphasis on property in the Western tradition has been on rights to production, to the fruits of bodily labour: ownership tempered by compassion for the dispossessed – a compassion that was steadily regulated out from the eighteenth century on (Linebaugh 2003). There has been less attention paid to the obligations of property, to the wastes, pollution and by-products that are also produced by labour.

Faulk re-engages with familiar ideas of rights through bodily labour. Here, however, the object under question (an abandoned hotel that is being renovated) is being *re*claimed through labour. Legal assertions of ownership are thus trumped by labour, which also demonstrates that the labourers have fulfilled obligations to the property object that the state has not. Having reasserted creative control over the forgotten waste of the hotel and their own lives, Faulk's informants show an alternative sense of ownership, tied to responsibility for both persons and things.

As the discussion above and Alexander's chapter also suggest, an emphasis on the daily engagements of care and maintenance suggests that the familiar subject–object relation of property ownership can itself be challenged by a relation of equality between subjects. Following objects beyond the point of manufacture, purchase or gift also shows that traces of former property relations remain. As medical supplies move from the point of donation to reception (Halvorson, this volume), the ritualized attempts to sever previous relations and recast the objects and exchange relations anew indicate the labour needed to exorcize previous lives of things. It is not, *contra* Appadurai (1986), simply a matter of objects moving between gift and commodity exchange relations. Things hang in limbo, are stored in warehouses, are dismantled, bear vestiges of earlier incarnations.

Traces of former lives are not easily eradicated, as Norris's chapter demonstrates well. While dismantling the clothes donated to charity shops in the global North, workers in Panipat factories muse on the clothes' origins, their owners, how and why they came to be ripped apart while still functional. Coat pockets shower down material stubs of previous owners' lives, but the workers also project imaginary routes through which the textiles in their hands have passed. As domestic things are fashioned from scraps and endlessly recontrived in contexts of material shortage (Alexander, this volume), clothes, domestic objects and indeed the urban landscape are palimpsests of former, present and potential things, momentarily coalesced into a form to which property rights may be asserted.

Macpherson (1964) famously outlined and condemned the principle of possessive individualism in classical liberal thought; the idea that an individual is the sole proprietor of his or her skills, which arises from the older sense that a free individual's body belongs to them. Possession, Reno suggests, of the products of one's body is not clear cut, particularly when those products can be used as part of the forensic repertoire to reconstruct a former life and person. Traces become an instrument to link present liability to past acts. Reno's discussion of contested rights over human waste plays with the notion that rights to the body end at its outer margins: the extent to which rights continue over detached parts of the body is increasingly the subject of legal debate. His focus is the narcotics trade in the contemporary USA, and the legal and scientific experts who try to make claims about drug practices by reusing waste as prime evidentiary material. While waste forensics offers trace glimpses into the movement of drugs through bodies and urban infrastructure, however, it is complicated by the sense of an enduring connection between people and their wastes and the rights of ownership that arise from this. At another level this can be seen in attempts to enforce producer responsibility. In this line of thinking, a manufacturer of cars or yogurt pots, for example, retains the obligation to deal appropriately with the used-up item, whatever exchanges the things has passed through.

While the drive to recover energy and materials from used goods is climbing political agendas (a high-end British retailer remarked to the editors of this volume that it 'made a good story'), it has also given rise to a massive global economy in recyclates and scrap that can provide an element of greenwashing. Recovering valuable materials can be dirty and dangerous work, often polluting lands, waterways and the air. While recycling ships, textiles or depleted uranium gains high marks in the moral economy of care for the environment, loosely understood, these processes often generate intensive, localized pollution in other places. As Garcier states, along with accepting depleted uranium for re-enrichment, the reprocessing factory takes on all associated property rights and obligations, including that of toxic contamination produced locally. Objects typically require clear limits before property rights can be asserted in them. Seeping, leaking, dispersible pollution in water, soil and air is a significant challenge to any effective property regime, as is control over objects that decay, change or are taken apart. Examining the rapidly shifting property obligations over recyclables reveals complex moral economies of global displacement and disregard.

Value added and multiplied Creation, recovery and the re-creation of value are at the heart of recycling. This much is relatively, but not entirely, uncontentious. However, there are several different forms of value that are unmade and remade in the course of moving stuff to *where* it can be recycled (typically marginalized places) dismantling it, reimbuing it with usefulness and reinserting it into mainstream material flows. In one sense, this is about the value-added of material transformation, in common with any productive activity. What a focus on recycling affords is an appreciation of the multiple, mutable values of a thing at any one moment in time: the nature of the thing itself, liable to transformation – its monetary price, whether trifling or huge, affected by market demands; the calorific value used and produced by different recycling or recovery technologies; the many positively freighted moral values of saving resources, providing labour, gifting items for reuse, which in turn need to be set against the unvalued people and places typically involved in the restoration of value to worn-out things.

The distinctions between the material, moral and monetary transformations of production and recycling are worth highlighting. We have seen how structural elisions commonly appear between marginalized labour, people and places, and how such elisions may be contested. The skills required for keeping things going, or crafting new objects from old, are not universally valued. This is particularly apparent in Alexander's chapter, where the once lauded and moralized ability to conjure a family meal from scraps or a garden hoe from oddments has become as outmoded and unregarded as the practitioners who find themselves beached, unable to turn with the tide. Moving from a domestic to an industrial setting, Bear and Faulk again show dissonances between how the practices of care towards things are conceptualized and valorized.

Halvorson's contribution investigates how the medical discards created by insurance regulations in American biomedicine attain new life in faith-based medical humanitarianism. Focusing on two American Lutheran aid agencies that supply an array of discarded and recovered medical materials to Madagascar, she documents the negotiation of moral, religious and historical values in working with used medical materials. At the same time, each actor at these various stages of circulation remains aware of the prior origin of the medical object as a used item, its former identity as another's waste product, and they act accordingly. This is evident from the ways that medical institutions negotiate the legal transfer of their waste to aid organizations and the ways that religious volunteers resist the description of their activity as a form of recycling. Arguably, those who manage the cast-offs of others could be said to possess the ability to transact between economic and environmental, moral and material values.

The global moral economy of recycling is frequently tendentious. The moral charge of saving the planet's resources accrues to shipping companies selling on end-of-life vessels for scrap; nuclear energy operators sending depleted uranium away for re-enrichment; e-waste collectors and brokers, donors of textiles to charity shops or hospitals redirecting unwanted medical supplies to needy countries. To the brokers of these flows and recycling processes, there is often considerable monetary and moral currency to be gained. But, all too often, in the places where materials are reinvested with value, employment is precarious and dangerous and unrecyclable wastes accumulate. The chimera of a global closed material system doesn't hold: flows do not keep going for ever, stuff wears out, fibres break, dust and wastes settle, as Norris's chapter demonstrates with such finality. Global flows of scraps and unwanted materials sharply juxtapose the action of recharging materials with monetary value with the places where these processes occur. Global margins are increasingly used either to dispose of wastes that have become too expensive to deal with, or to reprocess them.

As Gille (2007) argues, the toxicity of some wastes has a tendency to 'bite back', as they resist the frameworks (what she calls the waste regimes) that are used to process and control them. This is so because environmental processes and non-human agencies assert themselves through waste production and processing. Recycling technologies *do* stretch used materials. We do not suggest that they serve no purpose, only point out that there are limits to any such process and the hope of closed loops. This may mean that materials have a toxicity that cannot be dispelled, or that what 'resists' reuse and repurposing is a trace of an object's origin, a material quality that speaks of the former uses to which it was put. The forms of 'recycling' that Reno examines in his chapter seek to make waste into legal and scientific evidence by relying on the inertia of waste flows, their lasting connection to the relations, persons and bodies where they originated. Alexander discusses a similar material 'resistance' in her account of Soviet-era ideologies of material culture, where reuse is meant to affirm an object's identity as a comrade in the ongoing revolution performed at the scale of everyday life.

If the rag-picker standing aloft on a huge, stinking pile of urban detritus has become something of an icon for the dispossessed of the modern world, then the recycling cooperatives of Latin America seem to represent a different beacon, one of hope. This time, workers flung aside by the processes of neoliberalism have recovered and re-formed themselves into labour cooperatives. Organized *catadores* reject the title of waste people, reclaiming dignity and selves. Once again, however, a more nuanced ethnographic engagement with such organizations reveals additional layers of ambivalence, showing that the story is not straightforward. Fredericks's account of an NGO-inspired female waste cooperative has a strong flavour of the rehabilitative mission to re-form souls as well as things. Faulk's and Millar's chapters show the micro-politics of recovering value through such organizations, but also highlight the frailty of these cooperatives. Their viability relies on global commodity prices set elsewhere in the world, as much as that of any other organization subject to the vagaries of market demand.

One thing emerged unexpectedly as we started to write the chapters that follow; the language of recycling for materials and labourers alike is often tinged with connotations of Protestant redemption. Although this is clearest in Halvorson's chapter, it appears in other chapters too. Materials are salvaged, saved, recovered; sorting through trash is a common rehabilitative exercise for prisoners, intended to restore them to being social citizens. Conversion applies equally to the materials we have described here and to saved souls. Restoration is not merely extending the useful life of objects but, in a Christian eschatology, returns a corrupt world to a prelapsarian Eden. In this spirit, we end with a reminder of the secular apocalypse that shadows these pathways to material and moral salvation. There are limits to the eternal transformations suggested by much of the recycling rhetoric. And beyond those limits there are only hurt bodies, polluted lands and a handful of dust.

Notes

1 Technically, recycling is different from simple reuse, whereby objects may be repurposed but not necessarily transformed materially. For the purposes of this volume, however, the two terms are used interchangeably.

2 In March 2008, participants from thirty-four countries gathered in Bogotá, Colombia, for the first World Conference of Waste Pickers and the Third Conference of Latin American Waste Pickers, which was timed to coincide with the global event.

3 The term 'downcycling' is increasingly used for recycled things that fail to achieve prime-material quality. Werner Boote's 2009 documentary film *Plastic Planet* explores downcycling in recycled plastics.

4 The Navigation Acts of 1651, 1660 and 1663, for example, between Britain and the colonies, legally enjoined the colonists to buy goods from Britain.

5 Savas (1977: 4) notes, though, that the city of Mahenjo-Daro in the Indus river valley had 'rubbish chutes, at the foot of which were sometimes bins at street level'.

6 Urine would later also be collected to fix dyes, whiten laundry and as a medicinal component. Human and animal dung (known as pure) were essential for the tanning trade, hence the eye-watering aroma of Southwark – an area of London once famed for its soft leathers.

7 Moser (2002: 87) points out that French is more discriminating than English between types of waste: the singular and plural '*déchet*' allows the sense of waste as residue versus the notion of decay and corruption. Once it has become an amorphous, homogenized mass, 'an aggregate of heteroclite particles' (ibid.), different words again are used: '*gadoue*' or '*immondices*'.

8 Klima's novel *Love and Garbage* similarly sets up the urban ragpicker as one able to contemplate the follies of humankind from his marginal viewpoint.

9 Gibbs (2006) shows how infrastructure, people and politics can be added to the industrial ecology mix.

10 For example, the promotion of domestic recycling – in its conventional sense – in places like the USA during the 1970s and 1980s can be understood as a compromise form of regulatory oversight, offset to the household, in order to enforce a compromise between growing demands for environmental reform and the rights of private enterprise (see Rogers 2006).

11 As recognized by the activists of the Basel Action Network and other environmental NGOs.

References

Ackerman, J. (1966) *Palladio*, The Architect and Society Series, Baltimore, MD: Penguin.

Adorno, T. (1973) *Negative Dialectics*, London: Routledge.

Alexander, C. (2005) 'Value:

economic valuations and environmental policy', in J. Carrier (ed.), *A Handbook of Economic Anthropology*, Cheltenham: Edward Elgar, pp. 455–72.

— (2012) 'Value: economic valuations and environmental policy', in J. Carrier (ed.), *A Handbook of Economic Anthropology*, Cheltenham: Edward Elgar.

Alexander, C. and C. Smaje (2008) 'Evaluating third-sector re-use organisations in the UK: case-studies and analysis of furniture re-use schemes', *Resources, Conservation and Recovery*, 52(5): 719–30.

Allen, J. (2010) *America's Biggest Trade Export to China? Trash*, www.usnews.com/opinion/blogs/jodie-allen/2010/03/03/americas-biggest-trade-export-to-china-trash, accessed 15 September 2011.

Anderson, P. (1984) 'Modernity and revolution', *New Left Review*, 144, March/April.

Appadurai, A. (1986) *The Social Life of Things: Commodities in Cultural Perspective*, Cambridge Studies in Social and Cultural Anthropology, Cambridge: Cambridge University Press.

Ayres, R. (1989a) 'Industrial metabolism and global change', *International Social Science Journal*, 121.

— (1989b) 'Industrial metabolism', in Ausubel, Jesse and Sladovich (eds), *Technology and Environment*, Washington, DC: National Academy Press.

Barnes, D. (2006) *The Great Stink of Paris and the Nineteenth-century Struggle against Filth and Germs*, Baltimore, MD: Johns Hopkins University Press.

Barnes, D., F. Galgani, R. Thompson and M. Barlaz (2009) 'Accumulation and fragmentation of plastic debris in global environments', *Philos Trans R Soc Lond B Biol Sci*, 364(1526): 1985–98.

Bauman, Z. (2003) *Wasted Lives: Modernity and its outcasts*, Cambridge: Polity Press.

Baumgartl, B. (1993) 'Environmental protest as a vehicle for transition: the case of Ekoglasnost in Bulgaria', in A. Vari and P. Tamas (eds), 'Environment and democratic transition: policy and politics and Central and Eastern Europe', *Risk, Governance and Society*, 7.

Benjamin, W. (2002) *The Arcades Project*, Cambridge, MA: Harvard University Press.

Berman, M. (1983) *All that is Solid Melts into Air*, New York and London: Verso.

Bhuiyan, S. I. (2011) 'Social media and its effectiveness in the political reform movement in Egypt', *Middle East Media Educator*, 1(1): 14–20, ro.uow.edu.au/meme/vol1/iss1/3.

Block, A. (1985) *Poisoning for Profit: The Mafia and toxic waste in America*, New York: William Morrow and Co. Inc.

Boote, W. (director) (2009) *Plastic Planet*, Brandstorm Entertainment, Cine Carton Filmproduktion and Neue Sentimental Film Entertainment GmbH, Germany and Austria.

Bournay, E. and UNEP (United Nations Environment Programme)/GRID-Arendal (2006) *Vital Waste Graphics* 2, http://www.grida.no/publications/vg/waste2/, accessed 15 September 2011.

Branigan, T. (2009) 'From east to west, a chain collapses', *Guardian*, 9 January, www.guardian.co.uk/environment/2009/jan/09/

recycling-global-recession-china, accessed 15 September 2011.

Broadbent, J. (1998) *Environmental Politics in Japan: Networks of power and protest*, Cambridge: Cambridge University Press.

Bryant, B. (ed.) (1995) *Environmental Justice: Issues, Policies and Solutions*, Washington, DC: Island Press.

Bryant, B. and P. Mohai (1992) *Race and the Incidence of Environmental Hazards: A Time for Discourse*, Boulder, CO: Westview Press.

Calafate, F. (n.d.) *Recycling Markets of Secondary Materials: Price and Environmental Value*, MA dissertation, Goldsmiths, University of London.

Chaturvedi, B. (2009) 'A scrap of decency', *New York Times*, 4 August, www.nytimes.com/2009/08/05/opinion/05chaturvedi.html, accessed 15 September 2011.

Clapp, J. (2001) *Toxic Exports: The Transfer of Hazardous Wastes from Rich to Poor Countries*, Ithaca, NY: Cornell University Press.

Clark, J. (2007) '"The incineration of refuse is beautiful": Torquay and the introduction of municipal refuse destructors', *Urban History*, 34: 254–76.

— (2008) 'In the shadow of progress: the rise of municipal waste disposal in Britain', in T. Mizoguchi (ed.), *The Environmental Histories of Europe and Japan*, pp. 127–38.

Clift, R. and L. Wright (2000) 'Relationships between environmental impacts and added value along the supply chain', *Technological Forecasting and Social Change*, 65(3): 281–95.

Cooper, T. (2008) 'Challenging the "refuse revolution": war, waste and the rediscovery of recycling,

1900–1950', *Historical Research*, 81(214): 710–31.

— (2009) 'War on waste? The politics of waste and recycling in post-war Britain, 1950–1975', *Capitalism Nature Socialism*, 20(4): 53–72.

Daly, H. (ed.) (1973) *Toward a Steady State Economy*, W. H. Freeman & Co. Ltd.

Dasgupta, P. and G. Heal (1974) 'The optimal depletion of exhaustible resources', Symposium on the 'Economics of exhaustible resources', *Review of Economic Studies*, 41: 3–28.

— (1979) *Economic Theory and Exhaustible Resources*, Cambridge: Cambridge University Press.

Dawdy, L. S. (2010) 'Clockpunk anthropology and the ruins of modernity', *Current Anthropology*, 51(6): 761–92.

Dickens, C. (1998) *Our Mutual Friend*, London: Wordsworth Editions Ltd.

EEA (European Environment Agency) (2009) *Waste without Borders in the EU? Transboundary shipments of waste*, EEA Report 1/2009, Luxembourg: Office for Official Publications of the European Communities.

French, H. (1990) 'Green revolutions: environmental reconstruction in eastern Europe and the Soviet Union', Worldwatch paper 99.

Frosch, R. A. and N. E. Gallopoulos (1989) 'Strategies for manufacturing', *Scientific American*, 261(3): 144–52.

Gabrys, J. (2011) *Digital Rubbish: A Natural History of Electronics*, Ann Arbor: University of Michigan Press.

Gandy, M. (1994) *Recycling and the Politics of Urban Waste*, London: Earthscan.

Georgescu-Roegen, N. (1971) *The Entropy Law and the Economic Process*, Cambridge, MA: Harvard University Press.

— (1979a) 'Myths about energy and matter', *Growth and Change*, 10(1).

— (1979b) 'Energy analysis and economic valuation', *Southern Economic Journal*.

Gibbs, D. (2006) 'Prospects for an environmental economic geography: linking ecological modernisation and regulationist approaches', *Economic Geography*, 82(2): 193–215.

Gille, Z. (2007) *From the Cult of Waste to the Trash Heap of History: The politics of waste in socialist and postsocialist Hungary*, Bloomington: Indiana University Press.

Ginzburg, C. (1980) 'Morelli, Freud and Sherlock Holmes: clues and scientific method', *History Workshop*, 9: 5–36.

Gordon, W. J. (1890) 'How London lives: the feeding, cleansing, lighting and police of London', London: Religious Tract Society.

Gößling-Reisemann, S. (2008) 'What is resource consumption and how can it be measured? Theoretical considerations', *Journal of Industrial Ecology*, 12(1): 12–25.

Gregson, N. (2009) 'Challenging assumptions: recycling as policy and assemblage', *Geography*, 94(1): 61–5.

Grossman, E. (2006) *High Tech Trash: Digital Devices, Hidden Toxics and Human Health*, Washington, DC: Island Press.

Hardt, M. (1999) 'Affective labour', *boundary 2*, 26: 89–100.

Hart, K., J.-L. Laville and A. Cattani (eds) (2010) *The Human Economy*, Cambridge: Polity Press.

Harvey, D. (2003) *The New Imperialism*, Oxford: Oxford University Press.

Hawkins, G. (2006) *The Ethics of Waste: How we relate to rubbish*, Lanham, MD: Rowman and Littlefield.

Herbert, L. (2007) *Centenary History of Waste and Waste Managers in London and South East England*, Northampton: CIWM.

Hill, P. (2006) *The Japanese Mafia: Yakuza, Law, and the State*, Oxford: Oxford University Press.

Ingold, T. and E. Hallam (2007) 'Creativity and cultural improvisation: an introduction', in E. Hallam and T. Ingold (eds), *Creativity and Cultural Improvisation*, Oxford: Berg, pp. 1–24.

Jewitt, S. (2011) 'Geographies of shit', *Progress in Human Geography*, 35(5): 608–26.

Kang, H.-Y. and J. Schoenung (2005) 'Electronic waste recycling: a review of U.S. infrastructure and technology options', *Resources, Conservation and Recyling*, 45(4): 368–400.

Klima, I. (1993) *Love and Garbage*, New York: Vintage.

Kracauer, S. (1930) *Die Angestellten*, Berlin: Societäts-Verlag.

Laporte, D. (2000) *History of Shit*, Cambridge, MA: MIT Press.

Lefebvre, H. (1991) *The Production of Space*, Oxford: Wiley-Blackwell.

Lewis, I. (2003) 'Recycling Somalia from the scrap merchants of Mogadishu', *Northeast African Studies*, 10(3): 213–24.

Linebaugh, P. (2003) *The London Hanged: Crime and civil society in the eighteenth century*, London: Verso.

Locke, J. (1960) *Two Treatises of Government*, 3rd edn, Cambridge: Cambridge University Press.

Lukacs, G. (1971) *History and Class Consciousness*, London: Merlin.

Mackenzie, D. (2006) *An Engine, Not a Camera*, Cambridge, MA: MIT Press.

Macpherson, C. (1964) *The Political Theory of Possessive Individualism: Hobbes to Locke*, Oxford: Oxford Paperbacks.

Marx, K. (1998) *The German Ideology*, New York: Prometheus Books.

Massari, M. and P. Monzini (2004) 'Dirty businesses in Italy: a case-study of illegal trafficking in hazardous waste', *Global Crime*, 6(3/4): 285–304.

Maxwell, W. (1898) *Removal and Disposal of Town Refuse*, London: Sanitary Publishing Company.

Mayhew, H. (2010 [1851]) *London Labour and the London Poor*, Oxford: Oxford University Press.

Meadows, D., J. Randers and W. Behrens III (1972) *The Limits to Growth: A Report for the Club of Rome's Project on the Predicament of Mankind*, New York: Universe Books.

Medina, M. (2000) 'Scavenger cooperatives in Asia and Latin America', *Resources, Conservation and Recycling*, 31(1): 51–69.

Melosi, M. (1981) *Garbage in the Cities: Refuse, Reform, and the Environment, 1880–1980*, College Station, TX: A&M Press.

Minter, A. (forthcoming) *Wasted: Inside the Multi-billion Dollar Trade in American Trash*, London: Bloomsbury (publication 2013).

Mitchell, T. (2002) *Rule of Experts*, Berkeley, London and Los Angeles: University of California Press.

Morris, L. (2002) *Dangerous Classes: The underclass, and social citizenship*, London: Routledge.

Moser, W. (2002) 'The acculturation of waste', in B. Neville and J. Villeneuve (eds), *Waste-site Stories: The recycling of memory*, New York, SUNY Press, pp. 85–106.

Mumford, L. (1961) *The City in History: Its Origins, Its Transformations, and Its Prospects*, New York: Harcourt, Brace & World, Inc.

Nakamura, S. and Y. Kondo (2002) 'Input-output analysis of waste management', *Journal of Industrial Ecology*, 6: 39–63.

O'Brien, M. (2007) *A Crisis of Waste: Understanding the rubbish society*, London: Routledge.

Parry, B. (2007) 'Economy or shadow economy: modes of commodification of human body parts and tissues and their implications for regulation', *Geoforum*, 39(3).

Pember-Reeves, M. (2008 [1913]) *Round about a Pound a Week*, London: Persephone Books.

Posch, A. (2004) 'Industrial recycling networks: results of rational decision-making or "organised anarchies"?', *Progress in Industrial Ecology, an International Journal*, 1(103): 112–29.

Rees, W. (1992) 'Ecological footprints and appropriated carrying capacity: what urban economics leaves out', *Environment and Urbanisation*, 4(2): 121–30.

Rees, W. and M. Wackernagel (1996) *Our Ecological Footprint: Reducing footprint on the earth*, Gabriola Island, BC: New Society Publishers.

Reid, D. (1991) *Paris Sewers and Sewermen*, Cambridge, MA: Harvard University Press.

Reno, J. (2009) 'Your trash is someone's treasure: the politics of value at a Michigan landfill', *Journal of Material Culture*, 14(1): 29–46.

Rogers, H. (2006) *Gone Tomorrow:*

The Hidden Life of Garbage, New York: New Press.

Savas, E. (ed.) (1977) *The Organization and Efficiency of Solid Waste Collection*, Toronto: Lexington Books.

Schmidt-Bleek, F., S. Bringezu, F. Hinterberger, C. Liedtke, J. Spangenberg, H. Stiller and M. Welfens (1998) *MAIA. Einführung in die Materialintensitätsanalyse nach dem MIPS-Konzept*, Berlin, Basel: Birkhauser.

Socolow, R. (1974) 'The economics of resources or the resources of economics', *American Economic Review*, 64.

Socolow, R., C. Andrews, F. Berkhout and V. Thomas (eds) (1994) *Industrial Ecology and Global Change*, Cambridge: Cambridge University Press.

Stallybrass, P. and A. White (1986) *The Politics and Poetics of Transgression*, Ithaca, NY: Cornell University Press.

Stedman Jones, G. (1976) *Outcast London: A Study in the Relationship between Classes in Victorian Society*, Harmondsworth: Penguin.

Stiglitz, J. (1974) 'Growth with exhaustible natural resources: efficient and optimal growth paths', *Review of Economic Studies*, 41.

Strasser, S. (2000) *Waste and Want: A Social History of Trash*, New York: Holt.

Swedberg, R. (2008) 'The centrality of materiality: economic theorizing from Xenophon to home economics and beyond', in T. Pinch and R. Swedberg (eds), *Living in a Material World*, Cambridge, MA, and London: MIT Press.

Takase, K., Y. Kondo and A. Washizu (2005) 'An analysis of sustainable consumption by the Waste Input-Output model', *Journal of Industrial Ecology*, 9(1/2): 201–19.

Thorpe, N. (2009) 'Downturn hits Romania's tinkers', *BBC News*, 17 January, news.bbc.co.uk/1/hi/programmes/from_our_own_correspondent/7833138.stm, accessed 15 September 2011.

Velis, C., D. Wilson and C. Cheeseman (2007) 'Early 19th-century London dust-yards: a case study in closed-loop resource efficiency', Paper in the 2007 Sardinia Waste Symposium.

Vidal, J. (2004) 'The UK's new rubbish dump: China', www.guardian.co.uk/society/2004/sep/20/environment.china, accessed 15 September 2011.

Whiteley, G. (2010) *Junk: Art and the politics of trash*, London: I. B Tauris.

Zimring, C. (2004) 'Dirty work: how hygiene and xenophobia marginalized the American waste trades 1870–1930', *Environmental History*, 9(1): 90–112, www.oecd.org/dataoecd/2/20/4425421.pdf.

Global waste flows

1 | Shoddy rags and relief blankets: perceptions of textile recycling in north India

LUCY NORRIS

Introduction

Following humanitarian disasters around the world, bundles of grey emergency relief blankets are often distributed to those in need by aid agencies. Affording warmth and protection by literally wrapping abject bodies in gifts, these rough blankets materialize wider networks of care and support, while making visible the recipients' liminal status and framing their apparent lack of agency.[1] But the freely distributed grey aid blanket is just one of the unexpected end products of a very different global flow of gifts and commodities that reconfigure categories of value: that of second-hand clothing discarded and donated to charities in developed economies. For these gritty, smelly, coarse and scratchy grey blankets are produced from second-hand Western clothing, shredded and recycled in north Indian factories. They are woven from regenerated yarn (hereafter referred to as 'shoddy'), and are usually designed to last for just one season, during which they fall apart.

Tracing these material connections reveals the transformations that occur across multiple economic, political and cultural registers as donations of unwanted old clothes are commodified, destroyed, regenerated and donated in a new form to those in need. The ephemerality of clothing and the refashionability of its constituent fabrics and fibres is key to both its use in liminal, transformational contexts, and its agency in creating movement and change. However, the chapter argues that although the production chain is bracketed by the apparent moral value of the gift, the process of creative destruction at its capitalist heart involves investing minimal value in social and environmental manufacturing conditions, a self-defeating strategy ultimately revealed in the disintegrating blanket.

The political economy of second-hand clothing

The value of the global trade in second-hand garments doubled from $1.26 billion in 2001 to $2.5 billion in 2009.[2] Most have been bought from charities in the developed world, which cannot sell all the mountains of donations they receive themselves. In the UK, for example, charities sell only 20 per cent of their donations directly, the rest being sold to commercial dealers who export them for reuse (a further 60 per cent), sell them on to recyclers (15 per cent), and throw the remaining 5 per cent away (Morley et al. 2009).[3] Global markets for reuse have developed rapidly, and there is an increasing amount of research into their development and impact (Hansen 2000, 2004a, 2004b, Norris forthcoming-a). Eastern Europe has become the primary destination for high-quality brands of all-season clothing, the African market buys good-quality, fashionable summer clothing, while Pakistan is the destination for the lowest-quality grades.

However, as developing economies are largely situated in warmer climates, the global market lacks the capacity to absorb high volumes of winter clothing, such as thicker wool, acrylic and mixed-fibre suits, trousers, jackets, jumpers and soft furnishings sold as bales of 'jazz'. Lacking any other avenues to avoid their wastage, these clothes form a low-value, residual category of 'recycling grades'. Yet, as remainders, they destabilize the homogeneity of that category since some are perfectly wearable garments in good condition. The consumption of second-hand clothing has become an integral part of many developing economies in the global South, but these obsolete leftovers of global capitalism remain largely unnoticed, and are sold for shredding to the machine wiping industry, the flocking industry and the Indian shoddy industry.

The pivotal place in this particular sequence of creative destruction is the industrial town of Panipat, north of Delhi. Drawing on ethnographic research in the town and its factories,[4] this chapter focuses upon the local perceptions of those working in the industry concerning where the clothing comes from (and why) and where it goes to, contextualizing these constructed imaginaries with a description of the embodied engagement of workers with used clothing. Thus it provokes comparison with Halvorson's work on donor imaginaries concerning charitable chains of medical discards from the USA to Madagascar (this volume); her work addresses the complexities of how waste is recategorized as a resource in redemptive economies, carefully avoiding the moral pitfalls of certain destructive practices. This chapter takes as its starting point materials that have already been transformed from discard to gift to commodity, and are precisely located at that point in the production chain where the means through which they are destroyed is not necessarily productive of successful recuperation.

What emerges from this ethnography are the moral tensions inherent in these processes of conversion, which are symbolized by the decomposing aid blanket. Framed by the moral value of the charitable gift, this recycling industry produces waste and pollution, processes rags in unregulated factories using unorganized labour, and creates disintegrating end products that may even fail to deliver the care expected of them (Norris forthcoming-b). Textiles cannot be infinitely recycled, but this industry cuts to the quick, rapidly downcycling materials into rock-bottom products; the shock is the sheer waste of the wealth of social, moral and labour value(s) that have been previously added in order to create marginal returns. The deregulated neoliberal Indian economy described by Bear (this volume) underpins the recycling industry dependent upon the exploitation of subcontracted labour, but here the landscape of waste materials comprises the alienated discards of Western over-consumption; they have been imported to be reconceptualized and regenerated.

The global recycling trade often processes materials in liminal spaces, before they are reintroduced back into the market, a key theme in this volume. Industrial textile recycling is demonstrably downcycling, where value is constantly falling, and I argue that the processes and products revealed here show how value systems fail to fully reintegrate and revalue these materials and the people with whom they are entangled. Instead they remain waste products in the shadowy margins of global capitalism, reproducing social and economic inequality and conjoining people and things as waste.

Panipat industry

India imports 220,000 tons of worn clothing a year, some of which is sorted for reuse and re-exported via the special economic zones around Kandla, Gujarat. Approximately 15 per cent of these garments legally enter India as wearable clothing under a strict quota system, but the rest consists of 'mutilated hosiery', clothing destined for commercial recycling that has to be slashed to allow it through customs. Panipat, north of Delhi, imports roughly 100,000 tons of worn jumpers, coats and suits annually,[5] to be shredded and recycled into 'regenerated yarn' in over three hundred mills and hundreds of smaller units; it constitutes the world's largest remaining shoddy processing industry,[6] and comprises between a third and a half of the total output of the Indian wool industry.

Panipat is an old hand-weaving town north of Delhi, and was a colonial wool centre. Industrial spinning and weaving was developed after Partition (1947). Because of the expense and shortage of imported long-staple wool, and the coarseness of black Indian wool, the shoddy industry was established as a cheaper alternative, importing used woollen rags from Europe and the USA, and second-hand, rag-tearing machinery from Italy and Poland.[7] By the 1980s, cheap rags were being imported in large volumes to be processed by growing numbers of migrant labourers. There have always been crossovers between the wool and shoddy industries depending on the market (Jenkins and Malin 1990; Malin 1979), with larger factories running shoddy mills alongside other manufactures, and new entrants finding it a low-capital start-up business.

The local industry body estimates that of the yarn, fabric and blankets manufactured, about 10–15 per cent is exported, the rest is for the domestic market. Yarn is exported to Africa, or woven locally into *lohi*, men's shawls, and fabric by the metre for jackets and school uniforms. Up to 100,000 blankets are made every day, mostly thin, grey, one-season blankets for the domestic market and the global aid market. More expensive, thicker, dull-coloured shoddy wool blankets, intended to last three to four years, provision institutions such as prisons, hospitals, railways and the military across the world, while higher-quality, brightly coloured, checked versions used to be popular with the Indian middle classes. By the mid-1990s, the industry had begun to import acrylic jumpers to make acrylic shoddy yarn, opening up a whole new market for bright fluffy blankets featuring animals, cartoon characters and flowers. The most lucrative export market comprises the international aid agencies' emergency wool blankets, of which over 90 per cent come from Panipat. These are delivered to regional depots in Africa and Asia for stockpiling in case of emergency, or transported directly to disaster zones.

Industrial organization Most of the factory labour comes from less developed states in the north-east and eastern part of the country, such as Uttar Pradesh, Bihar, Orissa and West Bengal, with up to half of these migrants permanently settled in the town. Now, approximately 85 per cent of the town is involved in the textile industry, of which 40,000 are in the shoddy industry. The more modern, integrated mills, with international contracts, are on the outskirts of town, while the smaller spinning, weaving and finishing units are in the old part, with unmetalled roads lined with filthy brick buildings covered in lint, and fertile green slime oozing down the outside walls into channels of coloured waste water and sewage. Foreigners rarely visit, though many of these firms are unofficially subcontracted to the larger companies.

The industry operates in the informal, unorganized labour sector (Parry et al. 1999). This even applies to some large mills with up to one hundred workers, which initially appear to be one factory but are in fact broken down internally into smaller units owned or managed by family members and partners (see Breman 1999b). An ILO report estimates the Indian informal sector to be 92.9 per cent and the formal 7.1 per cent (Jha 2006), but it stresses that there are no rigid lines of demarcation and much crossover (see also Breman 2003). Jha argues that the informal economy is neither innovative nor full of opportunities, but is a 'shock absorber' for competitiveness in an increasingly globalized capitalist system (see Harriss 2005; Harriss-White 2003). As Hart (2000) comments, the decline of the formal economy in India is directly linked to the deregulation of Indian capitalism, supported by the World Bank and development agencies, with, quite literally in this case, the periphery mopping up the waste of the centre.

Many mill owners invest very little capital in the equipment, buildings and raw materials, and directly employ only a few management staff and technicians to protect their interests. The resultant labour force is completely subcontracted via the *thekedar* (jobbing) system and is highly fragmented. As one mill owner explained, this avoided the constant 'problems' they had formerly had with unionized workers, who were 'going slow' and sabotaging machines, a common narrative among owners disparaging the 'commitment' of their workers (Breman 1999a; De Neve 2003). It also shifts the blame for low productivity away from their own low-capital investment on to the workforce (Breman 1999a). Another owner disparagingly remarked, 'you don't need brains to run the factory because someone else is doing it for you, you just have to pay by the kilo … the clever people are the *thekedari*'. The jobbers are driven by production targets (i.e. piece rates) to make their profits, and have to extract as much labour as possible from the workers. Spinners claim that this leads to workers having to fix moving machinery, with inevitable accidents such as losing fingers, hands and lower arms.

The subcontracted workforce has no job security or rights of association, is unlikely to receive the state minimum wage, and has no medical benefits or subsidized travel home. As migrants they are politically marginalized; labour laws applying to subcontracted migrant labour are unenforced. Strategies to exercise control over their labour depend instead upon their ability to manipulate relationships with jobbers, often restricted by community ties and loans paid to families back in the village (see Breman 2003; Gopalakrishnan and Sreenivasa 2009). Although a local union representative stated that there is no 'bonded' labour in Panipat, workers do get 'stuck' because of indebtedness to jobbers, a situation described by De Neve (1999) as 'unfree' labour. Locally, jobbers are also known as *lathis* (sticks) and *goondas* (thugs), referring to the potential for violence underlying their relationships.

Processing rags to make shoddy yarn Used clothing for recycling that arrives in Panipat will have already been manually sorted in the back of a Western charity shop (Gregson et al. 2000), re-sorted along the rag merchant's conveyor belts (Botticelli forthcoming; Hawley 2006), sold on to a specialist trader at the bottom of the market (Oakdene Hollins Ltd et al. 2006), exported to India and often re-sorted once more in the special economic zone at the port of Kandla, Gujarat. Western rag merchants claim to hardly recover the costs of these garments,[8] yet even more labour must be invested in them to extract an alternative sequence of values from the heterogeneous contents of the bales. In stark contrast to the moral value accorded to charitable donations fuelling the beginning of this global production chain in Western countries, and that accorded to the aid blankets that are produced at the end, the following descriptive narrative of a shoddy recycling factory reveals the typically poor labour and environmental conditions in which this double conversion is enacted. This is contextualized by the widespread belief of mill owners that the whole industry is unproductive, in decline and facing a dead end.

Clothing has to be manually prepared for feeding into a shredding machine; each garment passes through another four or five hands before reaching the shredder. Workers in a shoddy factory inhabit a soft, undulating landscape of worn garments, whose contours are always in flux; a man standing atop a shrinking mountain of sweaters flings different-coloured garments with a practised swing into the ring of smaller piles growing around him; a circle of women sit in a valley carved out between a pile of stuff waiting to be stripped and the pile they have completed. A mound of grey coats slowly disappears, as a dozen women retrieve a head-load at a time, take them outside to be chopped up into several more piles, and carried off to the shredder, dropping threads, fluff and dust in their wake. As stockpiles grow, heat builds up inside them, and rats scuttle around the edges of the warehouse floor. Working on worn clothing involves engaging their whole bodies, smelling its overwhelming odours released into the dusty warmth, scanning its colours and patterns to assess its value, feeling the prickly wool and plasticky acrylic, slippery linings and ridges of seams between practised hands. To transform a mountain of clothing into a pile of rags involves a profound sensory intimacy with each and every garment, a perceptual encounter with its invasive materiality.

METAL DETECTING One of the owner's managers, Anil the 'sorting master', supervises the unloading of bales of clothing arriving at the factory, which are stood on their sides with the clothing layered in vertical bands. First the outer plastic wrapper is cut off, and then the metal bands cinching the bale are snipped off with cutters, pinging open as the tension is released. Cardboard sheets at each end are peeled off, and the compressed bale begins to expand and fall apart like leaves of filo pastry. The first value to be extracted is from this protective skin around the garments; plastic sheeting is sold into the local market for reuse, while a scrap dealer on a bicycle buys up the metal wire and cardboard by the kilogram. Anil gets a commission from the owner for arranging the sale.

As the bale collapses, the men start throwing garments into a pile near to four or five women sitting in a circle. Squatting on the floor and using traditional metal vegetable cutters, their job is to slice off all the metal fasteners, leaving the worthless plastic to the next stage; zips, buttons, coins and chains are worth money in the market, and can damage machinery.

A buyer can remake zips, shortening them and making them 'fresh' if they are damaged by the cutters – Anil jokingly said, 'It's a specialized job', an 'Indian version of job creation' ... they are 'always making work for more people by dividing up the tasks, and there is always another penny to be extracted from the waste if you have the time to work on it', echoing the strategy of deconstructing clothing into its constitutive elements in order to release its value. Again, he takes a cut in return for arranging the sale of metal and exchanging foreign coins with specialist dealers.

The pockets of jackets, coats and trousers also need checking for

1.1 Opening the bales of clothing (photo: Lucy Norris)

'goodies' or dangerous items. These women skilfully work their hands into pockets to retrieve the deposits that another hand slipped in, many months or years earlier, an intimate, invisible contact with another life that inhabited the garment and lived in it in another world. Business cards with fax numbers and email addresses from around the world litter the shed floor. Dirty hankies, plastic snakes, sweet wrappers and till receipts are the leftovers from busy mothers' daily rounds of shopping, receiving and pocketing rubbish from small children and looking after toys abandoned for a new game. A Rastafarian hat with fake dreads, a special cap with hair on the front for people with receding hairlines, a plastic sou'wester: all become things of curiosity and play, tried on and left hanging on a nail on the factory wall.

The women like the decorative designs added to garments, so they also slice off small trimmings that they take a fancy to, for use at home on clothing, for children or for decorating the house. This may be a fur collar, a piece of rickrack or embroidery, beaded designs, shiny sequins, stars and gold or silver metal thread embroidery, quietly slipped under the piles they sit on. The women say the work is a small business, daily bread, but it is better paid than that of those women farther along the process, who simply sit cutting clothes in the yard; these women get Rs120 ($2.5) for an eight-hour day, while the cutters earn less than Rs80 ($1.5) a day. The women don't get a commission or a bonus on what they find, but if something really valuable shows up they'll get some *ladoos* and *rasgullas* (sweets) as a treat from their supervisor.

This team of the three men who unload and unpack the bales and the women who sit in a circle rummaging and slicing has its own male jobber, and they move around various factories together as required. But one of the women is also a sub-jobber, recruiting and paying the other women. To be a good jobber, she said, she has to 'manage a lot of responsibility, control advances and listen to people's troubles'. The women said they found it easier to discuss problems with female jobbers, and they agreed that being a jobber was not easy; the main requirement was trust between the jobber and her workers as sometimes a jobber will walk away at the end of a contract and pocket the money for him- or herself.

COLOUR SORTING The mill owner considered Anil's skill in feeling the fibre content of garments and finely sorting them by colour to be his greatest asset; he trusted Anil to put just enough wool in the blend and create only as pure a colour as is required for each order, and no more. Owners keep warehouses full of stocks, in order to be able to buy at a good price in the market, and offer a wider variety of yarns through blending wool content and separating colours. Rags are mostly purchased as (1) commercial all wool (CAW) hosiery, about 90 per cent wool knits, soft and easy to tear open; (2) original woollen rag (OWR), about 50–70 per cent wool such as worsteds and suiting that are much harder to 'open'; and (3) acrylic hosiery, processed in separate factories but using the same technologies. First, they are sorted for colour. Bright shades are at a premium, with sludgy grey mixes at the bottom of the scale: a red blanket might sell for over twice the price of an equivalent grey one, as red clothing is scarcer given the increasing Western preference for dull clothing, and a high percentage of wool is similarly more expensive.

The men sort into about twelve first-colour families, then a second sorting into roughly sixty subcategories. The colours have delicious, evocative names in a mixture of Hindi and English, recalling ripe fruits

1.2 Mountains of clothing are sorted into 'colour families' prior to being cut up (photo: Tim Mitchell)

and favourite foods such as *jamuni* (a fruit), lemon, *beighani* (aubergine) and chocolate, animals and birds such as mouse, camel, parrot and peacock, plants such as henna, precious metals and gemstones, as well as mythological characters and royal princesses. Each one can be further qualified as bright, light and dark, referring to depth of colour, shininess and purity of shade. 'Uni' (i.e. plain) clothes are the most expensive, 'fancy' (i.e. checks and stripes) are the cheapest, but one can make several types of fancy: '10 fancy' (fancy with ten colours in it), or red fancy, violet fancy, blue fancy. The poetic everyday naming of colours and grading of clothing by shade serves to place its subjective past as used clothing farther in the distance, and highlights its more valuable, abstract qualities.

THE CUTTING YARD A separate team of women cutters carry heavy head-loads of sorted garments back to their spot outside, sitting in and among the piles to get comfortable, rigging up a piece of cloth to provide extra shade as the sun moves round. Those nursing babies and young children lie them down to sleep on the piles of clothing next to them, placing a cloth over their faces to keep away the flies.

Sitting chatting, useful things are filched surreptitiously: a cotton lining thrown across to another woman, who promptly sits on it, and soft bits of cotton to be used as babies' nappies, secured with string. Younger kids play with bits of fabric in the yard, stringing buttons on threads, running around barefoot in tatty clothing. It is thought to be a very safe environment so long as children keep out of the machine sheds; they can safely climb up the piles and slide down. They don't think the factory is particularly dirty, simply dusty from all the clothing and fluff, but many children have skin sores, coughs and runny noses. Some managers used to give the women sweets to take the cotton dust down into the throat, but many workers are concerned about the risks of contracting TB from the dust.

These women have their own jobber, who also reports to Anil; living in nearby colonies, they are usually very poor agricultural migrants from Bihar and Uttar Pradesh, Orissa, Bengal and Andhra. Poverty forces young mothers and old women to work outside the house and bring their preschool children with them. Many of the women had moved to Panipat at or after marriage or had joined male family members there; some mentioned family difficulties back in the village, lack of jobs and loans to repay. They received about Rs2,000 ($43) a month for a daily eight-hour shift; after deductions for days off it was even less and they were heavily dependent on advances from their jobber. But several women considered the work to be fairly comfortable compared with working in the fields, while a couple of older women said that they liked the work, there was no 'worst job' in the factory, and they were not pressured to work too hard. They took regular tea and tiffin breaks among the piles, bringing in home-made rotis and dahl in tins. As we were chatting one morning, the break ended and they washed out their tins, swilling the dirty water on to the ground then wiping it round with an old jumper picked off the floor.

This matter-of-fact entanglement with the material they worked on stretched from sitting among old clothes and working on it with their hands to using it for tasks at hand for its absorbency or comfort rather than its fashionability. One man cheerfully sported an orange pashmina shawl, wrapped around his head as a turban, with a 'Made in China' label just visible. Most of the women were dressed in very old clothing, often too small, worn or mismatching, and they admitted that a certain number of 'spoils', such as warm hats, jumpers and shawls, are smuggled home.

It is when women deconstruct tailored garments that their embodied skills become most apparent. They keep the cutters really sharp,

1.3 A woman cuts up a tailored coat, removing plastic buttons, linings and interlining, thick seams and padding. The strips of 'cleaned' cloth can then be fed into the 'teasing' machine to be shredded (photo: Lucy Norris)

and all around the factory can be heard the sound of metal blades being sharpened on whetstones. Seeta, who had been working in the woollens factory for twelve years, could reduce a tailored coat to a series of piles in three to four minutes.

Reaching into the mound next to her, she pulled out a black woollen coat, a stylish double-breasted garment with a complicated structure of yokes, panels, collar and cuffs, assembled with thick overlapping French seams. It appeared to be in very good condition, with no obvious stains or signs of wear. First, she cut out the lining and put it to one side. She always started the coat itself at the centre back seam at the lower hem. Where possible, she sliced open the bottom stitches and ripped the rest of the seam apart with her hands. But with a thick seam that would jam the shredding machines, she had to cut away the cloth on each side and throw the tubular seam itself on to a separate pile along with plastic fasteners discarded as rubbish. Working through each section of the coat, she cut out as much as possible of the stiff interfacing that is stitched into structural pieces of the coat, such as collars, epaulettes and cuffs, throwing it away, and separated out the cloth pieces with thick fused grey interfacing that she cannot remove into another pile. Then she used her thumb and forefinger to prise apart the softer fusible white interfacing from the cloth and discarded that, and finally cut the larger pieces of black wool into smaller rags.

Seeta described the process as 'cleaning' the cloth, aiming to extract as many pure black rags as possible; the more complex the garment, the more piles are created from its decomposition. The black coat rapidly augmented the five heaps in a semicircle around her. First there were three grades of usable cloth destined for the shredder: A, the best-quality pure black cloth; B, junior quality that had grey interfacing attached; and C, the lowest-quality lumpy collars and cuffs, flecked with white interfacing. The rubbish pile contained plastic buttons and zips, foam shoulder pads, elastic waistbands, thick seams, interlining and labels, all of which was burnt in the boiler used for dyeing. Lastly, the synthetic linings, later sorted into dozens of shades of brown, grey and black and sold on to another factory for shredding, to be used to strengthen acrylic shoddy yarn made from synthetic jumpers.

Pure wool, which is now a premium niche fibre, is valued for its warmth, insulation and its natural flame retardancy; the wool percentage of aid blankets is usually specified at approximately 50 per cent, and a wide range of qualities are made for the domestic market. Depending on the percentage of wool required in the yarn, a batch of wool rag may be supplemented by more expensive wool hosiery. This blending of garments brings better-quality, perfectly usable jumpers on to the factory floor. One day I watched while a tractor tipped a load of multicoloured pure wool jumpers with classic Scandinavian designs on to the concrete next to Seeta. One had a label boasting 'Danish pesticide-free pure wool'; a particularly ironic end was in store for such an apparently high-value, sustainably produced fibre.

Every now and then, a foul-smelling smoke drifts across the concrete yards. Acrylic rags are often over-dyed to produce a uniform bright shade, as is the yarn added for strengthening wool. Vats are heated directly underneath by fires fed with plastic waste from the in-house cutting process, and assorted leftovers from local factories such as foam offcuts from flip-flops, rubber, dust from fibre processing, wooden pallets and old window frames. Treading on buttons, shoulder pads and zips scattered across the floor, barefoot workers stoke the fires, pumping air into the hearth with makeshift hoses and breathing in acrid fumes. After dyeing, the fibres are not fixed or rinsed, but laid out to dry in the sun, while the waste water gushes into local open drains or floods neighbouring wasteland.

SHREDDING WITH THE 'TEASER' Rag-pulling machines (known as 'teasers') shred the pieces of fabric in order to 'open' the fibres. In order to ease their processing and reduce static, rags need pre-soaking in 'batching oil' for several hours. This oil is unfiltered, unrefined, used transformer oil from the local power plant, to which have been added various other chemicals: the waste oil from nearby ghee factories, carbolic acid, MEG (methyl ethyl glycols) and caustic soda. The emulsifying properties of the batching oil are tested by pouring it into a typical *chai* (tea) glass with a kitchen ladle, and swirling it in the light: it is ready once the consistency of buffalo's milk is achieved. Workers complain that the batching oil smells awful, and they suffer from headaches, dizziness and coughing.

Teasers generate enormous quantities of dust and fluff, and are usually placed in a contained, dark room with few openings. Rudimentary set-ups rely on workers to manually gather up the stinking rags to feed the teaser, bag the fibres at the other end and load them into the hopper for the card machine. Emerging for a tea break with hair, eyebrows and shoulders coated with fluff, one woman working on the machine said it 'makes your eyes hurt, it's noisy and your arms and legs ache'; this was from picking up piles of oil-soaked rags from the floor and pushing them into the machine on long twelve-hour shifts. One manager had rigged the small teasers up on tripods and chains to try to stop them falling over during use, while the whole process is a high-risk fire hazard owing to the batching oil and the combustibility of the cotton content of rags. While the pay is higher for a woman than cutting, it is dangerous work; one described how the end of her sari had got caught in the machine, and she was lucky a co-worker near by quickly hit the stop button.

Spinning and jobbing Men working on the card machines and spinning frames work in teams run by jobbers, who are paid according to output, so both they and the workers want to work in a reliable, well-run factory. The slogan '*Kaam hii puja hai*' (work is prayer) was painted on the side of a card machine, 'Life is Work' on another, while sheds had shrines to Vishwakame, the god of machines and craftsmen who made the chariot for Bima in the Baghavad Gita. Everyday a *puja* (act of worship) was performed before the machines started up. As Sanjay, a young migrant jobber in charge of two spinning units, explained, to maintain output he has to negotiate with the owners, who frequently cut back the percentage of strengthening material added to the fibres, and fail either to maintain machinery or to provide good generators.

His work, mediating between the workers and managers, fills him with tension. The work can be hard, lifting heavy sacks of yarn, and the dust causes respiratory problems. He has to entice new recruits, he says, tongue in cheek, with 'a lot of lies and a little truth!' He promises that the wages are generous, the machines are good, the thread is strong, there is a reliable electricity supply, they can have advances when they want, and it is comfortable work. He recruits workers he knows from other factories, or people's brothers and relatives.

The smaller jobbers in units talk about having the right attitude and social skills for upward mobility rather than education or training, and put themselves forward as apprentices. A dye master, who initially began as a sorter and had worked in Kandla, explained that 'if you think high and want to get ahead you will achieve it, you need to go step by step: it is easy to be what you want to be if you have confidence and gain experience. Even if you are a labourer you can move up if you have the mindset.' From his perspective, low-paid work goes with people who don't think about it, so they stay low paid.

Producing blankets Simple grey blankets are woven on old power looms in windowless sheds, the weak yarn reinforced with synthetic warps every few inches just to hold the short fibres together. Once checked for defects, the rolls of shoddy wool cloth ought to be 'finished', i.e. 'fulled' to felt the fibres properly, then 'raised' to bring up the nap, but these are further stages where corners can be cut. Finishing units are usually at the back of integrated mills, or in the older ramshackle part of town, where open waste-water drains spill over into the rutted roads outside. Inside the brick-walled, dust-coated enclosures, boilers spew out plumes of filthy black smoke, fired by offcuts of wood, plastic factory waste and local rubbish. During fulling, starch in the form of *maida* (chapatti flour) or *namak* (salt) is often added to the water to increase the weight by up to half as much again.

The cloth is then stretched out over tenters on the roof to dry before being passed through the raising machine. This has spiked rollers to bring the pills and loose fibres up to the surface to be suctioned off before steaming; fibrous waste can then be sold back to the spinning mill to be mixed back into low-quality shoddy yarn until it is too short to be bound in (a local joke runs that the sign of a cheap blanket is that if you take it out and refold it, it loses half of its weight in the process; if you attempt to wash it, it could disintegrate entirely). The remaining grey dust is piled up at the back of the factory. Unlike Mr Boffin's dust heaps, combed and sifted for their potential value in

Dickens's *Our Mutual Friend*, the finely ground remains of old clothes are utterly exhausted, and are eventually taken away for fly-tipping.

Imagined lives Two younger women, sitting cutting up a pile of mixed 'fancy' in an acrylic factory, came across a multicoloured bikini top; they sat shyly giggling as they surreptitiously stretched the fabric between their fingers and studied the clasp. A sorter held up a backless sequined evening dress and laughed in amazement. When women work with mixed bales of clothing, they come across swimsuits, glamorous garments, short skirts and underwear in mixed bales, sometimes familiar from TV programmes, but rarely from personal experience. Women working in factories are expected to dress modestly, and appropriately to their status and community background. Women often laughed about the clothes and played with them, trying them on when there was no one but us as an audience. Comments were made about the size of clothing, and the fact that people abroad must be 'tension free' and 'mind free' to be able to eat so much that two or three Indian people such as themselves could fit into them.

But in constructing the imaginary worlds in which this clothing is worn, the styles and designs of women's clothing bring out contrasting views among the factory workers. For some, they represent a sexual freedom they are curious about. Several women spoke about their desire to travel, to see these countries the clothing came from, and how people live there. In contrast, an elderly woman chatting to a couple of friends laughed about a pair of scanty women's knickers, but later referred to the women who wear them as 'poor helpless things', in this instance an allusion to their imagined occupation as sex workers. A truck driver delivering worn clothing from Kandla to Panipat believed that the clothing represented a critical lack of control over women's sexuality, typified by the tourists he had seen kissing in public and behaving inappropriately. He linked wearing revealing clothing and eating meat to tourists' excess 'heat', a reference to Hindu beliefs about behavioural tendencies (*guna*), whereby interaction with material qualities can have moral consequences and vice versa, and which should therefore be appropriately regulated (see Bayly 1986).

Everyone agreed that working with second-hand clothing is clearly dirty, dusty work, and all unskilled, manual work has low status (see Parry 2005: 142), but when they compare their jobs to those of casual labourers working in the petrochemical factories and oil refineries or manual rubbish collectors, they feel the work is relatively easy and not so unpleasant. The clothes are not considered 'old'; poor workers described how they themselves use up cloth either through wear or as cleaning rags, throwing it out only when it is totally threadbare. The imported clothes are believed to be rich people's unwanted things that still have some use in them; just a little dirty from having been worn once or twice, and lying around the warehouse. These clothes are *pukka* (in this sense whole, complete) when first discarded. The mechanical slashing of clothing is understood by the factory workers as necessary in order to stop those people working at the port from 'stealing' *their* raw materials and depriving the shoddy workers of work and poor Indians of affordable blankets. The shoddy workers' livelihoods depend not upon the manufacture of new garments for the export trade, as is more familiar in the literature on global commodity chains, but in contrast on their total destruction (Crang et al. 2012).

Demonstrating the relativity of waste and value depending literally on where one sits in the processing chain, one woman stripping metal zips explained: 'The clothes come to make thread [yarn] for poor people ... it's not really waste, ... for my master, it's gold ... but for me, it [the cloth] is waste; it's the zips that are money.' The cutters' job was to then turn the mutilated clothing into *kachcha*, raw materials. They also had to 'clean' the cloth of extraneous material to provide the purest coloured rags, and so for them it was the buttons, seams and interfacing, etc., that became the rubbish by-products. The spinners, in turn, conceived of their job as revitalizing the raw materials; dyeing and spinning fibres recuperated them, and transformed them into *pukka* yarn.

Conversations about how and why the clothing reached India revealed startling beliefs. Few of the workers in half a dozen Panipat factories had any idea that the clothing had been freely donated to charities in developed countries, except for the brokers, rag importers and one or two well-travelled owners of larger mills. Indian clothing is typically handed on until it is used up or bartered away, and households sell off old newspaper, cardboard, plastic bottles, glass and metal tins to itinerant traders. It was therefore assumed that foreigners also thriftily sold their clothing to traders, but a curious story emerged as to why they got rid of such apparently wearable clothing on such a scale. It was widely believed to be due to an extreme water shortage in the countries the clothing came from. One supervisor who had worked with clothing importers at the special economic zone in Kandla suggested that water cost the same as cloth, and foreign governments imposed a penalty tax on people who didn't use up a certain amount of clothing in a given time frame. All believed that it is so expensive to wash clothing abroad, it is cheaper to sell it off to traders and buy new. It was the truck drivers coming from the port at Kandla who were identified as the source of the information that had spread across Panipat, but women sorters in the special economic zone also expressed the same belief, arguing that with washing machines available, it couldn't be the labour that was the problem. To back this up, a semi-literate supervisor interpreted the English garment labels' advice to 'dry clean only' as proof that there was no water.

Women workers did not consider that the speeding up of the fashion cycle, over-consumption or changes in a person's life played a significant role in riddance; it was thought that when people had so much money and no water, they could just go out and buy the same things again. The corollary to this belief was that it could never happen in India, a very poor country, as there is always enough groundwater to wash clothes; in any case, women would rarely put almost new clothing on the market, there being better ways to use up its value (Norris 2010). But in the context of a scarcity of water, the disposal route is understood as an economically sensible solution for foreigners.

In decline: mill owners' perspectives At a meeting of the shoddy mill owners' representative body in 2009, it was agreed that the industry was in terminal decline, 'providing only for the poor and downtrodden'. As a lobbying group, they frequently complained that labour costs in Haryana were too expensive, as were government taxes, the erratic supply of electricity and transportation. To make it worse, there was a declining global market for pure wool, which was directly linked to the falling quality of rags for shoddy; the proportion of mixed fibres in clothing has risen steadily. They all agreed that ten years ago they were making more profit, but now the industry was just about sustaining itself; some mills were in crisis, many had shut or were close to shutting down.

Another problem was a declining local blanket market. One manager claimed the winter season was getting shorter and milder owing to climate change. A four-month winter in north India was now just a two-month cold season, and sales at Diwali, the festival of lights, were down. But another privately remarked that 'it is a small industry, in a small town. The local [Indian] psychology is that recycling is a cheap thing; a gift must be new ... recycled blankets could be dirty, full of germs; no one knows what it actually is.' The growing middle classes were also switching to synthetics for clothing, carpets and bedding; 'everyone now wants the mink blanket', a thick, light, fluffy synthetic blanket imported from China, with attractive, digitally printed designs of lush tropical landscapes and exotic animals, and sold in smart, zipped bags of transparent plastic.

A leading manufacturer admitted candidly that the industry's survival depends upon international disasters, and could not last more than a couple of years without an earthquake, flood or civil war: the international relief sector buys one billion blankets annually. But, in the opinion of a successful mill owner in Amritsar, 'Panipat mills don't see themselves as making anything else, they have a fixed idea about what they can do.' A Panipat businessman went farther: 'it's part of the Indian mentality to stay on the same track that they are on ... why improve things? They [the mill owners] are not broad-minded.'

But the belief that there was no future in the industry was more profound; they were technically at the very end of the line that had spanned two centuries. The industry had 'developed to the maximum in Italy, and we are the last to hold it', as one elderly mill owner explained. No small entrepreneurs were coming into the industry, and even the big family firms were only upgrading step by step, investing as little as possible in second-hand Italian machinery to keep going, and lacking the skilled technicians to maintain more complex equipment.

The town has now successfully developed as an export hub for cotton home furnishings, and as a growing petrochemical centre, including a fertilizer factory and a large oil refinery; family firms have diversified into more profitable areas. Middle-class mill manufacturers who run an assortment of interlinked factories maintain houses in Delhi, schooling their children for degrees in foreign universities. The leading industrialists who are globally exporting home furnishings may hide a dingy shoddy factory behind their well-lit, airy workshops at the front. Shoddy mills are kept as a back-up for as long as they are viable, with owners taking out as much profit as they can and reinvesting as little as possible.

Shoddy mills offer a dead-end career for the sons of established family firms; Dileep, a young manager, admitted that he had not wanted to run his father's factory and had been offered a place in the USA to study IT, but his elder brother had already left and it fell to him. Dileep was trying to make direct contracts with international NGOs. When I asked about emerging markets for sustainable goods, he explained how difficult it would be to upgrade. 'Giving the industry a corporate shape', streamlining businesses, provide a good working environment with appropriate labour conditions, and making 'germ-free products' would cost so much, he said, that he would have to 'charge $6 for a

$2 blanket'; the industry survives on a 4–5 per cent profit margin on large volumes, and only if they could make 20 per cent profit could they afford to sell a blanket as a recycled product.

Moral frameworks

It is difficult to frame this Indian recycling industry as either socially or environmentally beneficial in its current state, and many local mill owners also believe it is unlikely to remain economically sustainable. The extraction of profit through low capital investment and the exploitation of unorganized labour conflicts with the (Western) moral framework in which charities broadly operate, and which brackets each end of the trade, thus potentially undermining those same moral value systems in the longer term (Crompton 2010). In classic anthropological terms, this complex example highlights the ever-present danger of the conflict between short-term individual gain and longer-term social and cosmological regeneration (Bloch and Parry 1989; Hann and Hart 2011), and the difficulty of maintaining an appropriate balance between the two. The moral problems associated with the commoditization of the charitable gift resonate with Titmuss's (1970) work on blood donation in the UK, and his thesis that far from rationalizing the system and maximizing returns, such commoditization processes reduce the quality of supply, increase inefficiency and threaten concepts of mutuality and social cohesion.

Old clothing moves in and out of limbo, caught up in temporal cycles of transformation and stasis; vacuum-packed, unwrapped and rewrapped, stacked in bonded warehouses and piled high in overflowing sheds, it is a classic instance of Hetherington's absent presence (2004), waiting for eventual destruction and transformation. The entanglement of the moral and economic value bound up within it is extraordinarily materialized through the final object itself, eventually condensed in the form of the aid blanket. This object, the final reconfiguration of recycled fibres and recomposition of social relations bound up into its weave, is itself inherently unstable; it quickly turns threadbare, unravels and disintegrates, unable to perform as a durable materialization of common values beyond the initial act of giving.

Used, often still wearable, clothing is reduced to a desperately poor-quality commodity through the destruction of almost all of its material and contextual value, yielding little profit for all but the biggest commercial middlemen dealing in the largest volumes. Yet those shoddy workers performing the labour of transformation at the margins of the second-hand clothing trade depend upon this violent destruction to earn their wages; the absolute loss of value highlights the profound separation between the imagined lives of former owners of the clothing and their own economic and social restrictions. As Hansen documents for Zambia (2004b), buying good-quality imported second-hand clothing has afforded many local consumers in developing African economies the chance to engage with modernity and fashion the self through careful selection. Here the reverse holds true; the shoddy factory workers remain alienated from the materials as clothing, yet barely earn a living through their skills as sorters, cutters and shredders; their repetitive bodily engagement with fabrics as 'stuff' to be deconstructed is inversely related to the imaginary former contexts which they have mentally assembled. The challenge for those charitable entities involved at either end of the global used clothing trade working towards broader humanitarian, social and environmental goals is to establish an overarching set of common values and an economic model that can incorporate the shoddy recycling industry, and work to bridge the economic and social distance between the consumers of fashion and those that must labour to destroy their discards.

Acknowledgements

I would like to thank Catherine Alexander and Josh Reno for their editorial enthusiasm and rigour, and Nicky Gregson, Mike Crang, Danny Miller and members of the Waste of the World project for comments on earlier drafts. Meghna Gupta assisted with fieldwork in 2009 and conducted further research in 2011, and we appreciate the generosity of all those working in the industry in Panipat. The research was supported by the ESRC (RES 000-23-0007), with additional funding granted by the British Academy (SG100952).

Notes

1 For example, the cover of a recent anthropological volume depicts refugees on the Canary Islands in 2005, wrapped in grey aid blankets (Von Schendel and Abraham 2005).

2 UN Commodity Trade Statistics Database 2009.

3 Following general usage in the UK second-hand trade, clothing that can be worn again is classified 'for reuse', while items that cannot be worn but have other purposes are 'recycled'.

4 I first began to research the outlines of the industry in Delhi and Panipat in 2000 and 2004 (see Norris 2005), returning in 2009 with Meghna Gupta as research assistant. In 2011, Gupta spent two months in Panipat and Gujarat filming a short documentary, *Unravel* (working title); this chapter also draws on her research.

5 The total import of rags, both woollen and synthetic, for the shoddy industry in 2007/08 was 92.47 million kilograms, down from a reported peak of 110.26 million kilograms the previous year. Figures from DGCI&S, Kolkata, quoted in Ministry of Textiles (2010: 110).

6 During 2007/08, 43 million

kilograms of shoddy yarn was produced (compared to 96 million kilograms of woollen and worsted yarn), 18 million blankets (both wool and shoddy) and 33 million metres of shoddy fabric (compared to 85 million metres of new woollen and worsted fabrics). Figures from IWMF, Mumbai, quoted in Ministry of Textiles (2010).

7 The shoddy industry developed in Yorkshire after Samuel Law invented the process of tearing rags to reclaim their fibres in 1813. Avoiding the costs of buying, preparing and dyeing raw wool, it provided cheap clothing, uniforms and blankets around the world, supplying the working classes, soldiers and colonial governments alike. Rag auctions were a standard feature of the market from the early nineteenth century onwards, and buyers regularly travelled Europe and beyond, sourcing particular garments as demand for certain fibres and shades changed (Jenkins and Malin 1990; Malin 1979).

8 See monthly reports on this sector in *Recycling International* over the past few years.

References

Bayly, C. A. (1986) 'The origins of Swadeshi (home industry): cloth and Indian society, 1700–1930', in A. Appadurai (ed.), *The Social Life of Things: Commodities in Cultural Perspective*, Cambridge, Cambridge University Press.

Bloch, M. and J. Parry (1989) *Money and the Morality of Exchange*, Cambridge: Cambridge University Press.

Botticelli, J. (forthcoming) 'Between classification, objectification and perception: processing second-hand clothing for recycling and reuse', *Textile: The Journal of Cloth and Culture*.

Breman, J. (1999a) 'The study of industrial labour in post-colonial India – the formal sector: an introductory review', *Contributions to Indian Sociology*, 33: 1–41.

— (1999b) 'The study of industrial labour in post-colonial India – the informal sector: a concluding review', *Contributions to Indian Sociology*, 33: 407–31.

— (2003) 'Labour in the informal sector of the economy', in V. Das (ed.), *The Oxford India Companion to Sociology and Social Anthropology*, Delhi and Oxford: Oxford University Press.

Crang, M., A. Hughes, N. Gregson, L. Norris and F. Ahamed (2012) 'Rethinking governance and value in commodity chains through global recycling networks', *Transactions of the Institute of British Geographers*, published online.

Crompton, T. (2010) *Common Cause: The case for working with our cultural values*, London: World Wildlife Fund UK.

De Neve, G. (1999) 'Asking for and giving *baki*: neo-bondage, or the interplay between bondage and resistance in the Tamilnadu powerloom industry', *Contributions to Indian Sociology*, 33: 379–406.

— (2003) 'Expectations and rewards of modernity: commitment and mobility among rural migrants in Tirupur, Tamil Nadu', *Contributions to Indian Sociology*, 37: 251.

Gopalakrishnan, S. and P. Sreenivasa (2009) *The Political Economy of Migrant Labour*, Independent research.

Gregson, N., K. Brooks and L. Crewe (2000) 'Narratives of consumption and the body in the space of the charity shop', in P. Jackson, M.

Lowe, D. Miller and F. Mort (eds), *Commercial Cultures: Economies, Practices, Spaces*, Oxford: Berg.

Hann, C. and K. Hart (2011) *Economic Anthropology: History, Ethnography, Critique*, Cambridge: Polity Press.

Hansen, K. T. (2000) *Salaula: The World of Second-hand Clothing and Zambia*, Chicago, IL, and London: University of Chicago Press.

— (2004a) 'Controversies about the international second-hand clothing trade', *Anthropology Today*, 20: 3–9.

— (2004b) 'Crafting appearances: the second-hand clothing trade and dress practices in Zambia', in A. Palmer and H. Clark (eds), *Old Clothes, New Looks*, Oxford: Berg.

Harriss, J. (2005) 'South Asia', in J. G. Carrier (ed.), *A Handbook of Economic Anthropology*, Cheltenham: Edward Elgar.

Harriss-White, B. (2003) *India Working: Essays on society and economy*, Cambridge: Cambridge University Press.

Hart, K. (2000) 'Industrial labour in India: the view from 19th-century Lancashire', *Critique of Anthropology*, 20: 439–46.

Hawley, J. M. (2006) 'Digging for diamonds: a conceptual framework for understanding reclaimed textile products', *Clothing and Textiles Research Journal*, 24: 262–75.

Hetherington, K. (2004) 'Second-handedness: consumption, disposal and absent presence', *Environment and Planning D: Society and Space*, 22: 157–73.

Jenkins, D. T. and J. C. Malin (1990) 'European competition in woollen cloth, 1870–1914: the role of shoddy', *Business History*, 32: 66–86.

Jha, K. (2006) *Organizing Migrant Workers*, New Delhi: AITUC in cooperation with ILO India.

Malin, J. C. (1979) 'The West Riding recovered wool industry ca. 1813–1939', in *Economics and Related Studies*, York: University of York.

Ministry of Textiles (2010) *Annual Report 2009–2010*, New Delhi: Ministry of Textiles, Government of India.

Morley, N., C. Bartlett and I. McGill (2009) *Maximising the Reuse and Recycling of UK Clothing and Textiles: A report to the Department for Environment, Food and Rural Affairs*, Aylesbury: Oakdene Hollins Ltd.

Norris, L. (2005) 'Cloth that lies: the secrets of recycling in India', in S. Küchler and D. Miller (eds), *Clothing as Material Culture*, Oxford: Berg.

— (2010) *Recycling Indian Clothing: Global Contexts of Reuse and Value*, Bloomington: Indiana University Press.

— (forthcoming-a) 'Trade and transformations of worn clothing', *Textile: The Journal of Cloth and Culture*.

— (forthcoming-b) 'Economies of moral fibre: materializing the ambiguities of recycling charity clothing into aid blankets', *Journal of Material Culture*.

Oakdene Hollins Ltd, Salvation Army Trading Company Ltd and Non-wovens and Innovation Research Institute Ltd (2006) *Recycling of Low Grade Clothing Waste*.

Parry, J. (2005) 'Industrial work', in J. G. Carrier (ed.), *A Handbook of Economic Anthropology*, Cheltenham: Edward Elgar.

Parry, J., J. Breman and K. Kapadia (eds) (1999) *The Worlds of Indian*

Industrial Labour, New Delhi: Sage Publications.

Titmuss, R. (1970) *The Gift Relationship: From human blood to social policy*, London: George Allen & Unwin.

Von Schendel, W. and I. Abraham (eds) (2005) *Illicit Flows and Criminal Things: States, Borders, and the Other Side of Globalization*, Bloomington: Indiana University Press.

2 | Death, the Phoenix and Pandora: transforming things and values in Bangladesh

MIKE CRANG, NICKY GREGSON, FARID AHAMED,
RAIHANA FERDOUS AND NASREEN AKHTER

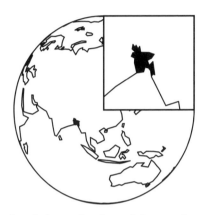

The ship as Pandora's box: death and destruction on the beach

Ships are both the glue and the grease of the global economy. The merchant vessel of the late twentieth century and early twenty-first century, combined with the technology of the big-box container, is how most commodities move around the world – although the central role of merchant ships and maritime spaces is all too often overlooked (Levinson 2006; Sekula 2001). But ships themselves are also commodities and they too change value and move through value regimes. In the case of their commercial life, which is likely to be twenty-five to thirty-two years, including periodic refits, ships progressively downgrade in terms of profitability and value. This chapter charts the passage of such vessels. We look at how these enduring and mobile objects, which, in life, link topographically distant ports into trading networks carrying commodities, cross into different networks of disposal and reuse, at their death. At this moment, they are linked to different locations, not in a trading network, but in a global destruction network, whose nodes are places such as breaking yards and re-rolling mills, where they are disassembled and become mutable. These breaking locations enable them to be reborn as new commodities in different networks of value. As in Thompson's (1979) formulation, the category of waste is a fulcrum point, where one form of value dies, yet another can be born. Here, we show how disparate networks are linked through processes of material destruction and transformation, enabling the rebirth of value.

Let us start with the story of a nondescript, fairly typical merchant ship – one of the 26,000 that at any one time keep the global economy moving – the Liquid Petroleum Gas carrier *Hoegh Galleon*, built in 1974 in Stavanger and 249 metres in length. For years, its capacity to deliver 87,600 cubic metres (cbm) of gas helped service ever-growing Western demand, on behalf of a string of owners, plying the seas variously as the *Mystic Lady*, the *Asake Maru*, the *Pollenger* and *LNG Challenger*. By the winter of 2008, the carrier was an elderly vessel named *The Lady Margaret Hill* and owned by US-based company LNG Partners, which acquired and then registered the vessel in the Republic of the Marshall Islands in the Pacific Ocean through a new shipowning arm, Maverick LNG, having paid a reported $45 million, although the ship's beneficial owner was its mortgage provider, Fortress Credit Corp. The latter, in late 2008, began to arrange a sale to scrap the vessel as its maintenance costs escalated and gas demand fell with the global recession. However, as it sailed towards its probable demolition in November 2008, it moored in Southampton in the UK, placing it under UK jurisdiction. NGOs contacted the UK's Environment Agency, which detained the ship on the grounds that, under European law, since it contained hazardous wastes, it was subject to the Basel Convention on trading toxic wastes, and thus could not be sold to a country outside the European Union for demolition. As an Environment Agency spokesman put it, 'because it was sitting in Southampton when they were looking to sell it as waste, it became our problem'. And so there it sat, immobilized and without value as either ship or scrap. In August, Fortress and the ship's new owner, Waller Marine, a shipping broker, gave assurances that it was going to be taken to Dubai for conversion into a floating gas storage platform, although ship trade agencies reported that it was to be sold by 'V Ships UK', its technical managers, to Indian breakers.

After three months of talks it sailed from the UK at the end of 2009. The vessel, after literally disappearing off the ship-tracking radar system, with a last report in Port Said (Egypt) on Christmas Day 2009, arrived in Dubai in February 2010, was renamed SS *Chill*, and re-registered to the Comoros islands, off the eastern coast of Africa. As the UK Environment Agency dolefully acknowledged, 'We know that she has been re-registered. What we do not know is where she is going.' Although they lobbied Fortress Credit 'to do the right thing', the agency was powerless to act as soon as the vessel had left UK waters. Meanwhile, Waller Marine's associated company, Polar Energy, had become the ship's owner. Reports from Dubai indicate that a locally based cash buyer (Argo Systems) purchased the vessel on behalf of ship-breakers in Alang, India. It was reportedly sold as a 23,400 light displacement tonnes[1] vessel for the then strong price of $359 per tonne, equating to around $8.4 million, on account of its 3,100 tonnes of high-quality nickel-steel. After all the controversy, the ship was reported as arriving variously at breaking yards in either China or Alang in the summer of 2010.[2]

This chapter looks at how some 800–1,000 ships make a similar final journey each year. As they do so they pass from a value regime that sees them as capital goods to one where they are seen in terms of material components – and where value is realized from the potential for reusing and reprocessing their constituent materials rather than their capacities as vessels to transport things. The chapter draws on ethnographic fieldwork between 2007 and 2011 conducted in and around Chittagong, Bangladesh, and is also based on following brokers and traders operating in the global trade in end-of-life ships. It works from a multi-sited team ethnography that traced connections beyond a single site to 'examine the circulation of cultural meanings, objects and identities in diffuse time-space' (Marcus 1995: 96). Unlike many products moving across value regimes, ships going to be broken are not passed intact along a series of sites; nor do they even attract symbolic layering and meanings on their way to becoming a final commodity. Rather, they are being unmade; stripped of symbolic associations (their names, their histories) as they are scattered into smaller parts. The work is destructive. It is about the labour of breaking things up, not putting them together (Gregson et al. 2010). And the process is dirty, dangerous and difficult. So, by the 1980s, in the USA and Europe, 'ship-breaking had become a nearly impossible business, for the simple reason that the cost of scrapping a ship correctly (i.e. with the necessary environmental controls) was higher than the value of its steel' (Langewiesche 2000: 35). In 2009, the vast majority of ships went to South Asia, with around a third sailing to Chittagong (Bangladesh), another third going to Alang (India) and a tenth to Gaddani (Pakistan). Another 15 per cent went to China, with 5 per cent going to Turkey and the remainder scattered across the globe. Each ship that went to South and East Asia was sailing into the grey area of whether or not the sale of such end-of-life vessels is legal, entailing as it does the movement of toxic materials across international borders. Each one traverses different regimes of value and makes a journey to where it is disassembled and reassembled into other things. Traders persistently exploit the ambiguities of maritime space and regulation. In the course of their day-to-day work, ships regularly cross international jurisdictions. They are flagged, and thus purportedly regulated as seafaring vessels by states such as Tuvalu, the Marshall Islands and even landlocked Mongolia. But it is only when they are travelling to be scrapped that they become subject to regulations on trans-boundary waste disposal. Ships, as waste products, are regulated by the last port from which they sail, hence the UK Environment Agency finding itself policing a Norwegian-built, US-owned, offshore-flagged vessel like *The Lady Margaret Hill*, until it left British waters, when it was beyond their control (Puthucherril 2010). The difficulty is that, almost until the hull grounds, it may not be legally provable that the ship is going for scrap, even if, as with *The Lady Margaret Hill*, everyone is certain that it is.

Ships may be sold several times in their lives, but the last sale is for scrap value: to recover the values of their constituent materials. As ships like *The Lady Margaret Hill* move from the second-hand 'sale and purchase' market to the 'demolition' market, the metric of their value is transformed from dead weight tonnes (dwt), or the amount they can carry, to light displacement tonnes (ldt) – that is, the weight of metal that composes their hulls. In this change of metric, we see them cross value regimes. In its life, the dwt of a ship is intimately tied to cargo capacities and charter freight rates. As it is scrapped, the ldt of a ship highlights the value of materials that may be recovered. *The Lady Margaret Hill*, valued for its gas storage capacity, ceases to be, and becomes the SS *Chill*, valued for the 23,600 tonnes of metal that is the fabric of the vessel. While still an object, a thing and a commodity, it is valued not for its current configuration but for what it will (or might) become – that is, for its potential as materials. The price depends on the evaluation of the complex heterogeneous conjuncture of materials that are more or less easy to extract through breaking and are then open to re-realization and revaluation.

The breakers look at a ship not for what it can carry but for how it will come apart. They are looking at the potential to take plates of metal from the ship, cut them into strips, and heat and roll those in a furnace to produce steel rods of various gauges. Irregular shapes or very thick elements have to be sent at greater expense to a plant with the capacity to melt the materials fully. So vessels like car carriers, ferries or liners, which have more internal structures, will both need to be sold to melting plants and increase the time taken to break them up. Not only does this delay realizing their value, it also accrues greater interest payments, and so is more expensive for the breaker.

2.1 Ship becoming steel: an end-of-life vessel being dismantled on the foreshore of Chittagong (*source*: the authors)

The result, for Bangladesh, is a preference by yard owners for the most hazardous vessels: tankers whose oily residues and inflammable gases pose a major fire hazard (Sawyer 2001/02: 548–9), but whose simple structures make them quick to disassemble. These ships may be anywhere on the globe when they are sold for demolition. Crews are quite often simply told to deliver their current cargo and then sail to a designated breaking yard. How a ship relates to the configuration of a given breaking yard is as important as its material composition. The 'yards' in Chittagong are actually just stretches of foreshore about one ship in width with varying gradients of beach, each suited to differing sizes of vessels. Having arrived on the foreshore at Chittagong, however, the ship enters a complex site of demolition, materials separation and segregation, reuse and secondary manufacturing.

While the massive hulls being broken on the foreshore make an awesome scene, it is also an awful one (Crang 2010). The ship-breaking beaches of South Asia have become poster children for the downsides of globalization. The conditions in which the vehicles sustaining our commodity culture are destroyed have attracted considerable attention, ever since the *Baltimore Sun* ran a Pulitzer prize-winning exposé in 1997, which depicted the breaking yards of Alang as 'mostly a place of death. It was not entirely wrong. Soon after [the journalists] left Alang, sparks from a cutting torch ignited the residual gases in a tanker's hold and caused an explosion that killed fifteen workers ... or fifty. Alang was the kind of place where "people hardly bothered to count"' (Langewiesche 2000: 37). The regular reports of deaths in the breaking yards of Chittagong produce contested numbers – whether one worker dies per month or per week – but incontrovertibly depressing reading. Meanwhile, scarcely recorded are the likely long-term effects from exposure to toxic chemicals from burning the paint of the ships, or revealing such materials as asbestos. A survey of workers in Chittagong yards found 50 per cent reported cutting of muscles, 25 per cent the breaking and fracturing of limbs, 6 per cent burning by gas flame, and 4 per cent loss of limbs, with very low awareness of possible chronic health problems from exposure to toxic substances such as PCBs (Polychlorinated Biphenyl), metals, asbestos, lead, waste oil and TBT (Tributylin) from antifouling paints (Hossain et al. 2008) (see Figure 2.1).

In terms of environmental contamination, the open beaching inevitably means that the paints on the exterior of the hull, full of toxic antifouling chemicals, are ground into the sands, while oily wastes and numerous other heavy metals and persistent organic toxins are released through the cutting. The result is that, after around twenty years of being used for ship-breaking, the environment has similar levels of contamination to heavy industrial sites used for 200 years in Europe (Srinivasa Reddy et al. 2004; Tewari et al. 2001). Studies of the Alang breaking yards' foreshore suggest around 96.71 tonnes per day of wastes (Srinivasa Reddy et al. 2003: 1613), including heavy metals contaminating the soils (Srinivasa Reddy et al. 2004) and plastic micro-fragments that persist for long periods in the marine ecosystem (Srinivasa Reddy et al. 2006). And yet this place is also a hive of activity. More than two hundred vessels like *The Lady Margaret Hill* are beached on the foreshore at Chittagong each year. As the photographer Sebastiao Salgado described it, labourers

> run these ships onto the beach at high speed; then they attack them
> from all sides, blow torches cut through its steelskin, giant hammers
> break up its iron and wood structure ... Everything from that giant animal lying on the beach has its use. Iron and steel will be melted down
> and given new roles as utensils. The entire ship will be turned into
> what it once carried: machines, knives and forks, hoes, shovels, screws,
> things, bits, pieces ... The huge bronze propellers will provide the
> most elegant of items – bracelets, earrings, necklaces, and rings which
> will one day adorn the bodies of working women, as well as pots from
> which men will pour tea. (Salgado 2005: 14)

This work is carried out by an estimated thirty thousand migrant labourers, hired by gangmasters from distant parts of Bangladesh, using blowtorches, winches and chisels. Thence the materials are trucked off the seashore and move through a complex of recycling firms in many directions (Gregson et al. 2012). From the foreshore, ferrous scrap is trucked to proximate re-rolling mills, of which over seventy are active in the greater Chittagong area. The mills roll sheet steel to form up to 80 per cent of the concrete reinforcing rods for the new houses and apartments springing up in Bangladeshi cities. Ship chandlery is resold to equip the coastal fleet. Electric motors and components are reconditioned and sold to land-based industries with, for instance, ships' boilers and compressors being used in the dyeing of fabrics and in generators to power the factories producing garments for the apparel sector. Indeed, the proud boast of the industry is that 99 per cent of an end-of-life ship is recycled. The examples we have chosen here focus on the furniture shops of Bhatiary, the transformations they effect, and the appropriation of ship-breaking furniture by the Bangladeshi middle classes.

Thus the demise of end-of-life ships is marked by their morphing through interconnected sites of translation, which work with the arts of transience (Hawkins 2006) to transform and revalorize objects and differentiated streams of material, through a plethora of secondary manufacturing, craft and retail activities. The resultant products are then distributed through Bangladesh's major cities, homes and workplaces. This focus on merchant ships challenges much work that looks at the valorization and revalorization of commodities in two ways. First, studies tend to focus on stable objects and identifiable artefacts. Here, though, the objects are destroyed and materially reconfigured. Secondly, these objects do not start as consumer goods or artefacts invested with great amounts of personal love and care. Like *The Lady Margaret Hill*, they are functional and intermediary things that are consumed in production and circulation, which become subsumed within, maybe obscured by, final commodities.

Phoenix from the cutting torch flames: sites of transformation and revalorization

In this section we take the domestic realm as our focus, showing how furniture derived from ship-breaking is revalorized through secondary manufacturing, craft and retail activities. As you drive along the Dhaka–Chittagong highway, the main trunk road in Bangladesh, both sides, from Chittagong City Gate through the district of Bhatiary to

Sitakunda, some nine kilometres north, are full of shops selling literally anything, from lifeboats to kitchen sinks and cooking equipment, from Western toilets to gym equipment and generators. The whole supply chain of these businesses depends upon the ship-breaking industry on the beach.

Originally, these shops were a means of simply disposing of the sundry, unvalued soft goods from the ships. Pioneer sellers tell stories from the early 1980s of 'poor people collecting leftover materials from the yards and selling them by the roadside'; of 'local people scavenging and making fences out of boards salvaged from broken ships or of using them as firewood'; and of ship-breakers chucking boards on the tidal foreshore as they broke up their ships. Scavenging and wasting are central to the narratives of the early pioneers in the business. Indeed, these pioneers portray themselves as originally taking unwanted materials off the ship-breakers' hands. In such narratives, ship-breakers saw no value in furniture, fixtures and fittings. 'Please release me from this burden' is a phrase commonly attributed by early furniture makers to the ship-breakers: 'at that time this stuff was nothing but trouble for them, they just wanted to get rid of it'. In their self-narrative, the furniture makers identify themselves as having seen the scope for entrepreneurial activities but without having the capital to enter the breaking business itself. Nowadays, ship-breakers hold auctions and the major furniture businesses, far from scavenging, send agents aboard the ships and then sell on up to a third of the materials to smaller operators.

To transform the board and fittings from rubbish into another valuable commodity required more than carpentry skills. It required a market of consumers. Initially, local understandings of ship-breaking furniture, based on its use as fencing and its abandonment by the roadside, dumped on the beach or in drains, emphasized its seeming poor quality and lack of durability. Added to this were local myths about the waterproof nature of ship furniture, leading to misuse, and also design anomalies that came from items being originally incorporated into the structure and fabric of the ship itself. Transferred to land, such furniture lacks many of the design features (such as backs) that are taken for granted in domestic furniture. Add to this their used condition, compounded by a lack of care devoted to the furniture's removal, and such items were never going to be easy to sell to the Bangladeshi middle classes for use in their homes. Indeed, to sell them at all required the nascent furniture businesses to develop repair and refurbishment facilities.

While initially retailers would sell goods 'as is' – that is, in the condition in which they came from the ships – the furniture sector has grown though moving into repair, renovation, reconditioning and refabrication work. In 2008 there were seventy-two furniture units clustered around the breaking beaches, and almost all have a refurbishment facility attached to the shop. Their work may vary from simple repairs, such as providing backs for cupboards no longer bolted to ship bulkheads, through to taking the boards as raw materials to produce almost entirely new products. The arts of transience here have far exceeded simple scavenging and reclamation, but have become institutionalized, embedded and elaborated. Indeed, the larger enterprises employ between thirty and forty people each, across the full range of carpentry and furniture-making skills: cutting board, constructing frames, doing joinery, gluing, upholstering, fixing surface materials (notably Formica), patterning and polishing. Most of these workers are migrants from Chandpur and Noakhali districts and are typically recruited through kinship networks. Their jobs, indeed the livelihoods of all those working in the furniture sector (estimated at ten thousand in 2008), are dependent upon a steady supply of materials from the ship-breaking yards, and therefore a constant flow of ships being broken. Neither can be assumed. Attempts by NGOs to stop the trade have moved from largely unsuccessful attempts to prevent ships like *The Lady Margaret Hill* in the developed world moving elsewhere, to legal moves within Bangladesh. The latter led to the High Court banning the importation of ships to break for periods of 2010/11.

The production of 'ship-break furniture', as it is known, offered new possibilities and patterns of value for the growing Bangladeshi lower middle classes. Previously, furniture in Bangladesh was made from teak. Expensive, extremely durable and handed down through the generations, it was, in Thompson's (1979) terms, a durable good, acquiring patina and value through use. Increasing scarcity and extremely high prices, however, provided an opening in the market for a different type of furniture. It was this gap which the nascent furniture businesses spotted and exploited. Selling their initial goods through a 'try it and see how you get on with it' narrative, they found that consumers began to value their newly acquired furniture precisely because of how it stood in opposition to teak. Thus, as we show in the next section, ship-breaking furniture came to be valued because it was cheap (compared to teak), and because, while it was hard wearing, it could also (unlike teak) be discarded, precisely because it was cheap and of less value. Ship-breaking furniture therefore could be

2.2 Chock-chocky furnishings: ship-breaking materials refurbished and covered in Formica (*source*: the authors)

given away to relatives, left behind if one moved, and thrown away if it broke. Its value, then, was in its transience as well as its price, and in the way it fitted in with the lives of an increasingly mobile Bangladeshi middle class.

Sun Furniture House illustrates the way adding Formica finishing re-enhances the products. The owner of the business, Mr Abdul Alim, tells the story of how his company's use of Formica enabled Sun Furniture to cover over the blemishes and marks of wear on ship-breaking furniture, to present it as shiny and new: in local parlance, *chock-chocky* (see Figure 2.2). Given that Formica can be produced in either a matt or a glossy finish, and with myriad patterns, Sun Furniture now fulfils bespoke orders from Chittagong's lower middle class, who desire, yet cannot afford, branded furnishings. Indeed, while Sun Furniture's chock-chocky may have started as an affordable alternative, it has now grown into a new ship-breaking furniture brand with its own cachet; its products are widely distributed throughout Bangladesh via wholesalers, retailing in Feni, Sylhet, Rajshahi and Noakhali. From the late 1990s, the market moved into a new phase, responding to a more modern, more self-consciously designed aesthetic, refracted through a spatial imaginary of 'international' styles whose putative globality both reflected and restated widening Bangladeshi middle-class horizons. Furnishings here are infused with a complex mix of national and global signifiers – or better, nationally understood signifiers of globality (Reimer and Leslie 2008).

The furniture shops and allied refurbishment workshops of Bhatiary show clearly how discarded goods, valued as rubbish by ship-breakers, were captured, transformed and revalorized. They show too how this revalorization is dependent upon creating markets for new products. That the furniture businesses of Bhatiary have been so successful in this regard is largely because they fabricate and recommodify goods whose value lies in their difference from other valued goods, particularly teak.

Domestic reincorporation and appropriation: shipshape and Bengali fashion

Having discussed how the Bhatiary furniture businesses revalorize the wastes of the ship-breaking businesses, we turn, in this section, to consider how these items are appropriated by Bangladeshi middle-class consumers. We draw here on thirty-nine detailed interviews with thirty-two households, conducted in Bengali, spread across the lower, middle and upper echelons of the middle classes, utilizing two households as exemplar cases. Both live in Chittagong City and were recruited through social networks and snowballing methods.

Mrs S is a widow in her mid-fifties living with one of her elder daughters, her husband and child in a small one-storey, rented house in the Noia Bazar area on the outskirts of Chittagong City. The house comprises two rooms alongside a kitchen and bathroom. The front room acts as a living room/bedroom with the other being the main bedroom. Space is at a premium in this home, yet it is crammed full of furniture – to the extent that it is almost impossible to move. In the bedroom, aside from a teak bed, which was her daughter's wedding gift, there is an upholstered sofa, a steel clothes rack and a wooden chair. In the main room is a second matching upholstered sofa, a bed-cum-sitting area, a small table and a cupboard/chest, on which stands a TV. All this furniture, with the exception of the teak bed, is ship-breaking furniture purchased in Bhatiary. Much of it was purchased relatively recently. Mrs S bought the second bed two years ago, partly on the advice of her neighbour, who stressed the competitive prices to be found in Bhatiary; she bought the rest subsequently. Mrs S talks about this furniture in a manner that emphasizes the multiple ways she values these items: in terms of affordability, as a worthy substitute for the unobtainable (teak), fashionable, varied in design and well made. She says:

It is very good and cherished by us [... it] is within the range of our ability and affordability. We can't buy teak furniture so it is very beautiful and attractive to us. People like us are basically the lower income group and the only option is ship-breaking furniture, both for design and by necessity.

Nevertheless, she emphasizes:

there is a big difference between today's products and previously. Ship-breaking furniture used to look second hand but the way it is made nowadays in Bhatiary with Formica and other materials is far better. Last year when I went to Bhatiary to purchase this sofa set I was really impressed to see all the different designs and that many of these items are chock-chocky.

Mrs K is in her mid-thirties and a schoolteacher. She has one child and her husband works for a private company. They live in a two-bedroom flat in Agrabad, a middle-class residential neighbourhood close to the financial and business quarter in Chittagong City. The flat has a living room, a dining room, a master bedroom, a children's bedroom and two toilets. Mrs K is from Dhaka originally and the couple moved to Chittagong shortly after their marriage, nine years ago. They started their married lives in a small one-bedroom flat, similar to that in the previous case study. Initially, they had no furniture for the flat. A friend told them about Bhatiary, where the furniture was ready made, ready to take away and reasonably priced. Mrs K explains:

When we went there for the first time we were so surprised to see that the whole of Bhatiary area is full of ship-breaking furniture and the price was so reasonable. It was really helpful for us to start a new life as a newly married couple with only my husband earning. First, we bought one bed and one wardrobe, which were essential items and desperately needed by us. Afterwards we also bought a dining table and sofa set – I really liked the furniture.

Today Mrs K's home has a mix of ship-breaking furniture and new international-style furniture and some teak. The main living room includes a large sofa in blue, gold and pink cloth, an ornamental table and an emergency bed for guest use. The master bedroom includes a teak bed, a chest of drawers from Bhatiary and two pieces of branded furniture: a wardrobe and a dressing table with mirror. The dining room, however, still contains the same oval table and set of chairs purchased 'as is' in Bhatiary when they were first married.

It is instructive to compare how Mrs K talks about ship-breaking furniture now compared to earlier on in her life. Acknowledging the impossibility of purchasing any other type of furniture as 'newly-weds', she now sees this furniture as 'cost effective but not fashionable'. Indeed, whereas for Mrs S chock-chocky connotes a stylish aesthetic, for Mrs K it does not. For her, using Formica has lowered the quality of the product and has had a negative impact on its appearance. She says: 'The glossiness of the Formica or the covering fabric of the sofas is very bright which I feel is less sophisticated.' The changing consumption of ship-breaking furniture within Mrs K's home over the years illuminates the ambiguities of ship-breaking furniture's entanglements with the taste registers of the Bangladeshi middle classes. For Mrs K, furniture is understood to convey social status. Ship-breaking furniture is prob-lematically, even negatively, positioned in relation to social status. Thus, chock-chocky is too brash, or too loud (to use an English translation). It is a marker of a lack of sophistication. In another sense, ship-breaking furniture is understood here as second hand, in its negative sense. As a consequence, in Mrs K's current home certain items of ship-breaking furniture have been relegated to the private areas of the house where taste matters less – notably a child's bedroom – and replaced with objects that accord with different taste aesthetics, assumed to be more modern. Paradoxically confirming this class aesthetic, however, other items of ship-breaking furniture – the 'as is' dining-room table and chairs – are proudly displayed in another public room. It is unadulterated and high-quality original furniture. The confines of Mrs K's flat therefore contain a conjuncture and collision of taste registers in which ship-breaking furniture is multiply positioned and thoroughly entangled.

By contrast, the upper-middle-class households that we interviewed had further relegated ship-breaking furniture and invested in teak. Here, in the upper echelons of this social class, where authenticity is affordable, it materializes through the historically traditional form of teak or in branded designs. Some associated ship-breaking furniture nostalgically with straitened times when they were establishing house-holds. Some passed it on again to relatives in the home village – whence it passes into another decommodified value regime centred on the rural economy and rural livelihoods – or gave it to servants, or simply dumped it to be scavenged and reused for its materials once more.

The broad contours of how distinction and taste work themselves out in the context of the Bangladeshi middle class will be familiar enough to those conversant with consumption debates. Running alongside this is a value grounded in disposability. That ship-breaking furniture can be discarded, and that it is disposed of through intra-familial gifting and the hand-me-down/hand-around social economy is a measure of its social worth. To be able to gift furniture in a country where 40 per cent of the population are without furniture, and to be able to place this furniture with poor relations living in rural areas, is both open to notions of care and responsibility towards family (or known others) and simultaneously a means of registering, in a highly material way, the social mobility of family members. Read thus, ship-breaking furniture begins to emerge as a type of furniture whose value lies in that it can be whatever the consumer wants it to be: a beautiful substitute for the unattainable (teak), offering comfort and convenience, fashionable, a nostalgic memory, disposable, conferring generosity and care. Such mutability in meaning is, we suggest, intimately linked to the conditions of the furniture's production and the seemingly infinite variety of its form. Ship-breaking furniture is not often second-hand furniture. The vast bulk of this furniture is fabricated from materials left over from the process of object destruction and steel scrap recovery on the beaches. Built on wastes and materials rather than objects, the furniture businesses are an instance of secondary manufacturing and founded on imagining and fabricating these materials into objects and commodities that resonate with the aesthetic tastes of the Bangladeshi middle classes. Epitomizing the arts of transience, these furniture businesses show that rubbish dumped on a beach can be reclaimed, revalued and re-enhanced, that the arts of transience can be a commercial success, and that waste can indeed be turned into value.

Conclusions – the dangers of revalorization

This chapter shows clearly Thompson's point: that rubbish is not an end point but a fulcrum, and that even with objects as seemingly global and durable as ships, the humble arts of transience are critical to rekindling value. In our story, we have followed the devaluation and revalorization of end-of-life ships as they decompose into new materials, and are both given new value and lead new lives. We have suggested that the crossing of value regimes with used products can involve global movements, from a place where materials are classified as problematic and toxic to places where, rather problematically, they are welcomed as resources. Rekindling thus binds global movement to places where the recategorization of materials allows their reuse. But that is not enough to explain the rekindling of value. There also has to be creation of new markets and the revaluing of refashioned products. Thus the story departs from much research on second-hand exchange and consumption, as well as from cultural work on salvage (Soderan and Carter 2008), which focuses on a stable object of devaluation and revalorization. The dismembered objects on Chittagong beach testify to rubbish value's connection to the material, its properties and capacities. Here material triumphs over things and value depends on the ability of materials to multiply and mutate. The ships cease to be vessels but revert to being thousands of tons of scrap steel and more. To stop seeing them as objects and to see them as conjunctures of materials requires a gestalt shift. The social sciences customarily focus upon objects, whether in material culture studies, museum studies or consumption research. A focus on end-of-life objects, however, insists on seeing that things are assemblages, ontological conjunctures of stuff, materials brought together and held together, but also coming apart and wrenched asunder.

Seen thus, things are inherently unstable, materially as well as in their meanings – hence the importance of repair and maintenance activities (Graham and Thrift 2007; Gregson et al. 2009). But repair and maintenance are unable to keep holding things together. Objects, even those as enduring and sizeable as *The Lady Margaret Hill*, eventually start to come apart, economically and physically, symbolically and socially. As such, the object is but a temporary moment in an endless process of assembling materials, a partial stabilization and a fragile holding together that is always inexorably becoming something else, somewhere else. To say this is not to celebrate it. The apparent virtue of recycling 99 per cent of the ship returns to haunt the discussion. With no distinction between materials, the furniture businesses and their agents strip out and rework their furniture from a range of boards: some benign, some made of toxic asbestos. The latter kind of boards are also sold extensively within the construction industry and therefore have been distributed widely across Bangladesh, notably in new-build apartments. The copper of the salvaged electrical cabling may be benign but the PVC sheathing is another matter: when it is stripped off and burnt in brick kilns it releases its energy content and PCBs in equal measure. Correspondingly, while the arts of transience suggest the phoenix of rekindled value, they show that the domestic construction boom of Bangladesh has let loose the demons of Pandora's box far beyond the beaches. We end the chapter, therefore, by sounding a note of caution regarding the arts of transience. While most materials have the potential to keep being assembled, there are some materials which would surely be better off corralled as 'wastes' and stabilized as wastes – even if thus sequestering them requires much by way of maintenance work.

Notes

1 See page 62 for an explanation of light displacement tonnes (ldt) and deadweight tonnes (dwt).

2 This account is compiled from numerous media and trade sources. Specific quotes, companies and figures are reported in the *Daily Echo*, 24 March 2010 (www.dailyecho.co.uk/news/5081678.Mystery_surrounds_future_of_impounded_ship), *MYNews India*, 24 February 2010 (www.mynews.in/News/Pos8sible_arrival_of_UK's_dead_and_toxic_vessel's_arrival_in_Indian_waters_N39045.html), the *Ecologist*, 18 February 2010, Cotzias sale and purchase monthly report, August 2009 (www.cotzias.gr/), BBC Hampshire, 13 August 2009 (news.bbc.co.uk/go/pr/fr/-/1/hi/england/hampshire/8200016.stm), *Lloyd's List*, 10 August 2010 (shipocean.webs.com/).

References

Buerk, R. (2006) *Breaking Ships: How supertankers and cargo ships are dismantled on the beaches of Bangladesh*, New York: Chamberlain Bros.

Crang, M. (2010) 'The death of great ships: photography, politics, and waste in the global imaginary', *Environment and Planning A*, 42: 1084–1102.

Graham, S. and N. Thrift (2007) 'Out of order: understanding repair and maintenance', *Theory, Culture and Society*, 24: 1–25.

Gregson, N. and L. Crewe (2003) *Second-hand Cultures*, Oxford: Berg.

Gregson, N., A. Metcalfe and L. Crewe (2007) 'Moving things along: the conduits and practices of household divestment', *Transactions of the Institute of British Geographers*, 32: 187–200.

— (2009) 'Practices of object maintenance and repair: how consumers attend to consumer objects within the home', *Journal of Consumer Culture*.

Gregson, N., H. Watkins et al. (2010) 'Inextinguishable fibres: demolition and the vital materialisms of asbestos', *Environment and Planning A*, 42(5): 1065–83.

Gregson, N., M. Crang, F. Ahamed, N. Akter, R. Ferdous, F. Mahmud and R. Hudson (2012) 'Territorial agglomeration, industrial symbiosis and learning from the South: Sitakunda-Bhatiary, Bangladesh as a secondary processing complex', *Economic Geography*, 88(1): 37–58.

Hawkins, G. (2006) *The Ethics of Waste: How we relate to rubbish*, Lanham, MD: Rowman & Littlefield.

Hossain, M. S., S. R. Chowdhury, A. Jabbar, S. M. Saifullah and M. A. Rahman (2008) 'Occupational health hazards of ship scrapping workers at Chittagong coastal zone, Bangladesh', *Chiang Mai J. Science*, 35: 370–81.

Langewiesche, W. (2000) 'The shipbreakers', *Atlantic Monthly*, 286: 31–49.

Levinson, M. (2006) *The Box: How the shipping container made the world smaller and the world economy bigger*, Princeton, NJ: Princeton University Press.

Mackenzie, D. (2009) *Material Markets: How economic agents are constructed*, Oxford: Oxford University Press.

Marcus, G. E. (1995) 'Ethnography in/of the world system: the emergence of multi-sited ethnography', *Annual Review of Anthropology*, 24: 95–117.

Nag, D. (1991) 'Fashion, gender and the Bengali middle class', *Public Culture*, 3: 93–112.

Puthucherril, T. G. (2010) *From Shipbreaking to Sustainable Ship Recycling: Evolution of a Legal Regime*, Leiden: Martinus Neijhoff.

Reimer, S. and D. Leslie (2008) 'Design, national imaginaries, and the home furnishings commodity chain', *Growth and Change*, 39: 144–71.

Salgado, S. (2005) *Workers: An Archaeology of the Industrial Age*, New York: Aperture.

Sawyer, J. F. (2001/02) 'Shipbreaking and the North–South debate: economic development or environmental and labor catastrophe', *Penn State International Law Review*, 20: 535–62.

Sekula, A. (2001) 'Freeway to China' (Version 2, for Liverpool), in J. Comaroff and J. Comaroff (eds), *Millennial Capitalism and the Culture of Neoliberalism*, Durham, NC: Duke University Press, pp. 147–59.

Soderan, B. and R. Carter (2008) 'The auto salvage: a space of second chances', *Space and Culture*, 11: 20–38.

Srinivasa Reddy, M., S. Basha, V. G. Sravan Kumar, H. V. Joshi and P. K. Ghosh (2003) 'Quantification and classification of ship scrapping waste at Alang-Sosiya, India', *Marine Pollution Bulletin*, 46: 1609–14.

Srinivasa Reddy, M., S. Basha, V. G. Sravan Kumar, H. V. Joshi and G. Ramachandraiah (2004) 'Distribution, enrichment and accumulation of heavy metals in coastal sediments of Alang-Sosiya ship scrapping yard, India', *Marine Pollution Bulletin*, 48: 1055–9.

Srinivasa Reddy, M., B. Shaik, S. Adimurthy and G. Ramachandraiah (2006) 'Description of the small plastics fragments in marine sediments along the Alang-Sosiya ship-breaking yard, India', *Estuarine, Coastal and Shelf Science*, 68: 656–60.

Tewari, A., H. V. Joshi, R. H. Trivedi, V. G. Sravankumar, C. Raghunathan, Y. Khambhaty, O. S. Kotiwar and S. K. Mandal (2001) 'The effect of the ship scrapping industry and its associated wastes on the biomass production and biodiversity of biota in in situ condition at Alang', *Marine Pollution Bulletin*, 42: 461–8.

Thompson, M. (1979) *Rubbish Theory: The creation and destruction of value*, Oxford: Oxford University Press.

Tolia-Kelly, D. (2004a) 'Materialising post-colonial geographies: examining the textual landscapes of migration in the South Asian home', *Geoforum*, 35: 675–88.

— (2004b) 'Locating processes of identification: studying the precipitates of re-memory through artefacts in British Asian homes', *Transactions of the Institute of British Geographers*, 29: 314–29.

3 | One cycle to bind them all? Geographies of nuclearity in the uranium fuel cycle

ROMAIN GARCIER

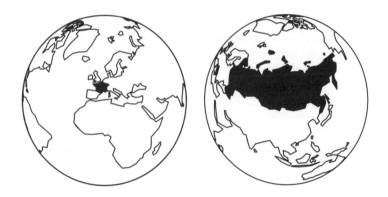

After a short decade of 'renaissance', the nuclear industry fell into crisis again in 2011 when the accident at the nuclear plant in Fukushima-Daichi contaminated a large zone in north-eastern Japan and raised questions about the intrinsic safety of nuclear energy production. Some countries, such as Germany, decided to abandon nuclear energy altogether, while others, France and the UK, stated their continued commitment to this form of electricity generation. On a global level, the Fukushima accident renewed debates on the relevance of nuclear for energy futures from both safety and economic perspectives.

In this chapter, I want to bring to the fore some of the discussions that pertain not to the nuclear plants themselves, but to their industrial supply infrastructure; more specifically to the 'nuclear fuel cycle'. Natural uranium requires considerable chemical and physical transformation before it can be used in nuclear plants: such transformations are performed in a succession of steps that constitute the 'fuel cycle'. One of the most fascinating aspects of industrial advocacy of nuclear power lies in its insistence that nuclear power is a *recyclable* – if not renewable – form of energy. Nuclear power extracts the energy contained in uranium atoms, which are themselves in limited supply on Earth and cannot be naturally replenished. However, spent nuclear fuel can be reprocessed to separate its constitutive materials, which themselves can be recycled and reused for electricity generation. The possibility of re-enriching and reusing uranium, and to a lesser extent plutonium, allows nuclear energy to benefit from the symbolic clout of recycling. Uranium abundance is increased by the possibility of recycling spent fuel: secondary uranium (and plutonium) resources theoretically allow 'peak uranium' to be pushed very far into the future (several millennia), provided some technological advances are made (Bouneau, David et al. 2009).

However, opponents of spent fuel reprocessing argue that it contributes to nuclear proliferation since plutonium extracted from spent fuel can be used to make bombs and, moreover, reprocessing threatens human health and the environment (Morichaud 2002). This opposition can be extremely heated. After reprocessing in France or the UK, materials that cannot be reused (high-level radioactive waste) or plutonium-based fuel elements, are shipped back to the Japanese or German owners of the original fuel. Apocalyptic scenes occur: militants chained to railway tracks, vocal demonstrations in harbours and train stations, swarms of cameras sweeping over vengeful banners. Other criticisms are directed at spent fuel recycling for economic (von Hippel 2001; Bunn, Fetter et al. 2003) or political reasons (Berkhout, Suzuki et al. 1990; Walker 1999). As William Walker puts it: 'Let it be stated clearly: reprocessing is not and never has been the option of commercial choice for utilities on grounds of energy cost, nor does it offer any significant gains in energy security. In Japan, as elsewhere, it is the scarcity of storage capacity for spent fuel that has driven utilities to engage with reprocessing and its associated technology of plutonium recycling' (Walker 2006: 759).

In other words, recycling spent fuel enables utilities to postpone and displace the time and place when and where the final disposal of radioactive waste will take place. For critics, therefore, recycling is not the logical outcome of an economic strategy but simply a way to keep matter circulating as long as possible, for want of a place where it can be permanently stored and disposed of. From this perspective, the physical and chemical transformations of recycling are only a pretext for a time-buying, spatial recirculation of cumbersome, high-activity materials within the nuclear fuel cycle. Moving, transforming and sometimes reusing materials push forward into the future the problem of scarce and contentious disposal sites.

Such circulations are seldom studied in the literature for what they are, essentially a geographical response to a management problem: local over-accumulation of unwanted materials.[1] This chapter addresses such a geographical response for recycled nuclear materials, and challenges two notions that are central to the nuclear fuel cycle. First,

I analyse how the nuclear fuel cycle is depicted and show that all representations are partial in terms of what is included and what is excluded. Second, I illustrate and explore the spatial strategies that structure material flows of low-activity, recycled materials inside the cycle. By spatial strategies I mean organized ways of enrolling geographical space as a management device for nuclear materials. Space and material flows matter immensely in the performance of the fuel cycle and two such strategies can be evidenced: physically moving unwanted materials to remote areas, and keeping them on site, unattended. The main hypothesis is this: at the core of spatial strategies lies the *qualification* of materials and matter within the cycle. In this, I extend Callon et al.'s argument (2002), that defining and making things singular through appealing to their qualities or characteristics is a highly contested, negotiated process of qualification. In this case, the qualities under scrutiny are those which may, or may not, define various materials, technologies and places as 'nuclear' and therefore part of the fuel cycle. As I discuss below, Hecht (2006) terms this subjective, technopolitical construction of what counts as nuclear 'nuclearity'. Thus, not unlike a famous ring, the nuclear fuel cycle narrative 'binds' materials and places while negating their contentious and specific spatialities and materialities. Even if they are controversial, images of the cycle and recycling both obfuscate how the 'nuclear status' of materials is constantly negotiated within the cycle, and obscure the spatiality of material transformations and circulations.

This chapter recovers the strategic dimension of fuel cycle geographies by analysing cases where such spatial strategies fail and the cycle-recycle imagery crumbles because material qualifications become contested. When, for example, France ships reprocessed uranium to Russia for re-enrichment, is this uranium classified as a waste or a resource? Re-enrichment creates depleted uranium, which has a very low fissile isotope content: there is a question as to whether or not this uranium should be considered as a nuclear material and thus inside the cycle. When reprocessing is performed, should radioactive residues be considered as industrial waste, and thus outside the cycle, or as nuclear waste? Such specific questions speak to more general debates: the variety of motivations behind recycling, its spatial organization and moral economy, but also the institutional devices that enable it. I suggest it is not possible to approach recycling without reference to its underlying geographies.

This chapter is organized as follows. The first part presents the standard nuclear fuel cycle and its geography, and shows how it is based on a highly selective approach towards the nuclearity of materials that enables them to be included in socio-economic processes. I then introduce a concrete example of the complex status of recycled materials within the fuel cycle and their importance for spatial strategies; this illustration is the controversy surrounding the flows of reprocessed uranium to and from France and Russia. The third part further explores the relationship between material qualifications and spatial strategies via the case of the uranium conversion plant in Malvési (France); this shows that spatial strategies not only involve shifting recycled material around but also requalifying it in place.

Defining the contours of the cycle, negotiating nuclearity

The circulation of uranium in the nuclear industry is generally analysed with reference to the 'nuclear fuel cycle' (Wilson 2001). The notion of 'cycle' is useful, because it articulates the succession of technical steps necessary for transforming, and retransforming, uranium into something useful.

The uranium cycle Uranium is a heavy metal, found in abundance on the Earth but generally in low concentrations (Falck 2009). Most of the uranium used today comes from primary sources (mines) but a significant proportion comes from secondary resources: decommissioned military uranium,[2] tailings from former uranium mines or recycled uranium. Global assessments of uranium resources take place every two years, under the observation of the International Atomic Energy Agency (IAEA). The latest instalment confirms that, in the near future, primary resources will still provide the bulk of uranium used in the nuclear industry (OECD-IAEA 2010).

One of the peculiarities of uranium among energy sources is the complexity and the number of technical steps that are necessary to tap into its energetic potential. Following extraction, uranium ore is ground, purified and concentrated to create yellowcake (uranium oxide). Yellowcake is further purified and then converted to a gaseous form (uranium tetrafluoride and hexafluoride). Uranium conversion is a necessary step before enrichment, which is the artificial increase of the fissile isotope $U235$, of which natural uranium contains only 0.7 per cent.[3] Once uranium has been enriched up to a level of 3.5 per cent $U235$, it is retransformed into oxide form. Enriched uranium oxide is the basic component of the many thousands of fuel pellets which are put together in fuel assemblies. Placed into nuclear reactors' cores, assemblies are irradiated for between three and four years before being removed and replaced. The 'front end' of the cycle refers to the steps needed to prepare the fuel; the 'back end' includes the processes of energy production, waste production, disposal and recycling; irradiation marks the limit between the front and back ends of the cycle and is the point where most radioactivity is created. Irradiated spent-fuel assemblies are extremely radioactive.

The back end of the cycle has two modalities. In the 'once-through' fuel cycle, all spent fuel assemblies are considered as waste and no form of recycling occurs. In 1979, the USA decided to forgo fuel reprocessing and started looking for options to dispose of spent fuel. Other countries, the UK and France, for example, decided to reprocess spent fuel, thus 'closing' the fuel cycle. Such countries separate spent materials into three constitutive parts: 'reprocessed' uranium (95 per cent), where the proportion of $U235$ is 0.8 per cent; a small proportion of plutonium (1 per cent); and about 4 per cent of 'fission products', highly radioactive elements considered as waste and generally vitrified and stored while a permanent disposal solution is found. Fresh fuel can be refabricated with reprocessed uranium and/or plutonium (a type of fuel known as MOx). MOx fabrication is a technical second best, the only way to put plutonium to civilian uses after the completion of atomic arsenals. Initially, fuel reprocessing was performed to furnish plutonium for bombs (Goldschmidt 1982); it was only in the mid-1970s that its civilian use in dedicated reactors (known as fast neutron reactors, or breeders) was discussed. This technical strand having failed for technical reasons (Finon 1989), MOx was invented as an outlet for existing and future plutonium inventories.

Geographically, these technical steps take place in distinct places, the spatial distribution of which is a legacy of the Cold War (Garcier 2009). The industrial infrastructures necessary for uranium transformation were developed when uranium's primary use was military. Uranium was mined and transformed inside each nuclear country's zone of influence (Helmreich 1986). For example, the USA drilled mines in the Western American deserts and established transformation plants across the mainland territory (Zoellner 2009); the USSR developed mining resources in Tajikistan and eastern European countries and performed final transformations in Russia (Kasparek 1952; Zeman and Karlsch 2008). Likewise, France used its colonial resources in Madagascar before developing mines in mainland France, where all transformations were also conducted (Caralp 1958). Civilian development of nuclear power in the 1960s led to a diversification of uranium sources and the creation of a commercial market for uranium. Numerous countries extract uranium today, but more than 60 per cent of uranium mined today comes from Kazakhstan, Australia and Canada (OECD-IAEA 2010). However, the emergence of a commercial market for uranium has not substantially modified the geography of transformation in the fuel cycle, because the technological and financial costs of entry into the market are extremely high and the quantities exchanged are low: global uranium demand now stands at between 50,000 and 60,000 tonnes.

This is why the industrial infrastructure underlying the uranium fuel cycle is particularly meagre: at each step of the cycle, there are only a few plants. For example, there are only nine uranium conversion plants in the world, belonging to four companies, and eight industrial-size enrichment plants. Only twenty-three plants in the world have the capability to manufacture nuclear fuel, and not even every type. At the back end of the cycle, the number of plants is even lower: there are four commercial reprocessing plants in the world, of which only one is currently commercially operational (La Hague, in France). The exception to such sparsity is the reactors themselves: about 440 are operational worldwide. As for the civilian high-level waste disposal sites, none is active today, although a few are projected.

Such a spatial structure for the industrial system explains why the uranium cycle hinges on a very specific geography that links a few nodes of uranium transformation which have many material flows between them. The nuclear industry depends on material circulations between places of production, consumption and transformation, whatever the uranium product under consideration: ore, concentrates, gases, fresh or spent fuel; hence the importance of transportation infrastructure. The fuel cycle's geography is predicated on port infrastructures, marshalling yards, warehouses, ships and lorries, which are all the more strategic as uranium mines are generally located in remote places. Uranium from Niger, for example, has to travel 1,500 kilometres by truck from Arlit to Parakou (Benin), before being loaded on to rail wagons headed for Cotonou harbour. From there, uranium is shipped to the port of Montoir-de-Bretagne, France.

Today, the uranium fuel cycle is globalized in that flows between industrial nodes now move beyond Cold War separations, as Figure 3.1 illustrates. Representing France's uranium supply, the figure shows that uranium is bought in nine different countries and enriched in three plants: Malvési (France), Metropolis (USA) and Seversk (Russia). Such diversity in uranium services providers guarantees energy safety because redundancy allows Electricité de France, the only nuclear utility in France, to protect itself from interrupted flows (Autorité de

3. Garcier

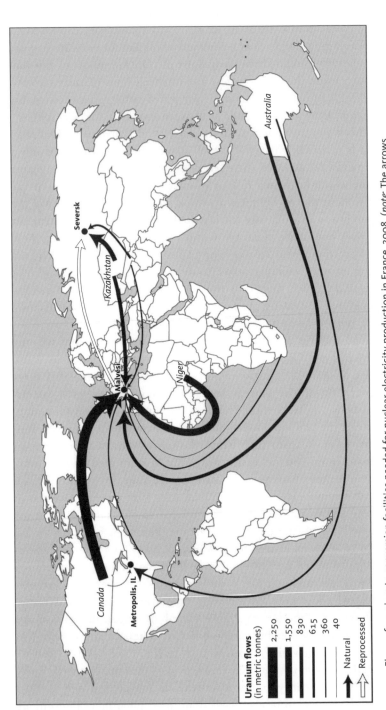

3.1 Flows of uranium to conversion facilities needed for nuclear electricity production in France, 2008 (*note:* The arrows represent flows, not actual transportation routes) (*source:* HCTISN 2010, copyright Romain J. Garcier, 2011)

Australia

Seversk

Kazakhstan

Malvési

Niger

Canada

Metropolis, IL

Uranium flows
(in metric tonnes)

2,250
1,550
830
615
360
40

Natural
Reprocessed

Sûreté Nucléaire 2010: 38). However, circulations inside the industrial system are still very much constrained by institutional devices that seek to prevent flows from endangering the environment and human health or contributing to nuclear proliferation (for example, the Nuclear Material Control and Accountancy performed by Euratom in Europe). As a consequence, natural uranium and, even more, transformed uranium is not freely accessible to economic stakeholders: states and international organizations such as Euratom and the IAEA are constantly involved and monitor uranium exchanges. Not all potential flows are thus possible. Until recently, for example, the absence of a bilateral treaty between Australia and Russia prevented Australian uranium exports to Russia.

The normativity of the cycle The above description of the uranium fuel cycle is useful, but does not exhaust the complexity of the fuel's constitutive geographies precisely because the notion of 'fuel cycle' is not a fact but a constructed representation. Let us take an example. Mining tailings are generally not considered a part of the nuclear fuel cycle: in France and the USA, they come under mining (and not nuclear) legislation and, as such, are not considered to be 'nuclear waste'. However, mining tailings are, by far, the primary material released by uranium mining: there are over 45 million tonnes in France, more than 200 million tonnes in Canada. To put this into perspective, it is worth noting that the total uranium ever extracted worldwide is 2.2 million tonnes (Price, Barthel et al. 2006). Mine tailings contain a significant proportion of radioactive materials, which is why tailings can be a secondary resource. Excluding tailings from the cycle indicates selection between materials and the forms they take; the value and social significance of a material vary depending on whether it is included in the cycle or not, and on the very limits and contours of the cycle it is included in.

Using the imagery of the 'closed nuclear cycle' and of 'recycling' to qualify the series of uranium transformations is deeply significant. It likens the 'uranium cycle' to other great fundamental natural cycles – the cycles of water, nitrogen and carbon – and thus suggests that, throughout the cycle, matter is conserved at an atomic level. This is not the case. The purpose of nuclear fission is precisely to perform atomic modifications. Such ambiguity is obvious in Figure 3.2, taken from the website of an association of former nuclear workers. It describes the closed nuclear fuel cycle but the drawing does not take material circulations into consideration, for the arrows join technical steps. The

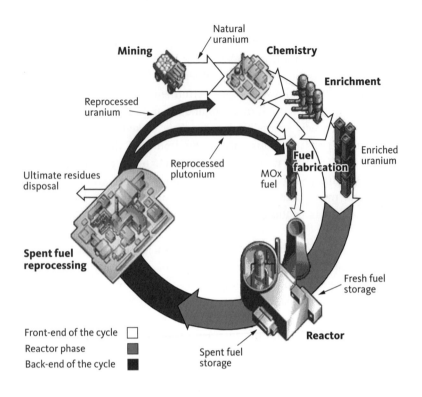

3.2 The 'closed nuclear cycle' (*source*: Union des Associations d'anciens et Retraités du groupe Areva, www.uarga.org, with authorization)

same arrows, specifically their constant size, let the reader think that all operations in the fuel cycle are conducted without any loss of matter – no leaks, no scrap, no waste – even though every technical step is concerned with a number of different transformations. Finally, the emphasis on recycling is dominant in this image, since only a small quantity of matter (the small white arrow labelled 'ultimate residues' on the left) appears to *exit* the cycle, while the larger arrows emphasize the importance of recycling flows. This way of representing the cycle is widespread in the nuclear industry; its power derives from the current semiotic resonance of the concept of 'recycling'. In Figure 3.2, many flows and intermediate material transformations are neither signalled nor spatialized, because they are deemed to be *outside* the cycle and are therefore condemned to invisibility. The focus is solely on uranium as the relevant matter for industrial and political responsibility.

Contrast Figure 3.2 with Figure 3.3, which shows exactly the same processes, but with a different take.

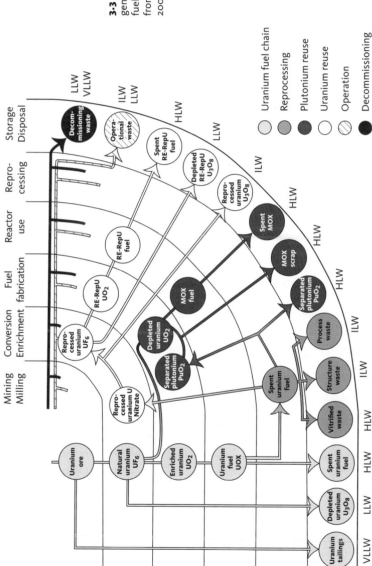

3.3 Waste and materials generated in the material fuel chain (*source*: Adapted from Schneider and Marignac 2008, with permission)

Mining Milling · Conversion Enrichment · Fuel fabrication · Reactor use · Repro-cessing · Storage Disposal

Uranium fuel chain
Reprocessing
Plutonium reuse
Uranium reuse
Operation
Decommissioning

Uranium ore
Natural uranium UF6
Enriched uranium UO2
Uranium fuel UOX
Reprocessed uranium U Nitrate
Reprocessed uranium UF6
RE-RepU UO2
RE-RepU fuel
Depleted uranium UO2
Separated plutonium PuO2
MOX fuel
MOX scrap
Spent MOX
Reprocessed uranium U3O8
Depleted RE-RepU U3O8
Spent RE-RepU fuel
Decom-missioning waste
Operational waste

Spent uranium fuel
Spent uranium fuel
Depleted uranium U3O8
Uranium tailings
Vitrified waste
Structure waste
Process waste
Separated plutonium PuO2

LLW VLLW · ILW LLW · HLW · LLW · ILW · HLW · HLW · HLW · ILW · ILW · HLW · LLW · HLW · VLLW

The focus is here on the plurality of by-products created by uranium transformation and recycling, specifically of the wastes generated at each step. Such wastes, diverse in type and level of radioactivity,[4] are seen here as constituent elements of the uranium cycle; foregrounding wastes like this is highly political, a way of confirming their 'relevance' for the nuclear industry. The figure's original authors are anti-nuclear experts and took the precaution of substituting the more neutral expression 'fuel chain' for 'fuel cycle', thereby implicitly criticizing the imagery and connotations of the 'cycle'. The chain they present is much more complex: they introduce *types* of uranium, eschewing the idea of complete fungibility for uranium forms along the cycle, even more so when recycling occurs. The figure shows that recycling does not create a single loop for materials, but parallel tracks of material reuse; recycling does not simplify material diversity, nor reproduce it identically, but introduces an element of increased intricacy in material and waste streams. Crucially, this complexity cannot be closed into a cycle, hence the depiction of a fan with irrecoverable waste streams rippling ever farther outwards.

Figures 3.2 and 3.3 are an excellent example of how the same technical processes and material flows can be represented by radically different imageries. Figure 3.3 is an implicit criticism of the material dispersion and dissemination introduced by reprocessing and recycling. What is being played out in such narratives, represented here in graphical form, is the prescriptive (or normative) dimension of the cycle and the recycling discourses: their capacity to perform or make things happen. Thus, excluding something from the cycle makes it invisible and removes it from pressing political concerns. This is not restricted to the nuclear industry; the same analysis could be made about the production of paper or plastics – every transformation, including recycling, that produces secondary materials or waste that are, literally and metaphorically, unaccounted for.[5]

However, such different representations raise another interesting question: what is the logic behind the definition of what is 'relevant' in the cycle? For example, how is it that mining waste is excluded from the cycle? I suspect an element of the answer lies in the differential allocation of nuclearity along the cycle, and it is to this question that I now turn.

Nuclearity, a geographical element Nuclear things belong to a set of specific imageries and legal and technical provisions, on grounds that Gabrielle Hecht has called 'nuclearity'. Counter-intuitively, a thing is

never 'naturally' nuclear: its nuclearity is the outcome of technopolitical negotiations (Hecht 2006, 2007). The nuclearity of uranium itself,
of all the material forms it might take and of all the technologies
necessary to tap into its power (most notably enrichment), is con-
ferred upon them. For example, uranium ore is generally regarded as
a mining product, and not a nuclear material, up until the enrichment
phase (International Atomic Energy Agency 1980): it is therefore not
the totality of the uranium cycle which is nuclear; things become
nuclear as they circulate along the cycle. The most striking thing is that
nuclearity has only distant links with radioactivity: it is not the level of
radioactivity of an object which defines its nuclearity. An aluminium
tube can be considered as a 'nuclear' object by the Non-Proliferation
Treaty if it can be used to build uranium enrichment centrifuges. For
Hecht, such considerations call for an analysis of why some things or
technologies are 'nuclear' – keeping in mind that nuclearity is neither
an arbitrary social construct nor a natural property of materials and
objects. Nuclearity is created for strategic ends, and is a defining
element in the social life of things.

Approaching nuclearity is integral to understanding the organization
of material geographies in the fuel cycle because nuclearity is not
simply a technopolitical creation but also a powerful *logistical* operator
in the nuclear industry. Nuclearity allows or precludes certain material
flows, enables materials to be circulated (spatial strategy no. 1) or left
on site, unattended (spatial strategy no. 2). By constantly changing
the definition of what is, or is not, nuclear, industry and government
can adjust their spatial strategies along the following principle: *the
less nuclear a material is, the more amenable it is to a spatial strategy.*
Saying that a mining residue is *not* nuclear greatly facilitates its being
left on mining sites. The 'nuclear fuel cycle', in all its guises, is not
simply a collection of technical steps but also a device for allocating
nuclearity, and facilitating the fixation/circulation of materials, and
thus the creation of value or the lowering of costs. Within the cycle,
allocating nuclearity unites physical transformations of matter with
qualification devices of a technical, legal and symbolic nature (such
as the powerful image of the cycle itself).

Such a line of reasoning is a useful way of unpacking spatial strategies deployed in the nuclear industry, for it connects actual geographies and the spatial distribution of material flows with qualifying and
nuclearity-allocating devices. To say what a thing is, or is not, modifies
its social standing, and the spatial properties that help structure industrial flows on a global scale. The following section introduces two

cases that flesh out how qualification inflects material geographies inside the cycle.

When spatial strategies fail (1): interrupted flows

The year 2009 was a difficult one for the French nuclear industry. Three TV documentaries challenged the dominant imagery for the fuel cycle, showing that it was far from being hermetically closed. The first one, entitled *Contaminated France: a scandal*, showed that huge quantities of materials left over from uranium mining in France were scarcely managed at all, notwithstanding their significant radioactivity (Lucet and Deconinck 2009). The second, *Uranium: a poisonous legacy*, broadcast in December 2009, was an investigation into uranium mining in Gabon and Niger. It showed that French-financed mining had very detrimental consequences on workers and the environment (Hennequin and Lorent 2009). Both films broke with the idea of a deterritorialized uranium cycle. Uranium mining, in France, as in Africa, was shown to transform landscapes, contaminate the environment and imperil human health. There were similarities in each country: the damages wrought by uranium mining linked, or bound, places and people half a world apart. In the films, the cycle was given a much darker imagery: ill workers, Geiger counters in ordinary bucolic landscapes, strong denials of negative effects by industry, heated accusations from environmental NGOs.

But the third documentary had a ripple effect that had an impact on policy, precisely because it directly engaged with the qualification of recycled materials within the cycle and challenged the legitimacy of their circulations. In October 2009, a TV documentary called *Waste: Nuclear nightmare* was broadcast on a public channel on prime time (Guéret and Noualhat 2009). Based on a lengthy investigation, the documentary showed that despite reassuring statements from the industry, the uranium fuel cycle had had a severe impact on the environment in the USA and Russia. But the documentary raised a much more controversial issue: unexpected flows of matter between France and Russia, the white arrow in Figure 3.1 that represents the shipments of reprocessed uranium from Pierrelatte (in France) to Seversk, in Siberia. The revelation of this particular flow shattered the image of a self-contained cycle and challenged the legitimacy of material flows within the uranium fuel cycle. Electricité de France (EDF) shipped drums of reprocessed uranium to Russia in order to have them converted and re-enriched in Russia by Tenex. It was not possible to re-enrich this uranium in France for technical reasons. Reprocessed uranium has a different isotopic composition from natural uranium; its isotopes can permanently contaminate non-dedicated industrial facilities (Secrétariat général – Haut fonctionnaire de défense et de sécurité n.d.).

Uranium re-enriched in Russia was shipped back to France to make new fuel, while depleted reprocessed uranium (90 per cent of all quantities) stayed in Russia. In the enrichment business, the ownership and obligations of depleted uranium are transferred to the enricher (HCTISN 2010). Since Russia had little use for depleted uranium, the journalists argued that France was sending waste to – or rather *creating* waste in – Russia. One of the most striking images in the film is the car park where thousands of drums were stored, without precautions.[6]

Such materials are not very radioactive and, in themselves, they are not truly dangerous, as the journalists acknowledged. What was troublesome was the idea that, in the fuel cycle, such secret circulations could occur, that geographically the cycle was not closed and some materials were 'left out'. Contrary to official communications on the subject, waste appeared beyond the specified limits, beyond the little white arrow, and industry did not seem to care or feel responsible. In other words, industrial stakeholders took into account the fact that some materials were leaving the cycle and thus their own remit and responsibility. The issue was deemed so serious by the French government that the Parliamentary Office for Science and Technology was asked to investigate the subject[7] and a report commissioned by the Ministry for Industry (ibid.).

Facing stern accusations, the government-owned EDF argued that the controversial uranium circulations were never secret: they had made the news some years earlier, when the *Montlouis*, a cargo transporting reprocessed uranium, sank in the North Sea in 1984 (Augustin 1985). In 2005, the flows had been mentioned during a national debate on nuclear waste (Commission particulière du débat public 2005: 34–5). It was therefore impossible to argue that EDF had knowingly kept the flows secret. Moreover, EDF were adamant that reprocessed uranium was not waste, even in its depleted form, it was a resource, insofar as it could be put to industrial uses now and in the future. However, the controversy was such that EDF stopped the shipments while waiting for an industrial route to become available in France itself.

This controversy is fascinating because it is precisely about reprocessed uranium, a recycled material that is the official reason why a closed nuclear fuel cycle exists. Uranium recycling and recirculation create uncertain materials, stranded somewhere between resource and waste; and cast a shadow of immorality over such recycling, because the places where it was performed were vulnerable. Transferring property rights over depleted uranium to Tenex was insufficient to boost the moral credentials of the whole operation; it just felt like a cheap way for EDF to disown its responsibility for the various materials that it had shipped. The Russian controversy called into question the legitimacy of the succession of technical steps, and the flows of to-be-recycled products between France and Russia, on the ground that they generated waste that became fixed in the place where the reprocessing took place. The controversy forced industrial companies to internalize, symbolically and economically, the same materials they had taken great pains to exclude from the cycle. In the process, it laid bare the level of arbitrariness that frames material qualification and boundary definitions in the nuclear fuel cycle.

When spatial strategies fail (2): requalified materials

The previous section illustrated the complexity of recycled uranium circulations. A second case study will illustrate another spatial strategy, fixing materials on site. The site is the Malvési plant, in southern France, which is pivotal for the global nuclear industry, and has been heavily affected by the uranium products that flow through it. For the company that owns the plant, it is economically and logistically essential to downplay the transformative power of its operations and thus to strip materials of their 'nuclear' nature when they enter the site.

The Comurhex plant at Malvési (Figure 3.1) is a fundamental node in the global uranium economy. The site produces a quarter of global uranium tetrafluoride (UF4), has a diversified and international customer base and covers up to 75 per cent of the French need for conversion services. The site was created in 1959, on the location of a former sulphur fabrication facility.[8] It extends over 247 acres near the city of Narbonne, 55 acres of which contain the industrial site *stricto sensu*. On the site's northern edge, there is a storage space large enough to accommodate 25,000 to 40,000 tonnes of uranium. In Malvési, uranium concentrates are dissolved in nitric acid, before being purified, concentrated, calcinated and fluoridated. The resulting uranium tetrafluoride is then shipped to another plant in Pierrelatte (in the Rhône valley), where it is transformed into uranium hexafluoride (UF6) and enriched. The refining processes used at Malvési produce large amounts of residues that are directed towards settling lagoons, large industrial ponds that spread over 45 acres north of the site. The nature of process residues is variable; they usually contain a high proportion of nitrates, but also uranium and its radioactive daughters. Because of the significant dangers presented by the site (notably large quantities of fluorhydric acid), it is classified as a high-risk industrial site and as such its operations are legally regulated by a Prefectoral Act.

Over the last fifty years, the plant's level of activity has dramatically increased along with the development of the civilian nuclear industry. While, back in the 1960s, the plant processed only about 1,000 tonnes of uranium annually, production increased from the 1970s onward and reached 10,000 tonnes a year in 1978. In 2011, the plant processed about 14,000 tonnes of uranium a year (Pourcelot 2008). All uranium processed currently is either natural or depleted uranium (Eury 2008). However, between 1960 and 1983, the plant processed reprocessed uranium from the French plutonium-producing piles at Marcoule, purifying and converting the uranium before it could be re-enriched. Such an industrial process had a very significant flaw: the mixed composition of incoming uranium meant that the purification residues contained a variety of radionuclides, including plutonium. It has been officially estimated that settling lagoons B1, B2 and B3, the oldest ones on site, contain over 300 tonnes of transuranic elements (ANDRA 2009). I now turn to these 300 tonnes of materials, produced from the recycling process, and the fascinating legal struggle to which they have given rise.

In 1998, and in 2000, plant managers asked for a change in the Prefectoral Act that set the plant's operating requirements. This was granted and changed, without publicity, the legal status of settling lagoons B1, B2 and B3. The new Act referred to them as 'permanent storage ponds' (*bassins de stockage*), as defined in the industrial facilities regulation legislation under nomenclature item 167B. It was an explicit transformation from their previous denomination as 'temporary storage ponds' or '*bassins d'entreposage*' (criiad, 2007). The significance of the transformation was huge. It amounted to creating a permanent waste disposal facility on site whereas, before, the legal implication of the basin status was that the residues would be dredged and disposed of in a specialized facility. The Act removed the residues from the cycle and its circulations. It cut short the expectation of another, further circulation of waste, and by the same token, wildly overlooked the 'nuclear' nature of the residues themselves. In a sweeping move, the administration court changed the nuclearity of materials and expelled them from the cycle. The problem was that, in French law, such a change of qualification needed a protracted public inquiry and planning permission, neither of which was conducted or granted. Despite such shortcomings in the planning permission process, the Act was not challenged in court within the required time (four years) and the new provisions were made permanent. Other administrative bodies took note of the change. In the 2002 edition of the French national waste inventory, the National Agency for Radioactive Waste Management (ANDRA) referred to the ponds as a radioactive waste storage facility.

On 20 March 2004, a violent storm downpour caused the basins to overflow, breached the dyke between basins B1 and B2 and led to the release of several tens of thousands of cubic metres of contaminated water and sediments. The event forced the prefect to pass another Act (5 December 2005), which not only confirmed that basins B1, B2 and B3 were a permanent storage facility, but authorized a 40 per cent extension of their surface area in order to accommodate the leaked residues. This time, however, an anti-nuclear NGO was informed of the Act and challenged it in court on 'abuse of power' grounds (criirad, 2007). The NGO argued that the content of the lagoons could be legally qualified, or categorized, as radioactive waste and that the Malvési plant itself was not a classic industrial plant (Seveso type II), but a nuclear one (*Installation nucléaire de base*) and should be regulated as such. What the NGO was in fact calling for was the requalification of the *totality* of the plant and the reaffirmation of its nuclearity. The mismatch between reality and qualification was staggering. Whereas ANDRA estimated that the 190,000 tonnes of sludge in basins B1 and B2 contained more than 56 TBq[9] of radioactivity (Chareyron 2006; ANDRA 2009: 191), the Malvési plant, an essential node in the global nuclear fuel chain, was never legally considered as a *nuclear* plant.

Faced with the risk of judicial humiliation, the prefect passed another Act (30 July 2008), which cancelled the previous one and once more referred to the lagoons as 'temporary storage basins' (Ferrando 2009). However, the situation had been brought to the attention of the nuclear regulator, who demanded that the basins be officially classified as 'installations for the packaging and temporary storage of radioactive substances' (*installations de conditionnement et d'entreposage de substances radioactives*) (Autorité de Sûreté Nucléaire 2009). This reclassification was undertaken in 2010 for basins B1 and B2, which now fall under nuclear legislation. Nuclear law is much more stringent than classic industrial legislation and is overseen by a different regulatory authority (Bringuier 2010). The requirement is therefore that the sludge will be managed in a technically more advanced way and possibly removed from site, at a much higher cost. Indeed, the stakes here are not simply legal or logistical, but financial. Requalifying the ponds not only opens up the possibility of a further, costly flow in the future, but changes the fiscal base for the plant. Plant managers would not comment on the specifics of this aspect. However, I estimate that the switch increased the taxes paid by the plant by 100,000 euros annually (Loi n°99-1172, 1999, article 43 and Décret n°2000-361, 2000). Hence, the judicial fiasco puts an end to a well-devised spatial strategy. By changing the storage ponds' denomination, the company changed the nuclearity of the waste materials they contained, removing them from the cycle and its series of circulations. The nuclear oversight authority brought that strategy to a halt when they asked for the waste to be reintegrated into the cycle and treated as nuclear waste.

Conclusion

In this chapter, I have analysed the material and geographical impli-cations of material recycling in the nuclear industry. I began with the imagery of the 'cycle' as a distinctive element of the civilian nuclear industry, suggesting it is a closed loop as all materials are endlessly transformed and reused. It is the dream of industrial ecology, as dis-cussed in the introduction to this volume. Whereas no one speaks about the 'paper cycle' or the 'steel cycle', the 'nuclear fuel cycle' is a common discursive trope. This chapter showed that the 'cycle' was much more than a discursive creation, or a factual statement, for that matter. The cycle works as a device for determining nuclearity for materials, things and places. By qualifying them as 'nuclear', the cycle discourse binds them together and circumscribes the remit and responsibility of industrial operators towards them. Hence, the cycle imagery is essential for working out the spatial strategies that are integral to the success of operations in the nuclear industry – and especially for fuel recycling: integrating or removing a material from the cycle by playing on its nuclearity enables the application of spatial trajectories which facilitate (and diminish the cost of) industrial uptake. In the two cases analysed in the chapter, industrial operators were forced to reintegrate into the cycle materials they went to great lengths to exclude in the first place, at great cost. Such cases, exceptional because they were made more or less public, illustrate the complexity of recycling fuel in the nuclear industry: a non-consensual process, recycling introduces uncertainties over the status of materials, and creates unexpected circulations and contested spatialities, well beyond the well-documented controversies over the status of plutonium.

Far from being an idiosyncratic case, it seems to me that the ura-nium cycle speaks to larger issues. It is an example of the contemporary political economy of materials created by global recycling flows, but it also points towards legal and technical devices that allow such a political economy to exist. Recycling flows rest on specific legal provisions – broad principles and conventions, but also minute acts and technical provisions that can make a huge difference in the social uptake of a material or object. A difficulty resides in the elusiveness of such technical provisions: as devices, they are most efficient when their legitimacy is not called into question by public scrutiny. The two cases we touched upon have been made public only because of controversial investigations or judicial challenges; the social life of recycled materials is generally sheltered from the public gaze.

A final conclusion points towards the instability of such a system. Because nuclearity and the contour of the cycle are open to challenges, the status of materials (including recycled ones) and the associated spatial strategies can never be taken for granted. This creates very serious symbolical and financial risks for industrial operators and weakens the strength of the bond created between materials and places in the fuel cycle. I suspect this line of enquiry is generally left out of the considerations about the future of the nuclear industry, as if it were only catastrophic, unforeseen events that had the power to stall its development.

Notes

1 This is reminiscent of David Harvey's famous analysis of the geographical movements of capital as a 'spatial fix' for local over-accumulation crises. See Harvey (2001) for a review.

2 Such a material loop is at the core of the US–Russian agreement of 1993 (which runs until 2013). Under the agreement, 500 metric tonnes of highly enriched military uranium of Russian origin will have been transformed into civilian fuel.

3 Some industrial strands make direct use of natural uranium and do not need enrichment.

4 Current radioactive waste classification systems generally distinguish between low-level (LLW), intermediate-level (ILW) and high-level waste (HLW).

5 Gille (2007) provides a fine example of the changing institutional co-production of waste and products between socialist and post-socialist Hungary. In the socialist era, waste was accounted for in the global balance sheet of the country and seen as a source of potential riches. After the Velvet Revolution, government and industrial companies lost interest in trying to value waste and removed it from their accounts.

6 The site and containers are visible on Google Earth at: 56° 37′09.04″ N, 84° 51′24.26″ E (accessed 1 August 2011).

7 'L'uranium de retraitement: défis et enjeux', audition de l'Office parlementaire d'évaluation des choix scientifiques et techniques, 4 November 2009. Transcript avail-

able at www.assemblee-nationale.
fr/13/cr-oecst/09-10/c0910005.asp
(accessed 10 May 2011).

8 The site can be seen on
Google Earth at: 43°12´51.40˝N,
2°58´45.28˝E.

9 Radioactivity is measured
in Becquerels, i.e. the number of
atomic disintegrations per second.
An activity of 1 TBq (terabecquerel)
means that a billion atoms disintegrate every second.

References

ANDRA (2009) 'Inventaire
géographique', *Inventaire national
des matières et déchets radioactifs*,
Paris, Agence nationale de gestion des déchets radioactifs.

Augustin, B. (1985) 'Le naufrage du
Mont-Louis et la sécurité nuclé-
aire', *AEIA Bulletin*, Vienna: IAEA,
Spring, pp. 28–31.

Autorité de Sûreté Nucléaire (2009)
*Décision 2009-DC-0170 de l'Autorité
de sûreté nucléaire du 22 décembre
2009 portant prescriptions
techniques pour les bassins B1 et B2
exploités par la société Comurhex
sur la commune de Narbonne
(Aude)*, Paris.

— (2010) *Plan national de gestion des
matières et des déchets radioctifs*,
Paris: ASN.

Berkhout, F., T. Suzuki et al. (1990)
'The approaching plutonium
surplus: a Japanese/European
predicament', *International Affairs*, 66(3): 523–43.

Bouneau, S., S. David et al. (2009)
'Construction d'un monde
énergétique en 2050', *Annales de
Physique*, 34(1): 1–101.

Bringuier, P. (2010) 'Droit nucléaire
2006–2009 (II)', *Droit de
l'environnement*, 177: 129–34.

Bunn, M., S. Fetter et al. (2003) *The
Economics of Reprocessing vs.
Direct Disposal of Spent Nuclear
Fuel*, Cambridge, MA: Project on
Managing the Atom, Harvard
University.

Callon, M., C. Méadel and V. Ra-
beharisoa (2002) *Economy and
Society*, 31(2): 194–217.

Caralp, R. (1958) 'Notes pour une
géographie de l'uranium', *Revue
de géographie de Lyon*, 33(2):
103–17.

Chareyron, B. (2006) *Impact
radiologique de l'usine Comurhex
(Groupe Areva) de Malvesi, Aude*,
Valence: Commission de Recherche et d'Information Indépendantes sur la Radioactivité.

Commission de Recherche et
d'Information Indépendantes sur
la Radioactivité (criirad) (2007)
*Mémoire de recours pour excès
de pouvoir contre l'Etat français
représenté par M. le Préfet de
l'Aude*, Tribunal administratif
de Montpellier, 23 March 2007,
34 pp.

Commission particulière du débat
public (2005) *Gestion des déchets
nucléaires. Compte-rendu de la
table ronde du 8 octobre 2005*,
Paris: Commission nationale du
débat public.

Décret n°2000-361 du 26 avril 2000
relatif à la taxe et aux taxes
additionnelles auxquelles sont
assujetties les installations
nucléaires de base en application
de l'article 43 de la loi de finances
pour 2000, *Journal officiel de la
République Française*, 100, 28 April
2000, pp. 6399–401.

Eury, S.-P. (2008) 'Entreposage
d'oxyde d'uranium appauvri
d'AREVA NC – Bessines-Sur-
Gartempe', *Rapports d'inspections*,
Orleans, 30 September.

Falck, W. E. (2009) 'Towards a
sustainable front-end of nuclear

energy systems', JRC Scientific and Technical Reports, Petten (Netherlands): Joint Research Centre, Institute for Energy.

Ferrando, R. (2009) 'Comurhex : cinquante bougies et des déchets encombrants', *Le Midi Libre*, Montpellier, 20 November.

Finon, D. (1989) *L'Echec des surgénérateurs. Autopsie d'un grand programme*, Grenoble: Presses Universitaires de Grenoble.

Garcier, R. (2009) 'The nuclear "renaissance" and the geography of the uranium fuel cycle', *Geography*, 93(4): 198–206.

Gille, Z. (2007) *From the Cult of Waste to the Trash Heap of History: The Politics of Waste in Socialist and Postsocialist Hungary*, Bloomington: Indiana University Press.

Goldschmidt, B. (1982) *The Atomic Complex: A Worldwide Political History of Nuclear Energy*, La Grange Park, IL: American Nuclear Society.

Guéret, E. and L. Noualhat (2009) 'Déchets, le cauchemar du nucléaire', *Arte Collection*, France: Sony Pictures Home Entertainment: 98 mins.

Harvey, D. (2001) 'Globalization and the "spatial fix"', *Geographische Revue*, 2: 23–30.

HCTISN (2010) *Avis sur la transparence de la gestion des matières et des déchets nucléaires produits aux différents stades du cycle du combustible*, Paris: Haut Comité pour la transparence et l'information sur la sécurité nucléaire.

Hecht, G. (2006) 'Nuclear ontologies', *Constellations*, 13(3): 320–31.

— (2007) 'A cosmogram for nuclear things', *Isis*, 98(1): 100–108.

Helmreich, J. E. (1986) *Gathering Rare Ores: The Diplomacy of Uranium Acquisition, 1943–1954*, Princeton, NJ: Princeton University Press.

Hennequin, D. and P. Lorent (2009) *Uranium, l'héritage empoisonné*, France: Nomades TV and Public Sénat, 52 mins.

International Atomic Energy Agency (1980) 'The convention on the physical protection of nuclear material', *INFCIRC274r1*, Vienna: IAEA.

Kasparek, J. (1952) 'Russia and Czechoslovakia's uranium', *Russian Review*, 11(2): 97–105.

Loi n°99-1172 du 30 décembre 1999 de finances pour 2000, *Journal officiel de la République Française*, 303, 31 December 1999, pp. 19914–90.

Lucet, E. and L. Deconinck (2009) 'Uranium: le scandale de la France contaminée', *Pièces à conviction*, France 3.

Morichaud, Y. (2002) *La Filière nucléaire du plutonium: menace sur le vivant*, Barret-sur-Méouges: Editions Yves Michel.

OECD-IAEA (2010) *Uranium 2009: Resources, Production and Demand*, Paris: OECD Publishing.

Pourcelot, L. (2008) *Etude radioécologique de l'environnement du site de Malvési (société COMURHEX)*, Le Vésinet: IRSN.

Price, R. R., F. Barthel et al. (2006) 'Forty years of uranium resources, production and demand in perspective', *NEA Newsletter*, 24(1): 4–6.

Schneider, M. and Y. Marignac (2008) 'Spent nuclear fuel reprocessing in France', IPFM Research Reports 4, Princeton, NJ: International Panel on Fissile Materials.

Secrétariat général – Haut fonctionnaire de défense et de sécurité (n.d.) *Estimation des importations et exportations de matières nucléaires à partir des données émanant du contrôle national relatif à la protection de ces matières contre tout acte de malveillance*, Paris: Service de défense, de sécurité et d'intelligence économique, Ministère de l'écologie, de l'énergie, du développement durable et de la mer.

Von Hippel, F. N. (2001) 'Plutonium and reprocessing of spent nuclear fuel', *Science*, 293(5539): 2397–8.

Walker, W. (1999) *Nuclear Entrapment: THORP and the politics of commitment*, London: Institute for Public Policy Research.

— (2006) 'Rokkasho and the future of reprocessing', *International Affairs*, 82(4): 743–61.

Wilson, P. D. (2001) *The Nuclear Fuel Cycle: From ore to wastes*, Oxford: Oxford University Press.

Zeman, Z. and R. Karlsch (2008) *Uranium Matters: Central European Uranium in International Politics, 1900–1960*, New York: Central European University Press.

Zoellner, T. (2009) *Uranium. War, Energy and the Rock that Shaped the World*, New York: Viking.

4 | The shadow of the global network: e-waste flows to China

XIN TONG AND JICI WANG[1]

Introduction

The rapid progress and pace of innovation in the global electronics industry has accelerated the rate at which these consumer products become obsolescent. This, in turn, has led to increasing amounts of electronic waste (e-waste). International regulations governing the disposal of such waste in countries of the global North have created incentives to export much of it to less developed countries. In March 2002, the Basel Action Network (BAN) and the Silicon Valley Toxic Coalition (SVTC) published a joint report entitled *The High-Tech Trashing of Asia* (Puckett and Byster 2002). Describing the transnational flows of e-waste from the developed to the developing countries of Asia, the report exposed the disastrous environmental pollution in some rural areas of southern China, which it traced to improper methods and techniques used in extracting secondary materials from the wastes. The exposé attracted much public attention to the management of e-waste in China; it also created a highly negative view of the recycling industry based on imported waste.

That same year, China's government formally accepted a new development strategy – the Circular Economy (CE) – aiming to 'alleviate the contradiction between rapid economic growth and the shortage of raw materials and energy' (Yuan et al. 2006: 4). Based on principles from the field of industrial ecology, the CE is an ongoing attempt to rein in the rapid urbanization and economic growth that have transformed China since the transition towards a market socialist economy began in earnest in the 1990s. Since then, the recycling sector in China has dramatically changed. In 2009, after a long debate among all stakeholders, China promulgated its own regulations on e-waste collection and recycling based on the principle of Extended Producer Responsibility (also called China's WEEE as the counterpart to the EU's WEEE[2]), which were enforced in 2011. These changes in development, at a national and sub-national level, cannot be isolated from the global dynamics that have shaped China's growth. New environmental reforms, for example, paralleled state efforts to rein in financial risk after the East Asian financial crisis of 1997. In this way, 'global' and 'local' economic processes are not independent of one another, but are mutually implicated in a more encompassing 'global production network'. Henderson et al. define 'global production network' as a framework that recognizes the diversity of priorities that motivate different political and economic actors and, hence, the relevance of location and value production in the study of development (2002: 446). Moreover, because the global production network framework fixes attention on the moments when local and global meet, it encourages scholars to pay methodological attention to the local and regional firms that are responsible for negotiating various inputs and outputs to national economies (ibid.: 447).

This chapter is based on investigations undertaken in 2002/03, right after the publication of the BAN and SVTC reports. It reflects on these reports and the different perspectives at that time regarding the unexpected consequences that the global dynamics of e-waste generation brought to local areas, and vice versa. This reveals an overarching global production network, encompassing the political as well as the personal, in the shadow of the global economy, as conventionally understood. Some of the company employees we interviewed struggled for years with this issue. This event changed not only their business, but also their daily lives, including their attitudes to and actions on recycling.

Transnational flows of e-waste

Discarded electronic products are among the most rapidly expanding types of waste in the developed countries (see, e.g., EU 1998; Gabrys 2011), and the management of e-waste has become an issue of global concern owing to the environmental degradation caused by transnational flows and their accumulation in particular sites. The trans-boundary movement of e-waste is driven by two forces. First, the disassembly of 'end-of-life' equipment is labour intensive with low value added, and secondly, compliance with environmental regulations can increase the cost of disposal. Most scholars tend to view the recycling of electronics as a useful but environmentally hazardous activity (see Lin et al. 2002). They point out that e-wastes contain toxic substances, among which are the following two broad categories regulated by the Basel Convention: (1) heavy metals, such as the lead contained in glass in cathode ray tubes (CRTs), or mercury used on printed circuit boards; and (2) brominated flame retardants (BFRs), found in abundance in fireproof plastics.[3] The impact of e-waste landfills and incinerators on the environment gives rise to spirited debates (see Osibanjo and Nnorom 2007; Kalana 2010; Chi et al. 2011). Advocates favour recycling of electronic equipment because it yields useful components and quantities of precious metals. But without proper pollution control equipment and technology, serious environmental problems may occur in the extraction of precious and non-ferrous metals from circuit boards or plastic-coated cables in electronic scrap. For example, heavy metals in the residues can contaminate soils and groundwater, and emissions of toxic substances from incineration of plastics containing BFRs can seriously aggravate air pollution. Since recyclers of secondary materials recovered from scrap in developed countries must cope with the rising costs of pollution control, many resort to exporting scrap instead of recycling it domestically (NSF 1999). In fact, the so-called 'pollution haven' hypothesis points out that the higher the costs of disposal caused by the increasingly strict environmental regulations in developed countries, the higher the incentive of recycling industries to move to the less developed world, where environmental restrictions are not severe (see Crang et al. and Garcier, this volume). Despite the EU's proximity principle, which encourages wastes to be dealt with as close as possible to their sites of origin, from a global perspective pollution continues to move from one place to another, rather than being treated adequately in regions where the polluting products are made and used.

Apart from disparities in environmental regulation, the gradual decline of transaction and transport costs also facilitates international trade in secondary materials. Thus, an international division of labour has evolved between developed and developing countries, whereby the former specialize in waste generation and recycling end-of-use products and the latter concentrate on the consumption and labour-intensive disassembly of secondary material (Beukering 2001). A good example is provided by a study of transnational flows of computers discarded in Australia, which were exported to the Philippines for disassembly, with some parts subsequently re-exported to China for reuse. In turn, shredded circuit boards were imported back by the Australians for extraction of precious or non-ferrous metals (Kellow 1999).

The international debate on recycling and the spatial dynamics of waste disposal has rarely addressed the relationships between the recycling of e-waste and electronics production. Similarly, the academic literature on global production networks has rarely addressed these issues, when this is precisely what a methodological focus on firms, labour processes and locality should encourage. Following the global production network framework, across interlocking paths of production and use, one is confronted with recycling economies occurring in the shadow of the global economy, conventionally understood. The close relationship between e-waste recycling and electronics industries is noted in an EU proposal for the regulation of wastes of electrical and electronic equipment (EU 2000). This document appears to confirm that recyclers of e-waste are mainly small- and medium-sized enterprises, found in most EU member countries, and that transnational transportation of such waste is concentrated in a smaller number of states. Movements of e-waste from developed to developing countries were largely ignored by scholars and government officials until the results of an investigation undertaken by BAN and SVTC in 2002 appeared (Puckett and Byster 2002). According to that report, over 90 per cent of scrapped computers that recyclers collect from users in the United States are exported to developing regions of Asia, with about 80 per cent destined for the coastal areas of China. It follows that China has become the largest recipient of e-waste exported by developed countries to be disassembled and dumped by informal recyclers and local firms.

Imported e-waste increased in coastal China at roughly the same time as the expansion of the country's electronics industry during the last decade. Figure 4.1, based on the UN Comtrade database (United Nations Statistics Division n.d.), shows that exports of electronics and electrical equipment from China increased dramatically from 1996 to 2003. Export-oriented electronics manufacturing is also concentrated in the coastal areas, where most firms are focusing on labour-intensive assembly for international brand-name companies. The export-oriented economic development policies promoted by the government of China have restructured the domestic electronics industry to the point that production and consumption respond fairly quickly to advances in technology.[4]

Most studies on e-waste problems in China have focused on its environmental impact (e.g. BAN and SVTC, 2002) or on the relevant international legal regulations (e.g. Lin et al. 2002); they seldom look closely at its impact on people's attitudes. The global production network combines people in different places through the exchange of commercial commodities. It also facilitates flows of opinions from place to place, which may later modify people's attitudes, even behaviour. However, these changes cannot be separated from the local context.

Outline of the investigation

Unfortunately, reliable statistical data on e-waste imports are virtually non-existent in China. We interviewed eight key experts employed by the government; non-governmental organizations (NGOs); and research institutes in Beijing which have been involved in the study and regulation of imported e-waste during the last few years. In order to obtain general background information, we designed a semi-structured interview schedule that we later used in our investigation of ten electronic producers and ten recyclers from 2002 to 2003. The electronic producers included three computer manufacturers, one mobile phone producer and one manufacturer of household appliances (all headquartered in Beijing), one producer of household electronic appliances in Qingdao, one mobile phone manufacturer in Ningbo, one computer producer in Suzhou, one computer manufacturer, and one automated office equipment producer in Shenzhen. All were drawn from a list of participants in a seminar on e-waste management sponsored by the Ministry of Information Industry in September 2002. We asked them about their attitudes towards e-waste management, their current knowledge about end-of-life requirements overseas, and their efforts to introduce environmentally friendly technological innovation and to increase the portion of secondary materials used in their products. Recyclers were selected through a snowball sampling procedure, which is suitable for studies involving difficult-to-find respondents (Bernard 2002). Because, by 2002, China's public media had created such a distinctly negative image of e-waste imports, and of the Chinese recycling sector that relies on imports of secondary materials, most recyclers, including those approved by the government, were reluctant to respond to our request for interviews. With the help of one of the leading specialists in Beijing, we were able to establish a reasonably good relationship with our interviewees in Ningbo and Taizhou. All interviews with recyclers were supplemented by a field study in these areas between May and June of 2002. Additionally, we visited the plants of the ten recycling companies in our study and five local secondary material markets. These included a secondary plastics market in Cixi

City, and four industrial material markets in the Luqiao Trade City (Luqiao Shangmao Cheng) in Taizhou City. The sample is relatively small, but most of our informants have been involved with a variety of relevant issues for many years, witnessing the industry's development from different perspectives.

Localization of imported e-waste recycling in coastal China

The development of e-waste recycling has played a significant role in China's local rural industrialization. Generally, imports of e-waste have been driven by the demand for low-cost raw materials to alleviate domestic shortages, and by the need to promote labour-intensive industries that generate employment opportunities for unskilled labor in rural areas (Lin et al. 2002). The demand for cheap industrial materials has grown in China since the beginning of economic reforms in the late 1970s. During the last decade, imports of secondary materials have increased rather steadily, as shown in Figures 4.2 and 4.3. Currently, China is one of the largest importers of secondary products in the world.

The recycling of imported e-waste is among the fastest-growing industrial sectors in several regional clusters in coastal China, including Taizhou City in the Yangtze river delta, and some areas in the Pearl river delta. Most recyclers are township- or village-owned enterprises employing unskilled workers and using unsophisticated equipment. Concentrated mainly in rural locations near seaports, with convenient access to sources of supply and to markets, they are difficult for government authorities to monitor and control.

Uncontrolled development of imported e-waste recycling has created fairly serious environmental problems. A survey conducted by China's State Environmental Protection Agency (SEPA) found that pollution in many localities in coastal China since the early 1990s was the result principally of e-waste recycling. The survey prompted the government to restrict (if not ban) not only China's imports of e-waste but also imports of scrap as well as other waste materials (ibid.).

In order to control recycling of imported e-waste, SEPA selected 460 enterprises from thousands throughout the country, and certified them as importers and processors.[5] By 2002, the number of such enterprises increased from 460 (1995) to 509. Guangdong in the Pearl river delta and Zhejiang in the Yangtze river delta are the two regions with the highest concentration of recycling activity. It is noteworthy that the increasingly strict controls have failed to curb the growth of e-waste recycling in coastal China. Aside from authorized imports,

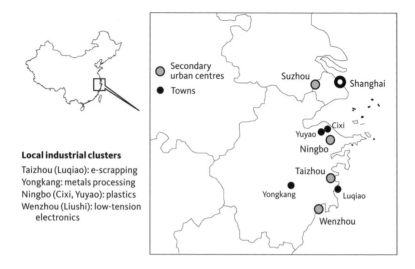

Local industrial clusters

Taizhou (Luqiao): e-scrapping
Yongkang: metals processing
Ningbo (Cixi, Yuyao): plastics
Wenzhou (Liushi): low-tension
    electronics

4.1 Industrial clusters related to recycling e-waste in the Yangtze river delta

inflows of e-waste also came from smuggling, aimed at refurbishing electronic products rather than extracting secondary materials. Had such enterprises been added to the count, the Pearl river and Yangtze river deltas would have shown an even more concentrated pattern of e-waste recycling relative to other areas of China.

On 26 January 2000, SEPA, together with three other government agencies, mandated a complete ban on imports of scrap computers, panel displays, television picture tubes and similar electronic equipment. However, the ban is largely ineffective because local government agencies lack adequate resources to enforce the regulations; furthermore, and more broadly, the command-and-control approach is not likely to fundamentally alter the basic forces that generate environmental degradation.

The number of small enterprises engaged in the recycling of imported e-waste is actually considerably larger than the number approved by the government. And it is difficult to obtain reliable data on the quantity of imports of e-waste, largely because such imports are frequently disguised as shipments of metal scrap or electronic products. The Beijing Zhongse Institute of Secondary Metals (2002) estimated the amount of e-waste imported in the Yangtze river delta at over 700,000 tons in 2001. And periodic exposés in the public media of unlawful processing tend to reflect the size and relative significance of activities in the underground economy. For example, an enterprise in Luqiao, Zhejiang province, uses discarded computer monitors to produce television sets, which supplied 200 units per month to an appliance store near by. There are also large markets for refurbished electronic products in most big cities, with thousands of disassembly and processing enterprises which have been operating for years. One inspection in Qingyuan City in Guangdong province revealed that over 14,000 used hard disks were sold to a buyer in Guangzhou in a single transaction (Ying 2002).

But notwithstanding the overwhelmingly negative public reaction and opposition to imports of e-waste, the recyclers interviewed told us a different story about the development of recycling in rural areas. Most believed it played an irreplaceable role in local industrialization when China was still at an early stage of transition to a market economy. At the time, most raw materials (such as iron and steel, non-ferrous metals and plastics) were allocated only to state-owned enterprises, and it was difficult for township- or village-owned enterprises in rural areas to procure such materials through formal channels of distribution. Thus, secondary materials became an important alternative, shaping the spatial pattern of China's recycling industry towards users of secondary materials. This complex portrait of development is in accordance with a global production network framework that does not take for granted what the impact of global flows will be, but traces the effects of local actors and institutions and their labour (see also Crang et al., this volume).

Figure 4.1 depicts several industrial clusters investigated by the authors in the Yangtze river delta that are related to the recycling of imported e-waste. Ningbo, a city near Shanghai and the second-largest seaport in the Yangtze river delta, is one of the major ports receiving inflows of recyclable goods. Over two-thirds of the e-waste inflows passing through the port comprised imported recyclable goods.

Taizhou, a city south of Ningbo, constitutes one of the largest clusters of recycling enterprises and secondary product markets in China. The development of recycling in that city, now known as an important centre in the global secondary materials market, began in the late 1970s. As one of our interviewees told us, there was little arable land here for agriculture. Peasants left their home villages to collect discarded goods in cities across the country in order to sell their finds to recyclers. At that time, industrial materials were strictly controlled by the state-owned planning economy. However, workers in state-owned factories were unwilling to collect discarded materials and dispose of old equipment, so this was subcontracted to peasants.

Some peasants refurbished the old equipment and sold it on to the township- or village-owned enterprises. During the transition from a planned economy to a market economy, a dual price system for industrial material existed; that is, there was one price system for exchange within the state-owned system, and another for exchange on the free market. The former was much cheaper than the latter, which created a substantial profit margin for collecting the discarded material of state-owned factories to sell as secondary material on the market. Before the 1990s, most recyclable goods were collected domestically, so the size of the industry was relatively quite small. However, since the early 1990s, imported waste has replaced domestic supplies as the major source of the industry's raw material.

Luqiao, a town whose location is shown in Figure 4.1, is the centre of trade and disassembly of discarded electrical and electronic equipment in Taizhou City. It is near seven specialized markets concentrated along National Road 104 between Shiqu and Fengjiang in Luqiao (about 2.5 kilometres) that buy and sell used machines, refurbished electric motors, gearboxes, non-ferrous metals, e-waste scrap, iron and steel scrap, and secondary materials. Secondary goods come from other cities in China, as well as from Japan, the United States, Russia and western Europe. In Luqiao and three other nearby towns, thousands of small enterprises are engaged in e-waste scrapping, of which only twenty-eight have been licensed by the government. State approval means passing pollution control inspections administered by the local environmental protection agency, and securing approval to import recyclable goods of the seventh category of China's waste imports regulation (i.e. scrap motors, waste electrical line and cable, metal and electrical appliance scrap). There are still thirty other large disassembly enterprises without import licences, and over 1,500 family-based firms working as subcontractors for these large scrappers. A measure of the scale of the activity is the fact that as many as 13,000 local workers and migrant labourers are gainfully employed in this industry within an area of less than forty square kilometres. And over 70 per cent of local families are directly or indirectly active in this industry, employed, for example, in buying, disassembling, processing and marketing products. Cixi, a city north of Ningbo, is the centre for producing plastic goods and recycling plastics in China. The plastics recovered from the waste of electrical wires, the shell and structure of electronic products, etc., are collected and sent here for further classification into acrylonitrile butadiene styrene (ABS), polypropylene and PVC, and subsequent processing into flakes or pellets. Consequently, the country's largest secondary plastics market is located in Cixi. Recovered materials are sent to nearby industrial enterprises, such as those in Yongkang, one of the leading industrial and metalworking clusters in China, which mainly depends on supplies of secondary metals.

Many rural enterprises have been active in refurbishing electronic products, regardless of restrictions on imports imposed by the government. For example, the low-tension electronics industry cluster in Liushi Town (Wenzhou City) originated in the disassembly and refurbishing of used electronic products exported to China. Although some of the enterprises have been upgraded to produce new products using primary materials, many still continue to refurbish and sell inexpensive products.

The Beijing Zhongse Institute of Secondary Metals (2002) reported that local demand for secondary materials provided the main economic motive for recycling e-waste in the Yangtze river delta. One of our interviewees, a recycling entrepreneur from Taiwan, reported that recycling e-waste in the 1980s had not been subject to controls in China. One of the first Taiwanese investors, he came to the mainland in the late 1980s, mainly because of increasing labour costs and environmental restrictions in Taiwan. However, differences in the cost of labour and environmental controls did not fully explain the recent development and expansion of his company on the mainland. As one of the recyclers we interviewed in Shanghai in 2002 told us, his first plant was built in Guangdong, where he imported most of the necessary materials from overseas, eventually exporting them after disassembly and subsequent processing. He built a new plant near Shanghai in the early 1990s, and became an active participant in the local business network, which facilitated sales of the company's products to customers near Shanghai.

The negative perception of, and attitudes towards, the processing of imported e-waste have been among the main concerns of the recyclers we interviewed. One recycler in Taizhou City, in business since the late 1970s, began his business scrapping used electrical motors and wires collected from other cities. His enterprise grew rather dramatically after he started processing scrap imported from Japan. The company secured all necessary licences from the government, made many efforts to comply with environmental regulations, and even hired academic consultants to improve pollution abatement techniques in the plants. However, the prevailing negative public attitude towards the recycling sector eventually dampened the entrepreneur's enthusiasm as well as his willingness to invest in more advanced equipment and technology.

All told, under central planning, China had an established and fairly well-designed system for the recycling and recovery of resources; this

4.2 The changing mode of competition in the global electronics industry

system has experienced difficulties during economic transition. This provides a useful point of comparison with the analysis provided by Gille (2007) to account for the shifting waste regime that accompanied Hungary's transition from socialism. Whereas Gille's focus is largely on changes in state-level regulation and policy and their impact on the lives of Hungarians, a global production network framework orients attention to firms as critical actors in the negotiation of forces and interests across different scales, not just the state and individual level. In the case of China, the privatization of the recycling sector presents a dilemma, as the sector has become economically more significant while government controls and inspection have become increasingly more disruptive. In the absence of large investments by local governments to re-establish a recycling system, some formerly state-owned recycling companies turned to importing goods, particularly those of the seventh category, which yielded comparatively higher profits.

Changing patterns of competition and innovation in the electronics industry

As noted above, most policies addressing the problem of imported e-waste were not designed in cooperation with the electronics industry. However, the situation is changing in response to the new principles governing environmental regulations relating to the management of e-waste.

Globalization prompts producers in less developed countries to emulate their counterparts in the developed world, where the emphasis is on mass production, mass consumption and disposal, on a massive scale, of products that have reached the end of their life. Producers in the electronics industry have adapted to the rapid pace of technological advancement by incorporating such practices as planned obsolescence in product design, encouraging consumers to discard old equipment for upgraded models.

To address such an unsustainable mode of development, environmental regulations in developed countries are gradually shifting towards various models of sustainable governance that attempt to redistribute property rights and obligations, including full life-cycle responsibility. Regulatory approaches have also expanded to provide increasing incentives for producers and consumers to change their behaviour at the earliest stages of material flows in the life cycle of products. Such a transformation will influence the pattern of innovation, production, consumption and recycling in the global electronics industry (Figure 4.2).

With regard to the management of e-waste, the principle of Extended Producer Responsibility (EPR) has been adopted by an increasing number of developed countries. According to the OECD (2001: 9), the key feature of the EPR policy is a 'shifting of responsibility (physically and/or economically; fully or partially) upstream toward the producer and away from municipalities'. This regulatory approach creates incentives for producers to consider, even at the design stage, the subsequent disposal and recycling of used products, and to participate as key players in the entire system of end-of-life management.

In 2002, a commission jointly organized by the Ministry of Information Industry (MII), the State Environmental Protection Agency (SEPA) and the State Economic and Trade Committee was established to develop regulations on e-waste management in China based on EPR. The three agencies cooperated in the legislative process, with each specializing in different aspects. The MII focuses on the impacts of new regulations on the competitiveness of industry, and thus promulgated the Regulatory Approaches on Pollution Control in Electronic and Information Products, which came into force in March 2007, directly responding to the EU policy on toxic substances in electronics, the 2002 Directive on Restriction of Hazardous Substances (RoHS). According to the provisions of Regulatory Approaches, producers are required to choose recyclable materials and 'environmentally friendly' design in production, and to label the material contents of products (RoHS 2003). The SEPA focuses on pollution control. In 2003, the SEPA published the Declaration on Strengthening the Management of Electrical and

Electronics Equipment, which recommended that local environmental protection agencies pay attention to pollution control in e-waste disposal and recycling activities, and suggested (but did not mandate) that electronics firms prioritize environmental concerns in production. The Technical Policy on the Pollution Control of End-of-Life Electronic Household Appliance and Electronic Products was also issued by the SEPA in April 2006, within the framework of two related national environmental laws, the Law of the People's Republic of China on the Promotion of Clean Production and the Law of the People's Republic of China on the Prevention and Control of Environmental Pollution by Solid Waste. This regulation aims to encourage electronic producers, users and recyclers to assume environmental responsibility in the production, consumption and recycling of electronic and electric equipment. The State Development Planning Commission took responsibility for establishing an overall system of e-waste management, particularly focusing on a take-back scheme. The directive on Regulatory Approaches towards Dealing with End-of-Life Household Electronic Equipment has been under development since 2001 and tries to address different elements of overseas experience. This directive was supposed to be promulgated in mid-2003; however, the legislative process was delayed because of disagreements on how to deal with the large informal sector in e-waste refurbishment, and criticism from the industry on several details of the distribution of responsibility among the stakeholders. The directive was eventually passed in early 2009, and was enforced at the beginning of 2010.

In order to promote the recycling of e-waste through the formalization of the recycling sector, the government and industry have cooperated in several initiatives at municipal and provincial levels for future national schemes. Several national pilot projects for WEEE recycling and management initiated by different government administrations and industries have been launched since 2004, including:

- A pilot project in Tsingdao City in Shandong province, which was initiated by Haier, one of the leading consumer electronics producers in China. The goal of this project is to set up a collection network and further develop recycling technologies.
- A pilot project in Zhejiang province, which is a provincial WEEE recycling project initiated by recyclers to develop disassembling and dismounting techniques and equipment. At the beginning, this will embrace major appliances, including washing machines, refrigerators, televisions and computers, as well as printed circuit boards.

- A pilot project in Tianjin, which was initiated by the Tianjin municipal government and Ziya eco-industrial park, where recyclers of imported scraps are concentrated. It was designed to develop into a WEEE recycling centre for both electronic production and consumption in northern China.
- A pilot project in Shanghai, which was set up by the Shanghai local administration and the Ministry of Information Industry to test a municipal-level take-back system.

In all the pilot projects, different players have to cooperate with each other. Figure 4.3 shows the ideal relations among different players in the e-waste recycling industry in China based on the EPR principle. The producers play the key role in the whole system because they control the most important aspect of the nature of product at the very beginning of its life cycle. The EPR system can promote the linkage between the producers and recyclers to enhance cooperation in upgrading recycling techniques and management. Producers also have the capability to educate consumers in how to deal with their end-of-life electronics products in a proper way through advertising channels. The government, as well as other public organizations, sets

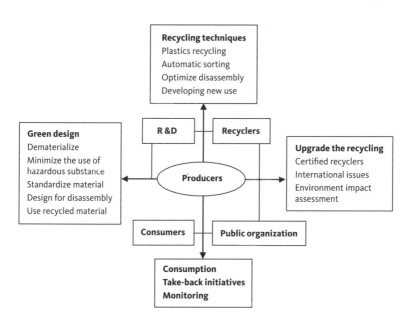

4.3 The role of different players in WEEE recycling flows

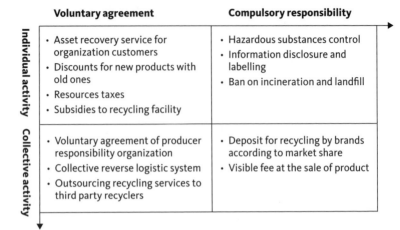

	Voluntary agreement	Compulsory responsibility
Individual activity	• Asset recovery service for organization customers • Discounts for new products with old ones • Resources taxes • Subsidies to recycling facility	• Hazardous substances control • Information disclosure and labelling • Ban on incineration and landfill
Collective activity	• Voluntary agreement of producer responsibility organization • Collective reverse logistic system • Outsourcing recycling services to third party recyclers	• Deposit for recycling by brands according to market share • Visible fee at the sale of product

4.4 Different approaches in the EPR system

the benchmark for the market and checks that all players are fulfilling their responsibilities.

All the roles of the various players should be enforced with various policy approaches. Figure 4.4 shows different policy approaches which have been used in other countries. They are grouped according to four criteria: 'voluntary/compulsory responsibility' and 'individual/collective activity'. Each approach has its advantage and weakness, thus the EPR system cannot be the only way forward; it is better understood as part of a package of solutions which combine different approaches. Also, it is worth noting that not all the approaches described in Figure 4.4 can be implemented at the same time. Some approaches will be easier for the stakeholders to put into practice than others. For example, it would be relatively straightforward for the producers to provide 'take-back' services to their large-organization customers, especially when the government has made green procurement compulsory for local governments, which are among the country's most influential consumers.

However, all these government-supported initiatives are facing difficulties in securing sufficient quantities of end-of-life products to keep the businesses running. While it is not difficult to import advanced technology and equipment for recycling and disposal, the challenge is to establish an efficient take-back system that is appropriate for China and provides supplies adequate for use by qualified recyclers.

There are two sources for the e-waste recycling industry in China: one relies on imports, the other depends on domestically generated waste. These input streams have been separated in policy. On the one hand, the government has tried to establish a recycling system for domestically generated e-waste, following the model of developed countries with the principle of EPR. On the other, international flows of e-waste are to be cut down, in spite of increasing demands for materials. During this process, different players, such as the electronics producers, consumers, central and local government, informal junk buyers and recyclers, have fiercely disputed the distribution of responsibilities.

The newly established formal e-waste recycling system has to compete with the informal sector to obtain e-waste from the users. It has been generally accepted that currently in China the existing informal collection network is much more efficient than the formal collection system applied in the government-sponsored pilot projects.

Informal recyclers make a good profit from recycling, while formal recyclers lose money in the recycling of many appliances. In order to get the end-of-life product from the users, formal recyclers have to pay the owners a price that competes with that offered by the urban junk buyers. Informal recyclers can obtain e-waste through the junk-buyer network at lower costs. They usually bargain with the users directly, and transport e-waste by tricycle instead of truck, thus reducing overhead costs. They have a vast multi-tier network for collection which is dispersed throughout the cities. It is not only cost efficient but allows for quick responses to market change. Furthermore, the final output of the informal recyclers largely goes to refurbish the second-hand market instead of being disassembled and shredded for material recovery. Therefore, the recycling activity of the informal sector is much more efficient than the formal one. Currently, all the national pilot programmes suffer from lack of input materials. Under the existing policy framework, formal recyclers will not be successful while competing against informal recyclers.

However, simply allowing the informal recycling network to function beyond regulatory oversight has an obvious weakness. E-waste cannot be profited from in the second-hand market flows to southern rural areas for material recovery; techniques for recovery here are very basic, leading to heavy pollution in those areas. The environmental cost cannot practically be incorporated into the informal recycling system.

Concluding observations

The report by Pucket and Byster (2002), which traced trans-border movements of e-waste to an environmental disaster in a small Chinese village, raised public awareness of the hazards and reinforced the negative perception of and attitudes towards China's recycling sector and the inflows of recyclable materials from developed countries. Our investigation leads us to conclude that the electronics industry in China needs a solid recycling system that incorporates environmental controls. We should note here, however, that the difficulties faced by the recycling sector have been almost completely ignored in public discussions prompted by the problem.

As China moves from state socialism to a market-oriented economy, local industries have been increasingly intertwined with the global production network associated with electronics. China became one of the main destinations of the global shift in manufacturing, which re-flected the north–south shift of material-intensive industrial processes. Policies of openness and reform have brought affluence to society in general, but changing modes of production and consumption have also resulted in large quantities of waste generated domestically.

New resolutions, based on the principles of EPR and industrial ecology, could become an effective way of linking production and recycling within a closed loop to reduce environmental impacts. We believe that a more flexible legal framework and improved institutional infrastructures could help China build an environmentally and economically sound e-waste recycling system. However, such 'top-down' transfer of responsibility promoted by central government still requires a broad consideration of the costs and benefits faced by producers and consumers, as well as recyclers at local, national and global levels.

Notes

1 The authors gratefully acknowledge financial support from the China Natural Science Foundation, grant no. 40401014, and wish to thank Professors Laurence Ma, C. Cindy Fan and Gerhard Werner, as well as the workshop on Environment Management in East Asia held in Okayama, Japan, in 2007, for valuable comments and assistance. Thanks are also due to all interviewees in China who shared their insights.

2 The Waste Electrical and Electronic Equipment Directive (or WEEE) became law in the European Community in 2003. It seeks to establish a framework for the governance of e-waste recycling and disposal.

3 See the United Nations Basel Convention on the Control of Transboundary Movements of Hazardous Waste.

4 Although the government pursues different policies relating to electronics production and e-waste recycling, both have been growing quite rapidly.

5 China established a declaration and inspection system for all imports of waste in 1996. According to Regulations on Waste Imports for Environmental Protection and Man-

agement (Provisional) (SEPA 2004), imports of the following materials had to be licensed: (1) animal bone; (2) metallurgical slag; (3) scrap wood and wood products; (4) scrap paper and paperboard; (5) scrap cotton and cloth; (6) iron and steel scrap, non-ferrous metal scrap; (7) scrap motors, waste electrical line and cable, metal and electrical appliance scrap; (8) dismantled ships and floating platforms; (9) other scrap for specific needs; and (10) plastic scrap. E-waste was mainly included in the seventh category for metal recovery.

References

Basel Convention (1989) *United Nations Basel Convention on the Control of Transboundary Movements of Hazardous Waste and Their Disposal*, www. ec.gc.ca/tmb/eng/ facts/basel_e.html, accessed 9 December 2004.

Beijing Zhongse Institute of Secondary Metals (2002) *Changjiang sanjiaozhou diqu feiza youse jinshu huishou liyong xianzhuang diaocha* [Investigation of the market for secondary metals in the Yangtze river delta], Unpublished report, Beijing: Beijing Zhongse Institute of Secondary Metals for the State Environmental Protection Agency.

Bernard, H. R. (2002) *Research Methods in Anthropology: Qualitative and Quantitative Methods*, New York: Altamira Press.

Beukering, P. van (2001) *Recycling, International Trade, and the Environment: An Empirical Analysis*, Dordrecht: Kluwer Academic Publishers.

Chi, X., M. Streicher-Porte, Y. L. Wang Mark and Markus A. Reuter (2011) 'Informal electronic waste recycling: a sector review with special focus on China', *Waste Management*, 31(4): 731–42.

EU (European Union) (1998) *Proposal for Directive on Waste Electrical and Electronic Equipment*, Brussels: Commission of the European Communities.

— (2000) *Proposal for Directive on Waste Electrical and Electronic Equipment and Proposal for Directive on the Restriction of the Use of Certain Hazardous Substances in Electrical and Electronic Equipment*, Brussels: Commission of the European Communities.

Gabrys, J. (2011) *Digital Rubbish: A Natural History of Electronics*, Ann Arbor: University of Michigan Press.

Gille, Z. (2007) *From the Cult of Waste to the Trash Heap of History: The Politics of Waste in Socialist and Postsocialist Hungary*, Bloomington: University of Indiana Press.

Graedel, T. E., D. V. Beers, M. Bertram et al. (2004) 'Multilevel cycle of anthropogenic copper', *Environmental Science and Technology*, 38: 1242–52.

Henderson, J., P. Dicken, M. Hess, N. Coe and H. Wai-Chung Yeung (2002) 'Global production networks and the analysis of economic development', *Review of International Political Economy*, 9(3): 436–64.

Kalana, J. A. (2010) 'Electrical and electronic waste management practice by households in Shah Alam, Selangor, Malaysia', *International Journal of Environmental Sciences*, 1(2): 132–44.

Kellow, A. (1999) 'Baptists and bootleggers? The Basel Convention and metals recycling trade', *Agenda*, 6(1): 29–38.

Lin, C. K., L. Yan and A. N. Davis (2002) 'Globalization, extended producer responsibility and the problem of discarded computers in China: an exploratory proposal for environmental protection', *Georgetown International Environmental Law Review*, 14(3): 525–76.

NSF (National Safety Council) (1999) *Electronic Product Recovery and Recycling Baseline Report*, Washington, DC: National Safety Council.

OECD (Organisation for Economic Co-operation and Development) (2001) *Extended Producer Responsibility: A Guidance Manual for Governments*, Paris: OECD.

Osibanjo, O. and I. C. Nnorom (2007) 'The challenge of electronic waste (e-waste) management in developing countries', *Waste Management and Research*, 25(6): 489–501.

Puckett, J. and L. Byster (2002) *Exporting Harm: The High-Tech Trashing of Asia*, www.crra.com/ ewaste/ttrash2/ttrash2/, accessed 8 December 2004.

Raymond Communication (2002) *Electronics Recycling: What to Expect from Global Mandates*, College Park, MD: Raymond Communication, Inc., www. raymond.com/durables, accessed 9 December 2004.

RoHS (Restriction of the Use of Certain Hazardous Substances in Electrical and Electronic Equipment) (2003) *Official Journal of the European Union*, L37: 19–23.

SEPA (State Environmental Protection Agency) (2004) *Feiwu jinkou guanli zanxing guiding* [Regulations on waste imports for environmental protection and management (provisional)], www.sepa.gov.cn/eic/6496475533 73011968/20021117/1035365.shtml, accessed 10 December 2004.

United Nations Statistics Division (n.d.) *UN Commodity Trade Statistics Database*, www.un.org/ esa/ desa.htm.

Ying, J. (2002) 'Anfang Guangdong Qingyuan yanglaji chang [Visit to imported waste recycling centre in Qingyuan Guangdong], *China Electronics*, 25 April.

Yuan, Z., J. Bi and Y. Moriguichi (2006) 'The circular economy: a new development strategy in China', *Journal of Industrial Ecology*, 10(1/2): 4–8.

The ethics of waste labour

5 | Devaluing the dirty work: gendered trash work in participatory Dakar

ROSALIND FREDERICKS[1]

Introduction

In the spring of 2003, the clogged transfer station for the Yoff community-based trash collection project had transformed into an enormous, unruly garbage pile (*dépôt sauvage*). Putrefying under the uncompromising West African sun, the stinking edifice of waste provided visceral testimony to all that had gone wrong with the project. It stood in dramatic contradistinction, moreover, to the often celebratory images of participatory trash management in the scholarly and non-government organization (NGO) literature. In the end, because of its location on the road to Dakar's airport, the clogged station was a politically untenable eyesore. When flocks of birds began swarming over the pile and interfering with planes' flight paths, the writing was on the wall. The national aviation authority stepped in to order the transfer station's closure, thereby signalling the end to one chapter in Yoff's participatory trash history. For the women who had been the central labour force on the project, its abrupt closure was bittersweet. On the one hand, it put an end to a contentious initiative that had starkly increased their dirty labour burden with little reward. On the other hand, it foreclosed the opportunities they hoped might eventually develop from their exemplary acts of 'participatory citizenship'.

The last twenty years have seen a withdrawal of state provision of urban public services enforced by structural adjustment, state budgetary crises and a paradigm shift in development policy towards participatory development across the global South. Part and parcel of the turn to participatory development has been an explosion of community-based waste management projects across Africa. Underpinned by a discourse of empowerment and entrepreneurial citizenship, participatory development projects in general have come under fire from a broad critical literature contesting their theoretical justification, efficacy and ethics. Though much less intensely studied, participatory waste management has been revealed to be especially problematic, given the onerous nature of the labour itself (Miraftab 2004a; Samson 2007). This chapter draws from ethnographic research conducted on one of the most notable experiments in community-based trash management in Dakar to probe the function and implications of this new paradigm of urban governance in Senegal. Indeed, garbage collection has been a front-running sector of community-based management strategies in Dakar, but there has been little critical analysis of how these projects have worked, nor of their impact on community members. In a critique of associated empowerment claims, the chapter interrogates the way these projects deploy exclusive notions of community and reconfigure the responsibility and reward for those who do the 'dirty work'.

Specifically, the chapter explores the community-based trash management project spearheaded by one of Senegal's best-known NGOs, ENDA,[2] in the early 2000s in the Tonghor neighbourhood of Dakar's Yoff district (*commune d'arrondissement*). More generally, ENDA's community-based garbage projects have been hailed as 'best practices' of participatory urban governance in Africa. Relying almost exclusively on neighbourhood women's free (or low-paid) labour as a replacement for municipal garbage services, they attempted to convert neighbourhood garbage management into a community responsibility. Drawing from project documents and interviews with participants, residents and those local government, NGO and community-based organization (CBO) officials involved, the analysis makes two, interconnected, interventions on the moral and material moves made by these projects. To begin, it explores how the 'images of community' (see Li 1996) that were produced in these projects through the space of participation turned on ethnic difference. The osmosis between 'formal' and 'informal' trash labour introduced through participatory trash management is thus revealed to solidify existing community hierarchies through reinforcing specific divisions and power relations. A key part of the justification for devolving trash management to the community level, moreover, is found to be a discourse of green values backing so-called appropriate technologies and environmental stewards.

Secondly, the chapter interrogates notions of empowerment in these projects through considering the way they instrumentalized gendered associations with household waste management in order to convert poor women into ideal participants and thereby extend their social reproductive duties into the neighbourhood space. It fleshes out the disciplinary particularities of trash work, given all of the loaded associations with waste, and the difficulties posed by the institution of a user fee for service. This allows for an exploration of the way in which the household politics of trash inform and reconfigure the landscape of neighbourhood trash politics and the role that women play as key transformatory figures in new governance agendas.

A concluding discussion will critique participatory development and glean insights from the analysis towards better understanding changing state–society relations during Senegal's neoliberal experiment.[3] In particular, it emphasizes the foundation of neoliberal development strategies in reconstituting the relations of social reproduction and exposes the particularly troubling implications of engaging people in the management of their own waste.

Description of the ENDA community-based trash project in Tonghor, Yoff

The ENDA community-based trash project in the Yoff district took place in the Lebou (one of Senegal's nine ethnic groups) neighbourhood of Tonghor. Dakar's Lebou neighbourhoods represent some of the self-proclaimed 'traditional' Lebou fishing villages that have occupied the Cape Verde peninsula for over five hundred years but which have now been absorbed into the rapidly growing capital city (Sylla 1992; UNESCO 2000). Uniquely situated as the 'original' inhabitants of the area, the Cape Verde Lebou have a long tradition of both incorporation into Dakar municipal politics as well as autonomy and self-determination in the face of urban development.[4] In certain areas – of which Yoff is an important example – the Lebou have retained an extremely insular and powerful customary authority base, even as their villages have been rapidly absorbed into the urban agglomeration of Dakar. This traditional political organization overlaps with the municipal authority with important effects.[5]

Despite being officially incorporated into the Greater Dakar Municipality, these Lebou neighbourhoods are disadvantaged in terms of receiving Dakar-based public services owing to their location on the periphery of the city and their traditional village plan. Built around the family concession and spatially limited in their expansion, the neighbourhoods are extremely dense and irregular, and most areas have only narrow, sandy pedestrian paths. Combined with a fierce politics of land and resistance to change imposed by the local customary authorities, these features pose a number of challenges to infrastructural upgrading and waste management. Whereas wastes previously were disposed of in 'the bush' surrounding the villages, these neighbourhoods are now often plagued with sanitation problems (Gaye 1996; Abdoul 2002; Gaye and Diallo 1997). These challenges were part of the justification for choosing Lebou neighbourhoods as the main sites of the participatory waste management projects spearheaded by ENDA in the 1990s and early 2000s, in the context of the wider turn towards community-based strategies of urban public service provision.[6] These projects have been a central thrust of ENDA's activities to improve Dakar's urban environment and have earned the organization some notoriety in international development circles.[7]

Tonghor is one of the oldest of Yoff's seven traditional neighbourhoods and had a population estimated at 6,891 out of Yoff's 53,200 inhabitants in 2002 (Ndoye 2005: 36). Though the majority of residents are employed in the fishing industry, declining fish stocks have contributed to widespread insecurity in that economic sector. Most of the residents of Tonghor are Lebou, though newcomers are moving into the area. A long-term population of *waa Geej Ndar*[8] fisherman of Sereer ethnicity have relocated to Yoff from Saint Louis for the fishing industry. Unlike most Lebou, who own their own property, most of the *waa Geej Ndar* do not own land, and they often live in even more cramped, irregular habitations near the water. They are generally understood to be the poorest, least educated members of the population and are still often seen as outsiders, despite having been in Yoff for generations in many cases.[9]

Tonghor was chosen as a pilot because it has long been seen as one of the most garbage-challenged neighbourhoods in Yoff (Ndoye 2005; ENDA 1999). Tonghor's garbage management challenges are generally attributed to the distance from most houses to the paved road where the city's trash truck passes to collect garbage. The sandy roads in the interior are often impassable for these vehicles, so most households have to walk some distance to the road when they hear the honking of the trash truck. A study conducted in 1997 as a baseline for the community-based trash project estimated that 60 per cent of Tonghor households disposed of their garbage on the ground or by burying it; over half of these discarded their garbage on the beach or in the ocean (Zeitlin and Diouf 1998: 4).

ENDA launched the pilot community-based trash project in Tonghor

in 2001 in collaboration with the neighbourhood's main CBO, the
Tonghor Management Committee (CGT).[10] Seed funding would come
from French and Canadian development funds, and the project was
to be maintained through a revolving savings fund based on household contributions (a user fee). The local government (Commune
d'Arrondissement de Yoff) and Yoff's main community association
(APECSY[11]) were official, non-contributing, partners in the project.
The project involved a door-to-door horse-drawn cart 'pre-collection'
system targeting over six thousand residents that would (in principle)
connect up with the city's trash system (ENDA 1999). Whereas, before,
women disposed of their household garbage through dumping it on
the beach or by the road to be collected by the city's garbage trucks,
the project ushered in a more refined system in which select women
would collect their neighbours' garbage. During the project's tenure,
the municipal garbage trucks ceased to enter Tonghor.

The project feasibility study performed by APECSY for ENDA emphasized the importance of local participation and the CGT was the
main player at the neighbourhood level (ibid.). The CGT created a
pilot committee and appointed a young male member as its volunteer
coordinator. The most important element of community participation was the six women chosen as 'animators' (*animatrices*) of the
project – or the liaison between the households and the three (male)
horse cart (*charrette*) drivers.[12] Two *animatrices* accompanied each horse
cart driver to collect the garbage from the homes and load it on to
the cart. Originally entirely volunteers, these women received a small
'token'[13] of 15,000 CFA per month for a few months until community
contributions waned and they received next to nothing. The drivers
were hired at 30,000 CFA per month ($60).

The collection process usually went as follows: each *animatrice*
would complete their household duties to start the neighbourhood
rounds by 7.30 or 8 a.m. They then walked door to door alongside the
horse cart, and, in many cases, entered their neighbours' courtyards
and homes to retrieve the garbage and load it on to the cart. In the
beginning, they did the rounds every day, but they eventually reduced
this to four days per week to lessen the burden. The cart drivers then
dumped the garbage at the transfer station, where it was, theoretically,
to be delivered to the city's dump, Mbeubeuss, by municipal trash
trucks.[14] On certain days, the *animatrices* had to solicit each household's
financial contribution (1,000 CFA per month) – a demand that was
often discomforting and frequently unmet.

The *animatrices* were also charged with assisting leaders of the CGT

5.1 An educational mural aimed at neighbourhood women on the wall of the eco-sanitation station in Tonghor, Yoff

in community outreach to educate (*sensibiliser*) neighbourhood women on how to properly store, separate and dispose of their garbage (see Figure 5.1). A key element of the education campaign entailed discouraging women from dumping on the beach or burying their garbage. In the face of persistent recourse to the beach, an ordinance was eventually enacted which prohibited all beach dumping and fined all perpetrators. This effectively forced neighbourhood residents to use the fee-based horse-cart system through placing the *animatrices* in the role of policing their participation.

Producing community and empowerment in the space of trash

The 'Community-based management of order and disorder'[15] Community-based waste management projects fit squarely within the 'revisionist' neoliberal discourse governing development policy in the 1990s and 2000s, claiming to enhance service delivery and local democracy by empowering the most marginalized, especially women (World Bank 1989; Mohan and Stokke 2000). Urban community groups are often hailed as the solution to urban problems for their potential to enhance operational performance and as a democratizing force challenging authoritarianism and stimulating new forms of inclusive citizenship

(UNCHS 1996). This mainstream development discourse has received a strong scholarly critique that raises key questions about the impacts and implications of community-based development as potentially 'the new tyranny' of market-based strategies aimed at rolling back the state and exploiting the poor (Hickey and Mohan 2004; Cooke and Kothari 2001). A key concern of the critical scholarship has been to unpack the ideas of community produced in these projects and the ideas surrounding 'culture' they are premised upon (Watts 2006). Conceptualizations deployed within development discourse of communities as undifferentiated 'sites of consensus and sustainability' are revealed to naturalize their boundaries and obscure social divisions that structure internal power relations and different community members' relationships to the economy (Li 1996). The obsession with community, moreover, is centrally implicated in the reconfiguration and respatialization of the state (Li 1996, 2000).

Drawing on these critiques, this research explored the work that the community-based waste management project in Yoff did towards producing a certain kind of community. The choice of the Lebou neighbourhoods, first and foremost, can be seen as much more than a simple choice based on sanitation challenges. Though these neighbourhoods on the city's periphery are among those most challenged by sanitation, they are not alone in this respect and their selection was explicitly made on ethnic terms.[16] Promotional literature on the ENDA projects often highlighted the historic legacy of Dakar's 'traditional neighbourhoods' and hailed the Lebou as a proud, independent people for whom community-driven development is a natural and long-standing truth. These images of tight-knit, traditional communities resisting the invasion of the metropolis have obvious charismatic appeal for funders. They also dovetailed with the Lebou elite's efforts to assert their autonomy and autochthonous ownership over Yoff.

Newly-in-vogue green values were also mobilized as justification for the turn to the community solutions to waste management. ENDA has an explicit environmental focus to its work, and projects are specifically targeted at sustainable and alternative approaches for a more green development path. In this light, it presented the choice of the door-to-door horse-drawn cart collection system as a more appropriate technology for these neighbourhoods' particular challenges, as well as one that could draw from the deep history of sustainable practice among the Dakar Lebou. Lebou women, in particular, were constructed as natural environmental managers.

In practice, the community activated by the project was exclusively

Lebou, despite the fact that the *waa Geej Ndar* areas are considered the dirtiest and most garbage-challenged areas in Tonghor. In fact, community-based organizations in Yoff almost always have an ethnic element to them that is rooted in the intent to preserve the Lebou's 'traditional' way of life – and hold on land – in the face of urbaniza-tion and settlement by non-Lebou.[17] Because autochthonous claims in Yoff are defined by ethnicity, claims to manage Yoff 'traditionally' yoke ethnicity with tradition. Although they do not explicitly exclude non-Lebou, both APECSY and CGT are understood to be Lebou organ-izations, in effect sidelining the *waa Geej Ndar* residents from most community decision-making processes. The waste project was no exception: the *waa Geej Ndar* were not consulted or involved in the project design. All of the *animatrices*, furthermore, were Lebou. This can be seen to stand in direct contrast to the inclusive rhetoric in ENDA's promotional literature and their supposed attention to the most marginalized members of society.

Also important here is the work that the ethnic identity of the project did in the interests of the Lebou elite to assert their autonomy from the local state – its competitor for power and authority over the Yoff community. Engaging their women in neighbourhood trash collection offered a productive opportunity for the Lebou to solidify their tenacious hold on their neighbourhood through the symbolic ordering of the neighbourhood by these Lebou 'municipal housekeep-ers' (Miraftab 2004b). A public service for and by the community, in other words, contributed to the independence that the Lebou have asserted since their absorption into the city through the performance of self-management. Extending the domestic waste management activities of Lebou women into the space of the neighbourhood thus acted to entrench Lebou authority and existing community hierarchies.

Interrogating empowerment: the production of trash labour value The production of community in participatory development is invariably anchored within a discourse of empowerment justifying the role of dif-ferent community members. Just as notions of community deployed in participatory development have received significant scholarly critique, associated notions of empowerment have been revealed to be quite slippery as well. More often than not, the simple *fact* of participation is often conflated with empowerment (Mohan and Stokke 2000). Studies illuminate, furthermore, how discourses of community participation built upon constructions of women's traditional roles and spheres have often been indispensable in harnessing women's labour at little or no compensation (Miraftab 2004a; Cleaver 1999). A more robust analysis of empowerment benefits demands a consideration of the reconfiguration of labour value resulting from participation, within a specific cultural context.

Social reproduction is a useful lens through which to consider the way formal and participatory labours are dialectically constituted. The categorical distinction between the realms of production and reproduction determines the nature and value of work through constructing labour taking place in the home in reproducing and maintaining labouring bodies as 'non-work' or work with no value. Katharyne Mitchell et al. term the 'compass of social practices and social relations' involved in maintaining households as 'life's work' (2004). These and other scholars explore the way in which neoliberalism has ushered in a crisis of social reproduction via the rollback of state welfare services across the globe. We can see how community-based waste management, as one element of the neoliberal turn in development discourse, is premised on tapping and reconfiguring relations of social reproduction, or the fabric of activities comprising 'life's work'. The Yoff project, more specifically, instrumentalized gendered associations with household waste management in order to idealize women as participants and thereby extend their social reproductive duties into the neighbourhood space.

As an element of women's duties as managers of the domestic space, waste work in the home is naturalized as intrinsically women's work in Senegal.[18] Project managers deployed these connections in envisioning women as the most practical interface with household garbage managers in the Yoff project, and thus the ideal *animatrices*. In the words of Malick Gaye from ENDA, 'as it's women who do the separation at the source, that's what motivated us to place women as key links in the chain' of the project.[19] Interestingly, this exclusive focus on women represented a distinct turn from the focus on youth that had dominated an earlier phase of neighbourhood participation in Dakar's waste sector that took place in the early 1990s (see Fredericks 2009a). It dovetailed well with the overall turn in ENDA's priorities – and in the wider development discourse, for that matter – by the late 1990s towards a focus on women's participation.[20] Mayor Issa Ndiaye, who had observed the roll-out of the project in his dual role as mayor of Yoff (from 1996 to 2002) and member of APECSY's executive board, further explained:

[The participation of women] was good because women can speak to other women ... It was a question of organization ... And so, the women, while the others went to the beach for money-making activities, they were taking care of the common interest! [They] had the capacity to withstand this work. Even if people spoke badly to them, they took it in [their] stride! They didn't create any problems. What interested them was the cleanliness of the neighbourhood ... So, whatever [community] reaction they received, they were incredibly diplomatic! Truly, they withstood lots of grief.[21]

The mayor's revealing statement echoes many of my interviews with those coordinating the project. Because household trash management is considered women's work, it was assumed that women would most easily influence the behaviour of other women. Also important was the notion of their role as community managers, or, in the description of the Rufisque project, 'their determining role in the education of children, the citizens of the future'.[22] Women's 'natural' attributes, including diplomacy, a non-confrontational style and their intimacy with the communities, as well as their altruistic choice to work for 'the common interest', were celebrated as their key skills as *animatrices.*

The six women from Tonghor chosen as *animatrices*, for their part, seem to have been taken by surprise when they were notified at a community meeting of their new roles. When they enquired as to why they were chosen, they were asked: 'Do you want to do your part to support your neighbourhood, your country?' Two of the women chosen knew their selection was motivated by their past involvement in garbage collection. Both had been deeply involved in the youth-based neighbourhood clean-up movement that took place in the early 1990s (*Set/Setal*) and then had actually worked for the municipality as paid trash collectors in an earlier phase of trash management.[23] Importantly, both had been fired from the formal trash collection force in a round of downsizing that had occurred just a few years before the initiation of the ENDA projects. The CGT leaders also emphasized that the 'neediness' of the women was taken into account in choosing these participants. They stated that they had purposefully chosen less well-off women who could make use of such an 'opportunity'. Three of the women were divorced or widowed heads of household, and three were over fifty years of age.

Despite a prevalent rhetoric in ENDA's promotional materials on its participatory waste projects that they were community designed and driven, furthermore, neighbourhood residents, including the *animatrices*, were in practice completely excluded from project design. In direct contrast with ENDA's emphasis on women's key roles as project leaders as a key metric of success, the *animatrices* were emphatic that they had not been consulted prior to the project's roll-out and that they would have designed it quite differently. The role of the community in designing the project was exclusively channelled through the two involved CBOs, CGT and APECSY, and took place between older male village elders and community leaders and ENDA's project managers. As such, the project reinforced existing community power dynamics.

The *animatrices* had no choice but to participate in the interests of preserving their reputations as good wives and housekeepers, but also out of a sense of obligation to their communities, as enforced by the power and authority of community leaders. In many respects, behaviour is tightly prescribed in Tonghor, and the intimacy of community gives the impression of neighbourly surveillance at all times. These women also participated, however, hoping that the work might translate into more lucrative opportunities. Because they lack the education and networks needed to land jobs, women in Dakar are at a stark disadvantage in terms of finding wage labour. The *animatrices* hoped that this project would be their ticket to paid work. In my interviews with all six participants, it was clear that their participation in the project had been quite onerous and that they were, in the end, deeply disappointed by the lack of compensation or other opportunities gained. One *animatrice* described her experience as follows:

> I'd wake up early to do my duties around the house then go meet the horse cart operator to do our circuit with the other *animatrice*. We left our kids, left our work at the house, to go rid people's homes of garbage. I would follow behind the cart, whistling and letting everyone know we were coming so they would bring out their garbage ... The work was really hard ... We continued on because we wanted to work ... we kept working. Then, you find that even before the end of the month, you'd have a sore chest and then, finally, that what you're supposed to receive, no one gives it to you. What we wanted was to work and that's the chance that God gave us, so we said we would grab that chance ... but it didn't help to fulfil any of our needs. You would work all day, go home, wash, do the cleaning, do our work, then the next day get back up to do it again.[24]

This reconfiguration of the space of household social reproductive activities into the community space built on the notion that women should be judged according to their skills and capacities as the managers of order and cleanliness in the home. This resonates with Dipesh Chakrabarty's observation in India of how 'housekeeping' – specifically household trash management – 'is meant to express the auspicious qualities of the mistress of the household' (1991: 20). These participatory trash projects extend the realm of that responsibility, to secure the cleanliness of the neighbourhood as the responsibility of its female residents – as a reflection of their 'auspicious qualities'. The notion that women in Tonghor are natural waste managers and community educators facilitated the negation of value of neighbourhood trash work as 'work' deserving of remuneration and placed the onus of neighbourhood waste work on women's skills as 'municipal housekeepers' (Miraftab 2004b). This resonates with other research on the instrumentalizaion of gender in cheap waste management solutions in neoliberal contexts, defended through a rhetoric of voluntarism, responsibility and skill acquisition (Samson 2007, 2008; Miraftab 2004a, 2004b).

Central to the targeting of women in these projects was a repudiation of the labours they already perform – i.e. all of the 'life's work' duties that the *animatrices* left behind as they went about their neighbourhood trash job – in the home, as well an extension of those unpaid activities into the neighbourhood. In this sense, we can see how the jobs ended up doubling their unpaid activities by extending the realm of social reproduction into the public sphere. This extension also came as a fundamental rejection of the value of women's labour in the official trash sector. Fired from municipal trash collection because they were not deemed worthy of those jobs, these women were then installed in the community-based project as idealized volunteers.[25] Quite in contrast with the early experience of women municipal trash workers, whose labours were masculinized when they entered the public space to collect garbage, the labours of women in the community-based system were devalued.[26] Although they toiled day in and day out alongside the horse cart drivers, the payment of these men was never in question and was never justified through a narrative of community responsibility. The drivers were clearly seen as workers, whereas the women were seen as *participants*, whose neighbourhood trash management labour was rendered an empowering duty undeserving of compensation. In this light, the case of participatory waste management in Dakar thus resonates with the growing body of research into the way that the crisis of social reproduction has worked through differentially disciplining gendered bodies through the devaluation of certain spheres of work (Mitchell et al. 2004; Fakier and Cock 2009).

What deserves further attention in the trash case, however, is the rooting of that discipline in the materiality of the labour itself. Drawing from Mary Douglas, we know that waste work is intensely stigmatizing, owing to the powerful symbolic associations around impurity (1966). Discourses around the danger of dirt produce social borders and classify people within a hierarchy of status (ibid.). The insidious power of these projects thus draws from the negative associations with waste and cleaning. Joining with the symbolic violence of being associated with waste was the arduous physicality of that labour process for the *animatrices*. Because standard trash receptacles are beyond the financial means of most Dakar residents, garbage is usually disposed of in small plastic bags or rice sacks, or dumped loose from an open plastic container. Owing to its high organic content, which included the stinking remains of the fish and other animals eaten the day before, and the intense heat of the uncompromising Senegalese sun, the garbage is often putrid. Supplied with only minimal equipment, if any at all, the *animatrices* did this work with their bare hands. By the end of a workday, they were filthy, forced to parade through their neighbourhood wearing the smelly remains of other people's waste. In an Islamic society where cleanliness of the body is of utmost importance in terms of spiritual and community standing, this is no small burden. Neither was the vulnerability to disease that came of this risky exposure for people with little or no access to healthcare. Despite their most fastidious attempts at staying clean, the work often led to infection and disease.

Thus, in contrast with the mechanized garbage truck, the intimate technology of the door-to-door horse cart system introduced an entirely different relationship between collector and garbage and new forms of subjection to waste management's symbolic and material discipline. The deployment of gender stereotypes in these projects entrenched their connection to waste, dirt and disorder through reserving them the dirtiest tasks in the household and the neighbourhood.[27] It also literally burdened them with disease. This highlights how the reconfiguration of labour value through such projects must be considered in light of the specific materiality and symbolic import of the labour itself.

Also important in interrogating the empowerment claims of the projects is the role of the user fee. The implementation of fees for service – or the devolution of the costs of basic services to the community – is one of the hallmark elements of the neoliberal model of urban public service reform and its associated reconfiguration of geographies of social reproduction. Consistent with wider trends, the Tonghor community-based trash project was rooted in the principle of the poor paying (more) for development or rescinding of the state's duty in reproducing the population. The project's feasibility study emphasized that the user fee for the door-to-door trash collection was as an important part of involving participants in a sustainable community-driven model of public service. Ironically, in this same document, only 43 per cent of Tonghor residents said that they would be willing to contribute financially to the project (ENDA 1999). Despite this early warning sign, the payment scheme was laid out in an appendix section entitled 'When the poor finance development' (ibid.: 136). Each household was asked to pay 1,000 CFA per month ($2), to be collected at the end of the month by the *animatrices*. A flat rate calculated per household, this fee was separate from the municipal Household Garbage Tax (*la Taxe d'Enlèvement des Ordures Ménagères*, TEOM), which is calculated based on property values.[28]

Although the vast majority of my respondents claimed to have regularly paid the user fee, the *animatrices* revealed that in practice they had faced intense resistance to paying. This impinged on their meagre salaries and those of the horse cart drivers, and was a key factor in the decline of the project. This resistance can be explained by exploring how the fee dramatically reconfigured the cost of waste disposal. For many, the amount demanded for garbage service was exorbitant for the lower- to lower-middle-class residents. Just before the project was launched these residents had benefited from trash collection by the municipality for 'free', given that the vast majority of the residents either did not pay the Garbage Tax or were unaware that they paid it. For those who actually do pay the tax, the new fee represented a doubling of their payment for garbage services. The fines imposed on those who continued dumping on the beach, moreover, acted to criminalize those who attempted to opt out. The user fee and efforts by the CGT to educate neighbourhood women on sorting methods most likely transformed the value and treatment of the garbage within the home as well. Charging for the garbage they put out – whereas before this service was taken for granted – in effect outsourced some of the burden of the new waste collection system on to the household members themselves, deepening their involvement in the management of their waste alongside their neighbourhood *animatrices*.[29]

Beyond their ability to pay, furthermore, was a resistance to paying out of principle. Most residents firmly believed that garbage collection should be a free public service and thus took the user fee as just one more symbol of the state's negligence and incapacity to serve the needs of its citizens. This sentiment was particularly strong among the *waa Geej Ndar*, who were not only least able to pay but also distrusted the

Lebou authorities. They viewed the project suspiciously as just one more scheme by the Lebou establishment and, as a result, exhibited the least buy-in of the Tonghor residents. The *waa Geej Ndar* residents' refusal to pay constituted a key reason that the project floundered. This highlights the fact that the ethnic definition of community deployed in this project in the end worked against its eventual sustainability. It also shows how unsuccessful the project was in actually winning over the community to the idea of individual and community responsibility for waste management.

The gendered landscape of household waste management and its connection to household bargaining power was also an important factor in the difficulties surrounding the user fee. As is to be expected, the gendered nature of domestic trash management informed household members' priorities regarding household expenditures and valuation of the service. Because they are in charge of managing and disposing of household garbage, women were more willing to pay for the door-to-door service as it alleviated their trash burden and obviated their need to risk dumping on the beach. However, because few women in Tonghor are financially independent, they found it difficult to make this contribution. On the other hand, asking husbands to pay for the service was often problematic because men did not prioritize the service as much as women. In this light, we can see how the user fee interfaced with family power dynamics to disproportionately burden women with the costs associated with maintaining the household.

Finally, given the controversial nature of these fees and their widespread rejection by community members, the *animatrices*' role in soliciting the user fee was a sticking point, to put it mildly. In effect, it cast these women as the taxman, supposedly drawing on their intimacies in the community, but in truth locating them on difficult terrain with regard to their neighbours. As some of the most marginalized members of the community, being asked to solicit money from their neighbours was highly problematic. Add to this stress the entrenchment of women's responsibility for dirty labour and the complete elision of participants' feedback, and the empowerment claims are revealed to be deeply flawed indeed.

Conclusions: a flurry of wings and the return of the trash truck

After less than a year of operation, the Tonghor community-based trash collection project was a shambles: many if not most residents refused to pay the user fee, the overworked *animatrices* were exhausted from – and no longer compensated for – their labours, and even the horse cart drivers were fed up with the increasingly irregular payment of their salaries. The dispute between the municipality and the neighbourhood authorities over the project, furthermore, precipitated disaster at the point of coordination near the airport. With the refusal of the municipality to participate, the transfer station had become a towering mountain of garbage. When the national aviation administration (ASECNA) weighed in over the bird problem, the project was definitively cancelled. Soon after the project dissolved, the municipal trash trucks began collecting along their usual circuit in Tonghor, with some changes made in an attempt to reach the hard-to-access areas. Much more recently, the service has improved markedly, tracking gains made by the municipal collectors' working conditions under the new mayor of Dakar since 2009.[30] Residents currently make do with this service, deploy creative strategies to manage their garbage, and periodically defy the ban and use the beach during collection crises. Besides occasional efforts by the neighbourhood's youth and women to clean specific areas when they become clogged with refuse, no comprehensive community-based project has been attempted since 2003. This chapter has aimed to expose how the project reconfigured the value of trash work and the image of the community, in the name of empowerment and efficiency, with key implications for local politics and state power in Senegal as well as participatory development in Senegal and beyond.

A closer look at the Tonghor project reveals how participation interfaces with local histories and power struggles with important effects. Quite in contrast with the often glaring omission of politics within development discourse and policy, this highlights how new development and governance agendas often reinforce the power dynamics they purportedly seek to eliminate.[31] Through a complex interplay of ethnic, gender and class differences, the project worked precisely through the activation of a notion of community that was exclusive, by directly interfacing with customary authorities that represented only one vision of the community. As such, the participatory agenda buttressed the Lebou elite's project of asserting their autonomy from the municipal state. Though considerable research of late has exposed the increasing intensity of localized political contests in urban Africa, much less has explored the nexus of participatory development strategies – still the dominant development paradigm – and autochthonous claims in different settings (Geschiere and Jackson 2006; Nyamnjoh and Rowlands 1998; Marshall-Fratani 2006). This research indicates that these connections demand closer attention.

Another striking feature of the turn to community seen here is the deployment of green values as part of a romanticization of the virtues of the 'local'. The discourse of community promoted by ENDA and reproduced by the local authorities endorses 'small is beautiful' and 'appropriate' technology solutions like horse-cart trash collection as the most natural and sustainable development approaches. Not only was the low-tech system assumed to be better suited to this particular type of community, but the Lebou were purported to be better suited for this green approach because of their historically and intrinsically 'green' lifestyles. The photos of horse carts might have looked good on ENDA's website, but the reality of women going door to door was less rosy. In the end, the project succeeded only in transferring the garbage from within the neighbourhood to a festering pile on its periphery. This raises the question of when green becomes greenwash in the service of projects which are no cleaner, more efficient or more sustainable than municipal services.

The analysis has also seriously questioned the claims of empowerment underpinning the turn to participatory trash management through considering the way it reconfigured the value of women's labour. The instrumentalization of women's connections to domestic trash work and the deployment of discourses of community management and diplomacy were a convenient way to harness the labour of the *animatrices* with little reward. The project not only extended the realm of their social reproductive duties but also placed them in disempowering positions with regard to their communities. For the women who had once been paid as municipal trash workers, this directly reversed the gains made for their labour value in the official trash sector. In this light, the Tonghor case resonates with much of the critical literature on participatory trash management elsewhere, which highlights the way that gender can be mobilized in the service of exploitative labour, defended through a rhetoric of responsibility and empowerment (Miraftab 2004a, 2004b; Samson 2003, 2007). It also contrasts with AbdouMaliq Simone's observations of the ENDA community-based waste project in Thiaroye sur Mer, which he contends offered neighbourhood women a 'platform for reaching the larger world' (2003). As such, this study highlights how notions of empowerment must be analysed in relation to the particular way they reconfigure labour within specific local political settings.

An analysis of empowerment must take on, furthermore, the expectations and experiences of those participating. The *animatrices* often articulated their motivation for participating in these projects as a hope for future 'opportunities' which might be made available. Instead, the *animatrices* witnessed a devaluation of their standing in the community because of the negation of their labour value, the nefarious implications of working with waste, and the uncomfortable tasks they were charged with as the new taxman. This experience stands in sharp contrast with the claims of empowerment that live on in the best-practices literature and highlights the way in which the crisis of social reproduction works through differently disciplining gendered bodies. And yet, as mentioned at the beginning, the end of the project was a bittersweet moment for the *animatrices* because of all of the sweat, hope and pride they had poured into their work. If we understand development to be 'the management of a promise', then 'what if the promise does not deliver?' (Pieterse 2000: 176). It is the mismanagement of hope which is perhaps the most disempowering element of these reconfigurations of value at Dakar's margins.

This case also deserves attention because of its focus on garbage. In many respects, this story has been a classic case of the flexibilization of labour under a neoliberal development logic. And yet, the emphasis on engaging people in the management of their own waste is a particularly revealing instance of the new configurations of labour value in the contemporary development climate. Trash is a special case, deriving from the power that is imbued in garbage and cleaning, because trash work is deeply implicated in the ordering of people as well as spaces. These factors make the material and moral conversions implied by community-based trash projects even more troubling. If those who work in garbage are burdened by the negative associations of their work, then those asked to collect their own garbage for free are 'trashed' in a double sense. Viewed through a more global lens, the reconfiguration of trash labour value at the margins casts stark light on not only the neoliberal development paradigm, but also the uneven geographies of wealth it is involved in sustaining and producing.

Finally, if community-based trash in Tonghor can be seen to extend women's social reproductive duties into the public space, then it was also part of a reconfiguration of the state's role in managing and sustaining the reproduction of labour power. In Senegal, structural adjustment and other neoliberal policies have resulted in a contentious struggle for power and resources between national and local authorities, and trash management has been at the centre of these struggles (Fredericks 2009a). Just as the battle to control Dakar's official trash sector reveals the contemporary political climate, this analysis prompts a discussion of the implications of the Tonghor project and participatory development in general for state power. Despite being an official partner, the Yoff local government was excluded from key project decisions and retaliated by ceasing to transfer the garbage to the dump. Rather than merely a 'technical problem', as labelled by ENDA, the transfer station disaster thus represents the tension between municipal and NGO-driven development agendas. Like many community-based initiatives, this project, in effect, cemented the neighbourhood's autonomy from the local state. This reveals that beyond a rhetoric of decentralization, outsourcing trash management to community organizations, which compete for power with the local state, may end up working against local state capacity and the decentralization of state power. This raises a host of questions about the implications of the turn to community for long-term governance agendas, given the short-term priorities and lack of accountability of NGO projects.

This research thus illuminates the fact that empowerment discourses accompanying participatory development may serve projects which are no cleaner, greener or more effective then municipal services and which are, in fact, disempowering for specific community members. As the new mayor of Dakar seems to understand quite clearly, associated resources would be better targeted at enhancing the capacity and sustainability of the urban public service itself. Perhaps the most hopeful lesson to be drawn from the Tonghor project, then, lies in its failure – or the rejection of this model by the Tonghor community and Yoff local government. As just one element of the ways in which, across Dakar, the trash workers and the communities they serve alike have fought the devaluation of trash labour, participatory garbage collection in Yoff may indeed point to a wider resistance to the neoliberal ethics of urban management in Senegal.

Notes

1 This chapter is based on research conducted between 2006 and 2010 in Dakar with funding from the National Science Foundation, Social Science Research Council, Fulbright-Hays as part of her doctoral dissertation research in the geography department at the University of California, Berkeley. The author would like to thank her research assistant, Ndeye Bineta Ndoye, for her valuable contributions to the research, transcription and Wolof–French translation. She is also indebted to Michael Dwyer, Asher Ghertner, Tracey Osborne, Sapana Doshi, Malini Ranganathan, Kendra Strauss and Michael Watts for comments on earlier versions of this chapter. A significantly shorter version was presented at the AAG annual meeting in Seattle

in November 2010. Finally, this research would not have been possible without the time and patience of CBOs, ENDA and, especially, the *animatrices* of the Yoff project. The author provided translation from French to English. Any mistakes that remain in the text are exclusively the author's responsibility.

2 Environnement et Développement du Tiers Monde (ENDA) is an international non-profit organization founded in 1972 and based in Dakar.

3 This chapter considers Senegal's 'neoliberal' era as the country's particular experience of structural adjustment, which began in 1979, and the policies aimed at liberalization that have followed on its heels, especially under Abdoulaye Wade since 2000. In contrast with 'overgeneralized accounts of a monolithic and omnipresent neoliberalism', this chapter joins with those approaches concerned with trajectories of *neoliberalization* in specific places, in light of their historical, cultural and political specificities (Peck and Tickell 2002: 381).

4 The Lebou declared their republic, independent of French authority, in 1790. The Lebou Republic lasted until 1857, when the Cape Verde peninsula was annexed into the French colony (Sylla 1992). Because of their claim to land on the peninsula, the Lebou constituted a large percentage of the *originaires* of the first four urban areas of Senegal, the *Quatres Communes* (Diouf 1998).

5 I use 'tradition' not to denote a static, unchanging nature, but, rather, to engage the discourse of tradition employed by the Lebou and the historical roots of their contemporary neighbourhood governance structures.

6 See Simone (2003); Soumaré (2002); Gaye and Diallo (1997); Gaye (1996).

7 For instance, the UNESCO Best Practices for Human Settlements report, as a case study for the Institute for Development Studies at the University of Sussex, and in the widely circulated article by Gaye and Diallo (1997).

8 '*Waa Geej Ndar*' translates directly from the Wolof to 'people from the Saint Louis sea'.

9 The *waa Geej Ndar* are the largest ethnic minority in Tonghor, and a very rough estimate would put them as constituting at least 10 per cent of the population.

10 ENDA's pilot in Tonghor also had a liquid sanitation element that was aimed at treating waste water with small-scale (off-grid) 'eco-sanitation stations'. Though this was not the subject of this research, it should be noted that the liquid waste project also experienced enormous problems and did not come to fruition. The mural in Figure 5.1 is painted on the wall of one of the stations.

11 Association pour la Promotion Social, Economique et Culturelle de Yoff (Association for the Social, Economic and Cultural Promotion of Yoff).

12 Though not originally from Yoff, the horse cart operators were locally based Sereer men who owned their own horse carts.

13 This is the language used by the project coordinators.

14 The project did not include a recycling element. All trash that makes it to the Mbeubeuss dump, however, is sorted by waste pickers and channelled into extensive informal recycling networks.

15 This phrase is taken from Diouf (1997).

16 For instance, Dakar's sprawling, disadvantaged suburb Pikine faces enormous sanitation and waste challenges but it is generally seen as lacking the actionable assets imagined in the Lebou neighbourhoods.

17 This is consistent with observations in other African cities revealing that autochthony claims often become more intense with urbanization. See Geschiere and Jackson (2006).

18 Cutting across the gendered division of waste labour in the home is differentiation according to marital status, age and location within family hierarchies, with younger wives, girls and maids generally allocated the most onerous waste duties.

19 Malick Gaye was the head of ENDA's Relay for Participatory Urban Development programme (*Relais pour le développement urbain participé*) (RUP). Most of the community-based sanitation projects (including that at Tonghor) were coordinated by RUP (personal interview, 14 November 2007, ENDA offices, Dakar).

20 For a concise overview of the history of 'mainstreaming' gender in development discourse, see Pearson (2005).

21 Personal interview, 25 November 2007, APECSY offices, Yoff.

22 This was taken from the 'Forum on household waste collection using carts: resolutions and action plans' for Rufisque, dated 22 December 1994, as reprinted in Gaye (1996: 122).

23 As discussed in Fredericks (2009a), the massive youth social movement *Set/Setal* aimed at cleaning up Dakar actually formed the foundations of the contemporary

municipal trash sector when the youth were formalized into a new trash collection force. Having been active in the youth movement, these two women had become incorporated into the municipal trash sector alongside their male compatriots in the mid-1990s. See also Diouf (1996).

24 Personal interview with *animatrice*, 19 November 2007, Tonghor, Yoff.

25 All of the women trash workers in Yoff were fired when the system was downsized in the late 1990s. The gendered basis of the firing was justified by the notion that the women are not primary breadwinners. On the contrary, both *animatrices* were the main breadwinners in their families (Fredericks 2009b).

26 Women brought into the municipal trash sector after *Set/Setal* actually experienced an increase in the value of their labour in material and moral terms. Because they were paid (albeit meagrely) for cleaning activities for the first time, and because they worked side by side with men, this worked to masculinize their labour (Fredericks 2009b).

27 This resonates with research on waste work and gender in other settings within the global South (Ali et al. 1998; Beall 1997; Miraftab 2004a, 2004b; Samson 2007, 2008). Though the concern here is primarily with the contemporary moment, parallels can also be drawn from other moments and spaces. Striking similarities can be found, for instance, with the notion of women as domestic angels, extending their care into the streets of the city, as part of the history of welfare in Britain in the nineteenth and early twentieth centuries (Alexander 2009).

28 The TEOM has infamously low recovery rates and is generally inadequate for covering service costs.

29 Data were not collected on how this reconfigured the use and value of materials in the home but it is easy to see the incentive for households to avoid paying the fee by reusing, recycling and dumping elsewhere.

30 See Fredericks (forthcoming) for a discussion of the municipal trash workers' union movement and recent gains related to salaries, healthcare, legal status and equipment under Dakar mayor Khalifa Sall (elected in 2009).

31 See Ferguson's seminal work on the politics of development in Lesotho (1994).

References

Abdoul, M. (2002) 'The production of the city and urban informalities: the borough of Thiaroye-sur-Mer in the city of Pikine, Senegal', in O. Enwezor, C. Basualdo, U. M. Bauer and S. Ghez (eds), *Under Siege: Four African Cities – Freetown, Johannesburg, Kinshasa, Lagos: Documenta 11, Platform 4*, Ostfildern-Ruit: Hatje Cantz Publishers, pp. 337–58.

Alexander, C. (2009) 'Illusions of freedom: Polanyi and third sector recycling schemes', in C. Hann and K. Hart (eds), *Market and Society: The Great Transformation Today*, Cambridge: Cambridge University Press, pp. 221–39.

Ali, M., J. Olley and A. Cotton (1998) 'Agents of change: the case of Karachi City's waste management', *Third World Planning Review*, 20(33): 255–66.

Beall, J. (1997) 'Thoughts on poverty from a South Asian rubbish dump: gender, inequality, and household waste', *IDS Bulletin*, 28(3): 73–90.

Chakrabarty, D. (1991) 'Open space/ public place: garbage, modernity, and India', *South Asia*, 14(1): 15–31.

Cleaver, F. (1999) 'Paradoxes of participation: questioning participatory approaches to development', *Journal of International Development*, 11: 597–612.

Cooke, B. and U. Kothari (2001) *Participation: The New Tyranny?*, London: Zed Books.

Diouf, M. (1996) 'Urban youth and Senegalese politics: Dakar 1988–1994', *Public Culture*, 8: 225–49.

— (1997) 'Senegalese development: from mass mobilization to technocratic elitism', in F. Cooper and R. Packard (eds), *International Development and the Social Sciences: Essays on the History and Politics of Knowledge*, Berkeley: University of California Press, pp. 291–319.

— (1998) 'The French colonial policy and the civility of the originaires of the Four Communes (Senegal): a nineteenth century globalization project', *Development and Change*, 29: 671–96.

Douglas, M. (1966) *Purity and Danger: An Analysis of the Concepts of Pollution and Taboo*, London: Routledge.

ENDA (1999) *Volet collecte des déchets et assainissement du quartier traditionnel de Yoff-Tonghor: Etude de faisabilité*, Dakar: Enda Tiers Monde RUP, République du Sénégal Commune d'Arrondissement de Yoff.

Fakier, K. and J. Cock (2009) 'A gendered analysis of the crisis of social reproduction in contemporary South Africa', *International*

Feminist Journal of Politics, 11(3): 353–71.

Ferguson, J. (1994) *The Anti-Politics Machine: Development, Depoliticization, and Bureaucratic Power in Lesotho*, Minneapolis: University of Minnesota Press.

Fredericks, R. (2009a) *Doing the Dirty Work: The Cultural Politics of Garbage Collection in Dakar, Senegal*, Berkeley: Geography Department, University of California.

— (2009b) 'Wearing the pants: gender and the politics of trash labor in Dakar', *Hagar: Studies in Culture, Polity and Identities*, 9(1): 119–46.

— (forthcoming) *Disorderly Dakar: The Politics of Garbage in Senegal's Capital City*.

Gaye, M. (1996) *Entrepreneurial Cities*, Dakar: ENDA.

Gaye, M. and F. Diallo (1997) 'Community participation in the management of the urban environment in Rufisque (Senegal)', *Environment and Urbanization*, 9(1): 9–29.

Geschiere, P. and S. Jackson (2006) 'Autochthony and the crisis of citizenship: democratization, decentralization, and the politics of belonging', *African Studies Review*, 49(2): 1–7.

Hickey, S. and G. Mohan (2004) *Participation: From Tyranny to Transformation?*, London: Zed Books.

Li, T. M. (1996) 'Images of community: discourse and strategy in property relations', *Development and Change*, 27: 501–27.

— (2000) 'Articulating indigenous identity in Indonesia: resource politics and the tribal slot', *Comparative Studies in Society and History*, 42(1): 149–79.

Marshall-Fratani, R. (2006) 'The war of "who is who": autochthony, nationalism and citizenship in the Ivorian crisis', *African Studies Review*, 49(2): 9–43.

Miraftab, F. (2004a) 'Making neoliberal governance: the disempowering work of empowerment', *International Planning Studies*, 9(4): 239–59.

— (2004b) 'Neoliberalism and casualization of public sector services: the case of waste collection services in Cape Town, South Africa', *International Journal of Urban and Regional Research*, 28(4): 874–92.

Mitchell, K., S. A. Marston and C. Katz (eds) (2004) *Life's Work: Geographies of Social Reproduction*, Malden, MA: Blackwell.

Mohan, G. and K. Stokke (2000) 'Participatory development and empowerment: the dangers of localism', *Third World Quarterly*, 20: 247–68.

Ndoye, N. B. L. (2005) 'Problématique de l'assainissement dans la Commune d'Arrondissement de Yoff: l'état de lieux d'une espace fragile', Mémoire de maitrise UFR Lettres et Sciences Humaines, Section Geographie, Université Gaston Berger de Saint Louis, Saint Louis.

Nyamnjoh, F. and M. Rowlands (1998) 'Elite associations and the politics of belonging in Cameroon', *Africa: Journal of the International African Institute*, 68(3): 320–37.

Pearson, R. (2005) 'The rise and rise of gender and development', in U. Kothari (ed.), *A Radical History of Development Studies: Individuals, Institutions, and Ideologies*, London: Zed Books, pp. 157–79.

Peck, J. and A. Tickell (2002)

'Neoliberalizing space', *Antipode*, 34: 380–404.

Pieterse, J. N. (2000) 'After post-development', *Third World Quarterly*, 21(2): 175–91.

Samson, M. (2003) *Dumping on Women: Gender and the privatization of waste management*, Cape Town: Municipal Services Project (MSPO) and the South African Municipal Workers' Union (SAMWU).

— (2007) 'Privatizing collective public goods – re-fracturing the "public" and re-segmenting labour markets. A case study of street cleaning in Johannesburg, South Africa', *Studies in Political Economy*, 79: 119–43.

— (2008) 'Rescaling the state, restructuring social relations: local government transformation and waste management privatization in post-apartheid Johannesburg', *International Feminist Journal of Politics*, 10(1): 19–39.

Simone, A. (2003) 'Reaching the larger world: new forms of social collaboration in Pikine, Senegal', *Africa*, 73(2): 226–50.

Soumaré, M. (2002) 'Local initiatives and poverty reduction in urban areas: the example of Yeumbeul in Senegal', *International Social Science Journal*, 52(172): 261–6.

Sylla, A. (1992) *Le Peuple Lebou de la Presqu'ile du Cap-Vert*, Dakar: Les Nouvelles Editions Africaines du Senegal.

UNCHS (1996) *An Urbanizing World: Global Report on Human Settlements*, Oxford: Oxford University Press.

UNESCO (n.d.) *Community Participation in the Management of the Urban Environment Senegal*, www.unesco.org/most/africa6.htm.

— (2000) 'Yoff, le territoire assiégé: un village lébou dans la banlieue de Dakar', in *Dossiers régions côtières et petites îles*, Paris: UNESCO, p. 90.

Watts, M. (2006) 'Culture, development, and global neo-liberalism', in S. A. Radcliffe (ed.), *Culture and Development in a Globalizing World: Geographies, actors, and paradigms*, New York: Routledge, pp. 30–57.

World Bank (1989) *Sub-Saharan Africa: From Crisis to Sustainable Growth*, Washington, DC: World Bank.

Zeitlin, M. F. and L. Diouf (1998) *Etudes Socio-économiques et d'assainissement du quartier de Tonghor du village traditionnel de Yoff, 16 Commune d'Arrondisement Yoff-Dakar, Sénégal*, Dakar: Programme Eco-Communautaire de Yoff (APECSY et Commune d'Arrondisement de Yoff) pour ENDA-RUP.

6 | Stitching curtains, grinding plastic: social and material transformation in Buenos Aires

KAREN ANN FAULK

El tema no es que sobra gente, el tema es que falta trabajo (the issue isn't an excess of people, but a lack of work) *Elena Ramos, Cooperativa BAUEN*[1]

19/20 December

More than a decade has now passed since Argentina gained international notoriety for defaulting on its crushing foreign debt. The convertibility plan, which had pegged the peso to the dollar at a 1:1 rate since 1991, collapsed in December 2001 under the weight of its own non-sustainability. Skyrocketing unemployment and widespread poverty led to massive street protests on the 19th and 20th of that month, bringing an end to President De la Rúa's *Alianza* government and, eventually, to the neoliberal economic model that it had inherited. In the years that followed, the country flourished, reducing social inequity and maintaining overall growth even during the 'global' economic crises that engulfed the United States and Europe a few years later. The case of Argentina has justly sparked renewed debate, particularly within Latin America, about the nature of the state and the feasibility of neoliberal economics. Questions as to the proper role of political direction in guiding economic policy have once again taken centre stage. Furthermore, the massive popular mobilization that spelled the ultimate end of neoliberalism's legitimacy in Argentina is seen as being reflected in similar mobilizations within the global

North, as financial speculation and deregulation become increasingly identified as responsible for problems with the current economic system and its effects on those living within it. The protests that brought about such drastic change in Argentina were the product of a general dissatisfaction and frustration with political representatives and the failure of democracy to allow citizens the right of choice concerning economic policy. Yet at this critical juncture, it is worth noting that the protests were also fundamentally concerned with ideas of work, legality, moral obligation and human dignity. Embedded in the many acts of protest and resistance that surrounded the Argentine crisis and its aftermath were discursive struggles over the nature of social life and the relationship of the state to society.

These discursive debates, far from being irrelevant, lay at the heart of the fundamental change that has occurred in recent years. In this chapter, I consider specifically how the idea of work has been a central point of conflict in Argentina. The nature of work, and the role of the state in protecting it as a basic right, has been a key notion around which actors have mobilized and sought legitimacy. I look at how this struggle has been defined and articulated by two separate groups united by the fact that each has *created* its own form of labour, in the absence of viable traditional options left by neoliberal-era structural reforms. The first group is a recuperated business, or an operation that was shut down by its owners and put back into production by its workers. The workers formed a cooperative that rebuilt and now operates a central Buenos Aires hotel under a principle of worker self-management. The other group I discuss is a cooperative of street recyclers, who take materials out of the garbage and turn them into a source of livelihood. In each of these, those discarded by a system no longer capable of employing them use their labour to physically transform objects that have been similarly discarded. In the process of these transformations, they effect a discursive change, denying their position as non-workers by insisting that their labour be counted as a legitimate form of work.

Focusing specifically on the notion of 'work' as used by these groups illuminates how members construct value-laden moral frameworks in response to the conditions in which they find themselves immersed. David Graeber's writings on anthropological theories of value show that the word 'value' is usually found used in one of three senses: 1) in a philosophical or moral sense; 2) in a classic economic sense, in terms of an assigned 'worth'; or 3) in a linguistic sense, à la Saussure, in terms of value as contrast or value as meaningful difference

(Graeber 2001: 1–2). Furthermore, Graeber makes the argument that these three senses are really all ultimately versions of the same thing. That is, that they correspond to some sort of symbolic system (however open, mutable or multiple) that defines the world in terms of what is important or meaningful.

I propose that the actions and words of the members of these two cooperatives demonstrate indeed how these three senses of value (economic, moral and linguistic) are inherently interrelated. By looking at the value of work in this way, we can see how what is meaningful here represents a departure from and a challenge to the dominant (neoliberal) symbolic system. Furthermore, I take it a step farther in focusing on the material aspects through which these symbolic notions of value are concretized, operationalized or put into practice. This is particularly salient in this case, as it is through the material conversion of 'waste' that these groups enact a revaluation of themselves, of the things they work with, and of the nation as a whole. As I will demonstrate, they take the ultimate in devalued material, waste, and propose an alternative valuation of the material. Through this medium they also enact a simultaneous revaluation of themselves as rights-bearing workers, and an alternative vision of national development and recuperation. Others have focused on the transformations in the identity or subjectivity of workers in Argentina in recent years (Battistini 2004; Dinerstein 2004; Fernández Álvarez 2004; Wallace 1999), or on the role of the body in confronting these systemic changes (Sutton 2010). I build on their insights but instead pay attention to the materiality of these conversions – focusing on the interrelation of people and things in enacting personal, cultural and national transformations.

The right to work

Key to these transformations is the way in which these workers seek to define themselves as such, after having been pushed out of the traditional labour market. Argentina's traditionally high employment rates in the formal sector has been a lasting source of pride and identity. Indeed, Argentina is notable among Latin American countries for a deeply ingrained sense of work as a right, to be enjoyed by all (adult) members of society. A long and vibrant history of activism around labour issues imbued the idea of labour with its associations to dignity and placed it as the anchor and ultimate source of social justice. As Argentine anthropologist Mariano Perelman has argued, 'In general terms, it is possible to say that "work" has constituted one of the most powerful disciplinary discourses of modernity, and in Argentina, it was one of the principal forms of social integration, and one that also reached those that were outside of the market of formal work' (Perelman 2011: 5; see also Perelman 2007b).

This recognition of a basic sense of equality and rights is noted by Maristella Svampa, who has argued that, in spite of the existence of various kinds of social hierarchies, Argentina has been distinctive within Latin America for its 'egalitarian logic in the social matrix' (Svampa 2005b: 47). The belief in upward mobility and social integration was supported by early state policies, such as those that instated universal education. This 'model of integration' (Svampa 2005a) grew to extend a broad swath of social rights to the popular classes under the first Peronist administrations (1946–55), including strong protections for workers' rights, state-run or state-supported healthcare systems and pension funds.

Guillermo O'Donnell's poignant article '¿Y a mí, qué mierda me importa?' playfully and effectively details the notion of work as a right (O'Donnell 1997). In it, he contrasts a hypothetical interaction between an Argentine service worker and a customer/client from a higher class with a similar encounter in Brazil. He argues that, upon feeling themselves disrespected, the Brazilian person may assay the worker with the phrase 'Você sabe com quem está falando?' ('Do you know who you're talking to?'), as a way of demanding the deference they expect to receive. An Argentine worker, says O'Donnell, endowed with a firmly embedded sense of rights, rather than accepting that they owe deference to their class superior, is more likely to believe that they are doing them a favour by providing service to the customer. Thus, such an injunction on behalf of the client would receive as a reply something akin to the title phrase, 'What the hell do I care?'

The role of the state in assuring the right to work was slowly eroded over the second half of the twentieth century, beginning with the military coup against Perón in 1955 and the overturning of the short-lived Constitution of 1949, which had guaranteed social and economic rights. In spite of moments of intense resistance from the labour sector during the following decade (James 1988), the weakening of the power of organized labour and the rolling back of the gains acquired in decades of struggle were to continue.

In 1976, the most recent and most infamous of Argentina's military dictatorships launched its Proceso de reorganización nacional, or the Process of National Reorganization. There are many connections between the repression and policies of this dictatorship (which lasted until 1983) and the era of neoliberalism that followed. One of these lies in the fact that the structural reforms that characterize neoliberalism, and which are deemed by many as responsible for the crisis that followed, did not begin in the 1990s. Rather, privatization of state-run industries, the erosion of workers' rights and protections, and the general lessening of government regulation of the economy were all aspects of the economic programme implemented by dictatorship-era economics minister José Martínez de Hoz. Furthermore, the brutal repression and severe weakening of the workers' movement during the dictatorship era were a necessary step in setting the stage for the later economic policies, which would have been much more difficult to implement had the workers' movement maintained its previous strength and vitality. Repression, the erosion of rights and the effects of state policies that fail to adequately consider the dire poverty in which so many millions of Argentines find themselves are intricately interconnected. As expressed by Barbara Sutton, 'Human bodies apparently disappear under the neoliberal logic, just as the last military dictatorship in Argentina disappeared the real, material bodies of many people who opposed precisely that kind of socioeconomic organization' (2010: 29).

Neoliberal workers The 1990s marked the height of the implementation of neoliberal reforms in Argentina.[2] The irregular and uncontrolled selling off of state industries and avid encouragement of foreign investment served more to line the pockets of well-positioned members of the traditional ruling classes and politicians than to stabilize the national economy. Over five thousand factories and businesses closed during the 1990s, and, by the end of the decade, un- and underemployment rates had reached all-time highs. Structural adjustment policies, which in Argentina included vast reductions in the number of state-employed workers, and the 'flexibilization' of workers, led to a marked increase in desalaried and black market work devoid of traditional protections, in a nation that had always prided itself on stable, salaried employment as a fundamental category of identity.

The 1991 National Employment Law, which established the possibility of short-term labour contracts, marked a change from previous legislation that emphasized job stability. Later laws, in 1994 and 1995, further eroded protections to workers' rights, limiting the liability that should be paid to injured workers, installing a 'trial period' for new workers, reducing the situations under which employers must pay social security and its amount, and eventually eliminating altogether the obligation to give severance pay to many workers.[3] The 1995 rewriting of the Law of Insolvency and Bankruptcy – *Ley de Concursos y Quiebras* (24.522) – was a clear expression of the marked neoliberal commitment to redefining the role of workers and redesigning the political economic system.[4] This move gave legal backing and justification to the continued transformation of Argentina into a market-driven society. Under the 1995 law, workers were redefined as neoliberal citizens whose rights are determined in terms of their degree of insertion in the market (Svampa 2005a; Faulk 2008). For the thousands of workers affected by the five thousand or so factory closures that ensued in the 1990s, the new law oversaw their rights. Fundamentally, it placed workers as creditors, alongside investors and debt-holding providers. However, it ranked workers at the bottom of the list in terms of receiving indemnity following the auction of the bankrupt business.[5] In practice, this led to the workers rarely if ever receiving much compensation in terms of back pay or other debts, and absolved the owners of many of the previously held obligations towards workers in such situations. Having already taken on centrality in political discourse and economic practice, property rights now became the focus and language of determination in the juridical sphere as well.[6]

The era of neoliberalism in Argentina fulfils in many ways the description of millennial capitalism offered by Jean and John Comaroff (2000). They use the term 'millennial capitalism' as it captures two key aspects of this historical moment: as occurring around the turn of the twenty-first century and revealing 'capitalism in its messianic, salvific, even magical manifestations' (ibid.: 293). Not only was the Argentine manifestation of capitalism in the final decade before the millennium representative of the changes within the global political economic system, particularly those affecting primary goods-producing nations, but the sense of catastrophic implosion grew to be ever more heightened throughout the decade and culminated in the political upheaval of December 2001.

The idea of work is being conceptualized and deployed in new ways in this millennial climate. Before the 1990s, owing to the strong political and juridical guarantees of good wages and a strong social security system, 'Workers did not see themselves solely as selling their labor on the market, but as contributing to a larger sense of societal security through their labor' (Perelman 2007b: 10). In the years leading up to and immediately following the crisis, precarious, informal work and under- and unemployment became the norm. Santiago Wallace and Osvaldo Battistini each take up different aspects of the changes in workers' subjectivity with the atomization of the neoliberal era (Wallace) and in the immediacy of the millennial moment (Battistini and contributors), focusing on the ruptures and reconfigurations produced in the construction of identity owing to the destabilizing effects of the increasingly precarious nature of work and dire unemployment rates (Wallace 1999; Battistini 2004). As they and others have noted, the new conditions of labour brought about by neoliberalism and its collapse have also led to drastic reconfigurations of the meaning of work from the bottom up, by those who resist the erosion of work as a social as well as an economic category.

In exploring the permutations that work has undergone in recent years, I focus on the material transformations that enable, condition and concretize the processes of change. One example of this comes from the Cooperativa BAUEN, a workers' cooperative that forms an integral part of the recuperated businesses movement. With some 13,000 jobs created, this movement consists of factories or businesses that, after being closed or abandoned by their owners, are reopened by their workers. The Cooperativa BAUEN operates a central Buenos Aires hotel, under the principle of worker self-management. The other example I describe comes from the *cartoneros*, comprised of organizations and individuals that recover and, in some cases minimally process, recyclable materials collected from consumers. Here I also use the example of a particular cooperative, in showing how the source of labour they themselves created is engulfed in legal and moral battles over legitimacy. With the heightening of the crisis of unemployment and the collapse of political and economic viability, rather than advocating for social assistance programmes, that would leave the unemployed in the position of being recipients of government handouts, the *cartoneros* and *cooperativistas* insist on their right to hold on to the source of labour they themselves created, as workers. This insistence on work as a right cannot be read as either an entirely new phenomenon or as a return to a previous era.[7] Rather, an examination of the actions and words of these groups reveals the way in which historical patterns and trajectories have been revitalized in innovative ways. By bringing into focus the material imbrications of these changes, the things and objects which are reconfigured, reconstructed, altered, reworked and transformed, we can see the concrete processes through which changes in ideological discourses and practices are accompanied and enabled by changes enacted on the material world.

The BAUEN

The Hotel Bauen is one of the most emblematic examples of the recuperated businesses movement. Located at the intersection of Callao and Corrientes in the centre of Buenos Aires, it was originally built using state loans as part of the preparations for Argentina's hosting of the infamous 1978 World Cup. Later, it was a favoured meeting spot for the political elite. However, years of self-interested management practices and the diversion of profits into other investments left the four-star hotel with accumulated debts worth millions of dollars/pesos. The workers relate the feeling that they had been 'discarded' (*descartados*) and 'thrown out on to the street' (*nos tiraron a la calle*) when the business closed during the peak of the 2001 economic and political crisis. By early 2003, some former workers had begun to meet representatives of other recuperated businesses and the umbrella movement the Movimiento Nacional de Empresas Recuperadas (National Movement of Recuperated Businesses, or MNER). The MNER advised them to gather as many former employees as they could and occupy the installation. Finally, on 20 March 2003, a small group of workers entered the hotel. Shortly after, they registered as a workers' cooperative.

Once inside, they were faced with the utter desolation that abandonment and pillage had left. In the year that had intervened, the former owner had stripped the hotel of everything of value, in violation of laws mandating the sale of the goods and proper allocation of proceeds to creditors, including the former workers. Before the workers could reopen for business, they needed to rebuild the hotel. They manually reconstructed the installation, sewing bedspreads, laying phone lines, rebuilding floors, etc. As such, the first few years became a constant process of rebirth. They often place this material conversion of the building, alongside their own reconversion into workers, but now as autonomous, self-managed workers rather than as employees. I focus first on this process of converting found and gathered materials into the physical trappings of a four-star hotel.

Sewing curtains, laying wire: the Bauen reborn In 2004 and 2005, the members of the cooperative were constantly engaged in manipulating the material components of the hotel.[8] Workers learned to repair wiring and electrical systems, replaster walls and lay tiles, in the effort to bring the hotel back to a usable state. Video documentation of these first months and years of the BAUEN cooperative by the Grupo Alavío captures this element. Their substantial body of documentary footage from this time shows cooperative members engaged in the many physical labours that were needed to reconstruct the hotel.[9] This focus on physical production and the making of things caught my attention, particularly as, unlike many of the other *recuperadas* or recovered factories which were firmly located within the industrial sector, a hotel is quintessentially part of the service sector. This distinction can, of course, be as illusory as it is omnipresent, yet I was struck by the marked importance given to the production and repair of material things both in the daily practice of the workers and in the way they spoke about their experience within the BAUEN. Throughout this process, the recuperation of material was *creating the conditions for labour*, as the hotel could not function unless they first recovered the materials it needed to do so. Lacking funds to invest in materials, the cooperative members combined ingenuity with a careful stewardship of abandoned materials to refashion and reconstruct everything from flooring to electronics.

In one video by Alavío, cooperative member Gladis Alegre explains the need to use the materials they already had. As she sits busily sewing curtains on a sewing machine, she tells the camera, 'Every day we are building [*construyendo*] more for our hotel. We are trying to take [new materials] as little as possible, to have a few more pesos, to survive, for ourselves and our families.' Another scene has two members working on the hotel's extensive telephone system. One refers to his *compañero*, saying, 'This guy's trying to juggle with what we've got.' He connects one phone after another to a cord, testing to see whether any of the old telephones from the rooms can be made to function again. 'There's another one,' the first guy says. 'Nope, not this one either,' replies the other with an ironic laugh.[10]

In enacting these material transformations, the cooperative was able not only to repair but also to expand the usable portions of the hotel. They invested much of their profits in renovations, and in 2004 were able to open to the public a new full café/bar. By 2005, 80 per cent of the hotel was in operation, and the ground floor hosted a bookstore, a hair salon, a gift shop and point of sale for the new line of originally designed and manufactured shoes by the recuperated factory CUC (Cooperativa Unidos por el Calzado, formerly Gatic). However, as the hotel became profitable, the pressure from both the former owners and political forces whose interests lay in the protection of property rights increased. Each of these has mounted persistent legal attacks against the cooperative's right to occupy and operate the hotel.

Property rights versus the right to meaningful equality The cooperative members respond to this pressure by 1) asserting their own right to operate the hotel based on the right to work as a fundamental right; and 2) denying the owners' attempts to displace or control them through a detailed examination of the illegality of the owners' actions while at the helm of the business. In examining the claims made by each side, it becomes clear that the arguments presented by former owners and the cooperative are built upon different moral frameworks. The workers insist on their constitutionally guaranteed basic rights to a dignified manner of employment, fair and honest treatment by the owners of the business, and the right to be remunerated with a wage that covers their basic needs and access to social benefits like retirement support and healthcare.[11] In this view, the state as representative of the people holds the obligation to protect the rights of workers. Within the recuperated businesses movement the idea of work takes on the added dimension of an effort having been realized by the workers themselves. They emphasize their organization around a principle of worker self-management (*autogestión*), one that is rooted in an ethic of cooperativism and which includes a responsibility towards society as a whole. For the business owners, operating under the logic of neoliberal capitalism, the emphasis is placed on moral responsibility to shareholders and the maximization of profitability. The state in this view takes on the role of defending the right to private property and the free operation of business. Fundamentally, these differences can be classified around the basic split between the primacy of the right to property (the owners) and the primacy of the right to meaningful equality (the cooperative). This tension, inherent in classical liberal political philosophy, once again reasserts itself at the heart of the debates left in the wake of neoliberal restructuring.

In making their case for the right to operate the hotel, the cooperative argues that the former owners acted both illegally and immorally in allowing the hotel to decline into bankruptcy. From this point of view, the corrupt practices of the former owners and the impunity afforded to the business class under the era of Menemist politics are seen coming together to form the principal cause of the severe unemployment and extreme debilitation of the primary and service industries in Argentina around the turn of the twenty-first century. In referring to the widespread practice of fraudulent bankruptcies, Rebón notes:

> This behaviour by the businesspeople is perceived as 'intolerable',
> making space for acts of resistance. In this perspective, it is important

to point out that in the literature [on recuperated businesses] and the
consciousness of the workers moral explanations of the 'inappropriate
behaviour by the owners' as determining the business crisis abound.
These hypotheses don't take into account that the very nature of
capital is the maximization of gain and its reinvestment. If the conditions for the realization of the cycle of accumulation don't exist, withdrawal at the lowest cost is the morally capitalist alternative to follow.
(2004: 65)

Nonetheless, the workers also highlight that even under the capital-
friendly laws passed or decreed during the era of neoliberal reform,
many of the actions of the business owners remained illegal, and
that this illegality was in fact an integral part of the system. The
weight given to profitability in the 1990s often led to business owners paying little regard to the continuity of the business and placing
exaggerated emphasis on the transportability of capital, manifested
both in widespread capital flight and preferential investment in other,
often foreign-based business. Indeed, the corrupt business practices
the owners utilized are singled out by the cooperative as part of the
widespread 'habitus of impunity' (Fajn 2003) that tolerated and even
encouraged such practices in the economic ethos of the era.

In addition, the fact that the former owners first allowed the hotel
to fall into disrepair and then stripped it of its useful parts is itself
seen as criminal by the workers, as wasteful and disrespectful of
the place of work. This is one of the most painful features for many
members of the cooperative, who invested many years of their lives
in the care of the hotel. The 'recuperation' of the businesses in this
case holds a double meaning. For the members of the recuperated
businesses movement, the dominant meaning of having 'recuperated'
the factory or business is of having recuperated a source of labour.
In the case of the BAUEN, this also includes the physical recuperation of the hotel. The nation's productivity is being recuperated after
the crisis one business at a time, in direct opposition to the long
decline of Argentina's self-held identity as an industrialized country.
In this sense, workers often cite how the word 'Bauen' itself carries
the meaning 'to build' or 'to construct', in its original German, and
they thus make a symbolic connection between their efforts and the
rebuilding of the nation. These debates over who deserves the right
to operate the hotel are, even more crucially, embedded in debates
over what the hotel *is*, i.e. waste or a workplace.

Through the language used to legitimize their actions both legally and morally, the cooperative is concerned with demonstrating the various, interrelated transformations they enact: of themselves, from discarded workers into full rights-bearing citizens; from those labouring under a system of exploitation to self-managed producers of goods and services; and of the hotel, from yet another closed business stripped of its infrastructure to a vibrant and vital service provider, rebuilt from the detritus left in the wake of its abandonment.

Cartoneando: from discarded workers to workers of waste

The interrelation between material transformation of objects discarded as waste and the transformation in subjectivities is also evident in the *cartoneros* movement. This section concerns these street recyclers, or those who recover and, in some cases, minimally process reusable objects from the garbage for resale.

Though actual numbers are difficult to calculate, there are an estimated 40,000–50,000 people in the Greater Buenos Aires Metropolitan Area engaged in the recollection and selling of recyclable materials pulled from garbage (Magnani 2006).[12] This represents at least a threefold swelling of the ranks of the traditional *cirjuas*, i.e. those who engaged in this activity prior to the late 1990s. The increase in numbers has led to increased visibility of this activity. The attention paid to street recyclers by the media and academics reveals and partially constructs the discursive battles in which the recyclers have become embroiled. As was the case with the BAUEN workers, these battles take place on grounds of legality and within competing moral frameworks.

The figure of the *cartonero*, and the gradual replacement of the word *ciruja* as that most often used to describe this increasingly notable social activity, is a result of the end-of-millennium crisis. As more and more Argentines fell into poverty, including wide swaths of the middle classes, the number of people involved in exploring income-generating alternatives to salaried work caught the attention of the mass media and *cartoneros* became symbols of national degradation. At that same time, formerly despised activities gained a new significance, and the *cartonero* became a new subject position that allowed those engaged in street recycling, and the journalists and academics who talked about them, to re-evaluate and revalue a traditionally deprecated practice (Paiva 2008). To the extent that the recyclers engage in these assertions of public redefinition, it has been primarily through the medium of the cooperatives that they have expressed themselves and fought for public policies that attend to and accommodate their needs and the service they provide.[13]

With only a few scattered precedents, street recyclers first began forming cooperatives in the latter half of the 1990s. This first wave of cooperatives was organized mainly by traditional street recyclers, i.e. those who had been engaged in the activity throughout their lives and, in many cases, had inherited the practice from their parents and even their grandparents. They came together in search of better conditions, particularly as the crisis of neoliberalism changed the basic organization and possibilities of scavenging.[14] A second wave of cooperatives came slightly later, and included more of the newly impoverished middle class. These were largely comprised of or given impulse by people who had little or no previous experience collecting garbage, but began to do so as a result of new unemployment. As Argentine sociologist Verónica Paiva notes, the formation of cooperatives was especially prevalent among this group, as a way of alleviating the feelings of indignity and desperation brought about by the loss of salaried or regularized work (ibid.; Fernández Álvarez 2004).

The Cooperative Tren Blanco is one of the cooperatives of street recyclers that operate in the Greater Buenos Aires Metropolitan Area.[15] Formed in 2004 by some ten *cartoneros*, it sought to increase the value of the collected recyclables by partially processing the materials. Rather than continuing to collect materials themselves, the cooperative focuses on buying the materials collected by others from their locale (Suárez, Partido of San Martín) along the (now defunct) Tren Blanco line.[16]

With the support of microcredit loans from the NGO LaBase,[17] the cooperative is able to access a much higher return on collected materials through separation, washing and grinding, primarily of PET plastics.[18] For example, microloans from LaBase allowed the Cooperative Tren Blanco to buy a machine to grind recovered plastics on their own, thus greatly multiplying both the quantity of material that they can transport at a time and the profit they can get upon selling it.

In the case of the *cartoneros*, as with the recuperated businesses, these cooperatives actively contest the value placed on their labour morally, economically and linguistically as they define their activities. One example that demonstrates this is a case from 2002 that was brought before the Supreme Court of the City of Buenos Aires, in an attempt to declare as unconstitutional the dictatorship-era clause in the City Ordinance (from 1977) that made street recycling illegal (Perelman 2007a: 255–6; also Perelman 2011). Those in favour of overturning the ordinance argued that it violated the *cartoneros'* right to work by making their labour illegal. Opponents argued that the right to work cannot be used as a shield for illegal activities.

Cartoneros also frame their activities in moral terms. They argue that they have transformed themselves, re-becoming labourers by '*cartoneando*'. Many *cartoneros* cite how this work, as difficult as it may be, is still preferable to simply receiving government welfare payments,[19] for the sense of dignity it allows them. The ethics of work remains very strong in Argentina, and being a recipient of welfare (*beneficiario*) rather than a worker (*trabajador*) is a difficult subject position to assume. In addition, their labour is contrasted with delinquency. As Francisco Suárez has argued, 'The activity of recuperation shows the internalization of a culture of work and not of crime ... There, where work doesn't exist, they invent it, they self-employ. They invent or generate work out of what others discard' (Suárez, cited in Perelman 2007a: 263). As with the BAUEN, it is the recuperation of materials which is *creating the conditions for labour* by literally taking hold of the abandoned means of production, in this case garbage, before they rot away or are removed permanently from the production cycle.

The issue of environmental sustainability is another terrain on which the battle is waged. Though the increase in the number of street recyclers is unquestionably due to rising unemployment and the lack of viable and stable work alternatives, a number of *cartoneros* have come to understand their activities as part of a broader project of remaking the nation and refounding the economy on sustainable environmental principles. Those living in Suárez, for example, are acutely aware of the problems produced by the need to adequately deal with the million and a half tons of waste produced yearly in Buenos Aires – their neighbourhood is built on top of an abandoned dump.[20] In addition, the model of economic/environmental sustainability that is invoked harks back to earlier, historically resonant ideas, in this case import substitution industrialization models. When the peso–dollar parity ended during the economic crisis, it made importing raw materials much more expensive, and the market and price paid for local substitutes increased dramatically. This increased demand for local materials was an important factor in making street recycling a viable option. *Cartoneros*, through the medium of the cooperative, make a moral claim to national sustainability through their role in developing and supplying local industry.

For those with a stake in the lucrative waste collection industry, rather than being a part of the solution, *cartoneros* have often been presented as part of the problem. Resistance to the *cartoneros* by waste collection companies may be partly explained by economic motivations. Not accidentally, the 1977 prohibition on scavenging accompanied the moment when privatization of this service was beginning. Until 2005, the businesses that held the contracts to collect garbage in the City of Buenos Aires were paid according to tonnage collected. As such, materials pulled out of the line of collection led, in theory if not in practice, to a reduction in their profits. Since 2005, they have been paid by area cleaned. However, recycling is still a potentially lucrative industry, and there are those who attempt to reserve the monopoly of waste for a concentrated number of actors. These interest groups code the activities as being undertaken by scavengers or thieves. Waste collection companies have also insisted on their ability to collect recyclables more efficiently, cleanly and safely. They allege that the *cartoneros* are performing an activity that is disorderly, unsafe and dangerous – to themselves, but also to the residents of the wealthy neighbourhoods which they enter in order to collect material. These claims play in large measure on the fears of some of the inhabitants of the wealthier neighbourhoods, who view the poor as 'invading' their living spaces, bringing filth, danger and disease into visibility. *Cartoneros* themselves are seen by many of these residents as matter out of place.

Faced with this stigmatization, those who have taken to collecting recyclables, as with the Cooperative BAUEN, find validation in proactively defining their activities as work. The importance of this category as a source of social identity in Argentina makes this assertion a powerful source of legitimacy.[21] I find it instructive to consider this idea of work as forming the centrepiece for a regime of value akin to the kinds described by Graeber, mentioned earlier in this chapter. In doing so, these groups advance a regime of value that challenges that embraced by many of the economic elite who oppose their actions. The notion of work as put forth by these groups can be considered in terms of those value meanings outlined above:

1 Morally, in that these groups treat the notion of work as a moral value, and, specifically, their right to dignified work as a fundamental right that the state must guarantee.
2 Economically, as a classical Marxian critique, in that they are challenging the features of capitalism that allowed labour to become an abstraction that can be commoditized (bought and sold). Rather, their valuation of labour reasserts its relationship to human creativity – that is, labour as the way in which human beings create their worlds and their social ties as well as their physical environment, through *autogestión*, which is not focused on maximizing profit but

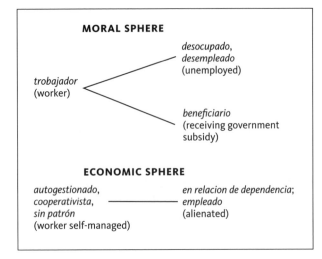

MORAL SPHERE

trobajador
(worker)

*desocupado,
desempleado*
(unemployed)

beneficiario
(receiving government
subsidy)

ECONOMIC SPHERE

*autogestionado,
cooperativista,
sin patrón*
(worker self-managed)

*en relacion de dependencia;
empleado*
(alienated)

6.1 Negative
equivalences
of linguistic
value

has other aims. As such, they are resisting the commoditization of labour by reinserting into it other kinds of social meanings.

3 Linguistically, in that the term 'worker' is contrasted to that of 'unemployed' (*desocupado*), or contrasted to someone who receives a government subsidy payment (*beneficiario*), which also gets at the relationship to the state and the citizen's right in relation to that state. Also, they define their work as that of *autogestionado, sin patrón*, in distinction to that of someone '*en relación de dependencia*'.

A map of these linguistic negative values or value as contrast is shown in Figure 6.1.

It is the notion of work through which this alternative regime of value is being expressed, in a unified way across these three senses. And furthermore, these workers demonstrate the relationship of the material to the discursive, how these ideas are concretized in practice, by utilizing precisely the moral equivalent of the discarded worker (material waste) in enacting these conversions.

Conclusion

Since the mid-twentieth century in Argentina, work has been seen as a 'natural part of life' (Perelman 2007b: 11), with all adult members of society deserving of a stable and salaried source of employment. Yet in practice this 'natural part of life' is a contested category that shapes the political, legal and economic system within which the workers are inserted. In this chapter, I have sought to show how, through the material conversion of things, post-crisis workers in Argentina seek their own conversion, from a discarded surplus of labour into workers, a social category that carries significant weight and profound importance. In this process, they contest neoliberal notions of work, which reduce the labour force to a commoditized, flexibilized variable and define rights in terms of an individual's level of insertion in the market. They seek to define their legitimacy on a contrasting set of moral and linguistic grounds. To return to the words of cooperative member Elena with which I opened this chapter, '*El tema no es que sobra gente, el tema es que falta trabajo* (the issue isn't an excess of people, but a lack of work)'. As her words reflect, primacy is given to an ethics of social and national, rather than individual, benefit. The current discursive battles surrounding the cooperatives of workers in recuperated businesses and of street recyclers focus on redefining their place in society, as productive members engaged in dignified activities that continuously (re)construct the nation through the slow but determined reconversion of discarded materials.

Notes

1 Some names have been changed.

2 On neoliberalism, see Greenhouse (2010); Harvey (2005); Saad-Filho and Johnson (2005). For an overview of neoliberalism in Argentina, see Teubal (2004).

3 See especially Ley Nacional de Empleo 24.103 (1991), Ley 24.465 (1995), Ley 24.557 (1995) and Presidential Decree 2609/93.

4 See Fassi and Gebherdt (2000) for a detailed study of this law. Modifying this law, especially in ways that give primacy to the reinitiation of activity, has been a priority for a number of the *recuperadas*, and has served as a focal point for their actions.

5 A new law for cooperatives, proposed by CNCT and presented by the ruling Kirchnerist party, was approved by the Argentine Senate on 2 June 2011. It prioritizes the solvency of the business, giving the workers legal protection to operate the establishment as a cooperative and to use all credits, indemnizations, back pay and other unmet obligations towards the workers as payment. The law is likely to face legal challenges.

6 Carlos Forment, personal communication.

7 See García Allegrone et al. (2004) for the historical context of such takeovers.

8 The Bauen Hotel (lower case) refers to the hotel installation itself, as well as the name of the hotel when it was operated by the former owners. The cooperative is called the BAUEN, which stands for Buenos Aires, Una Empresa Nacional (Buenos Aires, a national company), and itself encapsulates the fundamental message of the workers in insisting on the hotel as being in the service of the public, national good.

9 For more on the Grupo Alavío, see www.revolutionvideo.org/agoratv/index.htm; www.revolutionvideo.org/alavio (in Spanish and English). For an interview

with one key member, see Rodríguez (2010).

10 These clips can be seen at www.revolutionvideo.org/agoratv/ programas/empresas_recuperadas/ defensa_bauen_1.html, mins 14:26–16:00 and 17:13. In Spanish with English subtitles.

11 Article 14 and 14bis of the Argentine Constitution detail the rights of workers along these lines.

12 Sutton cites numbers for 2002 indicating 70,000–100,000 *cartoneros* in the Greater Buenos Aires Metropolitan Area (2010: 40).

13 Perelman makes the argument that traditional recyclers, or those who have engaged in this practice for an extended period of time pre-dating the current crisis, are more likely to view their activities as 'work', while those who have begun street collecting more recently are more likely to see this as a temporary survival activity, as an interruption in their trajectory as workers (Perelman 2007a, 2011). While not disputing Perelman's findings, I am arguing that the most vocal assertions of a vision of '*cartoneando*' as a category of work from *cartoneros* themselves come from those who have formed cooperatives. Among these, many of the *cooperativistas* are those with previous experience in a more formalized labour market, who thus seek to build and interpret their current experience within a revitalized framework of 'work'.

14 Principal among these changes were the modification, in 1997, of the law that determined the mode of garbage collection in the City of Buenos Aires, and the end of the pegging of the Argentine peso to the dollar, in 2002. See Paiva (2008, esp. pp. 75–94).

15 Other examples are discussed in Paiva (2008); Medina (2007); Schamber and Suárez (2007).

16 A 2003 documentary film, *El tren blanco*, by Nahuel García, Sheila Pérez Giménez and Ramiro García, traces the lives of users of the train. This train service, started by TBA in 1999, sought to keep *cartoneros* off the commuter train lines that link the provincial areas that ring the City of Buenos Aires with more central neighbourhoods. The service was ended under the administration of Mauricio Macri on 28 December 2007, leading to forceful protests by its users. Though a system of transportation by truck was theoretically put in place to replace it, as of this writing the City of Buenos Aires has yet to provide a truly functional alternative.

17 Part of the NGO The Working World. See www.theworkingworld. org for an overview of the organization, and www.labase.org for open information on the cooperative and their loans. A short film on the organization and the Cooperative Tren Blanco can be found at www.theworkingworld.org/tren BlancoLarge.mov.

18 See Magnani (2006) for a brief overview of the cooperative.

19 Under the Jefe y Jefas de Hogares, or Heads of Households, plan, the un- and under-employed living in poverty are entitled to monthly payments.

20 This statistic is taken from www.buenosaires.gov.ar/areas/ med_ambiente/basura_cero/?menu_ id=30973, and is based on data from 2004. Greenpeace Argentina reports that the City of Buenos Aires sent 2,110,122 tons of garbage to landfills in 2010. Under the 2005 Law Basura Cero, or Zero Garbage (Ley 1854), the city is required to

reduce to zero the amount of waste sent to sanitary landfills by 2020. Many organizations have strongly criticized the inability or unwillingness of the Macri administration to make responsible progress towards this goal. See, for example, Eduardo Videla, 'La ley de basura cero no es bienvenida', *Página 12*, 11 June 2011; Carina Quispe, 'Una ley que todavía no se aplica', *La Nación*, 19 June 2010.

21 Even so, the idea of *cartoneando* still frequently appears as an incomplete form for many of those engaged in the activity, as reflected in the way many define their activities as work, but when asked whether they are unemployed will immediately respond 'yes'. As such, it is considered as more of a form of work than begging or receiving a subsidy payment, but less than holding a salaried job. For this point I am indebted to Mariano Perelman (see especially Perelman 2011).

References

Allegrone, G., F. P. Verónica and M. I. Fernández Álvarez (2004) 'Los procesos de recuperación de fábricas: una mirada retrospectiva', in O. R. Battistini (ed.), *El trabajo frente al espejo: continuidades y rupturas en los procesos de construcción identitaria de los trabajadores*, Buenos Aires: Prometeo Libros, pp. 329–43.

Auyero, J. (2006) 'The political makings of the 2001 lootings in Argentina', *Journal for Latin American Studies*, 38: 241–65.

— (2007) *Routine Politics and Violence in Argentina: The Grey Zone of State Power*, Cambridge: Cambridge University Press.

Battistini, O. R. (2004) *El trabajo frente al espejo: continuidades y rupturas en los procesos de*

construcción identitaria de los trabajadores, Buenos Aires: Prometeo Libros.

Comaroff, J. and J. Comaroff (2000) 'Millennial capitalism: first thoughts on a second coming', *Public Culture*, 12(2): 291–343.

Cotarelo, M. C. and N. Iñigo Carrera (2004) *Looting in Argentina: 1989–90 and December 2001*, Leiden: Society for Latin American Studies Annual Conference.

Dinerstein, A. (2004) 'Más allá de la crisis. La naturaleza del cambio político en Argentina', *Revista Venezolana de Economía y Ciencias Sociales*, Central University of Caracas, 1/2004: 241–70.

Fajn, G. (ed.) et al. (2003) *Fábricas y empresas recuperadas: protesta social, autogestión y rupturas en la subjetividad*, Buenos Aires: Centro Cultural de la Cooperación.

Fassi, S. and M. Gebherdt (2000) *Concurso y Quiebra (ley comentada)*, Buenos Aires: Editorial Astrea.

Faulk, K. A. (2008) '*If they touch one of us, they touch all of us*: cooperativism as a counterlogic to neoliberal capitalism', *Anthropological Quarterly*, 81(3): 579–614.

Fernández Álvarez, M. I. (2004) 'Sentidos asociados al trabajo y procesos de construcción identitaria en torno a las ocupaciones y recuperaciones de fábricas de la Ciudad de Buenos Aires: un análisis a partir de un caso en particular', in O. R. Battistini (ed.), *El trabajo frente al espejo: continuidades y rupturas en los procesos de construcción identitaria de los trabajadores*, Buenos Aires: Prometeo Libros, pp. 345–65.

García Allegrone, V., F. Partenio and M. I. Fernández Álvarez (2004)

'Los procesos de recuperación de fábricas: una mirada retrospectiva', in O. R. Battistini (ed.), *El trabajo frente al espejo: continuidades y rupturas en los procesos de construcción identitaria de los trabajadores*, Buenos Aires: Prometeo Libros, pp. 329–43.

Graeber, D. (2001) *Toward an Anthropological Theory of Value: The False Coin of Our Own Dreams*, New York: Palgrave.

Greenhouse, C. (2010) *Ethnographies of Neoliberalism*, Philadelphia: University of Pennsylvania Press.

Harvey, D. (2005) *A Brief History of Neoliberalism*, Oxford: Oxford University Press.

Iñigo Carerra, N. and M. C. Cotarelo (2003) 'Social struggles in present day Argentina', *Bulletin of Latin American Research*, 22(2): 201–13.

James, D. (1988) *Resistance and Integration: Peronism and the Argentine Working Class, 1946–1976*, New York: Cambridge University Press.

Magnani, E. (2006) 'Pirámides de papel: el negocio de la basura', *Página 12*, 26 March.

Medina, M. (2007) *The World's Scavengers: Salvaging for Sustainable Consumption and Production*, New York: Altamira Press.

O'Donnell, G. (1997) '¿Y a mí, qué mierda me importa? Notas sobre sociabilidad y política en la Argentina y Brasil', in G. O'Donnell (ed.), *Contrapuntos: ensayos escogidos sobre autoritarismo y democratización*, Buenos Aires: Paidós, pp. 165–93.

Paiva, V. (2008) *Cartoneros y cooperativas de recuperadores*, Buenos Aires: Prometeo Libros.

Perelman, M. D. (2007a) '¿Rebusque o trabajo? Un análisis a partir de las transformaciones del cirujeo en la Ciudad de Buenos Aires', in P. J. and F. M. S. Schamber (eds), *Recicloscopio: miradas sobre recuperadores urbanos de residuos de América Latina*, Buenos Aires: Prometeo Libros, pp. 245–68.

— (2007b) 'Theorizing unemployment: toward an Argentine anthropology of work', *Anthropology of Work Review*, 28(1): 8–13.

— (2011) 'La construcción de la idea de trabajo digno en cirujas de la ciudad de Buenos Aires', *Intersecciones en Antropología*, 12.

Rebón, J. (2004) *Desobedeciendo al desempleo: la experiencia de las empresas recuperadas*, Buenos Aires: Ediciones P.ica.so/La Rosa Blindada.

Rodríguez, J. C. (2010) '"El cine militante es el cine abierto a la demanda de los compañeros": una conversación con Fabián Pierucci del Grupo Alavío y Ágora TV', *A Contracorriente*, 7(2): 294–314.

Saad-Filho, A. and D. Johnson (2005) *Neoliberalism – a Critical Reader*, London: Pluto Press.

Schamber, P. J. and F. M. Suárez (2007) 'Cartoneros de Buenos Aires. Una mirada general sobre su situación' in P. J. and F. M. S. Schamber (eds), *Recicloscopio: miradas sobre recuperadores urbanos de residuos de América Latina*, Buenos Aires: Prometeo Libros, pp. 25–46.

Sutton, B. (2010) *Bodies in Crisis: Culture, Violence, and Women's Resistance in Neoliberal Argentina*, New Brunswick, NJ: Rutgers University Press.

Svampa, M. (2005a) 'Ciudadanía, estado y globalización: una mirada desde la Argentina contemporánea', in J. Nun (ed.), *Debates de Mayo: nación, cultura y política*, Buenos Aires: Gedisa Editorial, pp. 263–90.

— (2005b) *La sociedad excluyente: Argentina bajo el signo del neoliberalismo*, Buenos Aires: Taurus.

Tedesco, L. (1999) *Democracy in Argentina: Hope and Disillusion*, London: Frank Cass.

Teubal, M. (2004) 'Rise and collapse of neoliberalism in Argentina',

Journal of Developing Societies, 20(3/4): 173–88.

Wallace, S. (1999) 'Trabajo y subjetividad. Las transformaciones en la significación del trabajo', in S. and N. Wallace (eds), *Antropología social y política, hegemonía y poder: el mundo en movimiento María Rosa*, Buenos Aires: Eudeba, pp. 359ff.

7 | Trash ties: urban politics, economic crisis and Rio de Janeiro's garbage dump

KATHLEEN M. MILLAR

Theories of marginality and metaphors of waste

In September 1978, garbage trucks began arriving in a neighbourhood called Jardim Gramacho (literally 'Gramacho Gardens') to unload roughly three thousand tons[1] of Rio de Janeiro's waste into the mangrove swamp at the edge of the neighbourhood. Despite federal guidelines that prohibited solid waste dumping in waterways,[2] as well as a federal law that established mangrove swamps as protected environmental areas,[3] the City of Rio chose the one million square metres of mangrove swamp located in the neighbouring city of Duque de Caxias as the new destination for the metropolis's refuse. The establishment of a garbage dump in Jardim Gramacho was considered a development project, sponsored and coordinated by FUNDREM, the Foundation for the Development of the Metropolitan Region, which was created by the governor of the state of Rio de Janeiro in 1975 in an effort to incorporate Rio's neighbouring cities into urban planning projects. Since 1978, well over fifty million tons of garbage have been dumped in Jardim Gramacho. Ninety per cent of this waste has come from the City of Rio de Janeiro.

Jardim Gramacho not only transformed from a small community of migrants and fishermen into what is now Latin America's largest garbage dump, it also became the workplace of roughly two thousand people, known as *catadores*, who reclaim recyclable and reusable materials on top of the dump for a living. For three months in 2005, and from 2008 to 2009, I conducted ethnographic fieldwork in Jardim Gramacho, living in the neighbourhood and collecting materials with *catadores* on top of the dump – first cardboard and later, when the price of cardboard plummeted, a range of different kinds of hard plastics. In the first few months, I learned, first and foremost, the *luta* or the everyday struggle of working as a *catador*. *Catadores* arrive on the dump at dawn in order to collect for several hours before the sun becomes unbearably intense, or they work at night with a flashlight under the chin, a light attached to a headpiece, or with no light at all. They must collect quickly and close to the unloading garbage trucks in order to gather as much material as possible before the tractor comes moments later to bulldoze the pile. They work in the sun and rain with no shelter aside from beach umbrellas that they sometimes find in the garbage and stick into the tops of filled sacks. They breathe the fumes from pipes that collect and burn off methane gas produced from the decomposing garbage beneath them. And they spend hours bending over, racing to avoid the vehicular traffic, and carrying heavy loads.

'Jardim Gramacho is a hell,' a friend from Rio told me.

Indeed, the most common reaction to my research that I have received – a reaction to the idea of people sorting through refuse for a living – is shock, disgust and horror. As the brief description of working conditions on the dump suggests, there is certainly much to be said about the struggles and suffering of *catadores* (as well as their pleasures, desires and life projects), both on and off the dump. However, this reaction rarely opens up to a discussion of what the struggles of *catadores* actually are and mean to them, but instead centres on a sensationalized image of people working in garbage. In this image, the garbage dump becomes a sign of social exclusion and social misery par excellence. *Catadores* become victims, the poor left out and left behind in the global capitalist economy. And their work of reclaiming value from waste becomes nothing more than a strategy of survival.

In this chapter, I am interested in exploring and unsettling the associations often made between garbage and marginality. In his insightful discussion on the stigmatization of scavenging, Joshua Reno notes that the news media 'often uses scavenging as an index of global inequality' (2009: 32). Many times during my fieldwork journalists came to Jardim Gramacho not to cover a story about *catadores*, but to report on a health or social issue related to urban poverty in Rio. Scenes of *catadores* racing after an unloading truck or trudging through mud with a barrel of plastics became the backdrop, the illustration of their

7.1 *Catadores* scramble to collect plastics as a tractor-trailer unloads a mound of waste

report on unemployment, poor health conditions or newly released poverty statistics.

I am especially concerned, however, with tacit associations of garbage and marginality in new theoretical approaches in the sociology and anthropology of urban poverty. In recent years, studies of urban poverty have revived the concept of marginality, or adopted the related term social exclusion, as a way to capture the impacts of neoliberal capitalism on social inequalities and social suffering in cities of both the global North and South (Caldeira 2009). Much of this literature argues that there is something qualitatively different and more severe about conditions of urban poverty in the neoliberal age. Loïc Wacquant has argued that 'advanced marginality', defined as the 'novel regime of sociospatial relegation and exclusionary closure', differs from the marginality of the 1960s and 1970s in that urban poor are now for the first time completely severed from the life of the city: from wage labour employment, public services and associational life, and state protection (1996, 2007, 2008). Studies of urban poverty in other parts of the world have similarly argued that the urban poor today are excluded, disconnected, cut off, relegated or in exile (see Auyero 1999; Escorel 1999).

Seeking to draw attention to the exclusion of the urban poor, this literature has often turned to metaphors of waste, remnants and residue. No longer integrated into the formal economy or the state through public services, the urban poor are described as 'redundant' (Wacquant 2008: 266), a 'surplus humanity' (Davis 2004: 23–7), 'super-fluous' (Escorel 1999), and even 'human waste' (Bauman 2004, 1998). Here, rather than garbage signalling marginality, marginality becomes understood in the metaphor of waste.

This conceptualization of urban poverty, of course, is not entirely new. Marx and Engels defined their concept of the lumpenproletariat as both the 'refuse of all classes' (Marx 1963 [1852]: 75) and as a mass 'living on the crumbs of society' (Marx 1964 [1895]: 50). While recent literature on marginality and social exclusion does not share the same disparaging attitudes towards the urban poor as found in Marx and Engels's writings on the lumpenproletariat, it retains the sense of the lumpenproletariat as those left behind by economic development or the poor who are no longer productive or functional in the capitalist economy. Philippe Bourgois and Jeff Schonberg, for example, make this very distinction in their explicit adoption of the term *lumpen* to theo-rize the subjectivity of homeless heroin addicts in San Francisco: 'To understand the human cost of neoliberalism in the twentieth century, we are resurrecting Marx's structural sense of the lumpen as a vulner-able population that is produced at the interstices of transitioning modes of production. We do not, however, retain his dismissive and moralizing use of the term *lumpen*' (Bourgois and Schonberg 2009: 18).

Jardim Gramacho is a site in which the associations of garbage with marginality take on double significance. Brazilian historian Marlucia Santos de Souza (2002) has called Duque de Caxias, where Jardim Gramacho is located, 'the periphery of the periphery of the city of Rio de Janeiro'. The few studies of urban poverty in Rio that include Duque de Caxias or other peripheral cities of the metropolitan region have noted that these areas are far worse than many *favelas* in the South and North Zones of Rio in terms of employment opportunities, housing and living conditions, sanitation, health indices and homicide rates (Alves 1998; Goldstein 2003; Perlman 2004, 2010). Most *catadores* are not originally from Jardim Gramacho, but have come from across the entire metropolitan area of Rio to be able to make a living by collecting on the dump and, for some, to be able to build a house of reclaimed construction debris on invaded swamp land at the edge of the neighbourhood. It is easy to view Jardim Gramacho as a dumping ground for Rio's poor.

The 8,000 tons of waste that pour into Jardim Gramacho each day further stigmatize this community as a place of marginality and *marginais*, a derogatory term in Brazil for the non-working poor: beggars, drug addicts and criminals. Glória, a *catadora* who had worked in Jardim Gramacho since she was eleven years old, loved to tell a story about a time two fairly high-ranking gangsters from a neighbouring *favela* came to Jardim Gramacho to hide out during a police invasion of their headquarters. 'It happened to rain,' Glória said, laughing, 'and they spent four days cursing the fucking mud that destroyed their brand-name shoes and cursing Jardim Gramacho as a place that could only be for beggars.'

In what follows, I tell three stories that challenge this image of Jardim Gramacho. Because much of the recent literature on urban poverty suggests that today's urban poor are excluded economically, politically and socially and constitute a residual class that is superfluous to the global capitalist economy, I have chosen stories that reveal Jardim Gramacho's connections to the world beyond its muddy streets. I begin with the history of the neighbourhood. Tracing the story of how Jardim Gramacho was transformed from a small fishing community to the primary waste disposal site for the metropolitan area of Rio, I show how this history unfolded at the intersection of large-scale rural–urban migration, Rio de Janeiro's industrialization and the strategic interests of Brazil's military dictatorship. I then examine more recent linkages between Jardim Gramacho and the surrounding metropolitan area through a story of inter-municipal battles in which Jardim Gramacho has taken centre stage. Finally, I turn to the work of *catadores*. Through an analysis of the impact of the 2008 global economic crisis on *catadores*, I examine how the materials that *catadores* collect integrate them into national and global industries and show how *catadores* understand their everyday labour as part of global processes and events. I conclude by arguing that waste has not marginalized Jardim Gramacho, but has rather been the medium through which this community has forged local and global ties.

Part 1: The perils of social inclusion

Origins and memories

'Jardim Gramacho was a paradise.'

Deca, a bar owner on the main road through the neighbourhood, Avenida Monte Castelo, told me this as he uncapped a bottle of beer. 'This road was just a dirt path when I came to Jardim Gramacho. I think my house might have been the seventy-eighth in the whole neighbourhood. We were surrounded by natural springs and fruit trees and when the tide came in, pools formed where we would go swimming. The pools were full of fish, and it was easy to catch crabs among the mangroves.'

I asked Deca what it was like when the garbage began arriving in Jardim Gramacho, whether Rio's waste management company, Comlurb, had informed the residents, and what they had thought about this change to their neighbourhood.

'They told us that Monte Castelo would be paved. We were told about the dump, but none of us knew to what extent the garbage would affect our lives.' Deca spoke deliberately. His words weighed heavily, as if laden with silent meaning, with sadness or perhaps *saudades*, the bittersweet remembering of something loved and lost.

'Did you know my wife?' Deca asked me. 'Did you arrive here before she died?'

I shook my head, but told him how often I had heard others in Jardim Gramacho speak of his wife's kindness.

'She had breast cancer,' he continued.

We fought it. We did the mastectomy and the reconstructive surgery. After five years, the cancer came back. When it comes back, there is nothing to be done. There are so many diseases in Jardim Gramacho. Cancers. Tuberculosis. Skin diseases. Other horrible diseases. I think that it is the garbage. The dust that we breathe in Jardim Gramacho is dust like no other dust, a dust that comes off the garbage trucks on their way to the dump. The leachate drips from the trucks on to our streets. All this toxicity causes these diseases.

Like Deca, other residents who lived in Jardim Gramacho prior to the inauguration of the dump described the neighbourhood as a place with dozens of natural springs, bordered by a mangrove swamp teeming with fish that entered from the Bay of Guanabara to lay their eggs. 'There were many people who used to fish inside here,' Seu Edmo, another long-time resident of Jardim Gramacho, told me. 'The mangrove swamp was rich with fish, with crabs, all kinds of shellfish. This was not a place of misery. Only if a person was lazy and did not have the disposition to fish. I would have to dry the fish I caught on my tin roof, because I didn't have a refrigerator and I caught too many for my family to eat, too many even for my neighbours.' Like Deca, other original settlers spoke of the degradation that the garbage brought to Jardim Gramacho and the ways the waste intimately touched their lives. 'I used to wake up to the smell of green foliage,' recalled Dona Ani, 'but then the garbage trucks began arriving, a truck with a dead horse or a truck dripping with rotten water, and that stench remains on the street.'

Jardim Gramacho and the Baixada Fluminense: a brief history The story of how Jardim Gramacho became the destination of Rio's refuse begins with the history of the Baixada Fluminense and Rio de Janeiro's urban development. The Baixada Fluminense generally refers to the lowland area of swamps and flood plains to the north-west of Rio de Janeiro. However, as José Cláudio Souza Alves (1998) illustrates in his political history of violence in the Baixada Fluminense, the Baixada has long been defined by *cariocas* (natives of Rio) not in geographic terms but in social ones: as 'barbarous' (in opposition to 'civilized' Rio de Janeiro), violent, underdeveloped and poor. Several scholars have noted that journalists reporting shootings or other violent crimes in a neighbourhood within the City of Rio have often mistakenly reported the location as the Baixada Fluminense (ibid.: 14; Marques 2006: 9).

In the eighteenth and nineteenth centuries, the Baixada Fluminense consisted of large plantations that cultivated sugar cane, rice, corn and beans (Ferreira 1957: 255). The Baixada's rivers also served as transportation routes between the inland gold mining region and the ports of Rio de Janeiro (Pires Junior and Santos de Souza 1996). However, beginning in the mid-nineteenth century, intensive logging destroyed much of the original forest of the Baixada, leading to increased flooding, pools of stagnant water, the proliferation of miasmas and malarial mosquitoes, and a general impoverishment of the region. Many residents abandoned the area. The population of Duque de Caxias, for example, fell from 10,542 inhabitants in 1872 to 800 inhabitants by 1910 (Beloch 1986: 22, cited by Cantalejo 2008: 22). Similar environmental and health problems are still common today in Jardim Gramacho. Parts of the neighbourhood lie below sea level; any rain turns dirt paths into rivers of mud and floods shacks built at the lowest points. Mosquitoes are so prevalent in Jardim Gramacho that one of the subsections of the neighbourhood, Maruim, is named after a type of small mosquito that thickens the air at dusk.

The founding of the National Factory of Motors (FNM) in Duque de Caxias in 1943 began a rapid transformation of the region into an urban industrial zone. Financed in part by funds from the USA to help industrial development of its allies during the Second World War, this factory became the first of many to line a newly constructed highway connecting the Baixada to downtown Rio de Janeiro. The Baixada as a location for new factories became an attractive option both because land with abundant fresh water was available there at a short distance from the City of Rio and because government officials of the Baixada welcomed industrial projects in the hope that they would bring urban development and much-needed infrastructure to the region (Cantalejo 2008: 25). As historian Cantalejo describes, the establishment of the Refinery of Duque de Caxias (REDUC) in 1961 provides a prominent example of this drive towards development both in the Baixada and in Brazil as a whole during this time:

> The opening of the refinery in 1961 helped to propagate even further in the region the vision that the city [of Duque de Caxias] was progressing. The country lived the developmentalism of the government of Juscelino Kubitschek, who pursued modernization by speeding up industrialization. This new image was also reinforced in material ways, as the refinery generated new funds for the city's coffers via taxes. (Ibid.: 51)

REDUC, which today produces 242,000 barrels of oil daily, lies only a few kilometres from Jardim Gramacho, making the blue flames of its smokestacks the only thing visible in the darkness of the dump at night.

The FNM, REDUC and other factories that sprang up in the Baixada Fluminense as part of Brazil's planned industrialization had the unintended consequence of building a strong labour movement in the region. Workers in the FNM factory began to unionize in the 1950s, supported by the Metalworkers Union of Guanabara. They organized the first general strike in 1961 for the end of overtime, an increase in salary, and the right to thirty days of vacation time (Santos de Souza 2002: 210–11). Workers at REDUC created the Union of Petroleum Workers and also joined forces with other unions in the region. In addition to the unionization and strikes in Duque de Caxias, food riots (*quebra-quebra*) broke out in the Baixada in 1962 in response to a shortage of rice and beans caused by price wars between producers and the Brazilian federal commission that stipulated prices of foodstuffs. Such events led Brazil's military dictatorship, which took power in 1964, to perceive Duque de Caxias as a union stronghold with communist tendencies that was unruly and explosive (Cantalejo 2008: 92). In 1968, the military dictatorship, citing the presence of the Petrobras oil refinery, declared the city of Duque de Caxias an 'Area of National Security', thereby justifying a takeover of the city government (ibid.: 96–100). The dictatorship governed Duque de Caxias from 1968 to 1985. During this period, Duque de Caxias signed the contract that established the dump in Jardim Gramacho. In other words, it was Brazil's military dictatorship, and not Duque de Caxias as an autonomous *município*, which established Jardim Gramacho as Rio's waste disposal site.

The urbanization of Rio was also a consequence of rural–urban migration in the 1950s–1970s. Land was much cheaper in the Baixada than in the City of Rio de Janeiro; those who still could not afford this land built houses on 'invaded' plots in the Baixada. A railway line connecting the Baixada to downtown Rio made it possible for migrants to live in the Baixada and work in Rio, though this commute was time-consuming, the trains overcrowded and the stations lacking security and known for high rates of armed robbery and violence. The earliest residents of Jardim Gramacho were part of this wave of migration, settling the area in the late 1960s. They were all migrants from other states of Brazil, particularly from the poor, drought-ridden north-east, who came to Rio in search of employment.

In summary, at the time that garbage trucks began arriving in Jardim Gramacho, the neighbourhood consisted of a small community of migrants who had come to the area in search of employment and who had built their homes on available land by a mangrove swamp in the more affordable periphery of Rio. Many subsidized their wages by fishing in the surrounding wetlands at high tide. Though there was no electricity, water, sewerage or paved streets, Jardim Gramacho belonged to a *município* that had the second-highest tax revenue in the entire state, funnelled from the heavy industries that had recently been established there, particularly the oil refinery, REDUC. Efforts to industrialize the Baixada Fluminense were part of the same state-planned developmentalist efforts that inspired the construction of the new capital city of Brasília in the interior of the country in 1960. These industries – both their political-economic importance and the unionization that they initiated – led the military dictatorship to take over the governing of the city of Duque de Caxias for over a decade. It was during this time of the dictatorship's control over Duque de Caxias that the city of Duque de Caxias signed a contract with Rio's waste management company, Comlurb, making Jardim Gramacho the new site of Rio's largest garbage dump. In short, as signalled above, the transformation of Jardim Gramacho from mangrove swamp to garbage dump occurred at the intersection of large-scale rural–urban migration, strategic industrialization and the security interests of Brazil's military dictatorship.

Part 2: At the centre of city politics

Blocking Rio's waste On 21 July 2005, Rio de Janeiro's main newspaper, *O Globo*, published the following letter to the editor: 'The mayor of Duque de Caxias does not want Rio de Janeiro's garbage deposited within his city. Now, imagine if the mayor of Rio prevented Rio's municipal hospitals from receiving residents of Duque de Caxias?'

These two terse lines encapsulate the complex unequal relationship between the cities of Rio de Janeiro and Duque de Caxias and point to the role that Jardim Gramacho has played in the inter-municipal battles of the metropolitan area. The letter appeared during a stand-off between then Caxias mayor Washington Reis and Rio mayor César Maia over maintenance of Monte Castelo Avenue, the access road to the dump in Jardim Gramacho. When Washington Reis took office in January 2005, he gave the City of Rio a period of six months to fix potholes on Monte Castelo created by the passage of heavy eighteen-wheelers to the dump, clean areas surrounding Monte Castelo of debris and dust, and pave an alternative access road that would enable garbage trucks to pass around the neighbourhood rather than cut directly through it. Washington Reis argued that these public works were the responsibility of the City of Rio and Comlurb, because 90 per cent of the waste deposited in Jardim Gramacho comes from the City of Rio. One Caxias city councillor complained to me in an interview, 'It's bad enough that they have to dump their garbage in our backyard; they also insist that they pass right on through our living room.'

The City of Rio did not heed Mayor Reis's demands. In response, on the morning of 18 July 2005, Reis ordered a sign placed at the entrance of Monte Castelo that stated that trucks with three axles were prohibited from using the road, and also sent several municipal police (*guardas municipais*) to enforce this interdiction. The garbage trucks that deliver waste to the dump from Duque de Caxias and from other cities of the Baixada are smaller compactor trucks, whereas most trucks carrying Rio's waste are large semi-trailers that have picked up garbage from transfer stations. The prohibition against trucks with three axles, therefore, kept out Rio's trucks exclusively. Within a few hours, the City of Rio obtained a judicial order requiring the City of Duque de Caxias to reopen Monte Castelo to all trucks. Mayor Reis removed the sign, but then ordered a bulldozer to break up the paved road so that no vehicles could pass. He insisted that this action did not impede Rio's access to the dump, because trucks could use the *via alternativa*, a road that circumvented most of the neighbourhood and which, he argued, was the responsibility of the City of Rio and Comlurb to pave. It happened to rain that day and the couple of eighteen-wheelers that attempted passage on the *via alternativa* sank deep into the mud. In reprisal, the City of Rio, which owns the property of the dump, closed the gates. By early afternoon, no trucks from any of the cities of the metropolitan area were able to deposit garbage on the dump in Jardim Gramacho.

Inter-municipal power struggles This incident is not the only case of disputes between the City of Duque de Caxias and the City of Rio de Janeiro, represented by Comlurb, over the dump in Jardim Gramacho. Five months previously, Comlurb closed the dump for two days in response to a fee of up to R$50 collected by the City of Caxias for each truck entering Jardim Gramacho. That time, the City of Caxias was successful in obtaining a judicial order establishing that any truck had a right to enter the dump, forcing Comlurb to reopen its gates. The former mayor of Caxias, José Camilo Zito dos Santos, who served two terms between 1997 and 2004, also engaged in multiple battles with Comlurb. In response to my astonishment at the bulldozed road, the closed dump, the commotion of dozens of journalists and the arrival of military police, a long-time resident of Jardim Gramacho standing next to me shrugged. 'Oh, this happens all the time, every few months.'

This dispute over the access road to the dump points to the ways that Jardim Gramacho has become a site where power struggles between centre and periphery in Rio's metropolitan area play out. The City of Rio has for decades taken advantage of the cities of the Baixada Fluminense as spaces for less favourable elements of the urban environment. For example, historian Maurício de Abreu (2006: 99) points to a law passed in 1930 that established an 'industrial zone' for the City of Rio as one of the principal causes of the urbanization of the Baixada. According to Abreu, neighbourhoods in the South Zone of Rio fell outside the established industrial zone, forcing the removal of the strong working-class communities and factories of Gávea, Jardim Botânico and Laranjeiras, which today count among the wealthiest neighbourhoods in all of Rio. Industries relocated to northern, poorer neighbourhoods along the Avenida Brasil, an area bordering the Baixada Fluminense, and into Duque de Caxias and other cities of the Baixada. And, as mentioned previously, the Baixada also became home to migrants coming to work in Rio in the 1940s–1960s. Perhaps surprisingly, given the degree of scholarly attention given to Rio's hillside *favelas*,[4] only 12.3 per cent of migrants in the 1940s settled in *favelas* within Rio, the rest finding residence primarily in the Baixada

Fluminense (ibid.: 107). This continued into the 1950s, with roughly half of new migrants settling in the Baixada or in the outskirts of Rio bordering the Baixada (ibid.: 121). As geographer Segradas Soares argued in the 1960s, 'The metropolis *needed* this area [the Baixada] to put its rapidly growing population and to locate its industries' (cited in Abreu 2006: 111, emphasis added).

The disputes between the cities of Rio de Janeiro and Duque de Caxias concerning Jardim Gramacho are therefore part of a larger, historical, ongoing relationship of inequality within the political economy of the metropolitan area. The letter to the editor mentioned at the beginning of this discussion summarizes these politics well through its problematic analogy between the dump located in Duque de Caxias and used by the City of Rio and hospitals located in Rio used by residents of Duque de Caxias. It is no coincidence that the primary garbage dump for the metropolitan area is located in Duque de Caxias, far from the wealthy areas of Rio, while the best hospitals for the metropolitan area are located downtown and in the city's elite South Zone. While some industries located in Duque de Caxias and the Baixada more broadly provide revenue for the city, such as the oil refinery REDUC, in large part the cities of the Baixada bear the brunt of the costs (both financial and environmental) of the industries and services that mostly benefit the City of Rio.

Mayor Washington Reis's efforts to block Rio's access to the dump were a way to expose and contest the City of Rio's exploitation of Duque de Caxias more broadly. It could be argued that the incident served the mayor's own political interests more than the residents of Caxias or Jardim Gramacho specifically, but such an interpretation would fail to account for the ways multiple interests and political differences can intersect in what Anna Tsing (2005) has termed the 'friction' of political encounters. Residents in Jardim Gramacho have long mobilized for improvements in their neighbourhood and for an alternative route to the dump by supporting city council candidates in elections and pressuring city officials to take action vis-à-vis Comlurb on their behalf. When the legal director of Comlurb was interviewed during the dispute over the road access, he stated that the 'City of Rio has made various investments in that region', citing the paving of roads around Avenida Monte Castelo and the building of a school, sports centre and daycare centre in the neighbourhood. Though meagre in comparison to the environmental consequences of the garbage dump in Jardim Gramacho, these examples are nonetheless benefits that residents have acquired through such incidents and through the exposure, debates and political struggles that they spark. *Catadores*, in turn, took advantage of the situation as grounds to meet with Duque de Caxias's Secretary of the Environment and to present not only their complaints about the current situation's impact on their ability to work but also long-term proposals, such as the construction of recycling centres in Duque de Caxias where *catadores* could work after the dump eventually closes.

Thus, far from the image of urban outcasts disconnected from the life of the city, residents and *catadores* of Jardim Gramacho have sought to further their interests by actively participating in the metropolitan area's political battles. These struggles certainly have their origins in deep social inequalities. However, the dispute over road access to the dump, which effectively obstructed waste collection in a city of 7 million people, reminds us that a place deemed remote – spatially, economically and politically – can nonetheless have an impact on the most basic functioning of a city's centre.

Part 3: *Catadores* and the global economic crisis

The work of catadores While battles between mayors over road access to the dump link Jardim Gramacho to the politics of the city, the trucks that leave the neighbourhood laden with bales of neatly pressed cardboard or plastic bottles link Jardim Gramacho to a global recycling industry that generates annually an estimated US$200 billion (BIR 2010). In what follows, I trace these linkages through the story of how the 2008 global economic crisis took shape in Jardim Gramacho. However, to provide context for this story, I first describe briefly the materials that *catadores* reclaim and the organization of their work on the dump.

Catadores differentiate the contents of the 8,000 tons of waste unloaded daily on the dump into four categories: (1) *podrão* (from the root word 'rotten'), that is food; (2) non-food *podrão*; (3) *material* (material); and (4) *lixo* (garbage). The first two categories of *podrão* consist of objects that are retrieved for their use value. *Catadores* frequently find shoes, clothing, books, electronics and household wares that they determine to be still in good condition or repairable. They set these items to the side of their sacks and often gift clothes and shoes of varying sizes to each other. Some *catadores* also reclaim food deemed edible, particularly packaged foods near or just past their expiration date. However, collecting *podrão* is very much a tangential activity to the *catadores*' main work of collecting *material*. This category refers to anything that can be sold depending on the market.

White paper, cardboard, aluminium, scrap metal, PET (polyethylene terephthalate, found in plastic bottles) and plastic film (the plastic of garbage bags and shrink wrap) were the most common materials that filled the sacks of *catadores* during my time in Jardim Gramacho. If one of these materials loses its value in the market, as occurred during the 2008 economic crisis (see below), an object can shift categories. The cardboard box that yesterday was *material* can today be garbage. Thus, contrary to popular images of scavenging as a subsistence activity largely directed towards personal consumption, most of the objects that *catadores* collect are tied to and determined by global markets.

Catadores work autonomously on the dump, meaning that they work for themselves, decide when and how long to work, and decide which recyclables to collect based on their personal preferences and the characteristics of the particular material. Some materials, such as cardboard soaked by the surrounding refuse, is very heavy, while other materials, such as plastic film, are considered to retain the worst stench. Garbage trucks unload on the dump twenty-four hours a day, every day of the week, enabling *catadores* to work at almost any time. At the end of the day or in the early morning, flat-bed trucks from the roughly 140 scrapyards located throughout the neighbourhood arrive at the top of the dump to pick up *catadores'* filled burlap sacks. *Catadores* either sell to these scrap dealers on the spot by the size of the sack or they ride down with the trucks, weigh their material at the scrapyard, and receive payment by the kilogram. The waste management company that operates the dump requires *catadores* to wear a numbered vest to collect on top of the dump and stipulates that they sell to the scrapyard that supplies them with their vest. However, *catadores* regularly circumvent these policies: sharing vests, making duplicates of vests, and hiding from scrap dealers to whom they are supposed to sell. In practice, therefore, *catadores* are generally able to sell to the buyer of their choosing, usually the one offering the best price at that moment.

Of the roughly two thousand *catadores* working on the dump, about fifty sell to a cooperative formed by the Association of Catadores in Jardim Gramacho (ACAMJG) in 2007.[5] Each member of this cooperative collects independently on the dump, but takes their material to ACAMJG's shed, where they sell it jointly at the end of the week. The earnings are divided among members in accordance with the amount of material they contributed. The cooperative takes the place of the scrap dealer and these *catadores* therefore receive higher prices for their recyclables.

7.2 Bales of plastic bottles, after being sorted and pressed at a scrapyard in Jardim Gramacho, leave the neighbourhood for a recycling plant in the south of Brazil

With few exceptions, all the materials that *catadores* sell eventually travel beyond Jardim Gramacho along their own separate trajectories, involving different commodity prices and chains, and production processes that ultimately transform them into yet other commodities. Scrap paper from Jardim Gramacho is transformed primarily into new packaging for products, and though its production is oriented towards national markets, the price of scrap paper in Brazil is tied to virgin pulp exports and varies according to fluctuations in the value of the US dollar. The steel, construction and automotive industries are the principal destinations for scrap metals, including scrap iron, stainless steel, aluminium and copper. Ferrous scrap from Brazil is increasingly exported to China, which surpassed the USA in steel production in 2009 (BIR 2009). Recovered plastics in Brazil are recycled at a number of corporations, many of which are multinationals, which export their products to Mercosul countries, the United States, Europe and parts of Asia. Most recycled plastics enter the textile industry, followed by the construction industry, and are transformed into a wide range of products, including fibre fill for stuffed toys and furniture, automotive carpets and roof linings, and cords used in yachting and water sports.

Crisis and global imaginings Nothing made Jardim Gramacho's ties to global industries more palpable during my fieldwork than the US housing market collapse and financial institution failures in September 2008 and the subsequent global economic crisis. On the morning of 17 September 2008, the day following one of the most severe drops in US stock prices historically, Glória and I stopped at a corner store on our way to the Association of Catadores so that she could buy a packet of cigarettes. The front page of the newspaper *O Dia*, which displayed a large diagram of stock markets around the world that had plummeted the previous day, caught her attention and she added a copy to her purchase. As we walked, Glória began to read the report, adding her own commentary: 'Bovespa fell over four points. Stocks in Petrobras and Vale went down.[6] Vale buys a lot of scrap iron; this means that the price of our scrap iron is going to drop. Plus, a lot of our steel is exported to the United States. If they aren't building anything, they won't need any steel, and that is bad for scrap iron. But the dollar went up against the *real*, so this should mean that there will be more exports of cellulose and the price of cardboard will go up.'

When we arrived at the Association, Glória continued discussing the economic news and the potential effect on the prices of recyclables with another *catador*, João. Throughout the day and throughout the coming months, I overheard numerous conversations among *catadores* and other residents of Jardim Gramacho about the '*crise*', the economic crisis. I learned a great deal about the recycling industry from these discussions. Indeed, as Glória explained to me as we walked to the Association that fateful day in September, the scrap paper industry had been struggling since 2007 when the dollar declined against the *real*, reaching below R$2 to the dollar. This is roughly the point at which it is not economical for the Brazilian pulp industry to export cellulose, resulting in a flood of virgin cellulose in the national market, lowering the demand for scrap paper (Vieira 2008a: 38; 2008b: 46–8). Unfortunately, though the dollar began to rise in September 2008, the demand for packaging dropped off precipitously, sending the scrap paper industry worldwide into near-total collapse (Baxi 2008). By November, the price of cardboard in Jardim Gramacho had declined from 20 cents a kilo (beginning in August) to 14 cents, 10 cents, 7 cents and eventually zero. That is to say, by the end of 2008 there was no longer a market for recovered cardboard. *Catadores* began saying that cardboard, once considered *material*, had become *lixo*, garbage. They began collecting other materials, especially plastics, which retained a relatively high price.

When the news hit of GM's and Chrysler's insolvency, another *catador*, Carlinhos, lamented that the price of scrap aluminium would most certainly fall, given its use in the automotive industry. Eighty-five per cent of scrap aluminium is consumed by the automotive industry (Vieira 2008a: 41). By carnaval, the time of year when *catadores* collect the most aluminium cans, a kilo of aluminium was worth only R$1, compared to the R$4 it had earned during the previous year's carnaval. After interrupting a debate between João and another *catador* concerning the 'normal' end-of-year fall in prices and whether price decreases could be attributed solely to this cycle, João explained that in January and February many of the larger scrap dealers and recycling plants close down for the holidays and routine maintenance and that this causes a small price slump. He had been arguing with his friend that the recent price drops were too great to be accounted for by this annual slump and that a part of the decline had to be caused by the 'crisis'. Not all *catadores* who joined the many conversations about the fall in prices of materials offered as prescient and detailed diagnoses as did Glória, Carlinhos and João. Most conversations made general references to the global economic crisis as a causal factor and some proposed more far-reaching theories, such as one discussion in which a *catador* argued that price declines were a direct result of 'Bush's war in Iraq'. What all of these conversations shared, though, was a sense of global connection, of Jardim Gramacho not as the 'periphery of the periphery', but as a place integral to the workings of a global economy.

Because the range of papers, plastics and metals collected and sold in Jardim Gramacho enter very different industries – from textiles to steel production – tracing all of the economic relations and processes that had an impact on the pricing of each recyclable is far beyond the scope of this chapter. Nonetheless, even the most basic sketch of these economic relations reveals how it would be wrong to interpret the economic activities in Jardim Gramacho in terms of a small-scale, local, informal economy. Many of the objects collected on the dump in Jardim Gramacho eventually travel across Brazil and worldwide, and the fluctuations of the recyclables market in the neighbourhood are linked to fluctuations in various global industries. It is important to remember too that it is not only the case that the global economy influences Jardim Gramacho. Very few cities in Brazil have formal recycling programmes (and those that do often involve the work of cooperativized *catadores*). Yet Brazil recycles more of its consumed aluminium than any other country and more of its plastic (PET) than any other with the exception of Japan.[7] Nearly all of this recycled material results from the work of *catadores*. The recycling industry in Brazil, which supplies raw materials to manufacturers nationally and internationally, depends almost entirely upon *catadores*.

Catadores, as well as scrapyards and repair shops in Jardim Gramacho, struggled financially as a result of the economic crisis. Conversations about prices often carried tones of discouragement and frustration. Zeca, who fixed and sold used refrigerators, replied to my observation that he seemed to have many more refrigerators in his shop than when I had last visited: 'Well, the crisis almost brought an end to this dump. The *catadores* are earning so little and they aren't working as much either. Do you think they are buying my refrigerators? You know, what started this crisis ... People just lost numbers. There is the same food and things in the world. What was lost was numbers. It is a crisis of numbers. And here I am with all these refrigerators.'

However, many conversations about the economic crisis also expressed a sense of connection and revealed how *catadores* imagine themselves and their work as tied into global processes and events. This recognition has deeply shaped the Association of Catadores, which was founded in 2004 by a small group of *catadores* and today is a major organizer in Brazil's National Movement of Catadores. A monthly newsletter that the Association produced in its first two years as a mobilizing technique included the subtitle 'From Jardim Gramacho to the World'. Just as the plastics, metals and cardboard that *catadores* collect travel far beyond Jardim Gramacho, so too do they envision their ideas and political projects as potentially shaping distant worlds.

Conclusion: waste and the making of social relations

The three stories of Jardim Gramacho traced in this chapter – the history of the neighbourhood, the battle over Rio's access to the dump, and the responses of *catadores* to the global economic crisis – illustrate in different ways the complex relationships between urban centres and peripheries. What is certain is that historical processes and more recent effects of neoliberal capitalism have not severed Jardim Gramacho's connections to city politics and global economies, but rather deepened them. This is not to say, however, that these connections are necessarily beneficial for the *catadores* who labour on the dump and for the other residents of Jardim Gramacho who endure the dust, stench and toxic leachate outside their doors. The global economic crisis, much like the residents' stories of a 'paradise lost', reminds us of the detrimental effects that *inclusion* in state politics and the global capitalist economy can have on the lives of the labouring poor.

Critiques of the marginality literature in the 1970s made similar arguments, that urban peripheries were not irrelevant to the metropolis, but rather connected to the centre through relationships of exploitation (see Perlman 1976). Given the renewed attention to concepts of marginality and social exclusion, these arguments are worth repeating. Certainly, conditions are different today in the post-Fordist, neoliberal context. The work of *catadores*, as a form of non-wage labour, is part of a general trend towards the informalization of work in cities of both the global South and North. The loss of wage labour, combined with the reduction of state services, constitute conditions of neoliberal capitalism that recent literature on marginality aims to denounce. However, as the stories of Jardim Gramacho make clear, what has transformed is not the connection/disconnection of the urban poor but rather the ways they are connected – that is, their relationships to forms of governance and capital. *Catadores* do not work as wage labourers in the often idealized Fordist model, but they are nonetheless tied into various global industries through the materials they reclaim and sell. To see the shift from Fordist wage labour to multiple forms of self-employment of the urban poor only in terms of a loss or disconnection prevents an understanding of how relationships of inequality are made and experienced in the urban world today.

Finally, the stories of Jardim Gramacho unsettle associations of waste with marginality. It is not only the case that Jardim Gramacho is connected to the world beyond its borders, but that its connections were often forged through the medium of waste. The garbage trucks that began arriving in the 1970s drew the small fishing community of Jardim Gramacho into the urban development of Rio's metropolitan area. Power struggles over access to the garbage dump have become a means through which *catadores* and residents of Jardim Gramacho have participated in municipal politics and voiced their own claims to city officials. And the objects that *catadores* retrieve from Rio's refuse connect them to global industries. In all of these instances, waste became productive of social relations, both relations of inequality and, as ACAMJ's slogan, 'From Jardim Gramacho to the World', suggests, relations of belonging and solidarity. These ties ultimately point us toward a reconceptualization of waste as not only decay, death and loss, but also as raw material, potential and possibility.

Notes

1 The amount of waste deposited in Jardim Gramacho has since reached 8,000 tons daily.

2 This refers to Portaria no. 53/59 of Brazil's National Council on the Environment, the Conselho Nacional do Meio Ambiente, CONAMA (Nascimento 2008).

3 See the federal law Lei no. 4.771, passed on 15 September 1965.

4 Janice Perlman (2010: 40) critiques what she sees as an overproduction of studies on the hillside, more 'picturesque' *favelas* near the South Zone (the wealthiest area) of Rio, whereas *favelas* in the North and West zones and in the Baixada Fluminense remain relatively unstudied.

5 Explanations for why most *catadores* have not become members of ACAMJG's cooperative extend beyond the scope of this chapter. However, a few reasons include weekly (versus daily) payments and a reluctance to adapt to some of ACAMJG's rules and leadership.

6 Bovespa is the São Paulo Stock Exchange. Petrobras is Brazil's largest semi-public oil company. Vale, founded in the Brazilian mining region of Minas Gerais, is one of the largest mining companies in the world and a leader in iron ore production.

7 In 2008, Brazil recycled 91.5 per cent of its consumed aluminium, compared to 90.8 per cent for Argentina, 87.3 per cent for Japan and 54.2 per cent for the United States (ABAL 2010). Brazil recycled 54.8 per cent of its consumed PET compared with 69.2 per cent for Japan and 27.0 per cent for the United States (ABIPET 2008).

References

ABAL (Associação Brasileira do Alumínio) (2010) *Números de Reciclagem*, www.abal.org.br/industria/estatisticas_recicla_latas. asp, accessed 3 August 2010.

ABIPET (Associação Brasileira da Indústria do PET) (2008) *Quinto Censo da Reciclagem de PET no Brasil*.

Abreu, M. de (2006) *A Evolução Urbana do Rio de Janeiro*, Rio de Janeiro: IPP.

Alves, J. C. S. (1998) *Baixada Fluminense: A Violência na Construção do Poder*, São Paulo: Universidade de São Paulo.

Auyero, J. (1999) 'The hypershantytown: ethnographic portraits of neo-liberal violence(s)', *Ethnography*, 1(1): 93–116.

Bauman, Z. (1998) *Work, Consumerism, and the New Poor*, Buckingham: Open University Press.

— (2004) *Wasted Lives: Modernity and Its Outcasts*, Cambridge: Polity Press.

Baxi, R. (2008) *Annual Report*, Bureau of International Recycling.

Beloch, I. (1986) *Capa Preta e Lurdinha: Ténorio e o Povo da Baixada*, São Paulo: Record.

BIR (Bureau of International Recycling) (2009) *Annual Report*, Bureau of International Recycling Annual Report.

— (2010) *The Industry*, www.bir.org/industry/, accessed 30 July 2010.

Bourgois, P. and J. Schonberg (2009) *Righteous Dopefiend*, Berkeley: University of California Press.

Caldeira, T. P. R. (2009) 'Marginality, again?!', *International Journal of Urban and Regional Research*, 33(3): 848–53.

Cantalejo, M. H. de S. (2008) *O Município de Duque de Caxias e a*

Ditadura Militar, 1964–1985, Master's dissertation, Postgraduate Social History Programme, Rio de Janeiro: Universidade Federal do Rio de Janeiro.

Davis, M. (2004) 'Planet of slums: urban involution and the informal proletariat', *New Left Review*, 26: 5–34.

Escorel, S. (1999) *Vidas ao Léu: Trajetórias de Exclusão Social*, Rio de Janeiro: Editora Fiocruz.

Ferreira, J. P. (1957) *Enciclopédia dos Municípios Brasileiros*, vol. 22, Rio de Janeiro: IBGE.

Goldstein, D. M. (2003) *Laughter Out of Place: Race, Class, Violence, and Sexuality in a Rio Shantytown*, Berkeley: University of California Press.

Marques, A. dos S. (2006) 'Baixada Fluminense: da conceituação às problemáticas sociais contemporâneas', *Revista Pilares da História*, 4(6): 7–16.

Marx, K. (1963 [1852]) *The Eighteenth Brumaire of Louis Bonaparte*, New York: International Publishers.

— (1964 [1895]) *Class Struggles in France (1848–1850)*, New York: International Publishers.

Nascimento, V. B. do (2008) *Estudo de Caso: Análise da Remediação Ambiental do Aterro Metropolitano de Gramacho-RJ*, Master's thesis, Escola Nacional de Saúde Pública Sergio Arouca, Rio de Janeiro: Fiocruz.

Peres, G. (2007) 'Mercado negro, escravidão e liberdade', *Revista Pilares da História*, 6(7): 26–31.

Perlman, J. (1976) *The Myth of Marginality: Urban Poverty and Politics in Rio de Janeiro*, Berkeley: University of California Press.

— (2004) 'Marginality: from myth to reality in the favelas of Rio de Janeiro', in A. Roy and N. AlSayyad (eds), *Urban Informality: Transnational Perspectives from the Middle East, Latin America, and South Asia*, Lanham, MD: Lexington Books, pp. 105–46.

— (2010) *Favela: Four Decades of Living on the Edge in Rio de Janeiro*, Oxford: Oxford University Press.

Pires Junior, R. and M. Santos de Souza (1996) 'Terras de muitas aguas', in *Socializando a Produção Escrita*, Duque de Caxias: Papelaria Itatiaia.

Reno, J. (2009) 'Your trash is someone's treasure: the politics of value at a Michigan landfill', *Journal of Material Culture*, 14(1): 29–46.

Santos de Souza, M. (2002) *Escavando o Passado da Cidade: A Construção do Poder Político Local em Duque de Caxias, 1900–1964*, Niterói: Universidade Federal Fluminense.

Tsing, A. L. (2005) *Friction: An Ethnography of Global Connection*, Princeton, NJ: Princeton University Press.

Vieira, S. (2008a) 'Os efeitos da crise mundial no setor de reciclagem', *Revista Reciclagem Moderna*, 13: 36–45.

— (2008) 'Papel: o último a sair apaga a luz?', *Revista Reciclagem Moderna*, 13: 46–8.

Wacquant, L. (1996) 'The rise of advanced marginality: notes on its nature and implications', *Acta Sociologica*, 39: 121–39.

— (2007) 'Territorial stigmatization in the age of advanced marginality', *Thesis Eleven*, 91: 66–77.

— (2008) *Urban Outcasts: A Comparative Sociology of Advanced Marginality*, Cambridge: Polity Press.

8 | Sympathy and its boundaries: necropolitics, labour and waste on the Hooghly river

LAURA BEAR

Necropolitics on the Hooghly river

This chapter examines a neglected aspect of biopolitics that I polemically call necropolitics. Necropolitics are the ethics that frame responses to the processes of decline and death that are inherent to capitalism and inevitable to life. Within this ethics, the physical signs of deterioration in objects, landscapes and humans and the destruction wrought by capitalism are selectively related to each other and demarcated as evidence of waste. This decay points to the necessity of further productive action. The act of labour is then an attempt to assert the creativity of human work against forces of decline. This necropolitics is visceral and affective because it links the reality of processes of decay in the world to the problem of regenerating economic life. It is often founded on theories of how animating forces inhabit the material world and how labour engages with these. It draws on diverse idioms of kinship, ritual and economics in order to locate waste and its antithesis, productivity.

My use of the term necropolitics brings into dialogue two of the most influential approaches to neoliberalism. Work is separated between that which explores the new forms of life it produces and that which addresses its destructive effects. Authors influenced by Foucault argue that it is the sustenance of life which provides legitimacy for both the state and the market within economic governance (Rose and Novas 2005; Lakoff and Collier 2004). Others have argued that neoliberalism is a new version of the creative destruction of capitalism that produces decline and accumulation by dispossession (Ferguson 2006; Harvey 2006). To explore necropolitics as I do here is to trace the attempts within biopolitics to recuperate its foundational remainder. This is both death itself and the forms of destruction neoliberal practices produce. My approach here is provoked by Veblen's definition of waste as expenditure, objects and forms of productivity that work against 'an enhancement of life and well-being'. But it is also grounded in the explanations of river workers and users of recent changes to the waterscape of the Hooghly in Kolkata. My overall point is that we cannot explain the resilience of utopian expectations of neoliberalism unless we examine the ethical framings of decline within which the creative destruction it produces are understood.

The banks of the Hooghly river in Kolkata are crowded with the corrosive effects of contemporary capitalism – derelict warehouses, ruined port quarters and rusting vessels. Newspaper articles frequently report rising silt levels that threaten trade and prevent the entry of ships to the docks at Kolkata and Haldia. Public debate frames these physical signs as evidence that decay threatens the circulations of rejuvenating life between the city, its citizens and the river. These discussions draw on a background sense of the river as the goddess *Ma Ganga* to make civic claims. In Bengali popular Hinduism and common speech the Hooghly is the Ganges and is strongly associated with *Ma Ganga*, who brings life to a world filled with polluting death (Ostor 1980). Public speculation about the decay along the Hooghly engages with the paradox that a life-giving deified river is dying. This trope has a long history in West Bengal. It was first proposed in 1937 in the environmental nationalism of Radhakamal Mukherjee, who argued that the Ganges in Bengal was declining because of silting caused by human activity.

In this debate people are most concerned by three kinds of waste: silting, human detritus and a waterfront that is empty of productive human exchanges with the river. Silting is widely attributed to a single cause, the immersion of thousands of idols at the end of the autumn *Durga puja* festival. The attribution of the decline of the river to these corpse-like forms condenses the sense that it is being overwhelmed by polluting death. People also frequently complain about deposits of human rubbish and industrial ruins that prevent them from taking the *gun* or qualities of the river. They suggest that the banks are *phaka* or empty of activity, useless and unproductive. These concerns were voiced to me across classes, including by the poor and sex workers

who live on the banks of the river. Environmental activists and architects campaign to reverse the decline of the river in ways that draw
on these popular concerns. Prominent figures such as Subhas Dutta
mount public interest litigation campaigns to the Kolkata High Court
demanding that the state Kolkata Port Trust clear rubbish, plant trees
and that immersion should be banned. Journalists follow these leads,
pressing for rubbish clearance, responsible immersion practices and
redevelopment of the waterfront.

Importantly these discussions assume that the processes of decay
are due to the negligence of state agencies, especially the Kolkata
Port Trust. There is also an assumption that their reversal can arise
only from the productivity of private enterprise. I will show in this
chapter that this public debate is one of several ethical accounts of
decay on the Hooghly that occlude the connections between private
capital and public deficit that have generated this waterscape. Each
of these ethical accounts attributes decay in a manner that cuts the
networks through which public and private economies are mutually
produced on the river. The conversions that objects, men and capital
undergo as they move along these networks are described as radically
altering their essences. These conversions on the margins of public
and private create the appearance of distinctions between two separate
domains of generative activity. In this chapter I will focus on the accounts of decay given by the men whose lives have been most affected
by changes on the river and whose actions contribute to its current
form. These are the officers in the marine department and business
entrepreneurs whose practices create the waterscape other inhabitants
of Kolkata seek to explain.

Senses of workmanship: labour, vitality and waste

My approach to the necropolitics of port officers and entrepreneurs rests on a critical reading of Veblen. In the 1910s–1920s Veblen
mounted a campaign against conspicuous consumption among the
American middle classes and the dominance of finance capitalists over
production. Veblen drew on contemporary debates among engineers
about scientific management to mount a broad attack against waste.
He found evidence of waste in non-utilitarian practices and objects.
These ranged from the middle-class housewife (who he argued existed
simply to 'adorn' the house) to craft pieces and the leisure classes as
a whole. In his work the attempts by engineers to introduce measures
of workplace efficiency that focused on productive potential rather
than financial profit were turned into a universal natural sense. This

transformation was achieved by his coining of the concept of the sense of workmanship. He argued this sense was biologically universal and neurologically traceable, but that it was particularly developed among engineers and working men. It should be, he argued, 'the court of final appeal in any question of economic truth or adequacy'. It, he suggested, 'disposes men to look with favour upon productive efficiency and on whatever is of human use. It disposes them to deprecate waste of substance or effort.' Veblen later argued that a utopian future could be created only if a soviet of engineers and workmen were in charge. His project was guided by the ethical question of whether work and technology 'serves directly to enhance human life on the whole – whether it furthers the life process'. Veblen's coining of the sense of workmanship out of debates among engineers alerts us to the various ethical projects within the industrial production process that define the forces of life and their counterpoints in waste. It also demonstrates that waste is the signifier through which people, including Veblen, attempt to explain the negative effects of capitalism. In Veblen's necropolitics a utilitarian sense of workmanship is a 'natural' solution to the problems of waste in capitalism. In the analysis that follows I examine the equivalent senses of workmanship and their associated necropolitics among marine officers and private entrepreneurs.

Importantly the various senses of workmanship I identify include evaluations of the connections between productive life forces and the vitality of objects. They rest on assumptions about the relationship between the material, the immanent and the transcendent. In acts of labour, technologies are experienced as related forms of life, repositories of workers' energies and as manifestations of fertile forces (Bennett 2001). The polyvalence of labour explored here shows that a singular management-speak of capitalist utility has not colonized notions of work and selfhood (Cosin-Jimenez 2008). Instead there are contemporary ethics of capitalism that are as potentially multiplex as those recorded for craft and small-scale family production (Venkatesan 2010; Dilley 2010; Simpson 2006; Hertzfeld 2004; Yanagisako 2002). Veblen allows us to conceptualize how we might explore this terrain, but we must also move beyond him. We need to focus on multiple senses of workmanship and how they create conceptual cuts in the fluid flows of capital between public and private that are central to the implementation of neoliberalism. To understand this process on the Hooghly river it is first necessary to explain the structural connections between public and private economies here. These have emerged from changing practices of public sector deficit policy during liberalization in India.

Neoliberalism, public deficit and private enterprise on the Hooghly

Since the 1990s the Kolkata Port Trust has devolved the realization of its schemes to private networks of entrepreneurs, brokers and informal labour. This is a situation similar to the processes of government outsourcing over the past twenty years in Britain and the United States. On the Hooghly these measures have created a coexistence of state and private sector enterprise and the extraction of value with low levels of infrastructure investment. Levels of trade have remained high; for example, in 2008/09 the absolute volume of cargo moving along the Hooghly was the third highest among the Indian ports. Yet this work is supported by decaying equipment and informalized labour. This derelict but productive industrial landscape is a valuable microcosm for exploring necropolitics within neoliberalism.

The variant of neoliberal policy practised here shares many features with its form elsewhere in its privileging of private enterprise and of governance beyond the state (Swyngedouw 2005; Hibou 2004). Yet it has been driven by a dynamic that has affected Europe and America only since 2008 as a result of First World sovereign debt crises. This is the increasing financialization of public sector debt, the emergence of an extractive central state and policy driven by the threat of recurrent fiscal crisis. Accounts of liberalization in India generally trace the impact of new capital flows and changes in the private sector following the deal made by the central government with the International Monetary Fund (IMF) for a $1.2 billion loan to cover severe fiscal deficit in 1991. Less attention has been given to changes in the fiscal regimes of public sector institutions that sought to draw money back to central budgets in order to pay IMF and other loans. The Ministry of Surface Transport had long been in a theoretical creditor relationship with the Calcutta Port, but in the 1990s it started to extract revenue from it by demanding repayment on loans that had been in permanent moratorium. A previous generation of social investment was transformed into a fiscal debt. In addition, the ministry greatly reduced public subsidies, especially those for dredging. It also pushed the port into funding itself by taking loans from other ports, national and foreign banks at commercial rates of interest. As a result the port trust was plunged into decision-making entirely driven by financial crisis in spite of its high levels of trade. It has reduced its permanent workforce since 1990 by two-thirds to 11,514 employees. The work of cargo-loading, ship repair and marine crew was outsourced to contractual day labour operating without unions or legal protection. These processes have taken on greater urgency since 2000 when the port experienced the most severe crisis in its history. A permanent hiring freeze was introduced. Anything that could be sold off was auctioned. All new infrastructure projects were discontinued. Repair of vessels and equipment halted and the ship-repairing department was closed. Men in the marine department watched as old forms of productivity were dismantled around them, and they were also agents in this process.

These developments created new forms of private enterprise on the Hooghly. A cluster of small family firms and labour brokers expanded their activities. They took up the work of maintenance on the river using adapted versions of technologies sold off by the port trust and other state agencies. Typical of these companies is India Private Ltd. It is a family firm run by the four Jaiswal brothers. It began as a jute transportation company in the 1950s under the great-grandfather of the current owners. It expanded into the midstream unloading of ships into barges in the 1960s–1970s. Until 2000 it was employed by the American Western Steamship Company to bring containers on barges into the docks. This work disappeared owing to the decline in central government funding which led to a reduction in the depth of the Hooghly and the ageing of dock infrastructure. But since 2000 India Private Ltd has become one of the many firms along the Hooghly that provides the port with low-cost solutions to the problems created by lack of public investment. For example, it was commissioned to produce low-tech dredging equipment and a virtual dock made of giant buoys. Using the expertise and prestige gained from these projects India Private Ltd bought vessels from state agencies and adapted them to the needs of clients. The firm expands and contracts its informal, non-unionized workforce according to projects. The prosperity of companies such as India Private Ltd emerges directly from state action.

Over the past twenty years there has been a systematic centripetal and centrifugal redistribution of the fixed capital and surplus value of labour generated in the port trust. The centrifugal redistribution has been to the central government and private banks, which claim the surplus value created by labour on the river in the repayment of loans. This includes the labour of informal workers in private firms on the river, who now often work indirectly for the state (Bear forthcoming). The centripetal redistribution has been through contractual payments and the transfer of technological objects into private sector companies. Yet, as I will show in the next section, these interconnections between public and private economies are occluded by the two entirely distinct senses of workmanship and necropolitics that exist among the marine department officers and in India Private Ltd. These senses of workmanship contain different explanations for the misfortune of decline and are based on contrary temporal structures. Men in the marine department emphasize the necessity of reviving a past of skill. In India Private Ltd future-oriented innovations are valued. These ethics in combination with the centrifugal and centripetal flows of capital produce the waterscape of the Hooghly. They fill it with the tangible, but misleading, material signs of a state that produces decay and a separate private sector that innovatively generates prosperity from old state objects.

A state ethics of preservation: *Ma Ganga*, pedigrees of skill and the marine department of the Kolkata Port

Men in the marine department claimed a strong affective relationship with the technologies that they patched and preserved. Many of them had personal archives of these technologies in their homes in the form of collections of old photographs, objects and documents. The most active among them had enthusiastically sent items to the archive that the port trust was setting up. Captain Reddy, the harbourmaster of the Kolkata Port, was exemplary of this ethic. He often described the docks as a 'living museum' and himself as a 'keeper' of its objects. Captain Reddy, like many of his fellow marine officers, was a product of two generations of working-class state employment. He had grown up in state railway colonies in Bihar, where his father was a railway mechanic. He joined the port in 1973 as a trainee pilot. He became a river pilot and in 1991 rose to assistant mooring master. He was commander of the pilot vessel from 1992 to 1997. He has been harbourmaster since 2000. His daily work was a calculation of how many risks he could take with the decaying infrastructure of reduced manning, decrepit tugs, lock gates and launches, and declining river depth without any major accidents taking place. He often took to the river, piloting ships, because of the shortage of pilots. From 2000 he had also implemented the hiring freezes, cutbacks, sales of vessels and introduction of contractual work among the marine crew. He was now at the centre of discussions about whether river pilots should also be placed on contracts. He was instrumental in arranging deals with private firms such as India Private Ltd and was close to men such as the Jaiswal brothers.

Captain Reddy's location at the heart of networks of outsourcing and his control of a declining infrastructure were accompanied by an intense enthusiasm for the port's material objects. In a manner characteristic of all the marine department officers, Captain Reddy was passionate about the heritage of the docks that he saw as alive in these objects. They evoked for him a living link to old technical knowledge of the river. They were solidified skill that needed to be preserved. Most of all they manifested the specialized sense of workmanship that was necessary to carry out productive acts on the river. If they decayed then this essential knowledge would be lost as well. Importantly such an assertion was also a claim about how necessary men such as himself who knew how to maintain these objects were to the business of the state on the river. The patching of objects was not merely a strategy to reduce public deficit for officers in the marine department, it was an assertion of the unique value of their own knowledge in a time of intense insecurity. Their own vitality was inextricably linked to that of the objects in their care. For them these machines were manifestations of living labour and of the vitality of men who had worked before them in the port.

Captain Reddy described this link through time between the labour of past and present state employees materialized in machines as the 'pedigree' of the port that you had to know in 'order to build a future'. This he understood as a projection of a lineage link back in time founded originally on a group of brothers, in the same way as he had calculated his own family history back four generations to two brothers from a village in Andhra Pradesh. His collection of old photographs of the industrial Hooghly manifested for him a visceral sign of this continuity. Captain Reddy had made a special compilation of photographs on his work computer that underlined this deep history. For each old image of a technological feat on the river he had taken a recent picture of the same place that replicated the vista of the historical one. He displayed these to visitors to the office one after the other, creating an effect that encouraged the viewer to project connections between the past and the present. The solidified pedigree of objects had also been activated to transfer what officers called the 'marine spirit' to new recruits. In particular, when the port began to recruit university graduates rather than ship apprentices as pilots in the late 1980s they set up training ships for them in Kolkata. These were two ancient paddle steamers on which obsolete technologies of the port were displayed. When the financial crisis in 2000 ended their upkeep the marine officers successfully campaigned for their exhibits to be included in the shipping section of the newly built Science City.

This tender care for objects was manifest in more practical forms in daily work. The work of preservation had intensified over the past ten years as infrastructure investment ended. Marine officers had to act vigilantly to maintain their means of production to guarantee their own continuing employment. For example, Captain Reddy's daily routine now involved monitoring of repair and watching for decay. Take, for example, one of the days I was in the Subhas Chandra Bose docks with him. Here a collapsing clock tower overlooks ruined warehouses and a slow queue of trucks loads containers. As usual container ships from Singapore and Sri Lanka were being offloaded. In the lock a port dredger, the *Subharnrekha*, was stalled because the gates had jammed owing to corrosion. Reddy spoke at length to the team attempting to fix them before ships started arriving on the next high tide at 4.30 p.m. He then went to oversee the dry dock, where a dredger was being repaired by contractual workers. Captain Reddy took me on to his next project – the swing bridge into the Subhas Chandra Bose docks, which he was repairing after years of disuse. A few men lifted mud and repaired its cracks with blow torches. Captain Reddy became enthusiastic as he spoke of the engineers who had built the bridge years ago and how he was reviving their achievements.

Captain Reddy and his fellow marine officers had recently affiliated their sense of workmanship to the ethics of regeneration associated with Hindu ritual practice. In 2006 Captain Reddy and his fellow officers had inaugurated the annual worship in June of the goddess *Ma Ganga* on the site of their old apprentices' boarding house. Until then a *puja* to her had been carried out only by the low-ranking marine crews on the dock waterfront. *Ma Ganga* is usually worshipped by low-caste boatmen, but the marine crew in the 1960s adapted the *puja* to their industrial labour. The marine officers were making further use of the ritual drawing on its structure of regeneration. *Ma Ganga* is a goddess who brings life to a world filled with polluting death. Her rituals and myth follow the classic form of cosmogony associated with Hindu ritual practice. Bhagirath and the sage Johumuni call *Ma Ganga* to earth to restore the life of Bhagirath's ancestors, who had been burnt to death in anger by another sage. She is controlled in her descent by the god Siva because otherwise her force would be destructive. The *puja* to *Ma Ganga* re-enacts this descent of the regenerating force of the Ganga. The imagery of the statue also shows the moment when Bhagirath and Johumuni, with their combined ritual acts, called her to earth to renew life. The power (*shakti*) of the goddess then regenerates the community that together eats her *prasad* (food offerings made auspicious by the goddess's consumption). As in other public *pujas* and domestic worship in Bengal, exchanges of life-giving forces are set in motion by acts of ritual labour on material substances. But the worship of *Ma Ganga* particularly underlines a mutual labour of renewal between worshippers and the goddess that fills the material world with life.

These meanings for the ritual were articulated by the marine officers on the day of the *puja*. But they linked them to the necessity of their skilled acts of labour to the renewal of the productivity of *Ma Ganga*. The place the marine officers had chosen for the celebration of the *puja* connected their ritual labour to their work and its time-honed skills. It was the garden of the unused quarters where they had all lived as trainee pilots. Many of the officers reminisced about their apprenticeship. They also talked about how wonderful it was to see the place filled with life again by the *puja* after so many years. As the day progressed men grew more expansive about the ritual. They said it showed their 'respect' for the river as a dangerous force that had to be mastered by marine skills, just as Siva had controlled the Ganga's force as she fell to earth. They said the *puja* was celebrated because there had been recent accidents on the river. These were attributed to the lack of marine training of the younger pilots. Conversations then circled around the inadequate knowledge of these younger river pilots, and the plans of the chairman to recruit non-marine staff as managers and to hire contract pilots. Each conversation would return to *Ma Ganga* and the fact that she could be mastered only by the skill of experienced marine men. These analogies placed marine officers on the one hand in the role of Bhagirath. Like him they were initiating the appearance of regenerating life by sponsoring the *puja*. On the other hand, they were also like Siva; through their skilled work they controlled the river. For the marine officers their ritual and professional labour produced a regenerating, productive exchange between men and the river.

But what was the necropolitics of this sense of workmanship? Past failures of productivity were blamed by marine officers on the destructive acts of the unions that had existed in the port until the 1980s, but these now collaborate with officers and are brokers of informal sector work. Current failures were attributed to the nexus of decadence and ignorance produced when high-level officials worked with private firms. These failures were epitomized by the new *Ma Ganga* pilot vessel. This had been built by a private shipyard to replace the much-loved pilot ship. It was an example of the new multi-purpose and low-cost technology that the high-level bureaucrats in the port desired. It was designed for the pilots to stay on in the monsoon months off Sagar Island before taking smaller vessels to board the incoming container vessels. The rest of the year it was used by the chairman as a pleasure cruiser for parties. All the marine officers complained that the *Ma Ganga* was the epitome of the short-sighted lack of marine knowledge of the senior management and useless machinery produced by private companies. They swapped photos on their mobiles of its already rusted and pockmarked hull. Typically Captain Reddy complained that it rolled unbearably on the waves. He explained that the pilots couldn't relax in the elaborately decorated smoking room or sleep at night because the rhythms of the vessel created severe seasickness. It was, he said, not practical at all, but had been built as a 'pleasure platform'. He contrasted it with the old pilot vessel. Sadly he added that he kept the bell and the commander's desk from the old pilot ship at home in his bedroom. The decadence of the *Ma Ganga* epitomized the decay of marine knowledges in its failures to fulfil a practical use. It was a materialization of the waste produced by collaborations between the private sector and senior managers.

The necropolitics of the marine officers is similar to that of the engineers who inspired Veblen in the 1900s. They were troubled by the new forms of scientific management that introduced the profit motive on to shop floors and they argued for other absolute measures based on the skill of technical men. Veblen claimed an inalienable relationship between such technical men and the instruments of production by suggesting these machines and their products were an expression of a natural human instinct that they had developed most. The marine officers were confronted daily by the effects of a ruthless extraction of value from fixed capital by a financialized public deficit economics. They countered this with an emphasis on their inalienable connection to machinery created from the surplus value of the labour of their predecessors. In addition they stressed their technically skilled acts of labour as the ultimate source of regenerative life on the Hooghly. Because of their shared valuation of technical skill both Veblen and the marine officers identify private capitalists and non-utilitarian consumption as decadent excess and waste. However, distinct theories of the relationship between the material, immanent and transcendent inflect these necropolitics. Veblen anchors productive life in the material world in a universal, trans-historical natural instinct that is neurologically irrefutable. It is nature inside and outside of us which is the life force of the economy. Marine officers draw on concepts of lineage-like connections between generations of brothers formed by their engagement in similar work. They affiliate this work to acts of Hindu ritual labour that create productive exchanges of life. It is labour acting on material which creates reciprocal flows of life and animates production.

Yet this work is a special kind of state labour. The sense of workmanship among marine officers has unintended, but significant, ethical effects. It prevents the formation of a common cause with technicians and workers in the informal private sector. It was the marine officers who outsourced work, laid off marine crew and negotiated deals with private firms. Their nostalgias for a marine spirit and sense of the pedigree of port labour supported an ethical disengagement from their acts of outsourcing. As far as they were concerned their work continued to be part of a long tradition of state skills and labour, even though they were privileged agents within a new productive form that exploited the deregulated labour of informal workers. Their rigorous preservation of machinery also contributed to the appearance of a materially tangible but illusory boundary for the wider public in Kolkata. This was between the decline associated with state inaction visible in rusting technologies and the prosperity formed by the dynamism of private capital manifest in innovative reuses of objects. Now the chapter steps across these irrefutable but hallucinatory boundaries into the world of private firms.

A private ethics of fluidity: Hanuman, trusted futures and India Private Ltd

I would often encounter the four brothers who run India Private Ltd in the dock offices making deals with marine officers, including Captain Reddy. From the first time I went to their office and shipyard I was struck by their enthusiasm for the limitless fluidity of the old state technologies they converted for projects. For example, one day Sushant Jaiswal (the eldest brother, in his fifties) and I were sitting in the yard office and he explained with excitement how they had recently converted for the third time a state-owned barge. He described how: 'We have to be creative in order to deliver on projects at a lower cost and in faster time than our competitors so we get the contracts. This is why we adapt existing barges into completely new forms in our boatyard.' The remodelled vessels were displayed proudly in the company brochure as a triumph of small business creativity. The company moored many of them on the river in the centre of Kolkata. In contrast to the ruined port vessels here, those of India Private were painted bright red and often carried spectacular high-tech objects such as giant power plant reactors.

The Jaiswal brothers were the third generation of a Jain family to work in port-related business. Their accounts of the history of the firm interwove the 'adaptations' of the family with the changes in industry on the Hooghly. Pedigree provided a literal connection between the productivity of generations of brothers in the paternal line and that of the river. Each brother would tell the story of the firm in a way that made this explicit. They began with their great-grandfather and his elder brother, who had a business together producing jute. But they explained that this business was uncertain and the two brothers quarrelled and separated. Their grandfather then bought his first barge for transporting jute. Their father gradually expanded this business with his three brothers and one cousin. When barge traffic declined in the 1980s their branch of the family moved to Goa to develop the iron ore transport trade. Their work in Kolkata was also being undercut by their father's middle brother, who had set up a rival business. But this feud healed in 1990 when they returned from Goa and started to transport containers on lash barges. When this business suddenly ended overnight in 2000, the brothers explained they had taken up contractual 'high-tech' work on the river for the port and private clients. Entirely absent was any sense that their opportunities were affected by state actions on the river. As Sushant put it, 'that is the world of government offices and consultants and we cannot wait for them to make decisions'. Their account instead was of the productivity of a family, its quarrels and seizing of the fluid possibilities of abstract capital. This capital inhered in objects and their task was to make the physical form of objects as fluid as this essential potential. Their family also had to be as metamorphic as capital itself.

The brothers emphasized that they used an untrained creativity that did not rely on formal technological knowledge, but on the ability to adapt. The quality that Sushant said they had learnt from their 'fore-fathers' was extensive relationship-building and adaptability. They were entirely oriented to future potential rather than to the inheritance of skill. They claimed also that their workers shared these qualities with them. For the Jaiswal brothers it was precisely because workmen had learnt their skills in their yard with no formal qualifications that they were able to convert vessels. This also meant of course that the men could be paid hourly rates, were non-unionized and could be laid off according to the availability of work. Sushant Jaiswal expressed this sense of workmanship in the following manner:

> The difference of our company is that not one of us is a qualified en-
> gineer. We have no master mariners. Yet all these big companies like
> Reliance, they all use us. Some companies have asked for permanent

tie-ups with our company, but we would rather be in the position of subcontractors. This is what gives us our specific advantage. We assemble what is needed just when the work starts.

Their workers were disposable elements in these assemblages. Sushant described how as projects were completed they would steadily reduce the numbers of workers. In this entrepreneurial world the historical formation of technical skill is entirely devalued. Instead it is the flexibility of response to the needs of abstract capital in a temporal present and future which is sought.

This service to fluid abstract capital was materialized in the state objects India Private Ltd stored and transformed into multiple reuses. The four brothers were fascinated by the potential of the vessels they bought at auctions. They repeatedly described the trajectory of two state objects in order to express this. The first was a pleasure boat they had recently made, the *Kolkata Riviera*, which had started out as a vessel sold off by the state-run Central Inland Water Transport Corporation. Sushant, for example, described its various forms one day: 'Now we are building an air-conditioned boat that will have a hall of 120 square feet. The French doors will open up to the deck where there will be a Jacuzzi and an artificial garden ... It will be used for corporate and private parties on the river. We will be converting the same barge that we used for replacing the spans on a railway bridge into this tourism boat.' Once the vessel was complete, Sushant insisted that I film him on it. The *Kolkata Riviera* had no engine and was a floating island with hanging baskets of plastic flowers and artificial grass. All the lifebelts had its aspirational name emblazoned on them. There was no sign of the Jacuzzi or garden as these would be added once it had generated some revenue. Orders for parties had been slow and Sushant discussed the inaction of the state which caused this lack of tourism: 'The government is doing nothing to beautify the banks ... They don't provide jetties either ... Everywhere else there are tourists for the sacred Ganga, but not here because of the port.' Within this sense of workmanship the port trust was unequivocally a source of waste on the river that betrayed its sacred and monetary potential.

The brothers' focus on the capital potential of objects was also expressed in accounts of a steam tug that they stored on the river near their yard. Sushant, for example, described how this was the oldest vessel that they kept for reuse. It had, he said, been built in 1888 in Holland and although it was 'heritage' they were keeping it for when it could be reused in a new way. Sushant kept the old steering wheel hung on the wall of their office and had made this the brand image for their company. For him this emblem expressed an ethic of production that benefited the nation as a whole: 'We are using the existing equipment available in the country by modifying it ... If you think on a country-level situation this is good. We are creating cheaper solutions which is good for the country also.' Along the muddy bank India Private Ltd stored many rotting hulks that had not yet found a use, expressing a hope in the future life and inherent flexibility of these objects.

Work routines and facilities in the yard reflected these senses of workmanship of flexibility, low investment and the metamorphosis of objects. The yard was a narrow, muddy stretch of ground joined to the waterfront by a platform welded together from remnants of vessels. Barges were tied up to this and converted on the river to reduce the area of land leased from the port. Minimum equipment was used for the remaking of the vessels – only welding torches and physical labour. Instead of a permanent dry dock there was a muddy wide ditch in the riverbank in which smaller vessels were repaired and transformed. The yard was filled with small parts and mechanisms that were being recycled by workers. In a large *godown* (warehouse) was a stock of rusted chains, old lifebelts, anchors, joints and handles waiting for the moment of revival. The yard office had been built from parts of a barge and designed so it could be transported to another location should the cost of leasing the land rise.

For the Jaiswal brothers one deity signified their ethic of workman-ship – Hanuman. All their vessels contained lithographs of Hanuman wielding his mace. Each office had an icon of him that was worshipped in the morning and evening. A giant painting of Hanuman stared down from the corrugated roof of the covered area of the yard. This choice of deity was odd. Hanuman is not important to the company's Bengali workers, who associate him with the rituals of migrant labour from Bihar. Although the Bharatiya Janata Party (BJP), Rashtriya Swayam-sevak Sangh (RSS) and Viswa Hindu Parisad (VHP) have since the 1980s promoted a revival of the worship of Ram's loyal henchman, the Jaiswal brothers did not support these groups. The Jain origins of the Jaiswal family also made such a choice odd. But the Jaiswal brothers were unified in their reasons for Hanuman's presence. He represented the assured future success that comes from a single-minded trust in and hierarchical service to a greater master. As Sushant put it: 'Hanu-man is a demigod in the Hindu religion and a symbol of service to his master ... His whole life, his whole service, his whole thought was

199

based in serving the master. If you look at it as ... a worldly thing then whatever you do in life ... if you dedicate your life ... to that job with a pure heart you have to have success.' It was Hanuman as an emblem of trust, service and hierarchy which provided an image of continuity and of a successful future achievable from short-term assemblages of men, state objects and capital.

The Jaiswal brothers' objects, especially the *Kolkata Riviera* in the middle of the decrepit waterfront, materialized the not yet utopian hope that Miyazaki has identified as characteristic of neoliberalism (2003). Unlike the *Ma Ganga*, which had represented decadence to the marine officers, the *Kolkata Riviera* floated as a tangible sign that objects never died, that pleasure could produce profits and that the future prosperity of liberalization had been made solid in the present. In this sense of workmanship, waste and decay were associated with the permanent skills, slow pace, inflexibility and regulations of the public sector. Within the company the storage and conversion of state objects tangibly manifested the ethical counterpoint to this. But the work of India Private Ltd took place within the niches created by central and local state action on the river. However much the Jaiswal brothers asserted their separation from them they were part of the networks of the port and had 'adapted' to changes produced by the rhythms of public deficit.

If we compare this sense of workmanship to those of Veblen and the marine officers it is strikingly distinct. It profoundly devalues the act of labour on the material world, which becomes sublimated to mental dedication to a higher master. Both Veblen and the marine officers emphasized technical skill and the knowledge gained from the act of work. The act of labour was the expression of a generative force. But in India Private Ltd labour in itself does not have a generative potential, it just releases the fluid potential of capital that essentially inheres in objects. Waste appears as anything from the state to regulated labour or the physical properties of objects that limit the accessing of this immanent force. Such a sense of workmanship cuts ethical ties to informal workers who labour for you and to state institutions that generate your work. It leaves you in precarious service to the fluid needs of capital alone.

Conclusion: necropolitics, the metabolism of cities, labour and waste

My account of the various necropolitics at work on the Hooghly river has touched on many themes that appear in literature on pollution and urban environments. In recent years much has been written on the limits of bourgeois environmentalism in Delhi and Mumbai (Baviskar forthcoming; Gandy 2008). But my discussion of necropolitics here suggests that to understand responses to the negative effects of capitalism, including pollution and urban informality, we have to analyse a complex ecology of ethical evaluations of the urban and of the act of labour. Certainly in Kolkata diverse ethical stances held across classes as well as within classes converge to occlude the structural origins and contemporary material practices that combine to produce the Hooghly waterscape. These draw on affective and ritual meanings to create divergent senses of the metabolism of the city and the place of labour in this.

Recent writing on environmental politics and the sacred meanings of Indian rivers has tried to explain the absence of popular support for campaigns for the improvement of water quality (Alley 2002; Haberman 2006). Alley attributes this to the inherent difficulty of perceiving of Ganges water as polluted because of its ritual associations with purity. Much of this work has been carried out in ritual centres such as Varanasi or with groups that are religious specialists (although see Doron 2009). This chapter supplements this work by showing that its findings are limited by its ethnographic sources. If we focus on the accounts of those who labour on the Hooghly and on urban civic discourses we find that there are plural and varied attempts to explain signs of pollution and decay along the river. These are rich and ethically compelling forms of necropolitics that attempt to explain the physical decay in the Hooghly and Kolkata caused by neoliberal policies. Waste is only ever selectively approached through and within these ethical framings, among which I would include that of environmental pollution.

Very often at the centre of these necropolitics are theories about the affectivity of the act of labour and what it achieves in relation to transcendent and immanent productive forces. Throughout this chapter I have placed these various theories in relation to Veblen's account of the sense of workmanship. This was to draw out the distinct valuations of capital, skill, labour and concepts of the material present in these explanations. But overall I want to suggest that there are some more general theoretical points to be made from this material. First of all, that in contemporary neoliberalism senses of workmanship have become fragmented. In particular they act to produce ethical cuts that hide the mutual production and obligations of private and public sector economies. Secondly, that we have profoundly underestimated the polyvalence of the act of labour within capitalism. This has been clearly demonstrated for the contemporary Hooghly river. However, we must also turn our analysis towards the senses of workmanship in more familiar settings. It has become a truism from Latour's work that modernity is marked by an impossible division between nature and culture that then produces apparently hybrid combinations that unsettle this separation (1993). Yet we have rarely examined how complicated and mysterious this makes the act of labour within capitalism. We have seen in Veblen's efforts to construct an instinct of workmanship in neurological and natural foundations such an attempt to get to grips with the complexity of labour as a social, natural and material life-giving act. I want to end by suggesting that the senses of workmanship on the Hooghly river show that we have much more to do in exploring the polyvalent productive powers animating contemporary capitalism. These distinct framings are an important site of analysis since they contribute to the forms of technological objects and assemblages of men and materials. In this case they also occlude the disenfranchisement that is inherent in the creation of value through public–private partnerships that involve informal labour. These senses of workmanship cannot be mobilized as a moral and political force as Veblen hoped those of technicians and workers could be against finance capitalists in the 1920s. Yet importantly, Veblen's approach reminds us that the identification of waste is always part of a necro-politics that has significant economic and political consequences.

References

Alley, K. D. (2002) *On the Banks of the Ganga: When wastewater meets a sacred river*, Ann Arbor: University of Michigan Press.

Baviskar, A. (forthcoming) 'Cars, cows and cycle-rickshaws: bourgeois environmentalism and the battle for Delhi's streets', in in A. Baviskar and R. Ray, *Elite and Everyman: The cultural politics of the Indian middle classes*, New Delhi: Routledge.

Bear, L. (2007) *Lines of the Nation: Indian railway workers, bureaucracy and the intimate historical self*, New York: Columbia University Press.

— (forthcoming) 'Making a river of gold: speculative state planning, informality and neo-liberal governance on the Hooghly', *Focaal*.

Bennett, J. (2001) *The Enchantment of Modern Life: Attachments, crossings and ethics*, Princeton, NJ, and Oxford: Princeton University Press.

Cosin-Jimenez, A. (2008) 'Working out personhood: notes on labour and its anthropology', *Anthropology Today*, 21(6): 10–12.

Dilley, R. (2010) 'Reflections on knowledge practices and the problem of ignorance', *Journal of the Royal Anthropological Institute*, 16(S1): 176–92.

Doron, A. (2009) *Caste, Occupation and Politics on the Ganges:*

Passages of resistance, London: Ashgate.

Ferguson, J. (2006) *Global Shadows: Africa in the neo-liberal world order*, Durham, NC: Duke University Press.

Gandy, M. (2008) 'Landscapes of disaster: water, modernity and urban fragmentation in Mumbai', *Environment and Planning A*, 40: 108–40.

Haberman, D. (2006) *River of Love in an Age of Pollution: The Yamuna River of Northern India*, Berkeley: University of California Press.

Harvey, D. (2006) *The Limits to Capital*, London and New York: Verso.

Hertzfeld, M. (2004) *The Body Impolitic: Artisans and artifice in the global hierarchy of value*, Chicago, IL: University of Chicago Press.

Hibou, B. (2004) *Privatizing the State*, London: C. Hurst and Co.

Keane, W. (2007) *Christian Moderns: Freedom and fetish in the mission encounter*, Berkeley: University of California Press.

Lakoff, A. and S. J. Collier (2004) 'Ethics and the anthropology of modern reason', *Anthropological Theory*, 4(4): 419–34.

Latour, B. (1993) *We Have Never been Modern*, Harvard, MA: Harvard University Press.

Miyazaki, H. (2003) 'The temporalities of the market', *American Anthropologist*, 105(2): 255–65.

Mukherjee, R. (2009 [1937]) *The Changing Face of Bengal: A study in riverine economy*, Calcutta University Readership Lectures, Kolkata University.

Ostor, A. (1980) *The Play of the Gods: Locality, ideology, structure and time in the festivals of a Bengali town*, Chicago, IL: University of Chicago Press.

Rose, N. and S. Novas (2005) 'Biological citizenship', in A. Ong and S. J. Collier (eds), *Global Assemblages: Technology, Politics and Ethics as Anthropological Problems*, Oxford: Blackwell.

Simpson, E. (2006) 'Apprenticeship in Western India', *Journal of the Royal Anthropological Institute*, 12(1): 151–71.

Swyngedouw, E. (2005) 'Governance innovation and the citizen: the Janus face of governance beyond-the-state', *Urban Studies*, 42(11): 1991–2006.

Veblen, T. (1924) *The Theory of the Leisure Class*, London: Allen and Unwin.

Venkatesan, S. (2010) 'Learning to weave; weaving to learn ... what?', *Journal of the Royal Anthropological Institute*, 16(S1): 158–75.

Yanagisako, S. (2002) *Producing Capital: Family Firms in Italy*, Princeton, NJ: Princeton University Press.

Traces of former lives

9 | 'No junk for Jesus': redemptive economies and value conversions in Lutheran medical aid

BRITT HALVORSON

Introduction

This chapter investigates how the medical discards created by in-surance regulations in American biomedicine attain new life in faith-based medical humanitarianism. I focus on two American Lutheran aid agencies, established in the early to mid-1980s in Minneapolis, that supply an array of discarded and recovered medical materials – ranging from respiratory tubing to X-ray machines – to the Malagasy Lutheran healthcare department (*Sampan'asa Loterana Momba Ny Fahasalamana*). Many scholars of waste practices draw attention to what might be termed 'redemptive economies' encircling work with rubbish, discards and other purported 'waste' forms (Hawkins and Muecke 2003: xi). Such cast-offs almost always bear a latent exchange value, even if they have been temporarily 'deactivated' as commodities, which enables them to be pressed into a new use (Kopytoff 1986: 76). I suggest in this chapter that faith-based medical humanitarianism, however, requires that we pay especially close attention to the productive ambiguities embed-ded in the notion of redemptive economies. The faith-based agencies upon which I focus negotiate moral, religious and historical values in waste work alongside more overt processes of commodification. Trans-forming biomedical rubbish into medical relief potentially confirms religious values of salvaging/saving, usefulness and the extension of an object's 'life'. But the activity of sorting donated medical supplies in the two NGOs, which most vividly captures the uncertainties inherent in recovering discarded goods, can also be seen to provoke ethical concerns about the colonial legacy of American Lutheran missionary evangelism in Madagascar. By selecting 'useful' biomedical supplies and sending them to Lutheran brethren overseas, Lutheran aid workers in Minneapolis endeavour to produce more equitable social ties with Malagasy Lutherans and, therefore, redeem certain histories of inter-action between Malagasy Lutherans and American Lutherans. In this chapter, I examine the ambiguities resonating between the economic, religious and historical registers of Lutheran biomedical waste work and their incumbent possibilities for renewal.

Established by former medical missionaries to Madagascar, the two Lutheran non-governmental organizations attempt to implement a strong ideological commitment to 'accompany' Malagasy Lutherans from afar by sending medical relief rather than human missionaries to the Malagasy Lutheran Church (*Fiangonana Loterana Malagasy*). Malagasy Partnership and International Health Mission (IHM) began as part of the same initiative in the early to mid-1980s. Following a socialist revolution that unfolded on the island between 1971 and 1975, Malagasy clinics faced shortages of medical supplies after years of government-controlled import and export markets. In the face of a state economic crisis in the early 1980s, former and retired American Lutheran missionaries pooled their resources to start a medical aid organization in Minneapolis/St Paul that would gather donated bio-medical materials from US hospitals and channel them to a central distribution centre in Antananarivo for Malagasy Lutheran clinics. What began as an emergent humanitarian response to the economic crisis in Madagascar has since become a more routine supply-chain relationship between the two American Lutheran aid agencies and the Malagasy Lutheran healthcare system.[1] Scholars have pointed out that Madagascar's 1980 World Bank agreement opened the island nation to a neoliberal order that established an unparalleled role for foreign NGOs in the provision of social services (Randrianja and Ellis 2009: 12; see also Raison-Jourde 1995). By tracing the acquisition and circulation of discarded medical technologies, I shed light on the unlikely alli-ance between faith-based humanitarian initiatives in former colonial mission sites and the risk economies in biomedicine that make their operations possible. In what follows, I primarily address the North American 'side' of this supply-chain relationship in order to develop a deeper understanding of the ambiguous position NGOs embody as new 'conversionary sites' in the fabric of global Lutheranism, or mediating locations that transform, produce and negotiate economic, religious and historical forms of value.

I focus in the chapter on one foundational paradox underlying the American supply of medical technologies to Lutherans in Madagascar and former mission sites: how do American Lutherans affirm their moral relationship with their foreign brethren through material things deemed by some to be institutional discards, ultimately cast off because of their non-usefulness or obsolescence in the US hospital setting? Building on field research conducted in 2005/06 and 2008 in the Minneapolis aid agencies and in Malagasy clinics, I suggest American Lutheran aid workers attempt to resolve this ethical dilemma by concealing the institutional life of the medical technologies, placing the technologies they collect into a social calculus of 'useful' and 'junk' supplies, and associating this classification system with a moral economy of blessings and sins. Waste forms like hospital discards are especially apt religious forms for creative manipulation because of their capacity for recovery and regeneration. At the same time, in the subsequent sections of the chapter, I examine how a range of social actors in the Minneapolis aid agencies recognize the limitations of remaking 'objects' of biomedical practice into new material things: how are notable stamps of their former institutional lives recognized, absorbed or otherwise negotiated through different regimes of religious and moral values? These competing values make medical technologies key examples of what Parry and Gere (2006: 140–1) call 'hybrid collectives', which are not fully formed 'things' but 'negotiated into being' through a variety of actors, debates, institutional sites of use and ethical standards.

Most recent scholarship examining processes of commodification in biomedical practice and biomedical science has focused on the problematic social entailments of human bodily materials like tissue, organs and DNA sequences. These forms defy traditional property divisions of persons and things and raise numerous questions about whether they constitute 'things' fully separable from persons (see Hayden 2004; Parry and Gere 2006; Sharp 2006). Despite scientific work to make such forms into 'biotechnological artefacts', some research shows that organ recipients forge intimate ties with traces of the persons from which donated organs were harvested, making organs difficult to categorize through property models (Sharp 2006). Others have pointed out that DNA sequences, for example, bear little resemblance to the 'donated parts' of the human body once the research scientists, technicians, funding bodies and institutions involved in reinventing them have 'mobilized new claims in, or to, them' (Parry and Gere 2006: 153). This chapter examines a biomedical form much less analysed in the recent scholarly literature on the relationship of property relations and biomedicine: hospital waste. Coming ostensibly as they do from the opposite side of the thing–person spectrum, the divisibility of these things from persons and from clinical practice is seemingly a given from the medical institution's point of view. Indeed, the thing status of biomedical discards goes hand in hand with their ability to be summarily expelled from the medical institution as waste forms.

Yet I suggest that, in different ways, biomedical discards bear qualities that more informally unsettle or call attention to the regulative limitations of property regimes. Their form often bears strong ties to their itineraries through the medical system and sometimes also to human bodies, particularly in the case of more 'personal' objects like spectacles or bedpads, which prompt different kinds of interaction from things used only in clinical encounters (e.g. respiratory tubing and syringes).[2] Many medical discards, in ways distinct from the tissue samples and cell lines discussed by Parry and Gere (ibid.: 140), 'unsettle the binaries on which so many regulatory regimes rely for clarity'. Because traces of other persons and former institutional lives remain unsettled or unresolved by the mere transfer of property rights, medical discards carry signs of what we might consider unresolved pasts. By examining how discarded medical technologies have become forms mediating relations between Lutherans in the United States and Madagascar, I explore the processes by which such materials participate in value conversions across property regimes central to biomedical practice. I also investigate how they occupy multiple statuses simultaneously (charitable donation, medical property, sacred gift, commodity with exchange value) as they move across cultural sites of waste, acquisition and dispersal. But these processes are not uniform or self-assured transformations across discrete values: instead, I suggest that they point to gaps in value production and social ambiguities that arise in faith-based medical humanitarianism, where medical discards are cast into several coexisting but not always compatible value regimes with ethical/moral, religious, economic and scientific dimensions. To better understand how aid workers engage in a broader moral practice with historical dimensions, we first need to address the historical context for Lutheran medical humanitarianism, as well as how the two Lutheran NGOs currently position themselves as exchange partners with foreign Lutheran churches.

Circulating things not people: NGOs as Lutheran global actors

Besides their original relationship to changing forms of governance in Madagascar, Malagasy Partnership and International Health Mission form outgrowths of the long-standing American Lutheran medical mission to southern Madagascar, which began in 1888. The French colonial government in Madagascar (1896–1960) initially prohibited foreign missionary doctors from practising medicine in Madagascar without medical training in France. Still, the American Lutheran missions, administered by the US-based Lutheran Free Church and Evangelical Lutheran Church, found a range of sanctioned ways to actively combine the healing powers of medicine with evangelism: many clerical missionaries carried and dispensed medicines such as aspirin as they travelled throughout the south; unofficial dispensaries inside missionary homes treated local Tandroy, Tanosy and Mahafaly people; and the American Lutheran church actively recruited single women nurses from the US Midwest, who worked in mission-run schools for Malagasy youth. In the late colonial period, following the Second World War, the French colonial government relaxed restrictions on medical practice by foreign missionary doctors, and the American Lutheran mission obtained French permission to build two hospitals in the south-east (Manambaro) and the south-west (Ejeda), which it staffed with Malagasy Lutheran doctors and nurses and long-term American Lutheran medical missionaries and administrators. Even though the independent Malagasy Lutheran Church (*Fiangonana Loterana Malagasy*, FLM) was established in 1950, it initially extended colonial mission structures of authority, with American and Norwegian missionaries holding a disproportionate number of the highest positions in the church hierarchy until well into the 1960s.

When the Malagasy Lutheran healthcare system was officially set up in 1979, it combined medical facilities that had originally been part of the American Lutheran and Norwegian Lutheran missions to Madagascar, eventually bringing some nine hospitals and thirty-nine dispensaries under its authority. As a centralized healthcare network providing administrative assistance to each medical centre, SALFA accrues a portion of the funds for its operation through charging a small service fee for the medical supplies it disburses to each clinic.[3] Interestingly, many donors in Minnesota are unaware that the medical materials sent from the two American Lutheran non-governmental organizations become revalued monetarily once they arrive in Madagascar. The medical relief agencies provide the necessary supply chain for this centralized institutional structure in Madagascar. Malagasy Partnership today sends four annual transatlantic shipments of medical relief to the port city of Tamatave, Madagascar, where the shipments are processed by customs officials and then transported by truck to

Antananarivo. Though IHM sent sea containers to Madagascar in its early years, it currently finances a portion of Malagasy Partnership's overseas shipping, pharmaco-therapy for patients in small communal treatment centres called *toby* (Malagasy, lit. camp), medical training and continuing education programmes, and medical and dental equipment. Even though the two Minneapolis-based agencies strive for a completely new relationship with Malagasy Lutherans, 'accompanying' rather than directing their efforts, it is possible to see that they bear notable ties with the history of colonial medical missions. These historical associations become the focus of active renegotiation by volunteer workers aiming for a more equitable, 'post-colonial' Lutheranism.

During my fieldwork in 2005/06, I noticed, for example, that concern over the legacy of colonial evangelism was evident in agency leaders' moral scrutiny and evaluation of fellow believers' aid projects, as well as official discourses promoted by both organizations. Gene, a former medical missionary to Madagascar in 1977/78, was a founding member of Malagasy Partnership in 1980 and IHM in 1987. Over time, he maintained Malagasy Partnership as a separate organization that sent materials only to Madagascar and gradually lessened his involvement with IHM. He implied this was necessary for cultivating the specific relationships Malagasy Partnership volunteers had with Malagasy Lutheran physicians, whom they knew by name, hosted during US visits, and prayed for in weekly prayer circles. Because of the many world regions where it sends medical relief, IHM did not focus exclusively on maintaining personal relationships between US volunteers and foreign clinicians; paid office staff conducted communications with a range of foreign hospitals, activities largely kept separate from the process of sorting medical supplies in the main warehouse.[4] Moreover, while both organizations stressed the equality of their 'partnership' with overseas Lutheran churches, they do so in different ways. Gene criticized fellow believers who referred to overseas clinics as 'mission hospitals'. He avoided the term 'mission' because it implied to him the problematic presumption that the hospitals were under the authority of the American church rather than the Malagasy Lutheran Church. Emphasizing the divine rather than human authority guiding its work, Gene preferred to describe Malagasy Partnership as 'one link in a chain of God's construction'. In an interview with me, the chair of the IHM board of directors, a former medical missionary to Madagascar and child of missionaries to Madagascar, likewise expressed her desire to not be a '*vazaha*' (Malagasy, foreigner/stranger/white person) who remained in Madagascar but to see Malagasy nationals fully in charge of their healthcare institutions. Using Malagasy language terms to evoke a generalized Malagasy point of view, she interestingly characterized the position of IHM as a 'supportive' and 'faithful' partner.[5] As in Gene's rejection of the term 'mission', my conversation with the chair of the IHM board of directors repeatedly evinced her keen awareness of the power of language in conveying an ethical practice that distinguished the agency from previous and less equitable approaches. I point out in this chapter that such ethical concerns extend beyond the official discourse of the agencies to the activity of sorting medical supplies undertaken by volunteer labourers.[6]

Both agencies adopt a rhetoric of business 'partnerships' to characterize as highly equitable their relationships with Lutherans in former mission sites. Their careful moral scrutiny of aid approaches espoused by fellow believers and their discourse of equity itself, however, imply an overarching concern with inequities of an abstracted past. Current practice is marked off from past approaches through an evaluative teleology that makes former approaches to 'charity' appear less equitable, less collaborative and perhaps even less appropriately Christian. Aid workers extend this moral scheme to contemporary approaches that bear the unfortunate stamp of resembling such older relationships of inequity between colonial mission structures and national churches, leading one to see these approaches as a sort of morally dangerous 'backsliding'. Yet, in a different sense, I would point out that the history of colonial mission involvement also forms a crucial backbone for the kind of global engagement pursued today through faith-based medical humanitarianism. In Madagascar, inequalities in capitalist accumulation were produced by the French colonial regime with which the American Lutheran medical missions to Madagascar originally formed an uneasy alliance in order to pursue their evangelical programme on the island. Recognizing the national and cultural sovereignty of the Malagasy Lutheran Church and other national churches in former mission sites has interestingly required American Lutherans to continue their interactions with their foreign brethren through new institutional structures, namely non-governmental organizations. Rather than staffing a foreign mission with human missionaries, the agencies sustain the historical involvement between these world regions through circulations of material goods. As I discuss in the next section, the agencies rely on a series of value conversions of medical discards in order to enact the 'partnerships' they see as an ethical divergence from the less equitable mission past. Communicating this ideological commitment interestingly requires them to downplay the equally crucial partnerships formed with the US hospitals that donate medical equipment and supplies.

Concealing the institutional life of hospital discards

For biomedical institutions, appropriate disposal of medical materials is an adherence to the germ theory of disease and hygienic measures for the prevention and isolation of infection, as well as a legal obligation. Through the disposal process, medical discards occupy multiple statuses simultaneously, and this makes the terms used to describe them imprecise but also particularly revealing. Calling them 'hospital waste' presumes the hospital's institutional perspective on such materials, only one among many coexisting views, which interestingly anticipates the materials' eradication from the hospital setting in assigning the waste classification. The term 'hospital waste' must also be distinguished from 'medical waste', which usually refers to 'biohazardous' materials contaminated with bodily fluids and used 'sharps' like scalpels and needles, all materials that hospitals are legally required to dispose of separately. Hodges (2008) alternates between calling the combined category of hospital waste and medical waste 'biotrash' and 'medical garbage', which she describes as the material remnants of the clinical encounter between patients and practitioners, including used syringes, plastic tubing, blood bags, pharmaceuticals and pharmaceutical containers, and even human tissue and fluids. The materials handled by IHM and Malagasy Partnership have participated to varying degrees in the clinical encounter described by Hodges (ibid.), with many travelling through the medical institution while remaining fully unused.[7] The IHM operations manager, Mark, once pointed out the crucial difference between recovered supplies and reused supplies, making the argument that many IHM supplies were in fact never previously used in the biomedical institution (see also Rosenblatt and Silverman 1992: 1443). Many of these medical supplies can be sent overseas only because they cannot be used in American hospitals owing to insurance regulations.

It is perhaps hard to overestimate the importance of risk economies as the engine that drives the Lutheran transition to global engagement through medical aid agencies. Insurance industry assessments imply that the presence of expired medical supplies or those close to reaching their expiration dates increases the 'risk' of legal liability for the medical centre and for individual healthcare workers (ibid.: 1441).[8] In receiving a donation, the faith-based non-profits assume this liability on behalf of the hospital.[9] In her discussion of the 'biomedical waste recovery industry' in Chennai, India, Hodges (2008: 13) attributes its growth more to the influence of transnational insurers than the Indian juridical system designed to enforce certain methods of medical waste disposal. She notes, 'Global insurers thus regulate medical commerce as well as attempt to maintain levels of acceptable risk: both financial and epidemiological. If these new regimes of regulation do anything at all, they create conditions for enterprising illicit, informal economies of waste' (p. 13). Medical risk is commonly perceived to be something that opposes the creation of value in the medical setting. I follow Hodges, however, in pointing out that risk economies critically underpin medical commerce. The IHM executive director, Curt, a Lutheran pastor and social worker, once explained to me that no major insurance companies, besides Lloyd's of London, would insure the medical aid organization because of the excessive liability ('risk') it assumed in acquiring discarded medical materials. Since the organization could not pay the high premiums required by Lloyd's of London, Curt characterized this insurance regime as an obstacle to the NGO's wish to make 'something good' from biomedical waste, but elided the NGO's deep reliance on the very same risk economies that make its operation possible. Curt's emphasis on the valorizing qualities of IHM's work further identifies it as a social and civic good but only obliquely references the risk economy that enables IHM to turn what Hodges (ibid.: 17) calls a 'public bad' (medical patient risk) into a 'private good' (medical humanitarianism). When bringing together these points, it is possible to see the interwoven relationship between medical-legal risk and biomedical humanitarian engagement, social practices that rely upon one another in constructing patient bodies, economic exchange value and transnational aid relationships.

If we return our focus to the disposal process, we can better appreciate, then, that disposal is a multifaceted property transaction for the biomedical institution which both devalues supplies as active property of the medical centre and revalues the materials as charitable donations. Additionally, multiple transfers of value underpin the movement of supplies between the medical institution and the NGO and perhaps overdetermine the transition as a shift in their value.[10] From a legal and business standpoint, the revaluation of donated items according to their 'fair market price' is a central part of the transaction, for it offers hospitals a monetary figure that may be claimed as a tax deduction. Non-profit organizations are legally prohibited in the United States from valuing their donors' gifts-in-kind, although they must do so for their own financial records. The transfer of ownership, signalled by copious paper documentation, gives the hospital the legal ability to revalue items monetarily that were otherwise designated as 'waste'.[11] Hodges (ibid.) suggests that hospitals also find valuable the paper trail documenting such transfers, which verify that the hospital has followed insurance regulations mandated by the state. Such adherence also makes the hospital eligible for continued accreditation, auditing processes and high accreditation ratings, all commodity forms inter-linked with appropriate waste disposal. Although conceived legally in the USA as 'non-profits', then, organizations like IHM and Malagasy Partnership play an integral role in property transfers that ultimately reconstitute the materials' exchange value. In other words, they enable the profitable exchange of different forms of capital (i.e. commodities and credits). The principle underpinning such transfers is the fact that for medical supplies to be considered valuable by both parties (i.e. the non-profit and the for-profit) they simultaneously must be without a use value for the hospital but still possessing an exchange value.

I suggest that the specific hospital and clinic 'contacts' made through repeated donations are also commodity forms transferred with the medical donations and equally as valuable, if not more so, as the medical supplies for the medical aid organizations. In the September 2005 monthly volunteer meeting, the IHM executive director, Curt, voiced his opinion that IHM should accept a large donation of unsorted supplies (approximately fourteen pallets of stethoscopes, blood pressure cuffs and hospital gowns) from the St Paul Area Service Guild in order to receive access to their 'network links' of cash and medical supply donors. Since the Guild was closing down its warehouse, its network links were 'up for grabs', he said, and would give IHM a stronger 'network of feeders'. Gene also once told me how his fifteen-year relationship with a large Minneapolis linens supply service, which he visited weekly to collect donations, gave Malagasy Partnership favoured status and the best pick of discarded linens among other competing agencies. Each of these examples indicates that supply acquisitions, from the perspective of the aid agency, are complex negotiations where value may be organized through a series of transactions subsidiary to the actual exchange of medical materials. From the perspective of the donor, too, medical donations accrue value in a number of ways beyond the mere assurance of a tax credit. Donations are often made on the hospital's or supplier's terms, meaning that NGOs must be willing to accept whatever a hospital or medical relief agency is willing to give, as was the case with the St Paul Service Guild. NGOs must provide the volunteer labour to sort through donations in order to determine what items may be useful and, sometimes, even what items are contained in donated boxes, bags and bins. IHM held a series of what the volunteer coordinator Dagmar called 'sorting marathons' in spring 2006 to sift through the forty-cubic-foot sea container of medical supplies it received from the Service Guild. In this way, medical suppliers and hospitals reduce labour costs involved in the disposal of supplies. Additionally, hospitals and medical relief organizations decrease the cost of disposal itself. If non-profit organizations subsequently find certain supplies unusable, they must assume financial responsibility for their disposal. To better understand how supplies enter the NGOs and continue their itinerary to overseas clinics, I turn now to the practice of sorting, a crucial juncture in determining and negotiating value.

Converting medical supplies into useful things

Converting medical supplies into objects other than hospital waste is a social and moral practice firmly rooted in the work of 'fixing propriety' in things, a second sense-meaning of property relations originally discussed by John Locke (see Verdery and Humphrey 2004: 5). Rather than focusing exclusively on the transfer of property rights as an incipient event for the relations of persons through things, I see the labour of handling, sorting and classifying the medical materials, or 'fixing propriety' in them, as an equally important process that endeavours to refine the material and moral qualities of the medical donations. Owing in part to the 'highly heterogeneous' composition of medical donations (Rosenblatt et al. 1996: 630), however, volunteer workers, myself included, were engaged in a constant process of questioning, seeking advice, making uncertain and temporary classifications, and reorganizing the supplies. Classifications were routinely overturned, items reordered, new materials arrived, some things appeared unclassifiable (e.g. stray tubes and machine parts), and disagreements arose as to how the supplies should be classified. I shall attempt, therefore, to illustrate in the next two sections the multiple ways in which volunteer labourers work to establish ethical relations with their foreign Lutheran brethren by negotiating, establishing and debating use relations of medical supplies in the sorting process that takes place in the two warehouses.

If we examine the sorting process more closely, we can see that placing an item in a biomedical classification is a first step in establishing its eventual institutional use – an act of reinstitutionalizing the medical discard – but not a practice that fully secures use value.

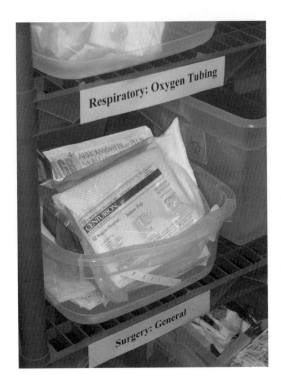

9.1 When volunteer labourers classify medical materials using labelled sorting bins, they begin a process of reinstitutionalizing the biomedical discard

In most cases, the act of sorting compartmentalized the supplies into predetermined biomedical categories. At IHM, more than twenty labelled plastic bins, such as 'respiratory' and 'anaesthesiology', existed in the sorting room (see Figure 9.1). At Malagasy Partnership, volunteers always consulted Gene first-hand when sorting materials, and he gave them specific verbal instructions for an item's placement, telling them that a surgical dressing, for instance, should be set in the marker-labelled 'sterile dressings' bin rather than classified as 'surgical supplies'. Uncertainty still existed, though, as to whether the classified item would be requested and needed by an overseas clinic. The possibility remained that biomedically classified goods would not find a use value in an overseas Lutheran clinic, owing to the different circumstances of biomedical practice or the ill fit of the supplied goods, and would be thrown away. Moreover, even as some volunteers threw things away at IHM in order to avoid sending non-useful things overseas, others quickly retrieved items from the rubbish bin to bring them home, giving them a use value outside the NGOs' official circuits of usefulness. Maude, a monthly volunteer appearing to be in her seventies with short, straight white hair, joined another volunteer named Harriet and me in the IHM supply sorting room one September afternoon. Maude observed a thin, clear plastic rectangular container with an attached cover that had been placed in the rubbish bag in the sorting room. 'It's a shame to throw this away,' she said as she gingerly picked the plastic tub out of the rubbish. Harriet nodded, observing the container as Maude rotated it in her hand. Maude said she could use the container 'for small things' she had at home and placed it beside her bag on the floor. Many of the volunteers at International Health Mission share Maude's concern with the moral implications of 'waste' and 'wastefulness', something which both draws them to IHM's work but also is constructed in the very experience of sorting, 'salvaging' and packing used and donated medical supplies (see Reno 2009).

Another way aid workers approached the ethical issues surrounding use was by suggesting that what made something useful was the anticipated duration of its use value in the receiving clinic. As we sifted through medical materials in the IHM 'sorting room' one afternoon, Lois, a Norwegian-American missionary to southern Madagascar from 1952 to 1982, described having once opened a box in Madagascar shipped from an American congregant only to discover that it looked as though the person had overturned what she termed their 'household junk drawer' into the carton. For Lois, the overturned kitchen junk drawer served as the negative image of thoughtful giving against which she organized her volunteer work at IHM. On several occasions she refused to package disposable supplies. A Baptist missionary couple stopped at IHM in October 2005 to pick up two duffel bags' worth of supplies for an orphanage they operated in the Philippines. Gesturing towards a box of facial tissues as we located items for the orphanage, Lois remarked: 'I don't like to send anything out that's just gonna be thrown away.' A substantial number of items in the warehouse were made for one-time use, although they were sometimes used beyond that in a clinic short on supplies. The design of materials by medical supply manufacturers, though, is increasingly geared towards disposability (see related points on reuse in Rosenblatt and Silverman 1992: 1443). It was important to Lois that anything coming from International Health Mission could be used more than once and be *useful* in the long term, not something that could turn to waste shortly after it arrived and be placed back in the social category (waste/rubbish) from which IHM attempted to 'recover' it. Lois did not draw attention explicitly to the religious significance of waste work but it is worth pointing out that her commitment to extending usefulness potentially echoes

219

salvationist discourses. Some productive ambiguity exists, therefore, between the religious principles shaping Lois's lifelong work and sorting practices that offer opportunities to confirm or reflect on these values in specific material engagements.

Lois questioned giving things simply to reduce one's own waste and its moral entailments, symbolized by the household junk drawer, but also wanted giving to extend the life and usefulness of an object, thereby limiting or delaying the waste of others. This stance partly communicated the notion that American Lutherans should take responsibility for the disposal of non-useful things, and the quality of their actions more generally, rather than removing or passing on their culpability to others. Moreover, Lois conveyed an overarching value in fostering the durability, and long-term commitment, of the transnational ties that she and others created through the exchange of medical materials. For Lois, this practice could also be linked to the important kinship ties she maintained through working as an IHM volunteer: at age seventy-nine, she saw her work as a way of 'staying connected' to Madagascar at a time when travel was becoming difficult for her, but also as a way of contributing something that could benefit her own family, who remained in the south. One of her sons, a US-trained engineer-turned-evangelist and Bible translator, married a Tandroy Malagasy woman, and they lived together with their son in the town of Tsiombe. Lois's son and family maintained ties with the Lutheran medical clinics in the southern region, which received monetary aid from IHM, and occasionally journeyed to the regional centre of Fort Dauphin/Tolagnaro for special care, supplies and visits with travellers to the area. Although we can see how Lois promotes multiple kinds of relations through her sorting work, her direct connection to people who frequented Malagasy Lutheran clinics was exceptional. For most IHM volunteers, the supplies' destinations and the people who would be receiving them were not differentiated but rather organized in a more general category of 'aid recipients' or 'brothers and sisters in Christ'.

Finding a use value for discarded medical materials further linked the circulation of medical relief to a broader moral economy involving divine blessings, which operated as a kind of return on the transmission of a useful object to foreign Lutheran physicians. IHM brochures commonly promised donors and volunteers blessings in return for their work: 'God bless your effort to serve Him by helping the hands that heal!' During the Christmas luncheon for volunteers in 2005, Curt told those seated that they were the 'life and blood' of IHM and 'make gifts of [them]selves' to the agency; the chair of the IHM board of directors concluded the programme by wishing 'blessings' to the listening volunteers. In narrating his exasperation at not knowing what to do with a school group arriving at the warehouse, Mark commented to me one afternoon that he worried he sometimes forgot to appropriately see the volunteers as 'blessings from God'. In one sense, this language of blessing placed the warehouse operation in a divinely orchestrated gift economy: volunteers could be divine blessings to the agency by giving their labour, much as they could receive divine blessings in return for their work. Prayer played a central role in securing material returns that could serve as socially recognizable marks of divine agency or blessings. After suddenly acquiring the adjacent warehouse in 2005, which enabled the agency to double its physical space, IHM volunteers commonly referred to the warehouse expansion as an 'answer to prayer'. In the May/June 2006 IHM newsletter, Dagmar later described the warehouse acquisition as a 'tremendous blessing'. These immediate, observable 'returns' for prayer and obedience reinforced the idea that the IHM operation was divinely 'blessed' in the general sense or woven into a sanctioned gift economy. But they also served to heighten volunteers' efforts to continue this cycle by securing 'blessings' in return for their work and attempting to ensure that the medical supplies operated as 'blessings' in the recipients' lives.

The best example of how volunteers asked for divine blessing for the medical supplies occurred during special container-packing sessions when the final preparations were made to ship materials overseas. At both agencies, just before the doors of the transatlantic sea containers were shut, volunteers formed a ritual prayer circle that faced the open doors of the container, where the cardboard cartons of the shipment were still visible. The placement and timing of the prayer is significant because it indicates how the prayer text suffuses the container with requested blessings just before it leaves the physical presence of the volunteers. The container doors were typically shut only after the prayer had ended. For example, in August 2005, IHM volunteers gathered in the warehouse before a container destined for a hospital in northern Cameroon. When the final box had been shoved into the tightly packed metal frame, the operations manager, Mark, suggested that everyone 'gather in prayer for the container'. Mark began the prayer, asking that the container 'be blessed'; that it have a safe journey; that Cameroonian customs officers 'be kind' and perhaps not charge as many tariffs as for the previous container; and that 'God bless the work' of medical doctors in Cameroon. In one special packing session at Malagasy Partnership, I observed a comparable request for

9.2 Harriet, a retired American Lutheran missionary nurse who spent thirty-six years in northern Cameroon, worked as an advisory medical professional in IHM's 'sorting room' in 2005/06

blessings for the transatlantic sea container just before its doors had been closed. One middle-aged engineer and regular volunteer, Theo, led a prayer circle for the container. His college-aged daughter asked that the things in the container 'bless and acclaim You'. In his turn, Theo prayed that 'the Lord would bless each item in the container' and that the items would 'be a blessing for and through You, Lord'.

Prayers for the supplies to be blessings can be viewed as one way in which discourses of usefulness intersect in complex ways with the blessing economy in each agency. For volunteers in both agencies one central tension arose in the system of divine blessing exemplified in container packing sessions: while it appeared to be a matter of faithfulness to trust that the medical materials would be turned into blessings (or useful things), it was also the volunteers' moral responsibility to demonstrate their faith by acquiring and selecting useful things. The possibility thus remained that the supplies might not have been sorted and selected with the volunteers' most rigorous attempts to prioritize the requests of overseas clinicians. Additionally, for volunteers, it was often unclear exactly how the supplies that they handled would be used in the foreign clinics where they were sent.

The geopolitical distance between the Minneapolis NGOs and foreign clinics in Madagascar, Tanzania and Cameroon further mystified the use relations of the medical materials but simultaneously contributed to the overall awareness among volunteers that the NGOs were linked to broader landscapes of divine activity. From this perspective, prayer helped to secure the potential for a supply, as Theo put it, to 'be a blessing for and through You, Lord'. Theo's language executed his wish to transform the sent materials still further and make the medical supplies into vectors of divine agency or blessings in the healing process. We can see, therefore, that spoken prayers for the supplies endeavour to reduce several distinct forms of uncertainty encircling the medical materials, such as their eventual use and the impact of their reception, as well as the relationship between American Lutheran volunteers and Lutheran clinicians in foreign hospitals.

Moreover, despite the extensive effort of sorting and reordering the supplies at both warehouses, some piles of stuff existed that no one knew what to do with, and these supplies sat in abeyance on the edges of countertops, in bags or on utility tables (see Hetherington 2004: 166). At IHM, part of this problem in establishing use can be attributed to the global scope of the agency's aid programme and its efforts to standardize the relief operation to fit numerous world regions. Several times, Harriet, a long-time volunteer and retired missionary nurse, expressed frustration and uncertainty about her own medical training being applicable to the many places where IHM sent supplies. As she explained to me, she was trained to practise medicine at one hospital in northern Cameroon, adjusting her practice to that setting over the course of thirty-six years, but she had retired and left Cameroon permanently some sixteen years earlier. IHM's use of retired medical professionals as arbiters in the sorting process resulted frequently in situations where they indicated some unease or hesitation about making blanket judgements concerning the appropriateness of certain medical technologies for the range of foreign Lutheran clinics with ties to IHM. Signalling small rejections of broader efforts to standardize aid responses, the unease of people like Harriet in making final judgements about a supply's usefulness contributed to the growing pile of 'odds and ends' that had no clear or easily ascertainable 'use' (see Figure 9.2). Harriet's refusal to categorize certain medical supplies and her decision to leave them in abeyance could be seen as part of an ethical practice of sending only 'useful' aid overseas. By contrast, aid workers frequently referred to non-useful medical supplies as 'junk' forms that vacated medical supply processing of the potential for receiving divine blessings. By looking at things deemed 'junk' medical supplies, we can see how the very materiality of the hospital discards in fact limited the NGOs' ability to infuse new value into discarded things and to create 'charitable donations' from them.

Sinfulness and 'junk' medical supplies

I have argued thus far that Lutheran aid workers engage in a variety of practices that attempt to dissociate hospital waste forms from their discard status. One subtle yet significant refinement to this practice, however, can be seen through a statement handwritten in marker at the bottom of a whiteboard posted in the IHM warehouse: 'Junk for Jesus is still junk'. The language of the sign is noteworthy: it advises the volunteers that sending 'junk' items overseas, even with the aim that they be used to do the healing work of Jesus, doesn't obviate the fact that these items are 'still junk'. In other words, certain medical materials have non-malleable 'junk' qualities that empty them of their potential for securing blessings while simultaneously verifying their non-usefulness. The scrawled reminder on the whiteboard suggests that it is necessary in their work at IHM for volunteers to create waste themselves, throwing things away that are not useful for foreign practitioners or patients. Additionally, the idiom 'Junk for Jesus is still junk' removes a layer of mediation between the 'giving' NGO and the intended recipient to suggest that medical practitioners in Tanzania, Madagascar and Cameroon are not necessarily the only or final recipients of the medical relief but instead Jesus forms one predominant exchange partner ('Junk for Jesus') with both NGOs and their volunteer labourers.

I came to realize shortly after beginning my research that the warehouse sign at IHM ('Junk for Jesus is still junk') originated in the language and policies of Technical Exchange for Christian Healthcare, namely its widely used adage 'No junk for Jesus'. Malagasy Partnership and International Health Mission constitute part of a movement of more than one hundred US-based Christian medical aid organizations, which has been known collectively since 1990 as Technical Exchange for Christian Healthcare (TECH). TECH agencies distinguish themselves from their predecessors and their contemporaries in two primary ways. First, TECH requires agencies to meet specific standards for the quality of their donations and the frequency of their communication with aid recipients before they can join the umbrella organization. Secondly, TECH's elected leadership openly criticizes non-member Christian agencies that send what they call 'junk' overseas. Some commonly referenced junk supplies include medical machine parts detached from their original equipment or respiratory tubes that likewise required equipment that had not been donated with them. As I observed at one TECH meeting in April 2006, in levelling their assertions about the unethical practice of circulating 'junk', TECH leaders make the broader argument that non-member agencies engage in a kind of hypocrisy and damage the reputation of TECH members with secular humanitarian agencies and non-Christians. Among TECH leaders and members, these accusations of hypocrisy stem from a specific association of 'junk medical supplies' with morally dubious behaviour and human sin. This sinfulness originates in an insufficient effort to match medical supplies with the expressed 'needs' of the people aid agencies aim to be serving – in this framework, sending non-useful things overseas is akin to sending 'junk medical supplies' overseas. TECH leaders indicated that this moral problem can be remedied by engaging God squarely in the accumulation of medical technologies by praying for guidance, communicating regularly with overseas partners, and requesting blessings in return for carefully and thoughtfully secured medical materials. Through their moral scrutiny and even censure of contemporary aid approaches through a discourse of sin, TECH members suggest that they see their work as an enchanted landscape on which small battles between human sin and divine justice play out in a variety of decision-making processes involving medical technologies. I find especially notable the emerging connection between this economy of sin and blessing and waste processes linked to institutionalized consumption, specifically in biomedicine.

Some IHM volunteers, like TECH leaders, explicitly connected 'junk' medical supplies with human sinfulness. In a conversation one afternoon, Richard, a retired engineer and regular IHM volunteer who repaired equipment and arranged pallets for shipment, likened storing 'junk' in the warehouse to 'keeping sin in you and not freeing it up' and added that the storage of junk was something that 'kept [people] from receiving blessing'. Richard's language attends to the way junk functions as a detrimental force, not merely a series of stationary, non-useful commodity forms, but a social act that shapes the relationship between people working in the organization and God. Junk supplies blocked the blessing a person might receive for acquiring and storing items to send overseas. By linking 'junk' analogously to sin kept inside the human body, Richard implied that the full effects of junk medical supplies may be obscured from view or unseen by volunteer labourers yet continue to be powerful nonetheless. Interestingly, in Richard's estimation, the medical supplies that remained at the warehouse, without a certain purpose or destination, were already junk because of their non-usefulness. To hold items in abeyance would be only to verify their junk quality, since their usefulness had not been readily identified. In some ways, it was the very ambiguity of their position in the circulation of medical supplies through the warehouse which had made them into junk.

Besides their embrace of TECH-sponsored signs, buttons and stickers emblazoned with the adage 'No junk for Jesus', volunteers at both agencies endorsed the more general view that sending non-useful things abroad would be morally questionable. One way of specifying that the warehouse supplies were explicitly non-junk was to designate them as divinely 'called' things. At Malagasy Partnership, Gene stipulated on several occasions in prayer that the medical supplies packaged within the warehouse had been 'called' by God and were not merely 'sent' by a hospital, a pivotal distinction. On one snowy February evening in 2006, before the group prayer circle that concluded the evening's work session, Gene narrated in detail the story of his interaction with a company that supplies the medical industry with Hemacue finger sticks, which are used to obtain blood samples for tests. Each small test kit (*cuvette*) costs about US$1.25, Gene explained, which makes it difficult for SALFA to stock all its clinics throughout the island with an adequate number of kits. Gene e-mailed the manufacturing company to ask about the price and tacked on what he called a short description of Malagasy Partnership. The response from a woman at the company, Gene said, was to say 'that's a really neat organization' and to offer two boxes of 200 finger sticks as a donation. Gene summarized plainly: 'So God brought the Hemacues.' Gene's story provided evidence of God's active role in directing supplies to the warehouse. Although he incorporated the detail about his own e-mail description of the agency's work into his story, he emphasized at the time that it was a 'short' paragraph, diminishing his own role in prompting the donation. Through his tone and phrasing, he also depicted the paragraph as virtually an afterthought, something he placed within the body of the message in order to share this information but without deliberate intent to persuade his correspondent to donate to the organization. Gene thus amplified the surprise and gift of the donation by narratively minimizing his role and constructing the near-absence of purpose in his e-mail interaction.

Gene reinforced the idea that the medical supplies were 'called' rather than simply sent through elaborate stories that he would tell about each medical item. One evening two families from Gene's church, totalling nine people, suddenly arrived at the warehouse during a regular work session. Gene provided the families with a brief tour and then brought all the volunteers together in the middle of the warehouse for introductions and a short prayer session. As we crowded together in the few open spaces within the warehouse, Gene pointed out to the guests how 'God has kept the warehouse busy' over the past few weeks. He gestured around us in a concentric circle, saying that each large carton or crate facing us 'has a story attached to it'. Gene turned around, drawing our attention to a small wooden crate in the corner of the warehouse nearest the office, partially covered by other cardboard boxes and rubber sorting bins. That box there, Gene explained, contains pieces of stained glass that have been requested for a small rural church. Above us, on second-storey-high shelving against the warehouse wall, was a large, appliance-sized cardboard box. That contains some cellos and a violin, Gene noted. A Korean American mission church had established a music programme at a school in Madagascar, and they needed a way to ship some instruments for their programme. At the back of the warehouse, in front of a bulging pile of boxes that filled the space from ceiling to floor, were a number of boxes that originally carried frozen chips. These contain some 5,400 pairs of spectacles, Gene said, noting that they came to the warehouse through his response to a posting on the TECH website. Extending the arc he drew around us with his finger still farther, Gene drew our attention to a stack of crutches atop another cardboard box on the second level of shelving. These would be sent to Madagascar, he said, for polio patients. By attaching stories to the supplies, Gene more implicitly denuded the previous lives of the medical materials in the biomedical institution and accentuated their role in the divinely orchestrated fabric of social relations. Moreover, the multifunctional stories played an instructional and interpretive role, since they included telling details about the ailments and programmes for which they would be 'used'.

In sum, the category of 'junk' brings the potential for moral backsliding into each aid transaction. Junk medical supplies effuse the negative values and personal moral implications of non-usefulness, non-circulation, lack of care and even sinfulness in medical supply acquisition. The sinfulness of junk medical supplies is an 'absent presence' that forms a crucial part of the two operations (Hetherington 2004: 163). By representing the possibility of sin within each and every medical supply transaction, medical aid workers co-construct the religious value of non-junk forms, make useful discards into embodiments of divine agency, and underscore their work of pursuing ethical relations with Lutherans overseas. The discourse on the sinfulness of junk medical supplies indicates that the NGOs are not only identifying usefulness as a positive ethical relation between persons through things. They also extend and tie the process of medical relief acquisition to a broader set of linked moral categories that establish negative values in these commodity exchanges. Moreover, through adherence to the TECH standards, the Lutheran agencies indicate that they are putting into place a category shift: 'waste' forms are things to be redeemed (Hawkins and Muecke 2003) but only under certain circumstances. Detaching the category of waste from a morally dangerous kind of destruction, differentiating among kinds of waste forms and practices, and perceiving waste as a productive process are all central components of this ethical endeavour.

Conclusion

I have argued that the paradoxical dimension of Lutheran medical relief work stems in part from the agencies' full reliance on medical property transfers and their active role in producing capital (tax credits) by assuming ownership of the 'rubbish' of the medical industry. With each medical supply acquisition, the organizations participate in a series of value conversions between two property regimes, medical property and charitable donation, and thereby rely on the medical system's categorization of the supplies as hospital waste in order to produce new use relations for these things. Producing new use relations ultimately requires the NGOs to symbolically reject the very foundation for their continued existence as non-governmental organizations. Put another way, the agencies' moral endeavour of supplying useful and needed things to their overseas 'partners' entails a rigorous insistence that the medical materials are precisely *not* waste and a social distancing from the hospitals' classificatory scheme. In determining the usefulness of medical donations, the NGOs momentarily silence the hospital classification that resulted in their acquisition. Even this process, however, is plagued by further uncertainties: will foreign Lutheran clinicians realize the supplies' use value identified by American Lutheran aid workers? The crisis in the materials' ontological status is produced by the NGOs' complex position at the intersection of several economies: the medical supply industry, hospital adherence to theories of practitioner/patient risk, the moral economy of historical relations with Lutherans in former mission sites, and the 'informal' economic channels of non-governmental organizations. I suggest, therefore, that working with the medical supplies, assessing their usefulness or non-usefulness and accentuating their potential use value is an ongoing and unresolved practice focused on building moral relationships with foreign Lutheran doctors while emptying medical discards of their relations to the US hospital system.

By engaging in a process of sorting the medical materials and assessing their use value, Minneapolis aid workers socially negotiate, reject and absorb the distributions of 'goods' (property rights, charitable donations, scientific tools, gifts, blessings) and 'bads' (risks, liabilities, sins) evidenced in circulating medical technologies (Hayden 2004: 118; see also Verdery and Humphrey 2004). The religious practices of caregiving, blessing and healing are not completely separate pursuits from the circulation of medical technologies, nor merely attached to them, but play a prominent role in morally 'redeeming' medical discards as social forms suitable for transnational aid. In making this argument, I have benefited from a growing body of scholarship refuting popular assessments of market relations in Protestant Christianities that sometimes oppose their moral and economic dimensions. I follow Simon Coleman (2004: 437) in arguing that such depictions mistakenly advance 'narrowly secular assumptions about the autonomy of the economic sphere in Western social life'. As Coleman (ibid.: 424) points out, these assumptions gain traction through a series of other related contrasts between short-term individual strategy and long-term relational moral responsibility/obligation; (secular) material returns and (sacred) non-material forms of transcendence; and 'religious hucksterism' involving money and more trustworthy dealings by religious leaders in the non-market realm. By focusing instead on the traffic between varying processes of according and denying value, I have pointed out that different kinds of economies play a role in 'regulating' the international circulation of discarded and recovered medical technologies (e.g. the conferral of blessings for forms with identified use values). Indeed, we can see how economies of blessings and sins collude in transforming medical discards into suitable aid forms. Furthermore, when taking into account the various kinds of possible 'returns' for medical relief (particularly blessings), it becomes evident that American Lutheran aid workers perceive multiple 'exchange partners' in their work: Malagasy Lutheran and other foreign Lutheran medical practitioners, Jesus, foreign 'brothers and sisters in Christ', and perhaps even moral inversions of themselves (see ibid.: 432).

Throughout this chapter, I have sought to make the case that faith-based medical humanitarianism is a particularly revealing crossroads, or 'conversionary site', among disparate value regimes. As the American

Lutheran foreign mission movement came to a close between 1970 and 1990, the two American Lutheran medical non-governmental organizations in Minneapolis filled a gap in global engagement vacated by the end of the foreign mission movement and the deprofessionalization of the missionary vocation. Non-governmental organizations, in particular, operate in the fabric of American Lutheranism as new kinds of converting sites that engage in a variety of transformative and potentially regenerative tasks involving waste forms. I suggest that these sites tie together social processes with spatial and temporal qualities. In significant ways, hospital discards constitute 'products of time' or institutional 'end products' that aid workers try to make into a new beginning by capturing the redeemable life of the material effects of an institution and pressing them into a social future (Hawkins and Muecke 2003: xiv). We can see that, at the heart of aid workers' practices of salvaging, recovering and sorting medical materials, is also a social recognition of the connections between destruction and renewal. I have argued in this chapter that this process simultaneously carries historical, religious and economic dimensions that ambiguously collude with one another and cannot be easily disentangled. By carving out a new ethical practice through their work with medical discards, Lutheran aid workers and former missionaries engage in a subtle process of converting their own practice and reforming it in relation to the negative image of other possible pasts. A heightened awareness exists that the NGOs occupy a space betwixt and between multifarious economies, or a 'gap moment [...] where value is yet to be decided' (ibid.: xiii). This serves as a powerful synecdoche for the practice of an 'economy of redemption' but also for making a break with the problems of a colonial past.

Notes

1 Although a full discussion of this 'economic crisis' exceeds the scope of this chapter, I heed Fassin's (2008) insight concerning the production of crisis moments as an underlying trope of humanitarian intervention.

2 I thank Chris Dole for bringing my attention to this point.

3 One criticism I have heard voiced about the centralized system is that smaller clinics or those existing in areas with what one person called a predominantly 'cash-poor' population will not be able to absorb across-the-board fees instituted for medical supplies by SALFA, creating a disparity in clinics' access to medical materials.

4 IHM shipped fourteen containers of medical relief to Lutheran hospitals in Tanzania, Cameroon, Papua New Guinea, Liberia and Nicaragua in 2005, and the dramatic expansion of the IHM headquarters in 2005 signalled its plan to send as

many as twenty-eight annual containers to those and other locations, including Bangladesh and southern India.

5 This is perhaps most evident in the organization's motto, 'Helping the Hands that Heal', which I address more fully in other writing (Halvorson 2012).

6 Gene runs Malagasy Partnership entirely through volunteer labour, personally taking on all electronic communications with local contacts, biomedical suppliers and Malagasy Lutheran practitioners. IHM employs four full-time office staff and managed a US$1.9 million budget in 2006, but relies predominantly upon a 150-person local volunteer workforce drawn from an 18,000-member national mailing list. As many as twenty-five people, primarily Euro-American retirees of self-identified Scandinavian or German descent, staff each regular volunteer shift, doing everything from packaging transatlantic sea container shipments of medical materials to installing the electrical wiring in the agency's headquarters.

7 Materials are donated to Malagasy Partnership and IHM from hospitals and clinics in Minneapolis/St Paul and the surrounding region for one or more of five central reasons. The items may be 'short-dated' and close to reaching their manufacturer's expiration dates with about three or four months of existent 'shelf life'. Furthermore, a new product vendor may have been chosen for a piece of equipment, making the former one outdated or superfluous (even if completely new). Additionally, a surplus could exist of a particular medical item owing to changing medical procedures at the hospital and the materials

required for their implementation. If more than the requisite number of supplies has been opened for a given procedure, an operating room situation that Rosenblatt et al. (1997: 478) call 'over-preparedness', they generally may not be assigned to another procedure at a hospital even if they have not been used. Finally, some items may remain unopened and unused but are no longer considered sterile as judged by the manufacturer's expiration date on the packaging.

8 On the rare occasions when they accept expired medical supplies, the agencies do so with the understanding that the specific type of medical supply may be resterilized at the receiving hospital, eliminating most surface microorganisms using the prevailing equipment of heat sterilization, the autoclave machine. Sterility is not required of all medical supplies, corresponding to sterile and non-sterile zones of the medicalized body (e.g. blood versus skin, respectively) that determine the appropriate preparation of medical items for a given procedure.

9 Materials may be deemed 'unsuitable' for US biomedical institutions as a result more of the 'legal and political climate' that surrounds biomedicine than because of their complete inability to be used for 'safe, effective patient care', as two medical professionals noted in their discussion of the recovery programme for unused surgical supplies at Yale-New Haven Hospital in Connecticut (Rosenblatt and Silverman 1992: 1442). Rosenblatt et al. (1996: 631) report that the nonprofit Yale-New Haven programme, entitled REMEDY, accrued operating theatre supplies valued at $500,000

between the inception of the recovery programme in June 1991 and the date of the journal article (1996). At the April 2006 Technical Exchange for Christian Healthcare (TECH) meeting, several people expressed concerns that a multinational corporation may become more involved in organizing a used medical supply market and siphon off the charitable donations they receive into a lucrative for-profit trade. This would make medical supplies less available to the hospitals served by organizations like IHM and Malagasy Partnership and require them to purchase more supplies from an international market. One could observe, then, that there is a separate incentive for non-profits in only calculating the monetary value of the medical donations for the purposes of their financial records, as required by law, but in not doing so for any other reasons. Some of the TECH members pointed out to me that it is also fiscally beneficial for the hospitals to continue making charitable donations rather than selling their supplies on a used medical supply market. They are able to value these supplies and/ or equipment at their 'fair market price' when they claim them as charitable donations, whereas the hospitals may not be able to acquire the fair market price if they were to sell them to a multinational supply distributor. In this calculation, the tax credit is worth more than the direct sale, a transaction I describe more fully in the body of the chapter.

10 I am grateful to Josh Reno for suggesting this point.

11 Donated manufactured medical supplies comprise part of the support received by US-based private voluntary organizations that exceeded $18 billion during the 2005 fiscal year alone (USAID 2007: 5). USAID unfortunately does not offer specific statistics on exactly how much of this total comes from biomedical donations, and I have been unable to track down a specific figure elsewhere. The USAID figure includes support of in-kind and private contributions from US citizens and private sources, but not that from governmental agencies like USAID.

References

Coleman, S. (2004) 'The charismatic gift', *Journal of the Royal Anthropological Institute*, 10(2): 421–42.

Fassin, D. (2008) 'The humanitarian politics of testimony: subjectification through trauma in the Israeli–Palestinian conflict', *Cultural Anthropology*, 23(3): 531–58.

Halvorson, B. (2012) 'Woven worlds: material things, bureaucratization, and dilemmas of caregiving in Lutheran humanitarianism', *American Ethnologist*, 39(1): 122–37.

Hawkins, G. (2006) *The Ethics of Waste: How We Relate to Rubbish*, Lanham, MD: Rowman & Littlefield.

Hawkins, G. and S. Muecke (eds) (2003) *Culture and Waste: The Creation and Destruction of Value*, Lanham, MD: Rowman & Littlefield.

Hayden, C. (2004) 'Prospecting's publics', in K. Verdery and C. Humphrey (eds), *Property in Question: Value Transformations in the Global Economy*, Oxford: Berg, pp. 115–28.

Hetherington, K. (2004) 'Secondhandedness: consumption, disposal, and absent presence', *Environment and Planning D*, 22: 157–73.

Hodges, S. (2008) 'Chennai's biotrash chronicles: chasing the neo-liberal syringe', GARNET Working Paper no. 44/08.

Kopytoff, I. (1986) 'The cultural biography of things: commoditization as process', in A. Appadurai (ed.), *The Social Life of Things: Commodities in Cultural Perspective*, Cambridge: Cambridge University Press, pp. 64–94.

Parry, B. and C. Gere (2006) 'Contested bodies: property models and the commodification of human biological artefacts', *Science as Culture*, 15(2): 139–58.

Raison-Jourde, F. (1995) 'The Madagascan churches in the political arena and their contribution to the change of regime, 1990–1993', in P. Gifford (ed.), *The Christian Churches and the Democratisation of Africa*, Leiden: E. J. Brill, pp. 292–301.

Randrianja, S. and S. Ellis (2009) *Madagascar: A Short History*, Chicago, IL: University of Chicago Press.

Reno, J. (2009) 'Your trash is someone's treasure: the politics of value at a Michigan landfill', *Journal of Material Culture*, 14: 29–46.

Rosenblatt, W. H. and D. G. Silverman (1992) 'Recovery, resterilization, and donation of unused surgical supplies', *Journal of the American Medical Association*, 268(11): 1441–3.

Rosenblatt, W. H., C. Ariyan, V. Gutter, K. Shine and D. Silverman (1996) 'Focused versus operating room-wide recovery of unused supplies for overseas reconstructive surgery', *Plastic and Reconstructive Surgery*, 97(3): 630–4.

Rosenblatt, W. H., A. Chavez, D. Tenney and D. G. Silverman (1997) 'Assessment of the economic impact of an overage reduction program in the operating room', *Journal of Clinical Anesthesia*, 9: 478–81.

Sharp, L. (2006) *Strange Harvest: Organ Transplants, Denatured Bodies, and the Transformed Self*, Berkeley: University of California Press.

USAID (United States Agency for International Development) (2007) *Report of Voluntary Agencies (VOLAG)*, Washington, DC.

Verdery, K. and C. Humphrey (eds) (2004) *Property in Question: Value Transformations in the Global Economy*, London: Berg.

10 | Evident excess: material deposits and narcotics surveillance in the USA

JOSHUA RENO

Introduction

When I worked at a Michigan landfill, Four Corners, during the course of my fieldwork, one of my closest friends was a young man I will call 'Eddy'. A labourer, like me, Eddy earned less than the unionized mechanics and machine operators and, often, sought out alternative sources of income. But whereas some of our co-workers earned extra cash by reclaiming sellable items from the waste or fixing up old cars, Eddy had been a drug dealer.

On one occasion, agents of the Drug Enforcement Administration (DEA) arrived at the landfill to arrest Eddy, whom they suspected of dealing illegal drugs from his home in Greater Detroit. Making the arrest at the landfill was significant, because some of the agents thought Eddy was being supplied from a source across the border that was smuggling the material in the trucks arriving at the landfill from Toronto. The arresting officers made this clear during their interrogation, when they tried to convince him to reveal his source, hoping to make more arrests and disrupt what they believed to be an international drug smuggling chain. From what landfill employees had told me, suspicions that such a narcotics network existed, in connection with Four Corners, were not entirely unfounded. On one occasion, a driver who had strayed from his route was found to have a large amount of cash in his cab; on another it was discovered that a driver leaving the landfill had tied a bag of drugs to the back of his trailer, so that when the waste was dumped, the bag remained secured to the inside.

However, these were only rumours and, in any case, they had nothing to do with Eddy. He was quite pleased when he learned of the DEA's speculation, in fact, because it meant that his friends and acquaintances would be protected from the investigation.

Waste disposal in the USA was, until recently, closely involved with organized crime, and this remains a recurrent trope in popular entertainment, despite complaints from the waste industry that they now run legitimate businesses. What interests me is not why such associations persist, nor whether they are correct, but the effort to recycle material flows of waste, and also money, into trace evidence, standing in for an informal market that is otherwise difficult to grasp. The twentieth-century idea of territorially bound economies became widespread because state actors and economic experts could bring it to life, measure it, regulate it (see Mitchell 2002). Informal economies, particularly illegal ones, are thought distinguishable from 'the US economy', because they escape state monitoring. Both the rumours of landfill employees and the speculations of DEA agents suggest the existence of a concealed market in drugs, money and waste that can be glimpsed only if the smooth path of illicit circulation is interrupted, made suddenly visible and interpretable.

In this chapter, I explore various efforts to capture glimpses of drug trafficking, dealing and use in the late twentieth-century USA. I review attempts to render the drug economy in formal legal or scientific terms using intersecting flows of waste, drugs and money, thereby making their associations visible to analysis and enforcement. I argue that the recent history of narcotics surveillance through waste deposits not only presents a conceptual challenge to accepted notions of privacy and publicity, discipline and subjectivity, but also revalues familiar habits and objects through which we transfer our waste on to sites like Eddy's landfill. Mundane devices like garbage cans, bedpans and toilets are thus deputized as witnesses to criminal or transgressive acts.

Money and waste are thought capable of providing access to the hidden world of narcotics because both seem to detach themselves and travel with relative ease. This apparent mobility belies their potential to serve as a material record of behaviour, prohibited and otherwise.

In social theory, associations between money and waste can be traced to Freud and theories of anal personality, but it was John Locke who first proposed the connection between money and waste as part of his justification of the natural right of property ownership. For him, the relationship between waste and money is political and social rather than psychological and existential. Locke positioned waste as

235

the dialectical antithesis of property, that which is excluded by it and at the same time makes it possible. This is most apparent in the 'spoilage' argument of his *Second Treatise of Civil Government* (1980 [1690]). In these passages, Locke offers a conceptual myth for the rise of private property and the origins of government. Before the creation of money, it would not be permissible in God's eyes to hoard fruit as one's own, letting it rot while others starve. With the introduction of money, Locke suggests that it is now possible to own more wealth than one can make use of without fear of spoilage. Now the meaning of waste has changed as well. It would be a misuse of resources if they were left to waste in common when private labour and industry could make far better use of them. Government becomes necessary as a force to secure prosperity and property and avoid this secondary form of spoilage. It is also for this reason that Locke is able to endorse private (European) conquest of the newly discovered continent of America: if removed from common use, he suggests, its bountiful resources might be reappropriated for the benefit of all. 'In the Beginning', Locke writes in the *Second Treatise*, 'all the world was America ... for no such thing as money was any where known' (ibid.: 29).

Given the critical role of currency as the basis for just government and international trade, it is clear why Locke considered the spoilage of money, through counterfeiting and 'clipping', as among the greatest moral offences of his time. In an illuminating discussion, George Caffentzis (1989) explains Locke's attempts to track these illicit practices by making money speak about its misuse. This was not long after the publication of Locke's *Two Treatises* and the founding of the Bank of England (1694), the first modern central bank. At this time he invited Isaac Newton to become Warden of the Mint in order to determine with precision the average portion of silver present in the empire's circulating coinage and, therefore, to diagnose the extent of the coin-tampering problem (ibid.: 19). What Newton found confirmed Locke's suspicions that coin clipping was rampant, threatening to devalue the national currency during an expensive war with France, thereby destabilizing Britain's position in the global competition for colonies among European powers.[1] While a number of proposals was hotly debated, one common means of avoiding clipping was to create the serrated edges we find on many coins today, in a sense establishing a material means of recording attempted acts of defacement. What all the proposals shared in common was increased management of the money supply and, more broadly, a growing concern about the hidden activities of the governed populace.

Newton's intervention offered a rare glimpse into a hidden economy of currency manipulation and evidence of the need to control it. He and Locke recognized the power of money not only as an abstract measure of wealth, but also as a material object that could be put to different use, as a sign of illegality and a means of enforcement. Regulation of a national mint and a centralized bank meant that money could be recalled, studied and modified as needed, as a material record and political tool. By the time of American independence, a national bank was understood to be indicative of sovereignty, the sign of a mature state, not least because of its importance for monitoring and governing populations.

According to Dominique Laporte (2002), the origins of the modern state in the liberal, Lockean sense, with its emphasis on regulating circulation on behalf of the people, also involved the ordering of material wastes, and not just currencies. He traces ideological investment in the presumed divide between 'private' and 'public' to the transformation of excretion into a secretive and shameful activity. Just before the time of Locke, waste was ushering in these divides by transforming the visibility of their interconnections. It was almost two centuries before sewage and garbage collection were, like banks, centralized and systematically managed in the USA and Europe, but they share a number of startling resemblances. Both waste management sites and banks are considered signs of advanced statehood, and complementary means of representing and securing a population's financial and bodily hygiene through its most common material circulations.

Coursing through sewers, banks, waste bins and wallets, money and waste possess a hidden mobility that allows them to be taken for granted as anonymous media of circulation (see Hawkins 2006: 61). But they also bear the potential traces of the persons and activities with which they were once engaged, traces that can be carefully converted through legal and medico-scientific means to serve as evidence against them, as Locke and Newton did with clipped coins. In Kevin Hetherington's terms (2004), these recovered materials are a trace that signifies an absent presence: the person (even more specifically the *kind of person*) to which they previously belonged. Their abandonment and forgottenness allows deposits of money and waste to take on new life as evidence of legal guilt or, alternatively, extensions of state protections of privacy and property.

In what follows, I review three moments whereby mundane materials, especially wastes, are recycled into signs of a hidden narcotics economy. The first two are examined through prominent cases in higher courts in the United States, where the use of recovered waste as legal evidence was debated and decided upon. The final example comes from the controversial new practice of sewer epidemiology, which was developed to monitor the drug use of urban populations, thereby creating a virtual map of the distribution of illegal behaviour.

Revelation and representation

As I have written elsewhere (Reno 2009), the collected waste of populations is a pluripotent substance that lends itself to multiple interpretations and valuations. An array of representational practices is required to reimagine the specific potential they possess and bestow them with renewed social purpose. The various representational practices that I explore below share a tendency to explore dissociated materials, not as a source of something new, per se, but as a record of the past. The emphasis is to determine what materials once were, what activities they were previously engaged in, not what they might yet become. At the same time this work of contextualization is meant to be socially transformative; the goal of such conversions is to make legible the underground narcotics economy and, ultimately, to control and eliminate it.

But recovered waste does not readily lend itself to formalized representation. Like money, as described by Hart (2001) and Graeber (2011), waste serves as a form of social memory; it allows us to make distinctions between what we want to endure and what we want to forget. Despite the apparent ease with which mundane materials like money and waste become detached from their previous owners, the senses of transferred ownership that result are never so clearly defined that acts of repossession avoid complication. And given the stakes for those whose private actions are being publicly exposed and judged, there is every reason for them to challenge the fragile process of evidence construction.

For much of the twentieth century, American garbage cans and toilets served as conduits between private consumption and the anonymity of mass disposal, making them critical, everyday sites of material traffic and moral transformation. The corollary to this is a sense of privacy and security, a performative removal of one's 'intimate self' from public view. In a way similar to the social metaphysics of money (Simmel 1990), the circulation of waste makes possible a form of freedom from attachment to things. Just as personal forms of waste are detached from one's possession and made invisible, so too are the hidden lives that people conduct in private removed from view. The significance of waste recovery, or 'garbology' as it is sometimes called, is as a challenge to these assumptions, short-circuiting the material transformation of intimate privacy and anonymous publicity by rendering hidden lives and transactions suddenly visible.

While similar representational activities have long been important to state actors, as the example of Locke shows above, the idea of unveiling the 'real person' concealed behind closed doors was a prevailing concern of twentieth-century states, increasingly paranoid about political subversives and radical movements. This interest culminated in the pre-war and interwar creation of secret police and intelligence agencies. Such agencies and their domestic operations boomed with the start of the Cold War, and they relied on discovering ways of surveilling activities hidden from view, but ones which could be detected, like Locke's clipped coins, through the recycling of material traces left behind.

In the USA, law enforcement agencies performed surveillance by manipulating and violating the public/private boundary, as well as rerouting the transfer of materials and messages across it. Along with wire-tapping, 'mail cover' and break-ins, so-called 'trash cover' was a frequently used surveillance technique of J. Edgar Hoover's Federal Bureau of Investigation (FBI) during the 1950s and early 1960s. The FBI routinely used trash cover against those deemed to be real or potential enemies of the state, including leftist radicals, organized crime and the Ku Klux Klan. The search for methods of apprehending secret selves was not the exclusive obsession of the FBI and state agencies, but was part of a wider set of assumptions and anxieties about conspirators, strangers and immigrants that shaped US social life and fantasy. Around the same time, a cultural fascination around subversive lives conducted in private inspired everything from the sex studies conducted by the Kinseys at Indiana University to the popular literature about serial killers and the dramaturgical sociology of Erving Goffman.

Hoover ordered an end to trash cover in 1965, along with other techniques deemed possible violations of civil liberties, in anticipation of the changing political climate ushered in by the Johnson administration (Powers 2004: 271). As useful as these techniques were, Hoover was concerned they would draw more scrutiny. Fulfilling Hoover's prediction, from the 1960s onward the Supreme Court made the issue of privacy central to its interpretation of the Fourth Amendment and its application to a number of cases (Allen 2004: 21).[2] Waste continued to be utilized in police surveillance throughout the country, not as a primary source of evidence, but typically as a means of convincing a judge that law enforcement had reasonable cause to search a domicile, car or other private enclosure. But Hoover's concerns would prove prophetic. The increasing influence of privacy discourse in the American legal domain culminated in federal and state Supreme Court cases *California* v. *Greenwood* (1988) and *Venner* v. *Maryland* (1976/77). Both established the rights of individuals in their own waste and outlined the practical and semiotic grounds according to which the state can convert that waste into legal evidence.

The garbage can as a house In 1984, a police investigator in Laguna Beach, California, had a local trash collector help him gain access to the garbage of suspected narcotics trafficker Billy Greenwood. Using evidence from the garbage, which was enough to convince a local judge of Greenwood's possible culpability, the officer was able to obtain a warrant to search the man's home. The mounting evidence against Greenwood eventually led to an arrest and an appearance in front of the Superior Court of Orange County. The court sided with Greenwood's defence that evidence gathered from his garbage was inadmissible because obtained through illegal search and seizure. This would in turn invalidate the legal warrant used to obtain access to his home. They decided that Greenwood had a 'reasonable expectation' to assume his rubbish would not be inspected by others, perhaps least of all the police. Asserting his Fourth Amendment rights was surely a way for Greenwood to avoid imprisonment, not to expand the cause of civil liberty per se, but it brought up what, for the California courts at least, had become a growing concern. Over a decade earlier, the California court had decided in a similar fashion in *The People* v. *Krivda* (1971), when they had ruled, in related circumstances, that 'by placing trash barrels on the parkway' criminal defendants had not 'forsaken their reasonable expectation of privacy with respect to the contents'.

Greenwood was not free yet, however. Owing to a change in the state constitution in 1982, evidence could not be suppressed where seizure violated only California (not federal) law. As a result, the California Court of Appeal asked the US Supreme Court to review the case in 1986 (*California* v. *Greenwood*, 1988). In May 1988 the Supreme Court stunned many by reversing the California Superior Court's decision, holding that the investigator's search of Greenwood's garbage did not constitute a violation of the Fourth Amendment and, therefore, was admissible as evidence.

The representational forms employed by American law enforcers as evidence can be usefully compared with the conjectural method described by Carlo Ginzburg in his essay, 'Morelli, Freud and Sherlock

Holmes: clues and scientific method' (1980). Ginzburg describes a common form of semiosis, generally classified as an indexical sign, wherein a hidden cause or reality is deciphered from the slightest traces it has left behind. He identifies this interpretative mode, among other things, with the practical detection skills of hunters, medical diagnosticians and psychoanalysts. What makes Sherlock Holmes or Sigmund Freud clever semioticians is their ability to focus on seemingly insignificant details. Their cleverness lies in forming associations between a sign/ symptom and the object/cause that it stands for.

Producing legal evidence is about more than establishing a value-neutral 'fact'. In the case of recovered deposits like money and waste, in the twentieth-century USA at least, there was a tendency to interpret their discard as a secret exposed. Arresting the anticipated flow of deposits from waste bin to landfill or incinerator allows investigators to restore their severed connections in potentially unexpected ways. A good detective or hunter doesn't just track their quarry; they catch them by surprise.

What is complicated about these interpretative moves is not how traces are identified and read, however, but their conversion into legal forms of evidence; that is, objects which not only bear traces of a person, but can serve as a tool of state prosecution. This form of revelatory representational practice does not necessarily translate easily to the formal domain of legal argumentation associated with the US courts. Sally Engle Merry (1990) and others have argued that this formal, rule-based discursive style appears to conflict with the moral reasoning of everyday people. Less obvious, perhaps, is how it might potentially conflict with the styles of reasoning associated with police investigation. From the 1960s onward, reinterpretations of the Fourth Amendment had their greatest impact on the practice of law enforcement, including in particular the formal procedures one has to follow to make a legitimate arrest (e.g. securing a warrant). This standardization of policing, in some domains at least, was meant to secure conviction by strategically avoiding the infringement of individual rights. The significance of the debate over Greenwood's case had less to do with protecting liberty than deciding upon the conditions under which rights in things are suspended.

California v. *Greenwood* is frequently cited as the definitive legal case in the USA for classifying the contents of rubbish bins left for collection as something other than private property. But the decision was far from unanimous. The property status of garbage raised difficult questions that had hitherto seemed unimportant. To what extent does my waste still belong to me even as others handle it? At what point is the transfer of property initiated so that others might lay claim to what has been formally abandoned? Between the majority and dissenting Justices there were substantial differences depending on what 'understandings' of the waste process 'are recognized and permitted by society' (*California* v. *Greenwood*, 1988). The point of view of those responsible for the majority ruling found it unreasonable for anyone to think that waste remains entirely private after it is deposited on the roadside for collection. Consequently, discarded objects are always at risk of being traced back to the person that once owned them:

> [I]t is common knowledge that plastic garbage bags left on or at the side of a public street are readily accessible to animals, children, scavengers, snoops, and other members of the public, and ... the occupants place their refuse at the curb for the express purpose of conveying it to a third party ... who could sort through the trash or permit others, such as the police, to do so. (*California* v. *Greenwood*, 1988)

Dissenting Justices Brennan and Marshall, on the other hand, envisioned a completely different understanding of waste management processes. If not completely private, waste is at least depersonalized, made anonymous, while it mixes with the materials detached from other persons. Justice Brennan writes:

> I suspect ... that members of our society will be shocked to learn that the Court, the ultimate guarantor of liberty, deems unreasonable our expectation that the aspects of our private lives that are concealed safely in a trash bag will not become public. (*California* v. *Greenwood*, 1988)

Brennan and Marshall point out what many waste producers implicitly assume, that most, if not all, of what is discarded will not resurface or recirculate. Though no longer private, garbage is not yet released from an expectation of privacy. Brennan and Marshall argue further that this expectation persists even after property is formally abandoned.

One might think of the other sense of deposit, that of a bank transaction. As with waste transfers, depositing currency means abandoning attachment to the particular medium transacted. However, when we deposit something in a bank we assume that the physical objects we've left behind, whether cheques or cash, have been recorded by some accounting mechanism, which separates the materiality of the transaction from our virtual balance. The primary difference, and what offers monetary deposits their desired durability and waste deposits their desired transience, is that the right of ownership and trace of personal connection are dissociated from the thing itself and accounted for separately. And yet, even in these instances, the material trace of the object's former biography cannot be completely extinguished. This is because, as in Ginzburg's examples, there are innumerable ways of producing such traces: from the serial numbers on the banknote itself, to the human cells that may have sloughed off and become attached to its surface. Then there is Newton's method of weighing each coin to establish its true metallic content.[3]

Clearly abandonment does not necessarily entail public exposure. But in the view of the dissenting judges in the Greenwood case, the reasonable citizen has much more to lose than property:

> A search of trash testifies eloquently to the eating, reading, and recreational habits of the person who produced it. A search of trash, like a search of a bedroom, can relate intimate details about sexual practices, health, and personal hygiene. Like rifling through desk drawers or intercepting phone calls, rummaging through trash can divulge the target's financial and professional status, political affiliations and inclinations, private thoughts, personal relationships, and romantic interests. It cannot be doubted that a sealed trash bag harbors telling evidence ... which the Fourth Amendment is designed ... to protect. (*California* v. *Greenwood*, 1988)

Brennan and Marshall thus identify discard as something that, though detached, has the capacity to reveal private information. It cannot be completely alienated, even when abandoned, because even as it mixes with other wastes it can be recovered and reattached to its former bearer, with potentially damaging consequences.

It is telling that several of Brennan's metaphors relate specifically to the house or the rooms and furniture within it. Radin (1993: 56–7) describes the house as the prototypical 'thing' that becomes commingled with the life and history of the person that uses it.[4] It is the home which is the original possession protected from search and seizure by the Fourth Amendment. Not surprisingly, to counter the opinion of the dissenting judges, those Justices in the majority argue for a radical, spatial separation between home and trash bin. If under the kitchen sink or in the toilet the garbage is protected from the incursion of the state, once outside 'the curtilage of the home' garbage has officially lost protection from search and seizure. The majority Justices leave the exact border between 'inside' and 'outside' the home's reach somewhat vague, except to point out that in Greenwood's case the placement of the garbage exceeded this boundary.

The dissenting Justices, in contrast, employ this spatial metaphor in a unique way. For them the rhetorical relevance of the home is as an enclosure which hides private matter from a public gaze. Particular forms of private property, those things from which the person cannot be completely eradicated, are marked by a material removal from public view. Such a physical boundary, like the walls of a house or a secret room, suggests by extension that garbage is also protected from invasion by the state or the wider public:

> Had Greenwood flaunted his intimate activity by strewing his trash all over the curb for all to see ... I could accept the Court's conclusion ... But all Greenwood 'exposed to the public' ... were the exteriors of several opaque, sealed containers. (*California* v. *Greenwood*, 1988)

Thus the waste bin is made a microcosm of the house, divided from the public by a material boundary ultimately impenetrable to observation.

The different spatio-material dimensions of Greenwood's waste emphasized by the Justices ultimately correspond to different publics as well. For the majority, the invasive sorting practices of waste workers set the standard for the potential appropriation of domestic waste by '... animals, children, scavengers, snoops, and other members of the public ... such as the police' (*California* v. *Greenwood*, 1988). Garbage on the kerb, separated from the home, enters a commons which seems to exclude no one (whether animal, snoop or investigator). Where all the Justices seem to agree is on the fact that the rubbish bin itself plays a crucial role as a mediator between publicity and privacy, object detachment and attachment. Where they seem to disagree most, it seems, is on whether it is reasonable for waste makers to take the role of the bin for granted, to ignore the potentially dire ramifications of its influence.

This is the core contradiction associated with the mobility of social media – bodily or otherwise. In one sense, to be accessible to others something must already have been given up to the public domain and rights to it therefore abandoned. In another sense, things like waste cannot be completely separated from persons, even after they've been deposited for others to receive. It is the uncertain moral and epistemological grounds of these evidentiary forms which have made them the subject of legal debate and intrigue in recent decades and have made property claims in waste important considerations for twentieth-century interpretations of the Constitution. This is because, drug profiteer or not, anyone's secrets might be made vulnerable through the appropriation of their material deposits.

Invited on to the premises of Venner When the detached thing changes from garbage to bodily waste, and its means of detachment from a quotidian technology (a garbage bin) to an exceptional one (a bedpan), the ways that courts legitimize surveillance activities change as well.

In 1973, an American in Morocco named Charles Venner swallowed at least two dozen balloons filled with hashish oil and smuggled them into the USA. During the plane ride, some of the bags ruptured and began to leak the oil into his system. Upon arriving at JFK, Venner was hallucinating, nauseous, and experiencing a number of other symptoms. He was admitted to a Baltimore hospital experiencing the effects of the drug, where he excreted each balloon, one by one, in his faeces. He was later arrested after hospital staff turned the excreted balloons, neatly delivered to them by his bedpan, over to the police as evidence of his crime. Venner appealed the conviction on the grounds that this transfer was illegal, leading to a landmark test of the Fourth Amendment that forced the State Supreme Court to outline under what conditions individuals forgo legal rights in their own bodily waste.

For *Venner* v. *Maryland* (1977) the main task for the court was to isolate a moment of abandonment where the waste converts from one body's effluent to the state's evidence. Deciding whether or not privacy rights apply is based on whether the person has abandoned their right to the body's labour, to use Lockean terms, and can therefore reasonably expect that it is secure.[5] What the court must decide is this: what counts as abandonment of bodily waste?

Venner's appeal was denied twice, but his property claim was taken very seriously in both instances. According to Appellate Judge Liss:

> It could not be said that a person has no property right in wastes or other materials which were once a part of or contained within his body, but which normally are discarded after their separation from the body. It is not unknown for a person to assert a continuing right of owner-ship, dominion, or control, for good reason or for no reason, over such things as excrement, fluid waste, secretions, hair, fingernails, toenails, blood, and organs or other parts of the body, whether their separation from the body is intentional, accidental, or merely the result of normal body functions. (*Venner* v. *Maryland*, 1977)

Judge Liss's concern is what Rabinow calls the 'body/person metonymy', the modern image that relates the fragmented part to the whole being (1996: 148). That Maryland police took something previously 'contained within' Venner's body is even more suspect, given the prevailing image of the violated house in the legal assessment of

Fourth Amendment jurisdiction. Like the garbage guarding its contents from view, Venner's body is a protected domicile blocking state access.

Historically, America's higher courts have not typically recognized property rights in one's detached body parts (ibid.: 142). *Venner v. Maryland* is therefore unique, as many have noted, in extending the regime of 'private property' into the domain of bodily cast-offs.[6] Despite the resonance of Venner's claim, the court disagreed that the confiscation of his excrement constituted a violation of his rights. For Judge Liss, the Fourth Amendment did not apply because Venner had abandoned property rights in his bodily waste in the context of the situation in question. However, unlike the Supreme Court Justices, Judge Liss seemed to feel that full abandonment of property in waste is an exceptional occurrence. In Venner's case, abandonment was assured in two ways. On the one hand, it resulted from the institutional context where things were formally detached; on the other, it was a function of the calm and complacent manner in which rights to the waste were allegedly transferred.

The 'perishable', 'non-durable' qualities of bodily waste make it a difficult thing to reify into a thing of property. Unlike garbage, once it has entered the waste stream an individual body's waste is not likely to be recovered and reappropriated except as an objective, fluid mass (i.e. 'sewage'), which no longer holds a semblance of attachment to individual identity. Medical institutions and procedures – including the bedpan – make possible the individuation of waste matter as an extension of the patient and their monitored health. In a Foucauldian reading, this careful exploration and categorization of bodily wastes is part of 'the progressive objectification and the ever more subtle partitioning' of medicalized subjects (Foucault 1977: 173). According to Judge Liss, individuals give themselves over to the hospital's discipline when they are admitted as patients:

> Venner would have been a naïve young man had he in entering the
> hospital not expected his human waste would be examined. Urinalysis,
> blood tests, and examination of one's stools are part of normal hospital
> procedures. (*Venner v. Maryland*, 1977)

With waste, as with currency, not only is it possible to find traces of criminal activity inscribed in the objectual form of the objects themselves, but the process of material release makes this process superficially simple. The reason that money and waste so readily serve as mobile signs of criminal behaviour is that, when they are surrendered to further circulation, it is usually anticipated that they will dissolve into anonymous material streams. So long as suspected criminals continue to deposit pieces of their person – whether literal or figurative – in conspicuous ways, detection is made easy. Escaping such detection, similarly, involves practices of hoarding, of stopping flows and perhaps rerouting them altogether. Money 'laundering' is a good example, where 'dirty money' is made clean by carefully accounting for its release into circulation. In an unusual case recently reported in the UK, an incarcerated man refused to defecate to keep from providing the police with evidence of drug use – they continued to feed him and kept him jailed until he had no control over the matter.

It is no accident that perhaps the most commonly depicted method of escaping drug detection during a raid is by flushing illegal material down the toilet. Here the release of material does seem to elude capture; more to the point, it is thought reasonable to expect that it should. This explains why Judge Liss found it even more damning that Venner's excreta was eliminated into a bedpan rather than a private toilet. Whether one is in a jail cell or a hospital room the matter is the same. The potential for hospital surveillance of Venner's body was apparent in the materiality of the 'petty mechanisms' all around him (Foucault 1977: 173). The situation would have been different, Liss claims, if Venner had eliminated waste 'in a lavatory in [his] own home' (*Venner v. Maryland*, 1977). In a sense, Liss argues that Venner invited the hospital staff into his body. The excrement was not gathered through a 'trespass upon the premises of Venner' but rather was implicitly accepted as a part of entering a total institution.[7] The bedpan is a perfect embodiment of hospital care and bodily control; it can elicit embarrassment and laughter precisely because it signals the breakdown of individual privacy and health at the most intimate level. The whole point of the bedpan is to make your waste mobile, to put it in another's hands so that they might dispose of it for you. As with the waste bin, it suggests forms of connection that constitute (and potentially disrupt) senses of privacy and freedom, memory and forgetting, association and dissociation.

However, Liss is not entirely comfortable with the notion of implicit consent. For Venner to alienate property in his waste, he must also express the proper comportment during the transfer. This is a unique perspective, one not echoed in *California v. Greenwood*, *People v. Krivda* or many similar cases. But it does offer an example of 'reasonableness' in legal interpretation taken to a logical absurdity:

This court holds that when one does nothing and says nothing to indicate an intent to assert his right of ownership, possession, or control over his body wastes, the only rational inference is that he intends to abandon such material. (*Venner v. Maryland*, 1977)

Judge Liss continues, 'Venner was lucid. We have no indication of any effort on the part of Venner to protest the removal of his excreta' (ibid.). In other words, abandonment is not simply a matter of practice (e.g. the placement of a garbage can by the side of the road for pick-up), but is also a matter of attitude towards the loss of the thing itself. Liss cites another case where the criteria for abandonment are described as 'a combination of act and intent' (*Venner v. Maryland*, 1977). Had Venner protested, we are led to believe, the institution would have had no right to pass on his waste to the police for use as evidence. More than any of the legal arguments we have encountered so far, this position entails a microscopic focus on the moment of material transfer itself. The extent to which bodily waste loses the 'reasonable expectation of privacy' depends on the moment of its detachment. The medical setting provides an appropriate context for such a transfer to take place, but it is above all Venner's calm acceptance of the bedpan which signals that he is submitting his waste to be examined and turned over to the authorities.

Sewer epidemiology

In Venner's case a toilet appears a relatively simple affair when compared to the precarious use of a bedpan. Yet toilets carry their own potential for the application of surveillance and the assertion of rights to privacy and property. I would like to consider one last instance of property claims in waste. Leaving behind the subject of hospital medicine and turning towards the proliferating field that David Armstrong (1995) calls 'surveillance medicine', the vulnerability of the defecator is once again at issue, this time relative to a sampled population.

The deputization of bedpans and waste bins into technologies of state surveillance relies on their peculiar role as conduits of material excess. In both cases, however, there is an individuation of discards; they are physically contained in such a way that they can be reattached to the persons who cast them off. This is not so with the mess of common material as it is allowed to collect and amass in public waste streams. But even this anonymization of materials does not prevent new projections from being extrapolated from the formless disorder. Where once discards were made to speak only against *individuals*, new developments in narcotics epidemiology use municipal sewage and used currency to create new (and purportedly more accurate) surveys of the drug use habits of *populations*. While advocates allege that this shift from an individual-juridical to a collective-scientific mode of surveillance reduces threats to personal privacy, the politics of dissociation remain. But rather than generating legal debate over the legitimacy of state dispossession, controversy now is concentrated in the details of epidemiological case studies and statistical analyses.

As I have argued, the possible manipulation of anonymous media of circulation, specifically their use as sources of evidence about the secretive lives of persons and populations, extends to both money and waste.[8] In the mid-1980s, for example, it was widely reported that a substantial number of paper bills contained traces of cocaine. Paralleling Newton's investigation into money tampering, in recent years European epidemiologists have actually begun using samples of old currency and performing chemical analysis to determine levels of drug saturation in a given context. According to a recent article in *Science* magazine:

> Epidemiologists have struggled to get a quantitative view of drug use for decades. But the traditional data – tons of drugs seized, the number of people seeking treatment for addiction, drug-related mortality, and responses to drug-use questionnaires – are biased and patchy ... By interrogating the environment rather than the people ... 'you can obtain data in real time' that are not only objective but also 'rather affordable.' (Bohannon 2007: 42)

Money circulates as an anonymous social medium that ideally contains no memory of where it has been, representing 'neither the identity of its former owners nor the nature of transactions in which it has previously been involved' (Graeber 2001: 94). Epidemiological studies reduce paper bills to their carbon substrate, lifting electrons stored in their folds and destroying them in the process. Converting currency into evidence of narcotics use means undoing its previous value form once and for all.[9]

With the advent of what is called 'sewer forensic epidemiology', Swiss-trained scientists have begun examining the levels of various narcotics in the sewage of Europe and the USA. The problem epidemiologists face is depicting the actual distribution of drug use, as a corrective to survey data – the only method currently available for assessing drug use in a given population. As with all forms of surveillance medicine, the aim is to map the relative normality and abnormality of populations, as opposed to the health and illness of individual patients. Specially trained scientists retrieve samples from particular sewer lines and break down the results by making assumptions about rates and amounts of excretion, in order to provide a more reliable portrait of local drug use. In that sense they serve as something like the epidemiological partner to archaeological garbology. As with the efforts of Locke and Newton, the ultimate purpose of this work is to effect some change in the reality one is striving to understand, to use the results to bring about social change, whether one is interested in legalization or enforcement.

A legal analogue to epidemiological studies of currency would be *United States* v. *Dill* (1982), where an appellate court weighed the legality of 'dye packs': incendiary, anti-theft devices that transform money into a source of evidence by literally marking the bodies and possessions of guilty persons. Dye packs make cash useless and stain the body, vehicle and clothes of those responsible for theft, sometimes using tear gas, homing signals or other techniques. Red dye sticks to the bills and the persons of those who attempt to steal them. They make virtual money *matter* once again in order to stop it from circulating.[10] Unlike with sewer epidemiology, however, individual rights are at stake because a trace has been put on currency to follow where it goes, rather than read from it to determine where it's been.

As it is currently practised, sewer epidemiology does not target individuals. Indeed, that would go against its central purpose. According to Armstrong, 'a cardinal feature of Surveillance Medicine is its targeting of everyone. Surveillance medicine requires the dissolution of the distinct clinical categories of healthy and ill as it attempts to bring everyone within its network of visibility' (1995: 395). The whole point is to understand the distribution of narcotics usage, yet urban officials in the USA remain resistant to adopting the methods. In addition to concern over a city's reputation, privacy issues are often listed as a core concern officials have, and with good reason. The uses of such data go beyond simply generating statistics. As one reporter from *Popular Science* suggests, 'Knowing where in the country heroin use is highest, for example, could help Drug Enforcement Administration agents target their investigations or track major suppliers. Local police might be interested in subtler differences. If daily monitoring shows a spike in the standard ratio of cocaine, it means that somebody probably flushed his stash down the toilet' (Hagerman 2008).

Indeed, sewer epidemiologists readily admit that their sampling methods could one day be incorporated into police surveillance activities and there are currently no laws that would prevent sampling targeted at specific homes or neighbourhoods, though both *California* v. *Greenwood* and *Venner* v. *Maryland* provide some precedent that might rule this out, at least in the United States. If the role waste has played in narcotics surveillance in recent years is any indication, sewer sampling for evidence is almost certain to occur in the near future. And, according to Armstrong, 'a surveillance machinery deployed throughout a population to monitor precarious normality delineates a new temporalised risk identity' (1995: 403). But if the examples of Greenwood and Venner are instructive, than this same machinery also opens up new possibilities for the assertion of certain kinds of possessive personhood.

In this case, the unassuming toilet, protected as it is within the sacred home, reveals its potential for mischief. As with all objects involved in waste transfer, the main role of a toilet is to convey waste out and away in a speedy fashion. By protecting the contents of their sewers, urban officials in Milan, San Diego and elsewhere are asserting ownership, as caretakers of sewage waste on behalf of the population. They no longer dictate the process of evidence conversion, as in the legal cases above, but serve only as gatekeepers who attempt to control access to collective discard and manage the public image of the wasting/drug-using populace. What is at stake is not only access to the cities' circulating substances, but their depiction. All of these efforts, from trash-cover to police searches and the chemical testing of bills and sewage, are efforts to register the effects of a hidden economy at the level of exchange and consumption. If garbology or medical examinations offer glimpses of the home and the body, respectively, as imagined self-contained wholes, sewer epidemiology depicts the city as a circulatory system (see also Marvin and Medd 2006).

The placement of toilets and drains throughout cities, each contributing to the collective waste managed by the government and unified by the pipelines that connect them and mix their contents with that of the whole, creates the possibility for a defecating public to be conjured, measured and surveyed, as well as protected from such things. The consequence is a realignment of what it means to be a population or a city government, ushered in by changes in what it means to flush.

Conclusion

The difficulties of visualization are not simply a concern when it comes to illegal economies. At Four Corners landfill, efforts to regulate the incoming waste loads are confounded by the sheer impossibility of inspecting every truck that came on site. This created some anxiety for local residents, who wondered, like Eddy's arresting officers, what might be hidden in the waste haulers coming from across the border.

In the cases under consideration, sewer epidemiologists and government officials are investing in activities of dissociation and the stability of formal means of interpreting them. Political objects and techniques enable such separations and surveillance, their taken-for-grantedness allowing them to fall into the background and, through the subtle work of detachment they perform, creating opportunities for waste to be taken and also reclaimed. In a sense, all things taken from the mass of common rubbish are reclaimed and revalued for new purposes – even if they only become assessed as a landfill gate fee. What prepares these materials for such revaluation, regardless of their eventual destiny, are the technical objects whose function it is to quietly contain and transfer, readying rubbish for a social afterlife.

Traces are extracted from heterogeneous materials to create meaningful connections to waste-generating individuals and populations, as drug sellers, smugglers and users. I would stress that the accumulated mechanisms of waste collection and disposal, supporting and reinforcing those I have highlighted, together structure these detachments and reattachments. It is important to note that in all of the cases under consideration it was higher authorities deciding whether and in what way waste belonged to its producers or could be made to reveal damaging information about them. Even so, I think an interesting facet of each instance was the extension of claims of privacy and personal rights into new realms. The toilet, the bedpan and the bin are not merely instruments of disciplinary power, in other words, but means by which personhood has been and can be further expanded, as people search for different ways to affirm waste, when its outright rejection proves too difficult.

Thus, a key dimension of this chapter has been about ways of gathering evidence. But unlike other forms of evidence gathering, the collection of DNA evidence from a crime scene, for example, the examples considered here require particular material objects to mediate the dissemination of 'proof'. Making discards into evidence of the narcotics trade is meant to collapse black market economies and private socialities into an encompassing moral techno-economy of guilt, revelation and discipline. But as modes of surveillance establish associations between persons/collectives and discarded objects, they also expose the fragility of their own methods.

Notes

1 One of the main problems with counterfeiting is that it threatened what Locke considered one of the state's fundamental responsibilities – to guarantee the security of contracts. A monetary exchange was, in effect, a contractual relationship mediated by state authority. It was also primarily in defence of the integrity of contracts that the English colonial authority imposed the first institutionalized use of fingerprinting in the Hooghly district of West Bengal (Ginzburg 1980: 27). See Bear (this volume) for a discussion of the Hooghly area's ongoing significance as a periphery attractive for experimental governance.

2 The Fourth Amendment protects against search and seizure by the government, requiring that a judge issue a search warrant to grant law enforcement officers private access.

3 Contemporary methods of analysis combine his methodical precision with material transformation: in laboratories identifying underlying biochemical compositions typically involves destroying the object under study. Similarly, when libraries 'digitize' physical books into pure textual information, they usually tear pages from the binding to allow for easier photocopying.

4 Given the importance of epidermal cells in DNA tests, furthermore, one could argue that the temporariness of our physical skin has played a role in changing regimes of privacy and property (see Parry 2004).

5 According to Locke, the sacred inalienability of the body is the first natural right from which all others spring (1980 [1690]: 19).

6 In this respect, *Venner* has relevance for the better-known case *Moore* v. *Regents of California*, where plaintiff John Moore sought compensation for a genetically engineered cell line that was taken from his removed spleen. The California Supreme Court rejected this claim, in part on the grounds that it would defile the sacredness of the person to the level of mere 'things' (Rabinow 1996: 144).

7 The most similar case that Liss finds to the one under review is *United States* v. *Cox*, where hair clippings from a haircut were taken from a prison inmate and later used as evidence against him. Once again it is assumed that the inmate is exposing himself to the gaze of the institution, along with its potential appropriation of his abandoned wastes by disciplinary practices.

8 There are other circulating materials that this could be true for. Water is another example, owing to its unbounded reach throughout urban infrastructures. One need only think about the medicinal injection of fluoride into drinking water in American cities and the various conspiracy theories that have developed around this practice. Or one could consider the vulnerability of the water supply to tampering for the purposes of political activism or terrorism. I thank Catherine Alexander and David Graeber for pointing this out to me.

9 As discussed in the Introduction to this volume, recycling is a one-way process: materials deform and lose value as they are successively reused.

10 A similar technique of theft prevention and surveillance is so-called *smartwater*, a nano-technological procedure that marks possessions with invisible but uniquely coded data that can be traced back to the original owners.

References

Allen, A. L. (2004) 'Privacy in American law', in B. Rossler (ed.), *Privacies*, Stanford, CA: Stanford University Press, pp. 19–39.

Armstrong, D. (1995) 'The rise of surveillance medicine', *Sociology of Health and Illness*, 17(3): 393–404.

Bohannon, J. (2007) 'Hard data on hard drugs, grabbed from the environment', *Science*, 316: 42–4.

Caffentzis, G. (1989) *Clipped Coins, Abused Words, and Civil Government: John Locke's Philosophy of Money*, New York: Autonomedia.

Foucault, M. (1977) *Discipline and Punish*, New York: Random House.

Ginzburg, C. (1980) 'Morelli, Freud and Sherlock Holmes: clues and scientific method', *History Workshop*, 9: 5–36.

Graeber, D. (2001) *Toward an Anthropological Theory of Value: The False Coin of Our Own Dreams*, New York: Palgrave.

— (2011) *Debt: The First 5000 Years*, New York: Melville House.

Hagerman, E. (2008) 'Your sewer on drugs', *Popular Science*, www.popsci.com/scitech/article /2008-02/your-sewer-drugs.

Hart, K. (2001) *Money in an Unequal World*, London: Textere.

Hawkins, G. (2006) *The Ethics of Waste*, Oxford: Rowman and Littlefield.

Hetherington, K. (2004) 'Second-handedness: consumption, disposal and absent presence', *Environment and Planning D*, 22: 157–73.

Laporte, D. (2002) *History of Shit*, Cambridge, MA: MIT Press.

Locke, J. (1980 [1690]) *Second Treatise of Civil Government*, Indianapolis: Hackett.

Marvin, S. and W. Medd (2006) 'Metabolisms of obecity: flows of fat through bodies, cities, and sewers', *Environment and Planning A*, 38(2): 313–24.

Merry, S. E. (1990) *Getting Justice and Getting Even: Legal Consciousness among Working-Class Americans*, Chicago, IL: University of Chicago Press.

Mitchell, T. (2002) *Rule of Experts: Egypt, Techno-politics, Modernity*, Berkeley, Los Angeles and London: University of California Press.

Parry, B. (2004) *Trading the Genome: Investigating the Commodification of Bio-information*, New York and Chichester: Columbia University Press.

Powers, R. G. (2004) *Broken: The Troubled Past and Uncertain Future of the FBI*, New York: Free Press.

Rabinow, P. (1996) *Essays on the Anthropology of Reason*, Princeton, NJ: Princeton University Press.

Radin, M. (1993) *Reinterpreting Property*, Chicago, IL: University of Chicago Press.

Reno, J. (2009) 'Your trash is someone's treasure: the politics of value at a Michigan landfill', *Journal of Material Culture*, 14(1): 29–46.

Simmel, G. (1990) *The Philosophy of Money*, New York and London: Routledge.

Legal cases cited

California v. *Greenwood*, 486 U.S. 35 (1988) (Brennan W.J. and Marshall T., dissenting).

Venner v. *Maryland*, 279 Md. 47, 367 A.2d 949 (1977).

11 | Remont: work in progress

CATHERINE ALEXANDER

Since my early years ... I've been afraid of 'remont' ... this was something my mother would do every summer. I hated remont because I
would not be able to read because all the books would be packed and
put away. Other discomforts included sleeping on the floor ... with the
smell of turpentine. This is how my mother would spend her summer
holidays. Instead of traveling somewhere, she would spend half of her
vacation making a remont in our home, and then, visit her mother's
home in a different city and do a remont there as well ... Remont was
not confined to ... private homes. Schools, kindergartens, institutes –
would also conduct their remonts.[1]

Introduction

In 'The emotional life of Moscow things', Alaina Lemon describes
exercises given to Moscow theatre students in the early 1990s in which
they were asked to depict objects (*predmety*). The first attempts were
simply performances of everyday objects: unbranded and working,
one might say, as perfectly as an ideal representation of function and
appearance. This, Lemon observes, sharply contradicted students'
daily experience of such things as: 'worn out, or broken, or "under
renovation"' (2009: 209), things, moreover, that demanded intimate
engagement, to be 'constantly wrestled with or repaired or stepped
around' (ibid.). In moving to the next assignment on the emotional
life of things, however, the students began to portray objects that
'communicate[d] and miscommunicate[d]' (ibid.: 210). The objects so

vivified were marked neither as socialist nor post-socialist but clearly gendered with performances that accentuated 'violent trajectories of destruction' (ibid.).

It is precisely these ideas of the performance and aesthetics of continual refurbishment in Soviet and post-Soviet contexts alike which interest me. While Gille (2007) highlights the importance of recycling in socialist Hungary, the aesthetics of this practice are not considered; nor is, as Lemon suggests, and I discuss here, how the daily struggle with recalcitrant objects also serves as a metaphor for broader political changes and indeed a way of understanding being in the world as a continual project in progress.

While practices of 'making-do' (De Certeau 2011), patching and repair are undoubtedly ubiquitous outside these regions (Whiteley 2010), I suggest they had, and have, a particular explanatory power for citizens of the former Soviet space in characterizing the specificity of their lives, cities and shifting political regimes. It is a concept that connects persons to domestic and wider political worlds in an economy of reshaping, which is both moral and material. Chronic shortages of consumer goods in the Soviet and early post-Soviet periods gave rise to repair and remaking as a common domestic practice, which also indexed political flux and the rapid, often surface, changes to urban environments. The importance of this notion is indicated in part by its proliferating connotations, in part by the endless tales that continue to centre on 'remont'.

Simply translated, 'remont'[2] is Russian for repair. But it goes much farther than that. Remont covers refurbishment, maintenance, renovation, remodelling, modifying and making things, and (re)decoration. It is a practice that restores the pragmatic or symbolic function of objects, or adapts them as material for another object (Gerasimova and Chuikina 2009: 1). It is also an evocative word summoning a world that seems to be ubiquitously and chronically *na remont*, under repair; for, all too often, one remont leads to another. This needs emphasizing. Graham and Thrift (2007) point out the prevalence of urban maintenance. There is no need to draw citizens' attention to remont in the cities of the former Soviet Union. From Christo-style wrappings of buildings *na remont* in blue plastic, concrete panels fencing off building lots, and roads apparently permanently dug up, to the constant thuds, whines and rumbles of hammer drills, saws, tile cutters, cement mixers, and the dust hanging chokingly in the air, remont is a constant sensory barrage.

Nor does one hurry home to peace and quiet from the building sites of the wealthier cities abuzz with construction. Those who could afford the outlay were busily redesigning their apartments to suit a dream of European modernity advertised on television and in a multitude of glossy magazines. This was Evroremont (Eppinger 2009; Patico 2003: 1): white walls, fitted, smooth kitchen units, new furniture, typically focused on the interior, while 'entryways, stairwells and doors to ... apartments are purposely kept shabby' (Balzer 2003).[3] The distinctions between privatized homes kept up to scratch and the common places that were allowed to fall into disrepair drew new contours of the limits of care. In Kazakhstan, some of the 'new Kazakhs'' villas blended Evroremont with an equally imaginary local flavour: cut-out circles in false ceilings revealing blue skies and clouds which suggested the *shanirak*: the top opening of the yurt, the new state's national symbol. The seemingly perpetual domestic upheaval that decoration entails is reflected in the Russian aphorism 'remodeling your apartment is a way of life and worse than a fire' (Mason 2006; Gluschenko 1998; Smolchenko 2005). One of my informants repeated another common maxim: 'Volcanos, fires, remont, and scandal are all good – from a distance'. A new anxiety reared its head. How would the redecorated apartment be judged? What did the new-look apartment say about the owner's social standing, wealth and taste?

This was post-Soviet remont, at least until the economic crisis of 2008 stilled the cranes. Abandoned building plots appeared, empty behind their fences, signifying bankrupt developers and obscure owner-ship rights, which left the plots to silence and weeds. A different kind of remont altogether re-established a natural equilibrium without the constant work of keeping things in order.

Such feverish building activity, eviscerating and refacing homes and urban landscapes alike, was typical of Kazakhstan's boom cities, Almaty and Astana, in 2002–07. But remont has also been taken to be characteristic of the Soviet period (Gerasimova and Chuikina 2009), with a focus on the small quotidian material engagements required to complete poor-quality, mass-produced goods, and to stretch the useful lives of things by darning, patching, mending and creating new things from materials begged, borrowed, stolen or reconfigured. Remont was pervasive in the Soviet period and is typically analysed as a response to the chronic shortage of usable consumer goods (ibid.; Degot' 2000; Gurova 2009). For something that still crops up regularly in conversa-tion and is so omnipresent, it has been addressed surprisingly rarely except as a history of everyday material practices. Perhaps, as the Russian artist Vladimir Arkhipov noted on his online archive devoted to home-made Soviet-era artefacts or 'thingamajigs' (www.folkforms.ru/), it often simply doesn't register as something worthy of note: 'In 1994

... Arkhipov remembered his own father's inventions, among them a TV antenna made from a set of aluminium forks, "Things like these had been around me all my life but were almost invisible to the naked eye"' (Arkhipov 2006). On the website devoted to an exhibition in Perm of 'Russian Povera', Arkhipov speaks of the 'impossible honesty' of the things he has collected, the unsanctioned functional creations of those who 'feel the world through their hands' (www.bednoe.ru/eng/arkhipov.html). Here is a bucket made from a tyre, a bedstead that has become a pier, a basket cut from a rubber ball.

Most of all, however, remont provokes thoughts of households turned upside down for annual top-to-toe spring-cleaning, repair and redecoration. For an average family of four, living in a two-room apartment, the upheaval was, and is, immense, as the epigraph indicates. During each summer of my fieldwork from 2000 to 2010 most of my informants would disappear from the usual social rounds for a week or two, banning visits to a tiny apartment in turmoil, and later recalling the complicated arrangements for moving elderly parents to stay with other family members, the difficulties of obtaining reliable builders who would finish a job satisfactorily and then the contentment of a job well done and ready to be displayed to family and friends. Wilson and Donaldson (1996) neatly evoked the wider world of remont in their observation that in early post-Soviet Russia

> time for repairs to be completed can be considerable. A successful shop owner who decides to remodel or expand the premises may need to close down the business for three months in order for the job to be completed ... the shop owner will not try to question the repair team's estimated completion time since they're experts. On the individual level a *remontnik* [repairman] is perhaps a friend of a friend who comes to fix a water heater, [or] install a door lock.

Here I stretch analyses of remont as a quintessentially Soviet practice in two ways. First, I consider Soviet remont as something that challenges conventional ways of seeing. I suggest that remont is a means of *conjoining* familiar categories that order social worlds: production and consumption; spatial divisions of micro- and macro-levels, margins and centres; sequential temporalities of past, present and future; ideas and things. Thus, to borrow Latour's (2000) phrase, if we look through the lens of repair and making-do, then we see that the moments when things fall apart and are reconstituted or patched up allow people and things to object to normative categories, relations and practices.

Hawkins (2005) calls for an ethics of waste, a more intimate engagement with material and wasting practices. Chronic material shortage in the Soviet bloc bred exactly this moralized thriftiness and skills in stretching, mending and making that also appear in other places at times of material shortage (Strasser 1999; Cooper 2009; Riley 2008), in the context of 'recession chic',[4] or quite simply the pleasure of making things, the affect of delight generated by such labour (Alexander, Smaje et al. 2009). Beyond this, however, Constructivist-inspired propaganda in the 1920s prescribed a radical reappraisal of the world of things: equality between humans and non-humans premised on the eradication of the commodity and subject–object relation. Things were to be comrades (Degot' 2000). This programmatic emphasis on the social and moral aesthetic of material care is arguably part of what made Soviet remont unique, along with the explanatory work it performed.

The second way of extending these analyses is through examining post-Soviet remont. If, as Gerasimova and Chuikina suggest, the Soviet economy can be characterized as a repair society, how can we explain its continued prevalence? Through her powerful exploration of the uses to which archaeological metaphors and their entailments have been put in critical theory, Dawdy proposes that modernity's cult of newness has tended to override continuity (2010: 778) and that 'reinvention means revolution ... [returning] to an earlier possibility before time splintered into antiquity and modernity' (ibid.: 776). In line with this, I suggest that while many of the moral inflections, material ontologies, relations and practices of Soviet remont have changed, the sense of eternal remont, to borrow the name of another blog about the post-Soviet world, remains. The idea of the world as a permanent work in progress, *na remont*, transforming and transformatory, simultaneously highlights the continuity of Enlightenment evolutionary notions and destroys them. Enduring transformation is not the same as progress.

The rest of this chapter is divided into two parts, each exploring these two aspects of remont in Soviet and post-Soviet contexts. Part I opens with a discussion of Benjamin's *Moscow Diary*, which is punctuated by observations on remont; the ubiquity of repair evokes a startlingly different city from more familiar accounts. I draw on Benjamin at length since this text illustrates so well the entanglement of people and things, of structural material shortage and individual ingenuity, the marginal activities that dominate the urban environment. These descriptions of a city woven together by the thread of remont are then juxtaposed with Constructivist ideas which formed the basis of Soviet ideology promoting the care of things. These accounts of ideology and experience vividly evoke the conjunction of times, production and consumption, subject and object – the performance of making-do that links the material refusal of an erratic lamp to function properly, to people, cities and political regimes engaged in self-transformation.

Part 2 outlines continuities and differences between how remont was, and is, moralized, conceptualized and practised; for this, among other sources, I draw on fieldwork I carried out in Almaty, Kazakhstan, from 2000 to 2009. This shows new fissures between generations, morally valorized practices and the domestic and public spheres. Many of these fractures hinge on the lack of substantive transformation in the political sphere, despite attempts to present it as radically new. Once again, a hastily constructed artefact is understood to be unfinished, poor quality and in danger of falling apart. Thus, although the rest of this chapter is loosely divided between Soviet and post-Soviet periods, the emphasis is on the continuity of the performance and aesthetics of remont.

Soviet remont in practice: from bedside lights to policy

In December 1926 and January 1927 Walter Benjamin visited Moscow. The detailed notes in his diary have been described as 'resist[ing] our impulse to taxonomies ... exceed[ing] the conventions of genre' (Smith 1986: 137). Richter (1995: 1) further observes that the notes 'have haunted their readers'. This categorical slipperiness, hinting at other, different layers of meaning dissolving into half-hinted genre permutations, echoes a sub-theme of the diary, which concerns the fragile contingency of a life where 'nothing ever happens as planned or expected – this banal formulation of life's complications is borne out ... implacably and ... intensely in every single instance here' (Benjamin 1986: 30). 'Everything ... here takes place under the banner of the remont' (ibid.: 36).

The latter observation alludes to the profusion of small shops for repairing household articles scattered across the city and, thereby implicitly, to the paucity of available consumer goods (ibid.: fn. 54). Paucity here refers both to empty shelves as well as the tendency for goods to be of poor quality, incomplete or inadequate. More often than not, this was part of the shortage economy that Kornai (1980) describes as affecting not only consumer goods but also inputs to the production process. Faced with late, haphazard or substandard inputs (Alexander 2004; Dunn 2004), products frequently only adumbrated their intended form, requiring a series of tweaks after purchase to make an item usable and, in so doing, perhaps, to modify the partly mass-produced item to particular requirements. Such hazy shadowings of form and function were not only to be found in goods for sale. If incomplete goods only suggested a future use or shape, other things, in turn, made their pasts legible. Benjamin notes that his companion Asja Lacis's 'new' dress is made from 'some old, already moth-eaten black fabric' (Benjamin 1986: 108), thus drawing attention to the contingency of form, of coalesced temporalities: what something is, was and could be; an excess of possibilities in an object's form.

Continuing the theme of shape-shifting, Moscow itself fails to 'really look like the city it is, rather it more resembles the outskirts of itself' (ibid.: 67). In 'the famous Sukharev Park ... The people simply lay out their merchandise on the snow. One finds old locks, meter rulers, hand tools, kitchen utensils, electrical appliances etc. etc. Repairs are also done on the spot; I saw something being soldered over a jet of flame' (ibid.: 68). This is a city without a front. It is busy making and remaking itself, constituted as an improvised thing engaged in keeping itself going, selling the wherewithal for patching, colonizing public areas of streets with ad hoc activities that speak more of domestic than external, urban, industrial settings. Marginal, backstage activities (following Goffman 1959), more properly located in the outskirts, seep across the urban landscape and come to define the city's pulse. There are parallels here with the literal liveliness of Rabelais's grotesque body that is exemplified by its edges, which are in a constant state of becoming (Bakhtin 1968; Richter 1995). Notably, this blurring of difference in areas and functions contravened Soviet guidelines for town planning on the clear zoning, separation and order that drew on organic metaphors (Cooke 1995). Constructivist theory was more than half a hop behind the exigencies of everyday life.

In Benjamin's hotel bedroom, the lamp's 'provisional' connection comes undone again – note that 'again'. His attempts to fix it only touch off a short circuit (Benjamin 1986: 80). If communism, in Lenin's well-worn phrase, was to be the combined power of electricity and workers' councils, the frailty of power in connecting the everyday and publicly organized life was immediately apparent, and remains so, even down to the paucity of sockets allowed per household (Arkhipov 2006). Whole histories, geo-socio-political relations and political economy analyses may be marshalled to explain the poverty of things. But, in the end, it is the immediate material refusal of revolutionary progress which engages the senses: from the wobbly light switch with its exposed wire entrails, the flash of blue fire and smell of charring that often still accompanies an appliance being plugged in, to the freshly tiled façade of an old building which still reeks of sewage and displays elderly guttering on its rear wall.

The random closure of cafés was said to be 'part of the remont policy' (Benjamin 1986: 100), as though the plethora of non-operational services and non-functioning goods were deliberate. The fragility of the city unites domestic and public lives. The instability of Benjamin's text, suggestive of multiple registers and genres, resistant to meaning-making taxonomies, describes a parallel world where things are palimpsests of former material selves: a dress reconfigures old, worn fragments. The prevailing sense is uncanny: conjunctions of the familiar and the strange, forms endlessly suggesting previous and future lives of components. And, in among this fluidity, which defies naming and knowing and depends on creative dexterity, Benjamin observes of the people who failed to demonstrate a comparable adaptability themselves, 'I learned another strange term, namely the expression "have beens" [byvshie liudi], applied to those citizens who were dispossessed by the Revolution and who have been unable to adapt to the new situation ... continual organizational changes ... will go on ... for years' (ibid.: 85). Fixity leaves these people beached; resilience (in the sense of continuation rather than return) is the capacity to engage in the mutual transformation of labour on the self and the world. Flexibility was a survival strategy during the Soviet period, as the joke from the Stalinist era quoted by Schlapentokh (1989: 32) suggests: 'answering a question on his political views, the hero of the *anekdot* replies that they are "to oscillate with the general line of the party"'. As I discuss below, in Almaty during my fieldwork there was a strong sense of yet another generation being left behind, dispossessed, unable to adapt to the new world. As this volume suggests, for all that the idea of recycling selves and materials is centrally important to understanding and being in the world, it is also an incomplete process generating discarded people and things unable to effect one more modification.

Soon after Benjamin's visit, in 1932, Trotsky examined the effectiveness of Soviet industry, comparing it with that of capitalist countries and finding it severely wanting. A litany of poor agro-industrial performance harps on quantity and quality: 'The products of machine manufacture, says the head of the heavy industries in an official report, "must be good quality and unfortunately are not"' (1960: 33), before turning to consumer goods. 'A unique law of Soviet industry may be formulated thus: commodities are as a general rule worse the nearer they stand to the mass consumer. In the textile industry, according to Pravda, "there is a shamefully large percentage of defective goods, poverty of selection, predominance of low grades." Complaints of the bad quality of articles of wide consumption appear periodically in the press: "clumsy ironware"; "ugly furniture, badly put together and care-lessly finished'" (ibid.: 34). While propaganda successfully promoted the moral value of Soviet-produced goods as *'nash'* (ours) over capitalist commodities, part of the attraction of foreign-produced goods was for a better finish, rather than the more open-ended Soviet object. Global brands continue to exert a fascination at odds with the satisfaction of locally made things.

A theory of comradely things Kiaer (2005: 1) opens her marvellous discussion of socialist objects with a quotation from the Russian Con-structivist[5] Aleksandr Rodchenko, writing home from Paris in 1925: 'The light from the East is not only the liberation of workers, the light from the East is in the new relation to the person, to woman, to things. Our things in our hands must be equals, comrades, and not these black and mournful slaves, as they are here.' This became a rallying cry for a new way of reconsidering, and living with, things. There are a number of radical entailments from this proposition. In the first instance, as Kiaer notes (ibid.), this was far from a call for material renunciation but, rather, a focus on reforming the *relation* between people and things. The new relation was not to be one of ownership, of a possessive relation towards the material world. If capitalism was centred on commodity fetishism, obscuring human labour relations, then the implication was perhaps that the new relation would be more one of stewardship and care towards the things of socialism. One consequence was the necessity of rethinking the subject–object relationship from both sides of the equation.

The comradely relation to which Rodchenko refers eradicates the subject-to-object relation: as in English, the Russian *'objekt'* can indi-cate both a positional relation to a subject and its incarnation as a tangible, or intangible, thing. The subjective value of a thing, to return to a Marxist lexicon, should no longer be eclipsed by the reification of its objective attributes.

What began as a general rallying cry to reconsider the relations and nature of all things became confined to the useful and intimate things of the domestic sphere. This was not so much a diminution of the earlier call, but a reinterpretation of the artist's role to engage with the lives of citizens on the most immediate level; *byt*, as everyday life, was the focus of these interventions (Bürger 1974, quoted in Kiaer 2005: 4; Buchli 2000). The shift in emphasis extended to embrace self-production, recalling the mutual transformation worked by labour on material and worker.

The Productivist Boris Aratov went farther in 'recognis[ing] the affective power of the mass-produced objects of modernity, proposing the idea of a socialist object as a co-worker' (Kiaer 2005: 26). More explicitly, Arvatov (1925) discussed how socialism would transform passive capitalist commodities into active socialist things as proletarian society removed the dualisms in which bourgeois society was trapped with its rupture between things and people, material and idea (Kiaer 2005: 30). His belief that mass-produced things have an agency which the human can develop through interaction prefigures interest in the social sciences in intersubjectivity between things and people (see, for example, Latour's discussion of the parliament of things, 1993: 142). Unlike Marx, Arvatov is not so much interested in restoring the primacy of social relations between people as in transforming the nature of things themselves as equal subjects through changes in the means of production (Kiaer 2005: 33).

The final point to draw from Kiaer's discussion of Arvatov is his emphasis on connecting artefacts to their creative genesis in order to promote and understand these relations of equality. It is, he argues, the very divorce between production and consumption which restricts interactions with things to private property relations. Separated from the creative act, the thing-as-commodity appears to be passive and immobile. By contrast, socialist objects would be the comrades of the productive worker rather than merely the possessed objects of the wealthy (ibid.: 252).[6] This, then, is about theorizing everyday productive consumption as a key site for transforming person and thing alike. There is a distinct and perhaps surprising difference between this and British state propaganda directed towards limiting material wastefulness during the Second World War, a time of acute shortage. This emphasized recycling for the war effort and the nation-as-collective through individual thrift (Riley 2008).[7]

Gerasimova and Chuikina (2009) draw productively on these ideas (see also Orlova 2009), following Degot' (2000), usefully drawing attention to the range of ways and contexts in which people create and work on things (restoring antiques, saving money, making things unique). There are three key points where I differ. First, they state that the Soviet economy as a whole could be characterized as a repair society, since the plan at its centre was in constant need of adjustment, unlike the self-regulating market economy (Gerasimova and Chuikina 2009). I suggest market economies are equally in constant need of adjustment and state support (Galbraith 2001), as the economic crises of the twentieth and twenty-first centuries have made abundantly clear. Secondly, as noted above, making-do and repair are familiar in other regions of the world. Thirdly, remont is still common in the post-Soviet era. Far from being peculiar to Soviet society, I suggest repair and adjustment, as labour on the self, the world and the body politic, are symptomatic of the human condition. The specificity of remont is not that it happens but in how it is performed, aestheticized and moralized, and has come to domesticate broader economic and political changes.

Post-Soviet remont

Remont, as the introduction and Lemon's article describe, continues. It is, perhaps, an essential part of remont that it endlessly continues. Closure is only a moment, always temporary. Either the thing itself continues to change, the repair itself engenders more problems, or the environment alters so that the thing or person are out of kilter with their context. The questions therefore are whether multiple practices and moral versions of remont coexist.

In this section, I start by juxtaposing two short accounts of middle-aged informants in Almaty which comment directly and indirectly on materials, domestic and political bodies. The narratives and quotations below are typical of the conversations I had during fieldwork in the first decade of the twenty-first century. Three themes constantly reappeared. First, there were new dissonances between generations over how the ability to work on materials was moralized. Secondly, changes wrought in domestic space meant that places, such as balconies and dachas, which had earlier been the places for storing tools, bits and bobs and making things anew, now increasingly became spaces for leisure and display. Thirdly, debates over the nature of a remade thing slipped to sardonic observations on the fake, literally superficial, making over of the urban environment and new political ideologies.

Necessity and virtue A conversation with my landlady, Sveta, in 2000 turned to the subject of cooking. Sveta, a Russian teacher in her fifties, proudly came out with a statement I came to hear many times: 'In the West, you had everything. Here we didn't have machines, ready-made food ... we often didn't even have bread, but with a strong arm and a sharp knife a Russian woman can make anything out of anything!' Thinking to join in with the conversation's general tone, I described my family, trained by a mother raised in wartime England to keep cupboards full of oddments in case of unspecified need. Sveta looked baffled. 'But *why*,' she said, 'when there's no *need*?'

I discussed this exchange with women of different ages. Aigerim, a young, urbanized Kazakh girl, laughed sardonically. 'Oh, she was talking about being a real woman – you know, a Russian woman who can stop a train with one hand while she cooks a meal for ten children out of one potato. Thank God we don't have to do that any more. I have no interest in cooking at all.' Older women, however, tended to proudly tell their own stories of culinary resourcefulness and ingenuity. As described below, this instance of triumphant domestic making-do was echoed in other tales of bricolage in apartments and dachas. De Certeau (2011) suggests that we see such everyday practices as tactics of resistance to a drearily uniform world, a monochrome cultural economy. I suggest that in a context of adversity or shortage, a further twist of moral virtue is added to the poetics of making-do.

Arguably, the lauding of creative prudence was honed in relation to deficit; these were skills that could be held up against the perceived material and technological abundance of Western outsiders. Habits of necessity became a virtue and lingered, for a generation that had grown up with them, as an embodied moral practice after pressing need dwindled. A goal-driven practice, in Weber's terms, became a practice that had a value in its own right, whether or not expressed as ingenuity or 'ecological'. Nevertheless, the context of need still framed the conspicuous virtue of thrift, which had largely become outmoded, as Aigerim's scorn indicates. This clash of values was not always as clear cut. Other young people of Aigerim's age moved between slightly pious recognitions of the worth of manually creative skills, sometimes to the point of dramatically rejecting anything that was not home made as dirty, poor quality and morally suspect one minute, and sighing after a four-wheel Lexus, brand-new house and expensive jewellery the next. Sveta was one of many of her age group who described themselves as unable to adapt to the new world, left behind. 'We have to rely on the new generation,' she used to say. Just as Benjamin recorded people who were washed up by the tide of revolution, the 'has beens', so another generation began to describe itself as left behind, unable to change nimbly enough to swim with the new current.

Private ingenuity and public fake Gennadi trained as a vet in the 1950s but was then promptly sent to work as a welfare administrator. Now, teetering on the edge of retirement, he worked as an official in the Social Affairs Department of Almaty's municipal administration. Between 2000 and 2008 he was moved from job to job five times, each time, as he observed, reinventing himself yet again and hoping to prolong his working life a little longer. While the national and local bureaucracies were officially undifferentiated ethnically, a 'creeping Kazakhification' process meant that certain policies favouring Kazakhs were being quietly slipped in. Learning Kazakh, Gennadi often ruefully remarked, was one such new demand on officials from the government, but at his age was just too much to ask; a person could only be remodelled so far. 'I can learn words and phrases,' he said, 'but that's what a parrot can do. I can't learn the language so I can talk, discuss, write reports and do my job. I can't learn it as a real language.'

Gennadi regularly invited me to his dacha in Almaty's mountains. In common with many dacha owners, Gennadi, with the help of his family, had slowly built his dacha in the 1970s from scavenged odds and ends, along with formally obtained materials from the building market. As an architect, his wife had been in a good position to procure surplus building materials or exchange her design skills informally for planks and nails: exchange relations were typically based on kin, neighbours or current and former work colleagues.[8] Even with his wife's expertise, however, the dacha was basically a large shed, with gaps between the planks and a corrugated iron roof. As with all dachas, neither heating nor hot water was supplied.

Gennadi was immensely proud of his dacha and took great delight in demonstrating how he had fashioned, for example, a stand for the portable gas stove from a crate, a cupboard from a sawn-up door and stepping stones across muddy patches from old radiators laid flat. The dacha had, he solemnly lectured me, two main, related purposes: economic and pleasure. Both were to be found in his large and lovingly maintained kitchen garden of fruit trees and rows of vegetables (see Mack and Surina 2005: 128). This had been essential, he said, in the 1990s, for simple survival, but was becoming a burden as acute economic hardship lessened and his children had shown no interest in weeding and patching, even before they had moved to Russia. Fences, stakes, windshields and gardening implements for keeping the garden in trim were all contrived from radiators, sawn-off steel rebars for reinforcing concrete, bent aerials and factory remnants from punched-out metal shapes. Plastic water bottles with the top third sliced off served as plant pots or containers for soft fruit.

Gennadi showed me a hoe. 'What is this?' he asked, grinning. 'It started life as a broom handle and a metal panel I cut with my friend's oxyacetylene burner. Since then, I've replaced the handle and then ... I had to replace the metal. Is it the same hoe that it was before? – and it never was a hoe before that!' The parallel was never made explicit, but later that evening he remarked, 'First they used to tell us we were socialist. Now they tell us we're capitalist. But you know, ordinary people, we're pretty much the same as we were. Things just look a bit different on the outside.'

Ingeniously built and maintained from scraps and borrowed tools, both dacha and garden also served as a storage place for a vast array of oddments of metal and wood, jars, broken cups, old tools, nails, wire and so on. During the Soviet period, storage spaces, such as dachas and balconies, were essential for smoothing over erratic gluts and shortages as well as for keeping the bits and bobs that might turn out to have an unforeseen use. Echoing informants in an inner London housing estate at the same time (Alexander, Smaje et al. 2009), Gennadi told me that he could not break the habit of keeping things 'just in case' they came in useful later on. Gennadi, and later his wife, both pointed out old toys they had kept but also, sadly, that were unlikely to be used now that their children had moved away. His children, he said, worked hard and earned more than he had ever had, but had little spare time. He pointed to his garden, some of which had been left to run to weeds as he could no longer care for it all.

Many balconies, stuffed with cardboard boxes, large cooking pots, cleaning equipment, tools, sacks of potatoes, extra stools, home-made cupboards, lines for drying laundry, plants in cut-down plastic bottles, were walled in during the 1990s, glazed and transformed into compact offices or simply places of display for ornaments and plants. Conspicuous consumption began to replace frugality and the uniform outer walls of panel apartment blocks turned into patchworks of individual aspiration. Both the dacha and balcony were themselves largely home made and acted as a nexus in informal exchange relations. Building materials and tools were originally sourced through such exchanges; the dacha and balcony then served to store tools and oddments, or, in the case of the dacha, grow food, that could then be used to make or repair things for kin and friends. Both instances also neatly illustrate the point that repair is an affective practice, which at once gives pleasure and creates a particular bond between the worker and the (re)crafted object. Increasingly, however, these domestic places were changing from being worked *on* and *in* via transformative labour, to static places of display and consumption, particularly as the work environment absorbed spare time and energy. The affect of practising skills of repair, however, was not simply negatively or positively valued. The broader context of perceived necessity also informed the extent to which such material practices were morally valued.

Gennadi had been instructed to show me his department's latest welfare buildings. Mischievously going well beyond his remit, he took me to visit a dilapidated hostel for the homeless in Turksib, a poor, outlying area. The hostel, he noted, had been renamed a rehabilitation centre, received a new sign and a second grand opening and had then continued to function as before with inadequate funds and in a district where, he said, 'the state chooses not to come'. He continued, 'The Akimat wants everything to be new but most of the time, things are just being renamed or have a new façade. Underneath, things are pretty much as they used to be.' This was a common theme during my first period of fieldwork, informants pulling me to the back of apparently shiny, new buildings in the centre to show me, with great glee, the rusting old pipes and crumbling bricks that lay beneath the clip-on, tiled frontages (see Alexander 2008; Buchli 2007).

There is a sharp contrast here between domestic ingenuity in crafting sustenance from scraps, new things from old, and political manoeuvres to pass off old things as new, whether material or ideological. The point was frequently made to me, but particularly vociferously by a local historian. Making the connection explicit between the physical city and the rapidly mutating ideologies of the new regime, he remarked that everything that appeared to be new was built on communist foundations; the apparently new political regime was merely an instance of metastasis. In other words, there was no genuine or organic base to the apparent changes, which were simply grafted on to pre-existing structures. 'New' buildings were simply seen as ruins-waiting-to-happen. While it might have been expected that professional middle-aged informants on the cusp of retirement would mourn the differences between the Soviet and the post-Soviet era, the fragility of the new-for-old era was equally a common topic among the young. The Soviet cynicism that Alexei Yurchak (1997) records had simply been replaced by a different kind of cynicism. In late 2009, for example, Kazakh students in north Kazakhstan, for whom Kazakh was their second language after Russian, repeatedly and explicitly linked policies to instate Kazakh as the primary official language with the rapid construction of Astana, the new capital,[9] and buildings shooting up across other major cities. 'It's all too fast,' they said, 'nothing is being done properly. It'll all fall down – just you wait.'[10]

Conclusions

Typically, both emic and etic analyses of post-Soviet space are divided into 'before and now' (*ranshe i sechas*), which refer to the Soviet period and the time since it ended. This chapter has also loosely followed this temporal heuristic. Arguably, however, the constant obsession with remont, as both a means of making the world liveable and understanding it metaphorically, is a way of domesticating these larger-scale epochal divisions and bringing them down to size. Once brought home, so to speak, these political shifts and changes, which are so tremulously written on the city's surfaces, become more tractable to De Certeau's tactical manoeuvres of daily life. The constant remaking of self, home and everyday things repeatedly performs the 'before and now' at a smaller, more intimate scale which does not merely recapitulate the content of large-scale history (from socialist to capitalist), but mimics its form and makes it more recognizable as the constant tinkering and self-making that is the human condition. The velocity and scale of change enjoined by political regime change are shattering compared with such steady, continual modifications. In some ways, the constancy of remont might be said to echo Herzfeld's (2005) notion of cultural intimacy where citizens, who ostensibly reject state-sanctioned norms and values, end up reproducing them in moments of crisis.

Alongside the familiar themes of continuity and change the very acknowledgement of genuine transformation is morally laden and profoundly contested. In one sense then, the aesthetics of recycling are concerned with the recognition of form in the midst of constant flux, the moment when idea and form coalesce and become knowable. This adds a further layer to the ethics of waste and recycling proposed by Gille (2007), which is more concerned with resource conservation and the most effective way of achieving this through considering material waste regimes at the level of political economy. Rather, through examining 'our most quotidian relations with waste, what they mean and how they might change' (Hawkins 2005: 3), what I have been exploring here suggests, in line with Hawkins (ibid.), that material ethics and aesthetics cannot be meaningfully separated. New forms and change that are not recognized as 'real' organic transformation are rejected as fraudulent, superficial, deceptive and frail. Buildings and ideologies that are built on communist foundations or too fast and carelessly are, quite literally, unsound (see also Buchli 2007).

Practices of recycling are intensely morally charged. As I discuss here, my informants, and indeed Benjamin, not only experience and construct recycling in terms of performance and aesthetics, but also through a series of related levels (person, city, nation) and domains: material, political and economic. Thus, in addition to thinking about objects that fall or are taken apart and reconstituted, this chapter has added, first, the domestic and broader environments in which recycling takes place and which are subject to change, and secondly, an indication of how recycling serves as a metaphor for ideological shifts and a way of being in the world – which also includes the shortcomings of recycling: objects break down irredeemably, people are left stranded on the shore.

An ethnographic approach to the process of recycling demands that we stand aside from familiar categories for ordering the world and dive into the experiential stream of ambiguity and negotiation. Thus, the very materiality of things carries traces of former and possible incarnations, former and possible social relations. A subject–object relationship between person and thing is upended by the refusal of things to obey function, by objects that object – and by the affective labour of care and repair. Affective labour, following Hardt and Negri (2001), is typically taken to refer to emotional labour, such as the service industries, household care or nursing, where one of the main goals is to produce a positive affect in others, whether consumers, patients or other family members. As suggested in the ethnography above, the labour of repair, finishing and re-creation also indicates that positive affect can be experienced by those who are directly making such objects; Cova and Dalli (2011) describe the element of 'finishing' as the 'co-creation of value' by consumers who, through their immaterial labour, add value to commodities they have bought. Perhaps the notion of completing objects is not as peculiarly a Soviet practice as Gerasimova and Chuikina (2009) suggest. Again, while Dawdy draws attention to 'the endemic ruination of capitalism, the social life of ruins and the folding of time in recycled artifacts' (2010: 763), I suggest that the challenges presented by the coalesced temporalities of recycled objects go beyond capitalist ruination to ontologies of the modern – whether Soviet socialist or capitalist.

Continuities aside, the barometer of change from Soviet to post-Soviet eras registers in two ways. First, there are distinct generational differences between the value accorded to transformational skills. Secondly, there has been a move from a world where alteration, making-do, repair and creativity linked the domestic and the public street (Argenbright 1999: 5), taking front stage, to one where change is merely apparent, a front for the gradual irreversible crumbling of the basic fabric; a front that fails to hold form and idea together in the present and only suggests, uncannily, layers of past lives and future decay.

Acknowledgements

The research was supported by the ESRC (RES 000-23-0007). I am particularly grateful to Josh Reno for his collegial help with this chapter.

Notes

1 This posting was by Zhanara Nauryzbaeva on the artpologist blog which was part of a project to document 'the world of the artist's studio ... located in and intertwined with an urban site of indiscriminate demolition and relentless construction activity' (artpologist.net/almaty/the-project/).

2 The Russian remont derives from the modern French usage of '*remonter*', which indicates returning vigour to something, either by replenishing stocks or oneself; '*un remontant*' is a restorative; '*remontant*' refers to plants that bloom repeatedly in one season. My thanks to Anna Lavis for pointing out these meanings.

3 Despite its continued prevalence, remont has become chic as a kitsch way of referring to the past. In Moscow a café called Maki, with an exposed concrete interior, has been described as remont-chic, playing on the idea that Russia is permanently being refurbished. Muscovite Alexei Borisov produced a disc in 2002 called 'Before the Evroremont', a sound collage of sawing, hammering, drilling and clattering. Ukrainian group 'Fleur' released 'Remont' in 2004 as a track on their album *Magic*. An art gallery called Remont opened in 2000 in Belgrade; remont, they suggest, is never ending. Their web page says: 'Remont is an untranslatable term used in Eastern and Southeastern Europe, which means repair, repair

of the existing mechanism for maintenance and adjustment (new) conditions' (www.remont.net/).

4 Class, in Britain, is intimately linked to different views of thrift and second-hand goods. While such goods and clothes may be fashionable or consumed as a moral statement by the middle class, working-class consumers tend to associate this more with poverty and social disadvantage; even if low income precludes adults from buying new, second-hand goods are shameful. New items are reserved for children as symbol of a household's desired path towards affluence (Alexander, Druckman et al. 2009).

5 Constructivism was a movement that started in Russia in the 1920s among artists, writers and architects, among others, who reimagined art, broadly understood, as being in the service of social revolution.

6 This revolutionary materialism was in the context of a temporarily resurgent market economy in the Soviet Union rather than Bolshevism (Kiaer 2005: 265).

7 Gille's (2007) account of organized industrial recycling in post-war Hungary again suggests an emphasis on the collective good rather than addressing the fundamental nature of humans and things.

8 Lonkila (1997) notes that offering and receiving repair skills formed a significant part of the Soviet economy of favours (*blat*) described by her informants.

9 Astana is itself also a transfigured rather than a new city. In 1997, Tselinograd was renamed Astana (after a series of less popular

renamings) and work began: old buildings were concealed behind new façades alongside new constructions.

10 See Sandomirskaja (1999) for further discussion of parallels between language change and remont.

References

Alexander, C. (2004) 'Values, relations and changing bodies: industrial privatisation in Kazakhstan', in C. Humphrey and K. Verdery (eds), *Property in Question: Appropriation, recognition and value transformation in the global economy*, Oxford: Berg, pp. 251–74.

— (2008) 'Waste under socialism and after: a case study from Almaty', in H. West and P. Raman (eds), *Enduring Socialism. Explorations of Revolution, Transformation and Restoration*, Oxford: Berghahn Books, pp. 148–69.

Alexander, C., C. Smaje, R. Timlett and I. Williams (2009) 'Improving social technologies for recycling: interfaces, estates, multi-family dwellings and infrastructural deprivation', *Journal of Waste and Resources Management*, 162(WR1): 15–29.

Alexander, C., A. Druckman, C. Osinski and T. Jackson (2009) 'Estimating household material flows in deprived areas', *Journal of Waste and Resource Management*, 162(WR3): 129–39.

Argenbright, R. (1999) 'Remaking Moscow: new places, new selves', *Geographical Review*, 89(1): 1–22.

Arkhipov, V. (2006) *Home-made: Contemporary Russian Folk Artefacts*, London: Fuel Books.

Arvatov, B. (1925) 'Byt I kul'tura veshchi (k postanovke voprosa)', *Al'manakh proletkul'ta*, Moscow: Prolekul't, pp. 75–82.

Bakhtin, M. (1968) *Rabelais and His World*, Cambridge, MA: MIT Press.

Balzer, H. (2003) 'Routinization of the new Russians?', *Russian Review*, 62(1): 15–36.

Benjamin, W. (1986) *Moscow Diary*, Cambridge, MA: Harvard University Press.

Buchli, V. (2000) *An Archaeology of Socialism*, Oxford: Berghahn Books.

— (2007) 'Astana: materiality and the city', in C. Alexander, V. Buchli and C. Humphrey (eds), *Urban Life in Post-Soviet Asia*, London: Routledge.

Bürger, P. (1974) 'Theory of the avant-garde', trans. Michael Shaw, in W. Godzich and J. Schulte-Sasse (eds), *Theory and History of Literature*, vol. 4, Minneapolis: Minneapolis University Press.

Cooke, C. (1995) *Russian Avant-Garde: Theories of Art, Architecture and the City*, London: Academy Editions.

Cooper, T. (2009) 'War on waste? The politics of recycling in post-war Britain, 1950–1975', *Capitalism, Nature, Socialism*, 20(4): 53–72.

Cova, B. and D. Dalli (2011) 'Working consumers: the next step in marketing theory?', *Marketing Theory*, 11: 231–41.

Dawdy, S. L. (2010) 'Clockpunk anthropology and the ruins of modernity', *Current Anthropology*, 51(6): 761–93.

De Certeau, M. (2011) *The Practice of Everyday Life*, Berkeley: University of California Press.

Degot', E. (2000) 'Ot tovara k tovarishchu: k estetike nerynochnogo predmeta' [From goods to good comrades], *Pamiat' tela: Nizhnee bel'e sovetskoi epokhi*, Katalog vystavki, Moscow,

7 November 2000–31 January 2001, pp. 8–19.

Dunn, E. (2004) *Privatizing Poland: Baby Food, Big Business, and the Remaking of Labor*, Ithaca, NY: Cornell University Press.

Eppinger, M. (2009) 'Nation-building in the penumbra: notes from a liminal state', *Hastings International and Comparative Law Review*, 32(2): 773.

Galbraith, J. (2001) *Inequality and Industrial Change*, Cambridge: Cambridge University Press.

Gerasimova, E. and S. Chuikina (2009) 'The repair society', *Russian Studies in History*, 48(1): 58–74.

Gille, Z. (2007) *From the Cult of Waste to the Trash Heap of History: The Politics of Waste in Socialist and Postsocialist Hungary*, Bloomington: Indiana University Press.

Glushchenko, I. (1998) 'In Russia, remont can turn you into a wreck', *Moscow Times*, 4 February 1998.

Goffman, E. (1959) *The Presentation of Self in Everyday Life*, New York: Doubleday.

Graham, S. and N. Thrift (2007) 'Out of order: understanding repair and maintenance', *Theory, Culture and Society*, 24(3): 1–25.

Gurova, O. (2009) 'The life span of things in Soviet society: notes on the sociology of underwear', *Russian Social Science Review*, 50(4): 49–60.

Hardt, M. and A. Negri (2001) *Empire*, Cambridge, MA: Harvard University Press.

Hawkins, G. (2005) *The Ethics of Waste: How we relate to rubbish*, Lanham, MD: Rowman & Littlefield Publishers.

Herzfeld, M. (2005) *Cultural Intimacy: Social poetics in the nation-state*, London: Routledge.

Kiaer, C. (2005) *Imagine No Possessions: The socialist objects of Russian constructivism*, Cambridge, MA: MIT Press.

Kornai, J. (1980) *Economics of Shortage*, Amsterdam: North-Holland.

Latour, B. (1993) *We Have Never been Modern*, Cambridge, MA: Harvard University Press.

— (2000) 'When things strike back: a possible contribution of science studies to the social sciences', *British Journal of Sociology*, 511: 107–23.

Lemon, A. (2009) 'The emotional life of Moscow things', *Russian History*, 36: 201–18.

Lonkila, M. (1997) 'Informal exchange relations in post-Soviet Russia: a comparative perspective', *Sociological Research Online*, 2(2), www.socresonline.org.uk/2/2/9.html.

Mack, G. and A. Surina (2005) *Food Culture in Russia and Central Asia*, Greenwood Press.

Mason, C. (2006) 'For Russian style, an extreme makeover', *New York Times*.

Orlova, G. (2009) 'Apologies for a strange thing: the Soviet person's little tricks', *Russian Studies in History*, 48(1): 75–88.

Patico, J. (2003) 'Consuming the west but becoming third world: food imports and the experience of Russianness', *Anthropology of East Europe Review*, 21(1).

Richter, G. (1995) 'The monstrosity of the body in Walter Benjamin's Moscow diary', *Modern Language Studies*, 24(5).

Riley, M. (2008) 'From salvage to recycling – new agendas or same old rubbish?', *Area*, 40(1): 79–89.

Sandomirskaja, I. (1999) 'Writing on the wall: remont, restoration, and identity', in F. Björling (ed.),

Through a Glass Darkly. Cultural Representation in the Dialogue between Central, Eastern, and Western Europe, Slavica Lundensia, 19.

Schlapentokh, V. (1989) *Public and Private Life of the Soviet People*, Oxford: Oxford University Press.

Smith, G. (1986) 'Afterword', in *Moscow Diary*, Cambridge, MA: Harvard University Press

Smolchenko, A. (2005) 'How to take the pain out of remont', *Moscow Times*, 2 February 2005.

Strasser, S. (1999) *Waste and Want: A social history of trash*, New York: Metropolitan Books.

Trotsky, L. (1960) *The Revolution Betrayed*, India: Aakar Books.

Whiteley, G. (2010) *Junk: Art and the politics of trash*, London: I. B. Tauris.

Wilson, D. and L. Donaldson (1996) *Russian Etiquette and Ethics in Business*, New York: McGraw-Hill.

Yurchak, A. (1997) 'The cynical reason of late socialism: power, pretense and the anekdot', *Public Culture*, 9(161): 179.

Afterword: the apocalypse of objects – degradation, redemption and transcendence in the world of consumer goods

DAVID GRAEBER

Death's invisibility enhances its terror. *Philippe Ariès*

'Have you ever seen someone die, David?'

I still remember the first time I was asked that, by the grave, very Christian old matriarch of a household in Antananarivo where I had been staying while working in the Malagasy National Archives. It wasn't the last time I'd be asked during my two years in Madagascar. Many of the people I came to know seemed to feel one of the most exotic things about Europeans was that many had never witnessed death. Not accidental or violent death – that was considered just as bruising and horrific in Madagascar as anywhere – but normal, peaceful death, the kind anyone would be expected to aspire to as the culmination of a successful life, in bed, surrounded by children, grandchildren and loving neighbours and well-wishers.

That the North Atlantic societies that gave birth to modern social theory were somewhat unusual in this respect we have been aware of at least since Philippe Ariès's *The Hour of Our Death* (1982). Death is hidden away. But so is childbirth. Both the beginning and end of human life are felt to be properly relegated to antiseptic sanctuaries far from the public eye; it's significant, for instance, that birth and death are both acts that one is not legally allowed to show on American television. The reason that Lutheran missionaries in Minnesota have access to medical supplies to donate to Malagasy people (as discussed in Halvorson's chapter) is that illness and death have been separated into a multibillion-dollar industry that allows for the easy recuperation and redistribution of healing artefacts to ... wherever.

This attitude toward death seems to have really taken hold only around the time of the birth of industrial civilization, and it's likely that's no coincidence. If nothing else there is a curious homology here. We don't like to have to see, or think too much about, the moment when living organisms come into existence, or dissolve away

277

out of it. It's the same with animals. It's the same with commodities. The factory floor and incinerator are considered just as properly kept out of sight as the hospital ward and crematorium. This in turn makes it easier to imagine manufactured goods, which then become the paradigm for all material goods, or human beings, as discrete, free-standing, self-identical entities, that just sort of leap into being and disappear again – rather than as themselves ongoing processes, patterns of change, fundamentally entangled in the world around them. As nouns instead of verbs. The world is full of things (to which we give names) rather than being a jumble of processes of growth and decay, crumbling and assembly, fermentation, preservation, quiescence, explosion, contamination, one where what might at times seem discrete objects usually disposed to melt into one another, where humans are always transforming everything around them, and where maintaining things in more or less the same form often requires even more attentive labour than transforming them. The notion that there is some fixed, usually immaterial, essence, to people and objects, existing on an abstract plane that is somehow prior to, but also higher and purer than, materiality, would appear to come directly out of the habit of looking at the world which eventually drove us to hide death and childbirth out of sight.

Cosmologies have consequences

What follows is a brief sketch, really only a series of preliminary reflections, on the relation of the peculiar cosmology underlying industrial civilization and the general question of recycling addressed in this volume – and by extension, the very notion of ecological sustainability on which it rests. I should emphasize right away – I wish I didn't have to – that I am not doing so in order to undermine the idea of ecological sustainability itself. No one in their right mind (I hope) would not wish to see the world move towards an economic system that did not threaten to visit ecological catastrophe on the planet, as the present one surely threatens to do. What I would like to do, instead, is to examine some of the reasons why existing efforts in this regard have been so woefully inadequate. We live, after all, at an extraordinary moment, when rapidly advancing climate change has made it utterly apparent that the global industrial system is already causing global destruction on an unprecedented scale, and existing institutions of global governance have proved absolutely incapable of addressing the situation. It's hard to imagine such a failure of such colossal proportions. It's hard to imagine this is a simple question of political deadlock; or, for that matter, of the interference of corporate CEOs, who after all do themselves have a certain interest in the continued habitability of the planet. Something about the ways we have been framing these issues must be profoundly flawed.

In this context, trying to map out the underlying principles about what might be termed industrial cosmology might well be a useful first step.

If nothing else, it's hard to understand the concept of 'recycling' without it. Here I think we have to begin with two questions:

1 Why is the trajectory of manufactured objects, from factory floor to market to domestic or commercial use, seen as similar to the human life-course?
2 Why are both trajectories imagined as circular, as 'cycles'?

The first seems to be our starting point: this is why production and disposal are to be pushed out of sight in much the same way as birth and death. The resemblance seems especially salient when a product nears the time of its disposal: it's then especially we hear about 'product life', or 'end of life products'.

The second is already presumed in the very term 'recycling'. To 'recycle' literally means to 'cycle again'. But why do we imagine the history of a manufactured product as cyclical in the first place? Presumably it is by analogy with a human life, but it's not clear in what way the course of a human life is in any way circular either. We grow up, but we don't really grow down again. It's true that we tend to gain in social prestige and power over the first two-thirds or three-quarters of our lives, and (often) decline fairly abruptly towards the end of it. But this is hardly a matter of coming around full circle; if there's a shape, it's more like a long ascending arc with a final crash; and anyway, dotage is not really a 'second childhood'. We can only imagine lives as circular if we concentrate solely on the fact that we end up in the same place that we began – in nothingness – which flows directly from the way that beginning and end are both seen as being fundamentally unknowable.

It's the same, too, with manufactured objects. They are imagined as having magically appeared, proceeding to 'circulate' (note that word again), and then, finally, disappear into that same abyss from whence they came.

Marxist philosophers from Georg Lukács (1968) to John Holloway (2003) have noted that our conception of the world, which starts from the existence of self-identical objects, 'the thing in itself', and only then asks how things change and come into relation to each other, seems to be a direct result of the market system. The idea that objects are intrinsically separate and self-identical seems to fly in the face of all common sense. Why then do we insist on maintaining the fantasy? Most obviously, because if what we take to be objects are really more like interlocking processes, it's very hard to see how one could buy and sell them. Many of our most basic philosophical conundrums ultimately derive from this contradiction between the need to apply clear property rights, and hence to define discrete units existing in some sense outside of time, to which they can apply, and the observed realities of actual physical existence. What, after all, is the easiest way to see something as moving and changing, yet ultimately remaining exactly the same? Obviously, to say that it is moving in a circle. The cycle is ultimately our way of imagining stasis, the steady state, the condition in which an object might be said to be in motion but still remains nothing but itself, just as in each daily or seasonal cycle, the nature of each day or year can be seen as exactly the same as any other.

Of course, all these cycles are artificial constructs; humans and objects do not simply appear and disappear again; as poets and philosophers spend much of their time reminding us. Everything is recycled in one form or another; in fact, almost everything around us contains (among many other things) elements of the decay and destruction of past human beings.

> HAMLET: To what base uses we may return, Horatio! Why may not imagination trace the noble dust of Alexander till he find it stopping a bunghole?
> HORATIO: 'Twere to consider too curiously, to consider so.
> HAMLET: No, faith, not a jot; but to follow him thither with modesty enough, and likelihood to lead it; as thus: Alexander died, Alexander was buried, Alexander returneth into dust; the dust is earth; of earth we make loam; and why of that loam (whereto he was converted) might they not stop a beer barrel?[1]

The conjuncture between human remains, pottery and alcoholic beverages (inert matter themselves imbued with a kind of 'spirit') is a particularly common poetic theme. Fitzgerald's Omar Khayyam, written, depending on how you look at it, some centuries before, or some centuries after, Shakespeare, had conversations with his cup, whose clay, he estimated, must surely be composed of materials drawn from the lips of former generations. But the overall image of the world as a series of interlocking cycles can always be salvaged in some way – for instance, by insisting that all this means is that the smaller cycles we usually think about are ultimately part of larger cycles, whereby all matter is recycled as part of some grander, cosmic unity.

The English word 'recycling' is first documented in 1926, originally employed as a technical term in oil refining and related industrial procedures. It took on its contemporary sense, of gathering reusable items of domestic trash for reuse, only in the 1960s – as part of a broader ecological awakening, a growing consciousness of the wastefulness and destructiveness of consumer economy, and a moral commitment to moving towards an industrial system based on principles of ecological sustainability. But it's significant, too, that in becoming a moral imperative, rather than a technical term, the word also moved away from its earlier reference to industrial practices to refer to the behaviour of individual consumers. And this despite the fact that consumers produce only a tiny proportion of the world's waste. As Luna Glucksberg (n.d.) observes:

> According to different estimates, the amount of waste produced in the UK that can be traced back to individuals varied between 4% to 9%. Even using the highest available data of 9%, that means not even a tenth of what goes to landfill is attributable to the behaviour of individual households. The current highest targets to recycle up to half of all household waste would still, in fact, only divert from landfill up to 5% of total waste arising: this would be a very optimistic estimate.

Yet when people speak of recycling, they now refer almost exclusively to domestic waste, or consumer goods thrown away in public places (plastic bottles at the mall, that sort of thing) rather than the principal sources of the waste products that fill our landfills: the largest single share of which is created by the construction industry, and after that by industrial production. It would appear in fact that if UK property developers simply stopped ripping down old structures and building new ones, and instead limited themselves to refurbishing existing buildings, this in itself would have twice the effect of that which would be obtained if every family in the country were somehow able to recycle, compost or otherwise divert every single ounce of garbage their household produces.

'It is reasonable', Glucksberg concludes, 'to ask why an activity that has, on the whole, a rather limited impact on the amount of materials that end up in landfills or incinerators is invested with so much value.' Indeed. In her own analysis, she follows O'Brien (2007) and Luke (1993), in suggesting that what we are seeing is a combination of a habit of treating moral questions as matters of individual conscience, and political expedience – it is much easier to appeal to the personal conscience of consumers than to create the kind of mass social movements it would take to seriously change the modus operandi of powerful capitalist firms.

We are used to finding a profound morality in anything having to do with waste, as the editors of this volume so astutely point out: the language we use to speak of such matters slips easily from a technical language of efficiency and expedience to one of degradation and redemption. Just as the classic media image of economic catastrophe is the sight of formerly middle-class housewives picking through garbage heaps for food, it's also hard not to ask, 'Why, when so many are so desperate, are there people throwing away edible products to begin with?' As is demonstrated throughout this book, particularly in the chapters by Bear, Faulk and Millar, to refuse the sin of waste, to turn waste into something valuable, is also to rise from degradation to a sort of redemption.

The question is why this morality has such a stubborn tendency to attach itself only to personal, or household, consumption. Is it just a tendency to view all moral questions from an individual perspective? Or do we need to begin thinking more carefully about the household itself?

On the significance of the prefix 'eco-'

To map out everything that has contributed to our sense that household waste is a privileged locus of moral transformation would be a complicated business. We would have to consider medieval Christianity, with its strange combination of redemptive messianic religion, and an Indo-European-style caste system. It can hardly be a coincidence that, after the collapse of the great Axial Age empires across Eurasia, we see the gradual re-emergence of empires in China and the Middle East, and instead the emergence of a much more chaotic, decentralized system based on caste hierarchies in precisely those areas where Indo-European languages predominated: a four-part system (priests, warriors, merchants and farmers) in India, and a three-part system (without the merchants) in Europe. In each case, too, there was a residual category composed of groups who performed what were seen as especially polluting professions, especially those involved in the disposal of waste: in Europe these included, according to Jacques Le Goff, fullers, dyers, launderers, bathhouse-keepers, leatherworkers, barbers, butchers and tripe-sellers, and even pastry chefs (Le Goff 1990: 47–8).[2] There was a profound tension, of course, between this overall hierarchical organization of society, with clerics at the top, and the fact that these same clerics acted in the name of a Redeemer who had lived, who by his own words continued to live, above all among the lowliest members of society, and who provided the promise of universal salvation.

All this is complicated enough. But lingering behind our moral debates on the relation of economy and ecology lies, I think, a third factor, equally important: the ancient ideal of the *oikos*, the self-sufficient household.

Nowadays, 'eco' has become a sort of shorthand abbreviation for everything associated with environmental politics. We thus speak of 'eco-consciousness', 'eco-friendly', 'eco-tourism', 'eco-activists', or even 'eco-terrorists' and 'eco-freaks'. Ecological imperatives are, generally speaking, seen as directly opposed to the maximizing, growth-oriented, productivist ethos enshrined in economics. It's thus all the more confusing to recognize that, etymologically, 'economy' and 'ecology' are very close to the same word. In either case the 'eco' derives from the Greek word *oikos*, the household, which was also assumed in pretty much all ancient discussions of the subject to be what we would now call both an economic and an ecological unit, the family farm. 'Economics' is, in Greek, simply the regulation or management of this family estate; 'ecology' technically means the study of this same *oikos*.

Scholars from Max Weber (1998 [1908]) to Moses Finley (1974) have emphasized that all ancient economic literature is driven not by anything we would now recognize as economic imperatives, but rather on a moral imperative that a free man should not be dependent on anyone else. A man's holdings should, ideally, provide him with everything he needs. This is not to say that profit was not a motive. It just meant that it only came into the picture after those needs were completely provided. 'The paterfamilias', as Cato put it, 'should be a seller and not a buyer.' As a result economics was the art of managing one's holdings, and employing one's wife, children, slaves and other dependants in such a way that all physical needs (food, clothing, etc.) were to be obtained from within one's own estate, rather than having to be purchased, leaving the master of the household a fully autonomous being, free to engage in the political life of the city – but also, ideally, in a position to sell a surplus to others, so as to acquire money, which was also useful for all sorts of political purposes. Economics was thus the timeless domain of cycles, human and biological reproduction, birth and death, planting and harvest, to which women and dependants were relegated, while the political sphere it made possible was the male domain of rationality and history.

The critical thing for present purposes, though, is that this conception of the *oikos*, from the beginning, contained both a notion of self-contained, self-sustaining equilibrium with nature, and of maximizing production and hence profits, *at the same time*.

The discipline we now refer to as 'economics' derives from what in the seventeenth century began to be referred to as 'political economy', the idea that it should be possible to manage political units – kingdoms – according to the same principles as an ancient household, as materially self-sufficient units that would thus not be dependent on foreign imports, but which would still produce a surplus to export, for cash, to the residents of other kingdoms. For that tradition, which culminated in the mid-eighteenth-century Physiocrats, the basic economic unit was still the agricultural household; only the task of administration was now to encourage interdependency between households so as to increase overall yields. The discipline began to take its contemporary form only with the Industrial Revolution, once the household came to be imagined not as a unit of production at all, but rather of consumption, and 'the economy' could be conceived as an autonomous domain of human activity wherein commodities travelled through a kind of life cycle, from production (a word which originally just meant 'putting out') in factories, farms or other workplaces, through the marketplace, to their ultimate destination in the hands of consumers – the English word 'consumption', significantly, originally meaning 'to burn, waste, or utterly destroy' (see Graeber 2011a).

As many have remarked, this conception of economic life as a cycle of creation and destruction sits rather oddly with much of how we actually treat our houses, books, furniture, appliances, and so forth, but it's certainly true that consumer economies have increasingly encouraged us to see material objects as disposable, or to create them in such a way that they do break down and need to be disposed of, in order to answer the need to continually expand production. The ecological movement was to a large degree motivated by a need to address the pernicious effects of this constant expansion of both production and destruction.

But what of the term 'ecology' itself?

The term is in fact quite late: it was coined by a German biologist named Ernst Haeckel in 1866, as *Öekology*, 'the investigation of the total relations of the animal both to its inorganic and to its organic environment' – as a scientific area of study meant to cover the same ground as the earlier term, documented from at least the sixteenth century, 'the economy of nature'.[3] *Oikos* was, again, a direct reference to the old Graeco-Roman family farm, as a place where ideally nothing is wasted, nothing should have to be brought in from the outside, where perfection is the attainment of a perfect equilibrium – though one which, somewhat paradoxically, yields a profitable surplus at the same time.[4]

Haeckel himself was a confusing and contradictory character, who tried to bring together virtually all the emerging intellectual currents of his day. He began as a classic liberal, a pacifist enthusiast for the free market, who saw his new science of ecology as a kind of combination of the insights of Darwin with the then emerging discipline of economics; but enfolding both within a variety of Spinozan monism that saw all of the material elements of the natural world as imbued with psychic qualities. A fervent opponent of all forms of Christianity, Haeckel ultimately dreamed of replacing the Church with a scientific, but at the same time mystical, religion of nature. By the end of his life this drove him in an increasingly conservative and nationalistic direction, and he abandoned his earlier egalitarianism, arguing instead that the study of biology demonstrated the inevitability of a dominant elite. This makes him a decidedly peculiar ancestor for the current ecological movement, but the tensions within Haeckel's thought were just a reflection of the intellectual tensions of his day.

What I would stress instead are two points: first of all, that as recent commentators have remarked (e.g. Kleeberg 2007), for all his opposition to organized religion, Haeckel was largely just reproducing the natural theology of his day, and secondly, that, partly for this very reason, ecology and economy emerged alongside one another, sharing very similar basic assumptions. The very notion of the 'economy of nature' was, originally, theological – essentially, based on the principle that God manages the entire natural world as if it were an *oikos*. But here again, we find the same internal tension. Consider here the following reflection on the work of Carl Linnaeus, who wrote his *Specimen academicum de oeconomia naturae* in 1749:

> By economy of nature, he meant the very wise disposal of natural organisms instituted by the Sovereign Creator according to which these organisms had common ends and reciprocal functions ... The economy of nature (otherwise called Divine Economy or Divine Wisdom) was essentially a concept according to which the interactions between natural bodies resulted in an *intangible equilibrium* that maintained itself throughout the ages. (Lévêque 2003: 205, emphasis added)

God was economical in the sense that he ensured that nothing was wasted, that the systems he created were self-sustaining. This balance of nature was often held out as proof of God's existence – as it was by Linnaeus himself. But at the same time, Linnaeus argued, nature was also 'designed by Providence to maximize production' (in Sideris 2003: 23)! It not only maintained itself as an equilibrium system, it was also capable of producing an endlessly increasing bounty to serve the purposes of man, who was assumed to be constituted over and above the natural world in much the same way the ancient male householder and his political sphere were constituted over and above the world of domestic production.

That tension – between a self-contained, self-reproducing system that remains in stasis, and a system of endless productivity, with both being simultaneously seen as moral values in themselves – continues to haunt both economic and ecological discourse as, in the nineteenth century, the two become secularized. The emphasis tends to shift back and forth. Hence productivism of early political economy (echoed in Marx) was soon followed by a turn to equilibrium models, under authors like Marshall and Walras, writing at almost exactly the same time as Haeckel was developing his own notions of ecological balance.[5]

The idea of markets as generalized equilibrium systems was to come to define neoclassical economics, and, indeed, to become the key to its moral power (markets know best). Yet at the same time, as Paul Worster (1977) has so clearly documented, the science of ecology, which drew freely on economic concepts, was by the middle of the twentieth century able to use its own equilibrium models to make if anything even greater moral claims, or at least the only ones capable of seriously challenging economic ones: becoming, as Worster was later to put it (1990: 3), 'a program of moral enlightenment – of "conservation" in the sense of a restored equilibrium between humans and nature'.

If proof were required that both these equilibrium models were, essentially, duelling moral projects, one need only consider just how much needs to be pushed out of the picture in order to make it possible, in each case, to argue that we are in the presence of a self-regulating system. In the case of markets, one must not only make a series of obviously impossible assumptions (that all actors, for instance, are rational and have perfect information), but also ignore huge swathes of actual economic activity. An image of economies as closed loops can hardly do justice to the continual trade and transformation of electronic wastes (Tong and Wang, this volume), ships (Crang et al.), clothing (Norris) or spent nuclear fuel (Garcier). The case of ecosystems is if anything even more extreme, at least if considered from the perspective of thermodynamics, since all ecosystems are dependent on the constant infusion of new energy from outside the planet entirely – sunlight – without which they would perish almost instantly. They are thus about as much equilibrium systems as a clock plugged into a nearby electric socket. In fact, just as ecosystems could be considered giant processors of solar energy, our current, productivist, industrial system is entirely dependent on coal, gas and oil, is powered by solar energy trapped and processed by now-fossilized remains of plant life of ages past. In the case of the sun, at least we have several billion years before we can anticipate any real problems. The kind of solar energy preserved in the fossil fuels that industrial economies have relied on for the last couple of hundred years is unlikely to last another generation.

Back to recycling

At this point, it's easy to understand what recycling represents. It's the latest in a series of attempts to impose a circular, equilibrium model on a system that is, at least in energy terms, as far from an equilibrium as anything could possibly be.

The idea of recycling is entirely dependent on the logic of property. It is property arrangements, after all, which allow the transfer of rights to objects through commercial transactions, and therefore allow the 'circulation' of objects from the sphere of production to the sphere of consumption in the first place. After all, if we clean a plastic bottle and put some new liquid in it within our households, or decide to print on the other side of old documents, we don't normally refer to this as 'recycling'. That's just reuse. Diverting an object to new use is referred to as recycling only when we abandon our property claims and allow the object to exit the household and have a commercial value once again attributed to it.

Money, of course, is what makes all this possible; it is what propels these objects along on their purportedly circular careers. In fact, in neoclassical economics, money is both the communicative medium that allows for market equilibrium and also (since such economists assumed a gold standard) the ultimate recyclable product. Consumer products might constantly cycle from creation to destruction, but money was always reused; once spent, it was still not spent, in the sense of depleted, but simply passed along to the next stage of the cycle to be spent by someone else. Just as gold was, for the alchemists, the perfect, eternal form of matter, the ideal to which all minerals aspired, so gold in the form of money was the eternal commodity, endlessly recycled, never losing value at any point. The analogy suddenly makes the notorious psychological identification of money and human waste even more poignant. We are still dealing with the dream of turning base matter into gold.

One theme that has cropped up repeatedly in the essays assembled in this book is how communities can themselves organize themselves like households, and at the same time transform themselves into something higher, through the labour of transforming waste into something valuable. The result can be anything from a degrading, exploitative sham – as in Fredericks's chapter, for example – to what seem to be genuinely hopeful experiments – the main factor in the difference, unsurprisingly, being the degree of autonomous self-organization on the part of the participants. But in order to break out of the cycle and begin to imagine genuinely sustainable economies, I think, we will have to begin by reconfiguring the categories of political economy entirely. This is why I began the essay as I did: with the hiding away of birth and death, production and consumption, so as to render them sites of a kind of sacred power, but at the same time allowing us to imagine the world as self-identical objects and people that somehow, cyclically, come into existence and disappear.

This is also what makes it possible for us to spend endless hours worrying about the morality of our treatment of domestic waste, without ever noticing that the ecological damage caused by domestic waste is almost negligible when compared with that caused by the construction industry. After all, if there is any form of economic activity that is difficult to reconcile with an image of the economy as the movement of commodities from factories to market to domestic units, it's the process of building and maintaining those factories, markets and domestic units themselves. Taking full account of that, in turn, requires us to rethink the way we think about the value of human labour. Both natural theology and political economy start from the assumption that value is primarily a power of creation; then try to argue that power of creation is held in check, organized, regulated, by some kind of spontaneous equilibrium. In fact, however, only a very small part of the time human beings spend working is spent in producing anything, at least in the sense of bringing new things – shoes, sausages, fluorescent light bulbs, even buildings – into being. Much more is spent adjusting, refashioning, repairing, maintaining, cleaning, rearranging or transporting things. For all the labour we spend transforming material goods, we probably spend even more on keeping them the same. And this is only counting labour that is primarily directed at material objects rather than in educating or caring for other people. It is no coincidence, I think, that the most radical political challenges to the established order documented in this volume are also precisely those (the Soviet and ex-Soviet logic of 'repair', the refurbishing of the Argentine hotel, which so nicely overcomes Locke's creationist assumption that 'mixing one's labour' with an object yields property rights only the first time one does it and never subsequently) that set out from these otherwise largely invisible forms of labour. If it were possible to create – and popularize – a new economics that started, precisely, from those forms of human activity, we might finally begin to overcome the conceptual barriers to creating a genuinely viable system for the maintenance of our lives and physical environments. And in doing so we would, almost inevitably, begin to imagine the natural world, too, in an entirely new light.

Notes

1 *Hamlet*, Act V, Scene 1.

2 Obviously in South Asia the system became far more formalized, and the priestly caste there was en-dogamous, rather than being drawn largely from the younger sons of the warrior caste, but otherwise simi-larities are striking, and strangely unremarked on.

3 'The ecology of organisms, the knowledge of the sum of the relation of organisms to the surrounding outer world, to organic and inor-ganic conditions of existence; the so-called "economy of nature", the correlations between all organisms living together in one and the same locality, their adaptation to their surroundings, their modifications in the struggle for existence, especially the circumstances of parasitism, etc.' (Haeckel's 1868 definition, cited in Acot and Müller 1998: 672).

4 Needless to say it isn't really because ancient households were dependent on slave labour that had to be imported, at the very least from other households, usually from abroad.

5 From Bartelmus (2008: 21).

References

Acot, P. and G. Müller (1998) 'The birth of scientific ecology', in P. Acot (ed.), *The European Origins of Scientific Ecology*, London: Routledge, pp. 671–83.

Ariès, P. (1982) *The Hour of Our Death*, New York: Vintage Books.

Bartelmus, P. (2008) *Quantitative Eco-nomics: How Sustainable are Our Economies?*, Dordrecht: Springer.

Finley, M. (1974) *The Ancient Economy*, Berkeley: University of California Press.

Glucksberg, L. (n.d.) 'Wasting the Inner-city: Waste, Value and Anthropology on the Estates', unpublished dissertation.

Graeber, (2011a) 'Consumption', *Current Anthropology*, 52(4): 489–511.

— (2011b) *Debt: The First Five Thou-sand Years*, New York: Melville House.

Holloway, J. (2003) *Change the World without Taking Power: The Mean-ing of Revolution Today*, London: Pluto Press.

Kleeberg, B. (2007) 'God-Nature progressing: natural theology in German monism', *Science in Context*, 20: 537–69.

Le Goff, J. (1990) *Your Money or Your Life: Economy and Religion in the Middle Ages*, New York: Zone Books.

Lévêque, C. (2003) *Ecology: From Ecosystem to Biosphere*, Enfield: Science Publishers.

Lukács, G. (1968) 'Reification and the consciousness of the proletariat', in *History and Class Consciousness: Studies in Marxist Dialectics*, Cambridge, MA: MIT Press, pp. 83–222.

Luke, T. (1993) 'Green consumerism: ecology and the ruse of recycling', in *The Nature of Things: Language, Politics and the Environment*, Minneapolis: University of Minnesota Press.

O'Brien, M. (2007) *A Crisis of Waste? Understanding the Rubbish Society*, London: Routledge.

Sideris, L. H. (2003) *Environmental Ethics, Ecological Theology, and Natural Selection*, New York: Columbia University Press.

Weber, M. (1998 [1908]) *The Agrarian Sociology of Ancient Civilizations*, London: Verso.

Worster, P. (1977) *Nature's Economy: A History of Ecological Ideas*, New York: Cambridge University Press.

— (1990) 'The ecology of order and chaos', *Environmental History Review*, 14(1/2): 1–18.

About the contributors

Farid Ahamed is professor of anthropology at the University of Chittagong, and of sociology at the South Asian University, New Delhi. His areas of specialization rest primarily on in-depth narrative-based applied anthropological research on livelihood, globalization-driven adaptation, emerging crises and survival strategies of diverse people and communities.

Nasreen Akhter was a research assistant on the Waste of the World project and is now a lecturer in anthropology at the University of Chittagong. Nasreen is currently taking a Master's degree in anthropology at the University of Edinburgh.

Laura Bear is a lecturer in anthropology at the London School of Economics. She is the author of *The Jadu House* (Doubleday, 2000) and *Lines of the Nation: Bureaucracy, Railway Workers and the Intimate Historical Self* (Columbia, 2007). From 2008 to 2010 she carried out research with workers on the Hooghly river, Kolkata, funded by the ESRC. During 2008–11 she was also director of the ESRC-funded research network 'Rethinking Contemporary Globalization: Conflicts in Time'. She has made four ethnographic films with the river workers with whom she carried out her research on the Hooghly.

Mike Crang is professor of geography at Durham University. He has worked on social memory and preserved landscapes, and as part of the Waste of the World programme of research he has been looking at the flipside of ruins and things that decay and fall apart. He has long-standing interests in visual methods and temporality.

Karen Ann Faulk is an anthropologist teaching in the Department of History and Global Studies at Carnegie Mellon University. She is the author of *In the Wake of Neoliberalism: Citizenship and Human Rights in Argentina* (Stanford University Press, 2012). Her current projects include co-editing two forthcoming volumes, *Work in Argentina: 21st Century Paradigms* and *A Sense of Justice: Legal Knowledge and Lived Experience in Latin America.*

Raihana Ferdous was a research assistant on the Waste of the World project and is currently undertaking a PhD in geography at Durham University, working on consumption and energy.

Rosalind Fredericks is an assistant professor at New York University. Her research and teaching interests centre on the political economy of development, global urbanism and post-colonial identities in Africa. With a background in cultural geography, her work is focused on urban politics and social movements in contemporary Dakar, Senegal. Currently, she is revising her PhD dissertation on the cultural politics of garbage collection in Dakar for publication, while launching a new line of research into the politics of hip-hop in Dakar and the Senegalese diaspora.

Romain Garcier is assistant professor in geography at the University of Lyon (Ecole normale supérieure), France, where he holds a junior chair in 'Environment, spaces and emerging risks'. He has researched and published on the social aspects of environmental pollution and is currently conducting research on material flows in the nuclear industry. His website is: garcier.net.

David Graeber teaches anthropology at Goldsmiths, University of London. He is the author of *Towards an Anthropological Theory of Value*; *Lost People: Magic and the Legacy of Slavery in Madagascar*; *Fragments of an Anarchist Anthropology*; *Possibilities: Essays on Hierarchy, Rebellion, and Desire*; *Direct Action: An Ethnography* and *Debt: The First 5000 Years*. He has written for *Harper's*, *The Nation*, *Mute*, and the *New Left Review*. In the summer of 2011, he worked with a small group of activists and *Adbusters* magazine to plan Occupy Wall Street. *Bloomberg Businessweek* has called him an 'anti-leader' of the movement.

Nicky Gregson is professor of geography at Durham University. She has published on waged domestic labour. Her current research interests are in the fields of consumption and disposal, 'recycling' and waste economies, and science in practice. She has just finished running a five-year ESRC-funded research programme, Waste of the World.

Britt Halvorson is a sociocultural anthropologist who received her PhD from the University of Michigan and has taught at Mount Holyoke College and Colby College. Her research examines the moral and ethical dilemmas of American Lutheran medical humanitarianism in Madagascar and elsewhere, focusing on the emerging exchanges, circulations and sites of post-colonial religious encounter.

Kathleen M. Millar completed her PhD in the Department of Anthropology at Brown University in 2011, where she was also the academic coordinator for the Center for Latin American and Caribbean Studies. Her research focuses on the configuration of labour in the context of informal employment and its relevance to anthropological understandings of work, social class and economies today. Her doctoral thesis, *Reclaiming the Discarded: The Politics of Labor and Everyday Life on Rio's Garbage Dump*, received the Marie J. Langlois Prize award.

Lucy Norris is senior research fellow in the Department of Anthropology, University College London, where she is currently working on issues of global textile waste. She is co-author of *Bali, the Imaginary Museum: The Photographs of Walter Spies and Beryl de Zoete* and author of *Recycling Indian Clothing: Global Contexts of Reuse and Value.*

Xin Tong is an associate professor in the Department of Urban and Economic Geography at Peking University. Her background is in industrial geography and she is currently interested in the spatial dimensions of industrial ecology. She worked on Extended Producer Responsibility in e-waste management in China, on which she has published several articles, and is now researching the relation between global environmental governance and technological change in developing countries more broadly. She has participated in several consultancy projects in China.

Jici Wang is a professor in the Department of Urban and Economic Geography at Peking University. She graduated in 1968 from the Department of Geology and Geography at Peking University. In 1978, when the Cultural Revolution ended, she pursued further non-degree education, with a major in economic geography. She joined the faculty of the Department of Geography of Peking University in 1980 and became a professor of economic geography in 1991. She was appointed a full member of the Commission on the Organization of Industrial Space, International Geographical Union (IGU), for the period 1992–2000. Drawing on her experience of research in China and active work in the Commission, she has been included in the Mentor Panel of the commission since 2000.

Index

dignity, human, 26, 144, 156
DNA sequences, legal status of, 209
Dona Ani, a Jardim Gramacho
resident, 169–70
donor imaginaries, 36
downcycling, 27 n.3, 37, 253 n.9 *see
also* recycling
Drug Enforcement Administration
(DEA) (USA), 234, 250
drug use: habits of populations, 249;
quantitative analysis of, 249
dumping of waste: and poverty, 167;
regulation of, 1, 17–19, 124, 132–3,
164 *see also* environmental pollution; toxic waste, dumping of
Duque de Caxias neighbourhood
(Rio de Janeiro), 167, 170; declared
Area of National Security, 171;
relation to Rio de Janeiro, 173,
174–5
Durga puja festival (India), 186
Dutta, Subhas, 187
dye-pack anti-theft devices, 250

e-waste: environmental problems of,
in China, 101; flows of (to China,
18, 98–116; reduction of, 113;
transnational, 99–102); recycling
of, in China, 103–8 (interviews
regarding, 102–3; negative views
of, 102, 113); smuggling of, 104
eco-, use of prefix, 282–7
ecological balance, 286
ecological footprint, 12
ecology, use of term, 284–6
economics, discipline of, 10–11, 16,
286
economy: connection with waste
management, 14, 15; representation of, 10; use of term, 283–4 *see
also* crisis, financial
education of consumers regarding
recycling, 111–12
Electricité de France (EDF), 88–9;
nuclear energy production by, 81
electronics industry, competition
and innovation in, 108–13
empowerment: discourses of, 137;

in trash management, 120–1,
124–33, 126–33 (questioned, 135)
see also community, gendered
participation in
end-of-life computer equipment,
disassembly of, 99
end-of-life ships *see* ships, end-of-
life
ENDA organization (Senegal), 120,
121–4, 127–9, 135, 137
energy, and matter, 10–11, 286–7
energy crisis *see* crisis, energy
Engels, Friedrich, 167
entropy, 12, 13
environment: good practices, 3;
regulation of, 16, 83, 109
Environment Agency (UK), 62
environmental nationalism, 186
environmental politics, 201
environmental pollution, 12;
controls over, in China, 114; from
e-waste recycling, 100, 101, 104,
113; from clothing recycling 37;
from ship-breaking activities, 64
see also dumping of waste
environmental sustainability, 156
environmentalism, and economic
policy, 16–19
ephemerality, 9; of clothing, 35; of
property objects, 22
Euratom, 83
European Environment Agency
(EEA), 14
European Union (EU): Directive
on Restriction of Hazardous
Substances (RoHS), 109;
regulation of electrical
and electronic wastes, 101;
Sustinability Unit, 12
Evangelical Lutheran Church, 211
Evroremont, 257
Extended Producer Responsibility
(EPR), 99, 109, 114

favelas, 167, 174
Federal Bureau of Investigation
(FBI), 239
ferrous scrap: exported from Brazil,

narcotics surveillance, in USA, 234–54
National Agency for Radioactive Waste Management (ANDRA) (France), 92
National Factory of Motors (FNM) (Rio de Janeiro), 170–1
National Movement of Catadores (Brazil), 181
nature, economy of, 285
necropolitics, ethics of, 185–7
neoliberalism, 147, 153, 182, 185–6, 189–91, 208; debate about, 143; rise of, 16; workers in, 147–9 *see also* crisis, of neoliberalism; liberalization, in India
Newton, Isaac, 236–7, 243
Niger, uranium mining in, 81
Ningbo (China), 102; e-waste recycling centre, 105
non-human entities, relations with, 26, 259; vitality of, 187–8
Non-Proliferation Treaty, 87
nuclear fuel cycle: representations of, 78 (as closed, 83–6, 89) *see also* closed systems, cycle
nuclear fuel processing, criticism of, 77
nuclear industry, 76–97; laws governing, 92
Nuclear Material Control and Accountancy, 83
nuclearity: geographies of, 76–97; use of term, 86–8

Öekology, 284
oikos, idea of, 283–4
organ recipients, 209
ownership, obligations of, 22–4; rights of, related to waste, 242, 244 *see also* human bodily materials; urban gleanings

Pakistan, 36
Palladio, Andrea, 21
Panipat (India), 20, 21; textile recycling in, 23, 36, 37–54
paper, scrap, prices of, 178

participation, 134; labour value resulting from, 127
paterfamilias, role of, 283
People, The v. Krivda (1971), 240
Perelman, Mariano, 145–6
Physiocrats, 284
Pierrelatte (France), uranium processing in, 90
plastic: recycling of, 5, 106, 155, 177, 178, 180
plastic bottles, recycling of, 176
plutonium, 77, 80, 91
podrão materials, 176
pollution: arising from e-waste recycling, 103; costs of control of, 100; of Ganges River, 201; polluting professions, 282; reduction of, 107
'pollution haven' hypothesis, 100
possessive individualism, 23
poverty: in Argentina, 154; urban poor, 182 (exclusion of, 166–8)
prayer, returns for, 221
privacy, 245, 247, 252; and security, 238–9; in US Fourth Amendment, 239–40; reasonable expectations of, 248
private–public division, 237
privatization, 147; of recycling, 108; of waste disposal, 157
proceso de reorganización nacional (Argentina), 146
property: fixed in things, 217; logic of, 287; private, myths of, 236
property rights, 22–4, 151, 209, 235, 280, 289; in detached body parts, 246; in relation to equality, 152–4 *see also* ownership, rights of
proximity principle for waste disposal, 100
psychoanalysis, 8–9
puja, worship of, 193–4

Rabelais, François, 261
rag-picking cooperatives, 2, 5
Ramos, Elena, 143
re-use exports, 17
recyclates, growing unusability of, 13 *see also* downcycling

in Rio de Janeiro, 164–84; representation of, 19; sorting practices of,
244 *see also catadores*
water quality, improvement of, 201
water shortages, imagined, 51–2
Weber, Max, 283
Wenzhou City (China), e-waste
recycling centre, 107
women: education of, in trash
disposal, 132; garment
dismantling workers, 20–1; in
trash collection work, 119–42
see also community, gendered
participation in
wool: declining market for, 52;
recycling of, 47
Woolf, Virginia, 8
woollen materials, recycling of, 43
work: concept of, 144–9; ethics of,
156; human, creativity of, 185 *see
also* right to work

worker self-management, 152, 157
working conditions: in ship-breaking
industry, 63–4; in shoddy industry, 40; in textile recycling,
45, 48, 49, 50; of *catadores*, 165 *see
also* accidents in the workplace;
deaths of workers; risk
workmanship, sense of, 187–8, 200,
201–2; ethical effects of, 196; in
port work, 192; necropolitics of,
194–5
World Bank, 39, 208

Yoff trash collection project (Dakar,
Senegal), 119, 121–4

Zambia, second-hand clothing in, 55
Zeca, a refrigerator trader, 181
zips, in recycled clothing, value of,
51
Ziya eco-industrial park (China), 111